The Treasury for Special Days and Occasions

The Treasury for Special Days and Occasions

More Than 1250 Anecdotes, Quotations, and Illustrations

Compiled by E. Paul Hovey

Fleming H. Revell

A Division of Baker Book House Co
Grand Rapids, Michigan 49516

Bill Finch

Published by Fleming H. Revell
a division of Baker Book House Company
P.O. Box 6287, Grand Rapids, MI 49516-6287

New paperback edition 1994

Printed in the United States of America

ISBN 0-8007-5538-3

ACKNOWLEDGMENTS

Acknowledgment is made to the following, who have granted permission for the reprinting of copyrighted material:

ABINGDON PRESS for selections: from Samuel M. Cavert in *Protestantism, a Symposium* by William K. Anderson. Copyright 1944 Commission on Courses of Study, The Methodist Church. From *Love Speaks from the Cross* by Leslie Badham. Copyright 1955 by Pierce & Washabaugh. From *Heaven and Hell* by John Sutherland Bonnell. Copyright 1956 by Pierce & Washabaugh. From *Prayer* by George A. Buttrick. Copyright 1942 by Whitmore & Stone. From *So We Believe, So We Pray* by George A. Buttrick. Copyright 1951 by Pierce & Smith. From *Ours Is the Faith* by Walter Dudley Cavert. Copyright © 1960 by Abingdon Press. From *The Seven Words* by Clovis G. Chappell. Copyright 1952 by Pierce & Smith. From *Sermons on the Parables of Jesus* by Charles M. Crowe. Copyright 1953 by Pierce & Washabaugh. From *Sermons for Special Days* by Charles M. Crowe. Copyright by Pierce & Washabaugh. From *Prayer and the Common Life* by Georgia Harkness. Copyright 1948 by Stone & Pierce. From Arthur J. Gossip in *The Interpreter's Bible*, Volume 8. Copyright 1952 by Pierce & Smith. From *How To Pray* by E. Stanley Jones. Copyright

1943 by Whitmore & Stone. From Henry Hitt Crane in *Your Life Counts,* edited by Hoover Rupert. Copyright 1950 by Pierce & Smith. From *Preaching Unashamed* by Joseph R. Sizoo. Copyright 1949 By Pierce & Smith. From *His Last Words* by William G. Skeath. Copyright 1939 by Whitmore & Smith. From E. Paul Hovey in *Speakers' Illustrations for Special Days* edited by Charles L. Wallis. Copyright 1956 by Pierce & Washabaugh. Used by permission of Abingdon Press.

Advance for selections: from "The World's Best Hope for Peace" by Ralph Bunche, Sept. 3, 1951; from "The Meaning of Thanksgiving" by Raymond Calkins, Nov. 16, 1953; from "Our Strength as a Nation" by John Foster Dulles, Feb. 7, 1952; from "People Are Afraid of Something," an editorial, Dec. 28, 1953; from "Poison" by Dorothy Canfield Fisher, Jan. 7, 1952; from "The Meaning of Pentecost in Our World Today" by Mrs. John D. Hayes, May 25, 1953; from "The Human Side of Lent" by Elsa Kruuse, Feb. 23, 1955; from "It's About Time" by James Willis Lenhart, March 3, 1952; from "A Place To

Promote Peace" by Henry Cabot Lodge, Jr., Aug. 24, 1953; from "In Remembrance" by Joseph Fort Newton, May 28, 1951; from "A Prayer of Thanksgiving" by Reinhold Niebuhr, Nov. 26, 1951; from "The UN and Our Religious Heritage" by Justin Wroe Nixon, Nov. 30, 1953; from "You Can Make Your Work Easier" by Norman Vincent Peale, Oct. 27, 1952; from "A Time of Reaffirmation" by James A. Pike, Oct. 19, 1953; from "Thanks Be to God" by F. Eppling Reinartz, Nov. 29, 1954; from "A Personal Disgrace" by Cornelia Otis Skinner, Jan. 21, 1952; from "And the Angels Are Still Singing" by Russell H. Stafford, Dec. 22, 1952. Used by permission.

American Magazine for selections: from God Is My Senior Partner" by Harry Bullis, *American Magazine,* Nov. 1952; from "Your Prayers Are Always Answered" by William C. Taggart, *American Magazine,* July, 1943.

AGRICULTURAL MISSIONS, INC. for selections: from "Grace at Meals" by Mrs. J. L. Goheen, *Bulletin,* Autumn, 1948; from "When We Give Thanks" by Herman J. Sweet, *Bulletin,* Autumn, 1948; from "The Spirit-Filled Family" compiled by Mrs. Edmund D. Soper, *Bulletin,* Spring, 1950. Used by permission.

THE AMERICAN BAPTIST PUBLICATION SOCIETY for selection: from *The Secret Place* by Earl Chanley, March 18, 1944. Used by permission.

THE AMERICAN BIBLE SOCIETY for selections: by James Z. Nettinga, *The Bible Society Record,* Sept., 1960; from "The Timeless Wonder," editorial, *The Bible Society Record,* April, 1959; from "Rejoicing in Hope" by Albert William Beaven; from "The Book To Live By" by John Sutherland Bonnell; from "The Light Shineth in Darkness" by Walter Russell Bowie; from "The Book That Has Power" by William T. Ellis; from "The Fountain of Life" by Alonzo W. Fortune; from "One World—One Book" by Ellis Adams Fuller; from "The Book of Hope" by Billy Graham; from "Attend To Your Reading" by Elmer George Homrighausen; from

"Searching the Scriptures" by Charles Edward Jefferson; from "The Book for Everyone" by Helen Keller; from "The Book for Everyone" by Gerald Kennedy; from "The Bible in a Time of Confusion" by Paul B. Kern; from "For the Healing of the Nations" by T. Z. Koo; from "The Light That Will Not Go Out" by Kenneth Scott Latourette; from "The Truth That Makes Men Free" by John Alexander Mackay; from "And Now . . . in a Thousand Tongues" by Eric M. North; from "The Bible, a Light and Guide" by William Walter Peele; from "What Darkness Cannot Dim" by Joseph R. Sizoo; from items by Robert Elliott Speer; from "Coverdale Speaks" by Charles Frederick Wishart. Used by permission of the American Bible Society.

MARIAN ANDERSON for selections: from "My Life in a White World" by Marian Anderson in the *Ladies' Home Journal,* Sept., 1960. Copyright 1960; from an address delivered on TV April 22, 1960.

APPLETON-CENTURY-CROFTS, INC. for selections: from *Our Country's Flag* by Edward S. Holden, copyright by Appleton-Century Crofts, Inc. Used by permission.

ASSOCIATION PRESS for selections: from Willard W. Strahl in *Strength for the Day,* edited by Norman E. Nyggard. Copyright by National Board of Young Men's Christian Associations; from *The Meaning of Prayer* by Harry Emerson Fosdick. Copyright 1915 by National Board of Young Men's Christian Associations. Used by permission.

Blue Book for selections; by Oren Arnold issue of Dec., 1955.

STEPHEN BIRMINGHAM for selection: from "Who Are Real Society?" by Stephen Birmingham in *Holiday,* Dec., 1959. Copyright 1959. Used by permission.

BOARD OF CHRISTIAN EDUCATION, the United Presbyterian Church U. S. A., for selections: from "The Greatening of Abraham Lincoln" by Edgar DeWitt Jones in *Social Progress,* Feb., 1940. Copyright 1940. Used by permission.

BOARD OF NATIONAL MISSIONS, The United Presbyterian Church U. S. A., for selection: from "The Communicant Member" by William Klein.

The Carolina Israelite for selections: from issues of Nov.-Dec., 1958; Jan.-Feb., 1959; and Sept.-Oct., 1959. Copyright 1958 and 1959 by Harry Golden. Used by permission of Harry Golden, Charlotte, North Carolina.

The Catholic World for selections: from "What's Happening to the Bible?" by Neil J. McEleney, C.S.P. *The Catholic World*, May, 1959; from "Albert Camus: Rebel" by Bernard G. Murchland, *The Catholic World*, Jan., 1959; from "Letters to a German Friend" by Albert Camus, *The Catholic World*, Jan., 1959. Used by permission of *The Catholic World*, N.Y.

EDWARD H. CHAMBERLIN for selection: from "Can Union Power Be Curbed?" by Edward H. Chamberlin in *The Atlantic.* Copyright. Used by permission of Edward H. Chamberlin.

THE CHRISTIAN EDUCATION PRESS for selections; from *Christian Hymnways*, p. 165, copyright Christian Education Press; from *Pathways of Prayer*, pp. 110, 247, and 359, copyright Christian Education Press; from *Gates of Beauty*, pp. 8, 50, 375 and from Ralph W. Sockman, quoted in *Gates of Beauty*, p. 364, copyright Christian Education Press, 1945. Used by permission.

CHRISTIAN FREEDOM FOUNDATION, INC., for selection: from "Would We Have Signed?" by Howard E. Kershner, editor of *Christian Economics*, issue of June 28, 1960. Used by permission of Howard E. Kershner.

CHRISTIAN SCIENCE PUBLISHING SOCIETY for selections: from editorials in *The Christian Science Monitor*, issues of June 14, 1955, and Dec. 30, 1955. Used by permission.

The Church School Worker for selections: from "The Minister or Director of Christian Education" by Herbert N. Allen in *The Church School Worker*, July-August, 1960; from "Informing becomes Transforming" by Patricia Risdon in *The Church School Worker*, July-August, 1960; from "Uneasy Conscience About Christmas" by Earl F. Zeigler in *The Church School Worker*, Nov., 1958. Copyright 1958 and 1960 by Fred D. Wentzel. Used by permission.

CHURCH WORLD PRESS, INC. for selection: "Go Down the Road to Bethlehem," copyright 1959 by Church World Press, Inc., Cleveland, Ohio. Used by permission.

CITY NEWS PUBLISHING CO. for selections: from *Vital Speeches* by Charles Anspach, Aug. 1, 1959; Adolf Berle, Jr., May 15, 1960; Wilber Brucker, Aug. 15, 1960; Lionel Crocker, Aug. 1, 1959; Henry J. Kaiser, Jr., May 15, 1959; Robert Milliken, May 15, 1960; Howard T. Mitchell, May 1, 1960; James P. Mitchell, Aug. 1, 1959; Ben Moreell, May 15, 1960; Gov. William Quinn, Aug. 1, 1960; Elmo Roper, June 15, 1960; Henry Wriston, Jan. 15, 1959. Used with approval of City News Publishing Co.

CLOISTER PRESS for selection: from *Advance into Light* by James W. Kennedy. Copyright 1948 by Cloister Press, Louisville, Kentucky. Used by permission.

COMMISSION ON ECUMENICAL MISSION AND RELATIONS for selections: from *The Tumbling Walls* by Marion and Edwin Fairman. Copyright 1957 by Board of Foreign Missions, United Presbyterian Church of N. A.; from *Red-Headed, Rash and Religious* by W. Donald McClure. Copyright 1954 by Board of Foreign Missions, United Presbyterian Church of N. A.; from *Remember* by Inez Moser. Used by permission of Commission on Ecumenical Mission and Relations of the United Presbyterian Church in the U. S. A.

The Commonweal for selections: from "French Youth in Profile" by Robert Barrat, April 3, 1959; from "A Word for Tolerance" by John Cogly, April 24, 1959; from "A Search for Morals" by John Cogley, March 11, 1960; from "Hope and the Christian" by Jean Danielou, April 1, 1960; from editorials of July 15, 1959, and July 15, 1955; from "Freedom and Education" by Alfred W. Griswold, Nov. 15, 1957; from "Concept of Faith" by Leonard F. X. Mayhew, March 11, 1960; from George N. Shuster, Feb. 27, 1959. Copyright 1955, 1957 and 1960 by *The Commonweal*, the weekly journal of opinion edited by Catholic laymen. Used by permission.

CONDÉ NAST PUBLICATIONS, INC., for selection: from "Success, Good or Bad?" by Michael Drury reprinted from *Glamour*. Copyright © 1959 by the Condé Nast Publications, Inc. Used by permission.

The Congregational Way for selection: from Archie H. Hook. Used by permission.

DAVID C. COOK PUBLISHING COMPANY for selection: from Fletcher Slater in the *Sunday Digest*, Oct. 7, 1955.

THOMAS Y. CROWELL COMPANY for selections: from *Two Together* by Robert C. Dodds. Copyright 1959 by Thomas Y. Crowell Company, New York, publishers. Used by permission.

DEFENDERS, INC., for selections: from a Lincoln creed; from "Father and His Family" by Grant and Ruth Stoltzfus in *The Defender*, June, 1960; from R. S. Beal in *The Defender*, May, 1960. Used by permission.

MARCELENE COX for selections: from *Ladies' Home Journal*, issues of June, July, Sept., Oct., 1959 and Feb., 1960.

DORRANCE & CO., INC., for selections: from *The Prayer Life of Jesus* by Guy Everton Tremaine. Copyright 1954 by Dorrance & Co., Inc., Philadelphia. Used by permission.

DOUBLEDAY & COMPANY, INC., for selection: from *Your Money and Your Church* by Richard Byfield and James Shaw. Copyright 1959 by Doubleday & Co., Inc. Used by permission.

WILLIAM B. EERDMANS PUBLISHING CO. for selections: from *The Seven Windows* by S. J. Reid. Copyright 1939 by William B. Eerdmans Publishing Co. Used by permission.

DWIGHT D. EISENHOWER for selections: from public addresses of June 3, 1947, January 10, 1957 and the 1953 Thanksgiving proclamation. Used by permission.

The Episcopalian for selections: from "A Yes-and-No Answer" by Mary Morrison in *The Episcopalian*, June, 1960; from "Our World at Work" by Bishop Stephen F. Bayne, Jr., in *The Episcopalian*, June, 1960. Copyright 1960. Used by permission.

ESQUIRE, INC., for selection: from "One Christmas Eve" by Adrian Anderson in *Coronet* magazine, Dec., 1946. Copyright 1946 by Esquire, Inc. Reprinted from *Coronet*, Dec., 1946, by permission.

Everywoman's Family Circle for selection: from "Let's Stop This Silly Worship of Youth" by Lester and Irene David, issue of May, 1959. Copyright 1959.

JAMES A. FARLEY for selection: from "What I Believe" by James A. Farley in *The Atlantic*, June, 1959. Used by permission of James A. Farley.

CHARLES K. FEWKES for selections: from *Central Truths of the Christian Youth Movement* by Norman E. Richardson. *Copyright 1936 by Charles K. Fewkes.* Used by permission.

THE FOUNDATION FOR ECONOMIC EDUCATION, INC. for selections: from *Notes From Fee*, Jan., 1959; from Percy L. Greaves, Jr. in *The Freeman*, Feb., 1959. Copyright 1959.

Fortune for selection: from "The Fabulous Future" by General David Sarnoff in *Fortune*, January, 1955. Copyright 1955. Used by permission.

Guide Posts for selection: from Gerald Horton Bath.

HARPER & BROTHERS for selections: from *From the Cross* by Gaius Glenn Atkins. Copyright 1937 by Harper & Brothers; from *The Prophets* by Julius A. Bewer. Copyright 1955; from *Journey in the*

Dark by Martin Flavin. Copyright 1943 by Martin Flavin; from *Taking a City* by Douglas Horton. Copyright 1934; from *Specifically to Youth* by Harry H. Kruener. Copyright 1959 by Harry H. Kruener; from *Reality and Prayer* by John B. Magee. Copyright 1957 by John B. Magee; from *The Art of Living* by André Maurois. Copyright; from *Free Speech and Its Relation to Self-Government* by Alexander Meiklejohn. Copyright; from *Giants in the Earth* by O. E. Rölvaag. Copyright 1927; from *Education and Moral Wisdom* by George N. Shuster. Copyright; from *Beyond Survival* by Max Ways. Copyright. Reprinted by permission of Harper & Brothers, N. Y.

Harper's Magazine for selection: from Charlton Ogburn, Jr. in *Harper's Magazine*, August, 1960. Reprinted by permission.

ALAN HARRINGTON for selection: from "The Personnel Interview" by Alan Harrington in *The Atlantic*, August, 1959; and *Life in the Crystal Palace*, published by Alfred A. Knopf, Inc., 1959. Copyright 1959. Used by permission of Alan Harrington.

His for selections: from "Foundations of the Christian Home" by H. W. Sutherland in *His*, Oct., 1958. Reprinted by permission from *His*, student magazine of the Inter-Varsity Christian Fellowship.

HOLT, RINEHART AND WINSTON, INC. for selection: from *Appeal to the Nations and Afterward* by Norman Thomas, published by Henry Holt & Co., N.Y. Copyright 1947. Used by permission.

Hot Springs (South Dakota) *Star* for selections: from Christmas meditations by E. Paul Hovey and Arthur Meyer. Used by permission.

HOUGHTON, MIFFLIN CO., for selections: from *The Affluent Society* by John Kenneth Galbraith, p. 5 and p. 9. Copyright © 1958 by John Kenneth Galbraith.

The Intercollegian for selections: from Emile Caillett, Feb., 1945; from John Deschner, April, 1945.

International Journal of Religious Education for selection: from "You Are Called" by Mildred B. Hahn in *The International Journal of Religious Education*, Nov., 1951. Copyright 1951. Used by permission.

JOHN KNOX PRESS for selection: from *Adventures in Parenthood* by W. Taliaferro Thompson. Copyright 1959 by John Knox Press. Used by permission.

W. LIVINGSTON LARNED for selection: "Father Forgets." Used by permission of William E. Larned.

Lewiston (Idaho) *Morning Tribune* for selections: from editorial by William Johnston Feb. 15, 1955; editorial March 29, 1959; editorial June 14, 1955; news story by Relman Morin. Used by permission.

Life for selections: from editorial April 2, 1956; editorial March 30, 1959; editorial Dec. 28, 1959; from Carleton Putnam in *Life*, July 11, 1960; George E. Carter in *Life*, July 11, 1960; from John D. Rockefeller, Jr. in *Life*, May 23, 1960; from Max Ways, Oct., 1959 (also Harper & Brothers publication); copyright 1956; 1959; 1960 © Time, Inc. Used by permission.

LITTLE, BROWN AND CO. for selection: from *The Soul's Sincere Desire* by Glenn Clark. Copyright 1925. Used by permission.

LONGMANS GREEN & CO., INC. for selection: from *Sins of the Day*. Copyright 1958-1959. Used by permission.

MACALESTER PARK PUBLISHING CO. for selection: from *The Three Mysteries of Jesus* by Glenn Clark. Copyright 1942 by Macalester Park Publishing Co. Used by permission.

THE MACMILLAN COMPANY for selections: from *Life of Jesus* by Maurice Goguel. Copyright; from *The Struggle of the Soul* by Lewis Joseph Sherrill. Copyright 1951 by Lewis J. Sherrill; from *Christ's Victory and Ours* by Frederick C. Grant. Copyright 1950; from *God with Us* by J. B. Phillips. Copyright 1957; from *Backwards to Christmas* by J. B. Phillips. Copyright. Used by permission.

McCall's for selections: from issues of March, 1959 and June, 1959. Copyright 1959. Used by permission. From "We Learned How To Live" by James F. Brown in *Redbook*, May, 1955; from Marlon Brando in *Redbook*, May, 1955. Copyright 1955. Used by permission of McCall's Corporation.

McCormick Speaking for selections: from "Marginal Notes on Higher Education" by Arthur McKay in *McCormick Speaking*, Dec., 1958; from "Communicating the Gospel" by Hulda Niebuhr in *McCormick Speaking*, March, 1958; from "A Living Hope" by Paul S. Wright in *McCormick Speaking*, October, 1959. Used by permission.

MEREDITH PUBLISHING COMPANY for selections: from "Man About the House" by Burton Hillis in *Better Homes & Gardens*, issues of Oct., 1958; June, 1955; May, 1959; July, 1959; August, 1959; Nov., 1959; and Jan., 1960; from "There's No Unanswered Prayer" by Margaret Blair Johnstone in *Better Homes & Gardens*, Dec., 1954; from "On the Spot" by May Richstone in *Better Homes & Gardens*, Oct., 1958. Copyright 1954, 1955, 1958, 1959, 1960 by Meredith Publishing Company, Des Moines, Iowa. Used by permission.

The Methodist Layman for selection: from Ernest F. Tittle in *The Methodist Layman*, Feb., 1950. Copyright 1950. Used by permission.

THE METHODIST PUBLISHING HOUSE for selections: from Harold L. Fair in *Adult Student*, Dec., 1957; from John M. Versteeg in *Adult Student*, Nov., 1949; from John Edward Lantz in *Bible Lessons for Youth*, July, 1946; from Helen and Myron Wicks in *The Christian Home*, Oct., 1958; from Thomas F. Chilcote, Jr. in *Daily Bible Lessons*, April, 1957 (now *Epworth Notes*); from "A Thanksgiving Prayer" by Percy R. Hayward in *Epworth Herald*, Nov. 16, 1935; from Henry C. Sprinkle, Jr. in *Prayer Manual for Week of Dedication 1952*, the Board of Missions. Copyright 1935, 1946, 1949, 1952, 1957, 1958 by the Methodist Publishing House. Used by permission of the Department of Church School Curriculum.

MISSION COUNCIL OF THE CONGREGATIONAL CHRISTIAN CHURCH for selections: from *Stewardship Notebook* by Warren H. Denison; from *The Church's Life* by Roger Hazelton and Robert V. Moss, Jr.; from "The Great Invasion" by S. Macon Cowles, Jr. in *Missions Today*, Nov., 1959; from *Missions Today*, May, 1960. Used by permission.

Monday Morning for selections: from William Hiram Foulkes, March 18, 1940; from "Learning To Add" by George A. Frantz, Feb. 15, 1954; from "Judgment by Sunlight" by George A. Frantz, March 14, 1954; from "Welcoming Christ" by George A. Frantz, March 29, 1954; from Hugh I. Evans, Nov. 15, 1943; from "Advent" by Donald Macleod, Nov. 5, 1956; from "The Wondrous Cross" by Walton M. Rankin, March 2, 1953; from "A Parent Speaks" by Eleanor Stone Roberts, Dec. 5, 1955; from "Reformation—Its Meaning for Us" by K. W. Schalk, Oct. 25, 1954. Used by permission.

MUHLENBERG PRESS for selections: from *For Today* by D. T. Niles. Copyright 1955; from *A Theology for Christian Stewardship* by T. A. Kantonen. Copyright 1956 by Muhlenberg Press. Used by permission.

The Nation for selections: from "The Fervor of the Faithful," editorial in *The Nation*, June 13, 1959; from "The Voice of the People" by Stewart Meacham in *The Nation*, Feb. 21, 1959; from "The God We Deserve" by Gabriel Vahanian in *The Nation*, Feb. 20, 1960. Copyright 1959, 1960 by The Nation Associates, Inc. Used by permission.

THE NATIONAL COUNCIL OF THE CHURCHES OF CHRIST IN THE U.S.A. for selections: from *Protestantism* by Hampton Adams; from *Pray Thy Kingdom Come* by Hampton Adams; from *Even as Christ Also Loved the Church* by Margaret Applegarth; from *The Power of God* by J. Harry Cotton; from *The Dynamic Leadership of the Holy Spirit* by Lloyd E. Foster; from *Christian Family Week 1960* by Elizabeth and William Genné; from *Prayer* by Harris Franklin Rall; from *Race Relations Message 1950* prepared by D. Elton Trueblood; from *The Glorious Liberty* by Cynthia Wedel; from a *Manual for a Community Call*; from *The Tried and the Untried*; the *Youth Ecumenical Service 1960*. Used by permission of the National Council of the Churches of Christ in the U.S.A.

National Council Outlook for selections: from "An Easter Message" by Eugene Carson Blake in *National Council Outlook*, March, 1956; from "The Meaning of Pentecost" by Samuel M. Cavert in *National Council Outlook*, May, 1959; from "Rainbow over Calvary" by Edwin T. Dahlberg in *National Council Outlook*, April, 1958; from an editorial in *National Council Outlook*, April, 1956; from an editorial in *National Council Outlook*, Oct., 1956. Used by permission.

NATIONAL FELLOWSHIP OF CONGREGATIONAL CHRISTIAN WOMEN for selections: from *What Doth the Lord Require?* by Doris Brenner Stickney; from *Guide Posts* by Doris Webster Havice in issue of Jan., 1960. Used by permission of the National Fellowship of Congregational Christian Women.

National Parent-Teacher Magazine for selection: from " 'Say Now Shibboleth' " by Matthew W. Hill in the *National Parent-Teacher: The P.T.A. Magazine*, Feb., 1960 p. 24. Used by permission.

The New Leader for selection: from "The Limits of Military Power" by Reinhold Niebuhr, *The New Leader*, May 30, 1955. Copyright 1955. Used by permission.

The New Republic for selection: from Joel Seidman in *The New Republic*, August 24, 1959. Used by permission.

Newsweek for selections: from Joost de Blank in *Newsweek*, April 25, 1960; from Senator Barry Goldwater in *Newsweek*, Feb. 1, 1960; from William Gowland in *Newsweek*, August 3, 1959; from F. A. Hayek in *Newsweek*, Feb. 15, 1960; from Henry Hazlitt in *Newsweek*, Sept. 7, 1959; from Murray Stedman, Jr., in *Newsweek*, April 27, 1959; from Burr Tillstrom in *Newsweek*, Sept. 7, 1959. Copyright 1959 and 1960 by *Newsweek*. Used by permission.

The New York Times for selections: from Ian Ballantine in *The New York Times* Book Review, Jan. 17, 1960, p. 6; from Allan Knight Chalmers in *The New York Times*; from Sidney Hook in *The New York Times Magazine*, July 9, 1950. Copyright *The New York Times*. Used by permission.

NORFOLK AND WESTERN RAILWAY for selection: from an advertisement in *Newsweek* of July 4, 1955. Used by permission.

BEN K. O'DELL for selection: from "Success or Failure?" by Ben K. O'Dell in *Specialty Salesman*, June, 1960. Copyright by Ben K. O'Dell. Used by permission.

KAY H. OWENS for a poem "Ladies' Choice" by Kay Owens in *Ladies' Home Journal*, Feb., 1960. Used by permission.

Parents' Magazine for selection: from "A Prayer" by Ralph W. Sockman in *Parents' Magazine*, Dec., 1959. Published by Parents' Institute, Inc., N. Y. Used by permission.

P E O Record for selections: from "The Power of the Home" by John Sutherland Bonnell in the *P E O Record*, Feb., 1954; from "Enduring Values" by Uretta A. Hinkhouse in the *P E O Record*, Dec., 1958; from "A Prayer for our Country" by Irene Avery Judson in the *P E O Record*, July, 1960; from "Motherhood" by Jeanne M. Lofgren in the *P E O Record*, May, 1959; from John H. Miller in the *P E O Record*, Oct., 1958; from Norman Vincent Peale in the *P E O Record*, Dec., 1958; from Ruth W. Rippey in the *P E O Record*, Dec., 1958; for a poem by Lillian E. Rogers in the *P E O Record*, May, 1960; from Augusta Rundel in the *P E O Record*, Dec., 1958; from "Setting Sail" by Myra A. Wiggins in the *P E O Record*, Jan., 1954. Used by permission.

THE PILGRIM PRESS for selections: from *On Coming to the Lord's Table* by Charles A. Baldwin; from *Problems of Christian Living* by Arlo Ayres Brown. Copyright 1913; from items by Fred Register, Edward J. Vobra and Mrs. James H. Woods; from "A Beatitude" by E. Paul Hovey in the *Pilgrim Elementary Teacher*, Oct., 1938. Copyright 1938 by Pilgrim Press. Used by permission.

Presbyterian Life for selections: from "A Paraphrase of Lincoln's Gettysburg Address" by John R. Bodo in *Presbyterian Life*, Feb. 15, 1959; from "The Desperate Choice" by Howard Lowry in *Presbyterian Life*, March 13, 1948; from "Thanksgiving Conquers Anxiety" by Park Hays Miller in *Presbyterian Life*, Nov. 28, 1953. Copyright 1948, 1953 and 1959 by Presbyterian Life, Inc. Used by permission.

The Presbyterian Magazine for selection: from an editorial, "From Everlasting to Everlasting Thou Art God" by Cleland B. McAfee in *The Presbyterian Magazine*, Jan., 1931. Published by the General Council of the Presbyterian Church in the U.S.A.

Presbyterian Outlook for selection: from "The Layman in the Church and the World" by D. Maurice Allen in *Presbyterian Outlook*. Used by permission.

Prophetic Realism for selections: from "The Pastor and His Youth" by Kenneth Beall in *Prophetic Realism*, Winter 1956; from "Realistically Speaking" by John Wick Bowman in *Prophetic Realism*, Summer 1956. Used by permission.

The Pulpit for selections: from "Pray for a Miracle" by Robert L. Eddy in *The Pulpit*, August, 1960; from "Big Enough for Freedom" by Donald Macleod in *The Pulpit*, July, 1960. Copyright 1960 by Christian Century Foundation. Used by permission.

PRENTICE-HALL, INC., for selection: from *'Twixt Twelve and Twenty* by Pat Boone. Copyright © 1958 by Prentice-Hall, Inc. Used by permission.

Pulpit Preaching for selections: from "The Meaning of the Supper" by Fredrich Rest, *Pulpit Preaching*, Oct., 1952; from "Translating Thanksgiving" by Fred R. Chenault, *Pulpit Preaching*, Nov., 1951; from "Gratitude—Thanksgiving" by W. P. King, *Pulpit Preaching*, Nov., 1951; from "We Three" by John B. Warman, *Pulpit Preaching*, August, 1959. Used by permission.

Rapid City (South Dakota) *Daily Journal* for selections: from an editorial, Feb. 12, 1952; from a Lenten meditation by I. B. Wood.

The Reader's Digest for selections: from "What Happens When We Pray for Others?" by Robert J. McCracken, *The Reader's Digest*, Oct., 1956. Copyright 1956; from "Living for the Fun of It" by Harry Emerson Fosdick, *The Reader's Digest*, May, 1930. Copyright 1930. Used by permission.

The Rotarian for selections: from "No Time To Live?" by Fred DeArmond in *The Rotarian*, Aug., 1959; from William Hazlitt in *The Rotarian*, March, 1960; from "Now" by M. E. Moore in *The Rotarian*, June, 1959; from "Line of Least Resistance" by Thomas Usk in *The Rotarian*, May, 1959; from Kendall Weisiger in *The Rotarian*, June, 1960. Copyright 1959 and 1960 by *The Rotarian*. Used by permission.

MARSHAL SCOTT for selections: from *The Christian and Social Action* by Marshal Scott. Used by permission.

ERIC SEVAREID for selection: from Eric Sevareid in *The Saturday Evening Post*, May 16, 1959. Copyright 1959. Used by permission.

MARIE RODELL AND JOAN DAVES, INC., for selections: from *Collected Edition of Heywood Broun* by Heywood Broun, published by Harcourt, Brace & Co., Inc. Copyright. Used by permission.

SOURCE PUBLISHERS for selections: from *Christian Faith for Today* by John Ferguson.

Specialty Salesman for selections: from Harold Blake Walker in *Specialty Salesman*, March, 1960; May, 1960. Copyright *Specialty Salesman*, 1960. Used by permission.

This Week magazine for selection: from "Father Was Tough" by Michael Griffin, *This Week* magazine, Feb. 11, 1945. Reprinted from *This Week* magazine. Copyright 1945 by the United Newspapers Magazine Corporation. Used by permission.

DOROTHY THOMPSON for selections: from "A Question of Value" by Dorothy Thompson in *Ladies' Home Journal*, Feb., 1960. Copyright 1960. Used by permission of Dorothy Thompson.

TIDINGS for selections: from "Evangelistic Opportunities at Easter" by K. Morgan Edwards, *Shepherds*, March, 1951; from *What Every Protestant Should Know* by Paul E. Folkers; from *I Take the Cup* by Eugene E. Golay; from *Learning To Pray* by Howard L. Stimmel; from *Rediscovering Christmas* by G. Ernest Thomas. Copyright by Tidings. Used by permission.

DOUGLAS TIFFANY for selection: from "A Modern Parable—The Delinquent Father" by Douglas Tiffany in the *Idaho Challenge*, Dec., 1956. Used by permission.

Together and The Christian Advocate for selections: from O. W. Bell, *Together*, Aug., 1960; from "Letter to an Innkeeper" by Michael Daves, *Together*, Dec., 1959; from Roy L. Smith, *Together*, May, 1959; March, 1960; August, 1960; from Lloyd C. Wicks, *Together*, March, 1960. Copyright 1959 and 1960 by Lovick Pierce. Used by permission. From Arthur H. Compton, *The Christian Advocate*; from Roy L. Smith, *The Christian Advocate*; from Harris F. Rall, *The Christian Adovcate*; from Rollin H. Walker, *The Christian Advocate*. Copyright Lovick Pierce. Used by permission.

UNIFIED PROMOTION for selection: from "Two for the Price of One" by Robert L. Bell. Unified Promotion of Disciples of Christ, Indianapolis, Indiana. Used by permission Robert L. Bell and Unified Promotion.

The Union Signal for selections: from Ada Simpson Sherwood in *The Union Signal*, May 28, 1960; from "Getting By" by Erma Kidd Hulburt in *The Union Signal*, March 26, 1960; from an editorial in *The Union Signal*, Jan. 23, 1960; from Erma Kidd Hulburt, *The Union Signal*, March 12, 1960; from Mrs. Herman (Edith) Stanley, *The Union Signal*, Dec. 26, 1959; from Mrs. Herman (Edith) Stanley, *The Union Signal*, May 14, 1960. Used by permission.

The United Church Herald for selections: from "The ABC's of Prayer" by Walter A. Mueller, *The United Church Herald*, March 31, 1960; from "Stewardship in an Economy of Abundance" by A. T. Rasmussen, *The United Church Herald*, March 31, 1960. Used by permission.

THE UPPER ROOM for selections: from *Finding God Through Prayer* by C. Irving Benson; from excerpts in *Dad*; from Bishop J. W. Lord, *The Upper Room Pulpit*, Sept., 1954; from E. Paul Hovey, *The Upper Room*, Jan. 10, 1947; from E. Paul Hovey, *The Upper Room*, Dec. 20, 1955. Copyright The Upper Room. Used by permission. From *Are Your Children with You?* by Edgar J. Helms. Reprinted through the courtesy of The Upper Room, Nashville, Tennessee.

THE UNITED PRESBYTERIAN CHURCH IN THE U.S.A. for selections: from Thomas A. Clark, *Gratitude to God*, A Source Book on Tithing; from "A Labor Sunday Offertory Prayer" by Hurd Allyn Drake, *Everyone*, Sept., 1940; from *When I Give Nothing* by John A. McAfee; from *The Soul of a Man Is in His Gifts* by Arnold H. Lowe; from "The Invitation to World-Wide Communion" by Marvin C. Wilbur; from *Come Before His Presence* by Mrs. John Hastie Brown; from *My Religion in Action, 1940* by Helen Welshimer. Used by permission Division of Program Materials, The United Presbyterian Church in the U.S.A., N.Y.

THE VIKING PRESS, INC., for selection: from *Times Three* by Phyllis McGinley. Copyright © 1959 by Phyllis McGinley. Originally printed in *The New Yorker*. Reprinted by permission of The Viking Press, Inc.

The War Cry for selection: "Prayer for the New Year" by Marie Barton.

A. WATKINS, INC. for selections: from *Begin Here* by Dorothy L. Sayers. Copyright 1941 by Dorothy L. Sayers. Published by Harcourt, Brace and Co., Inc. Used by permission of A. Watkins, Inc.

WHITTEMORE ASSOCIATES, INC. for selections: from *The Holy Bible* by Kenneth Clinton; from *What Prayer Means to Me* by Nels F. S. Ferre. Used by permission.

WESTMINSTER PRESS for selections: from *Intercessory Prayer* by Edward W. Bauman. Copyright © 1958 by W. L. Jenkins; from *The Significance of the Church* by Robert McAfee Brown. Copyright 1956 by W. L. Jenkins; from *The Inward Cross* by Charles Duell Kean. Copyright 1952 W. L. Jenkins; from *Entrusted with the Gospel* by David A. MacLennan. Copyright 1956 W. L. Jenkins; from *Making the Most of Your Best* by David A. MacLennan. Copyright © 1958; from *Mr. Valiant for Truth* by Harold McAfee Robinson. Copyright 1939 Board of Christian Education; from *The Teaching Ministry of the Church* by James D. Smart. Copyright 1954 W. L. Jenkins; from *Thine Is the Glory* by Florence Taylor. Copyright 1948 W. L. Jenkins; from *An Outline of the Christian Faith.* Copyright 1948 Board of Christian Education; from "The Sculptor Prayed" by Eda O. Borseth in *If I Be His Disciple.* Copyright 1953 W. L. Jenkins; from *Together We Grow* by Dorothy Arnim and Herman L. Sweet. Copyright 1958 W. L. Jenkins; from Jarvis S. Morris in *Follow Me,* May 31, 1937. Copyright 1937 Westminster Press; from Eliot Porter in *Forward.* Copyright; from "A Prayer for Father's Day" by Grace Helen Davis, *Forward,* Vol. 76 No. 24, 1952; from Franklin Gillespie in *Forward.* Copyright; from Sara J. Wescoat, *Discovery,* April-June, 1959. Copyright 1959 W. L. Jenkins; from *Westminster Adult Bible Class* by Earl F. Zeigler. Copyright; from "A Prayer To Greet the Day" by E. Paul Hovey, *Westminster Adult Bible Class,* March, 1943: from editorial, "The Angel Meant What

He Said," *Westminster Adult Bible Class,* Dec., 1942. Copyright Board of Christian Education; from Robert Lodwick, *Westminster Uniform Lesson Teacher,* July, 1943. Copyright 1943; from editorial *Westminster Uniform Lesson Teacher,* Jan., 1939. Copyright 1939; from "The Master Has Been Here" by E. Paul Hovey, *Westminster Uniform Lesson Teacher,* July, 1943. Copyright 1943; from "Everybody Does it" by E. Paul Hovey, *The Society Kit* Vol. III. Copyright 1945; from Henry Barraclough, *Today,* Nov., 1951; from Maurice Bone, *Today,* Summer Conference edition 1951; from George William Brown, *Today,* Oct., 1946; Walter Barlow, *Today,* April, 1952; George S. Bancroft, *Today,* Aug., 1942; James W. Clarke, *Today,* Jan., 1958; Walter D. Cavert, *Today,* Dec., 1958; Gilbert F. Close, Jr., *Today,* Jan., 1952; Lowell Russel Ditzen, *Today,* Oct., 1945; William Hiram Foulkes, *Today,* April, 1948; E. Paul Hovey, *Today,* Nov., 1944; William T. Hanzsche, *Today,* Jan., 1942; Toyohiko Kagawa, *Today,* June, 1941; Donald F. Lomas, *Today,* Dec., 1948; Peter and Catherine Marshall, *Today,* Sept., 1943; Arthur L. Miller, *Today,* June, 1950; Paul Calvin Payne, *Today,* Dec., 1941; William C. Skeath, *Today,* Nov., 1942; Harry Thomas Stock, *Today,* June, 1943; Frederick Udlock, *Today,* May, 1947; John Charles Wynn, *Today,* May, 1952; Lyman W. Winkle, *Today,* Aug., 1945. Copyright 1941, 1942, 1943, 1944, 1945, 1947, 1948, 1950, 1951, 1952, 1958 by Westminster Press. Used by permission Westminster Press.

Wesleyan Methodist for selections: from O. G. Wilson.

Ward County Independent for poem: from "A Prayer" by Huldah L. Winsted, *North Dakota—Land Of The Sky and Other Poems.* Copyright 1927 *Ward County Independent,* Minot, North Dakota. Used by permission.

MRS. WENDELL WILLKIE for selections: from Wendell L. Willkie. Used by permission.

The YWCA Magazine for selections: from the review of a Macmillan book by Frances Helen Mains, *The YWCA Magazine,* May, 1959; from "A Rich Spiritual

Climate" by Charles Malik, *The YWCA Magazine,* Jan., 1959. Used by permission.

Your Life magazine for selections: from "The Unknown Self Within You" by George Christian Anderson, *Your Life,* Oct., 1959; from Thomas Dreier, *Your Life,* Feb., 1960; from Imogene Fey, *Your Life,* July, 1960; from James J. O'Reilly, *Your Life,* Oct., 1959, Feb., 1960.

CONTENTS

THE TREASURY FOR

Special Days and Occasions

THE CHRISTIAN YEAR

1

The Christian year sets up the great human life. The building of the perfect man is the noblest work that can go on in the world. The seasons come and go, the harvests ripen and are gathered in, the mountains are built up and decay; but all these are sights that cannot match the dignity and interest of the spectacle of a full, strong man's life. First God prepares for him the place where he is to live. Then his life comes and takes place, a strong and settled fact. Then it puts forth its power and influences other men. Then suffering comes to it and matures it, but finally it issues out of suffering, refined and triumphant. And at last, when it has passed away out of the world into new regions of activity and growth, it leaves its power behind it to bless men after it is dead. There is nothing so round and perfect as such a life in all the world. It is the very crown of God's creation.

Such a complete life is pictured in the church's year. It has its Advent, Nativity, Epiphany, Lent, Easter, Whitsunday, Trinity Sunday. It fills the years with its increasing, slowly maturing beauty. This is the true meaning of the year, with all its sacred seasons. Let us be true churchmen and give it all its richness. Only, dear friends, we do not really honor the venerable beauty of the church's calendar when we make it a badge of our denominational distinction, or deck its seasons out with all the trickery of colored altar cloths, purple and white and green, but when we see in it the story of a human life slowly ripened from God's first purpose to the full-grown, glorified manhood standing before God's presence and sending forth God's power to its fellow men.—Phillips Brooks

NEW YEAR

2

From that January 1, 1502, when it is supposed Americus Vespucius first sighted the mainland of South America, on down the centuries the date has seemed to hold an important place in American history. That particular New Year's Day was destined to give the continents of the New World their names. Up to that time the newly discovered territory had been thought of as part of Asia, and Vespucius was one of the first to realize that it was an entirely new territory. He wrote a letter back, referring to it as the "Mundus Novus," or New World, and a geographer named Martin Waldseemüller quoted his letter and suggested that the new lands discovered by Americus should be called "the land of Americus, or America."

The famous ride took place in April, but Paul Revere was born on January 1, 1735, in Boston. Ten years later, on January 1, 1745, there was born on a Pennsylvania farm another boy who was to grow up and take a prominent part in the affairs of his country. Like Washington, he became a surveyor, and a trusted member of his community. This was Anthony Wayne, known to history as "Mad Anthony" Wayne, because of his courage and daring during the Revolution and the Indian wars that followed.

On Paul Revere's seventeenth and Anthony Wayne's seventh birthday—that is, on New Year's Day, 1752, was born Elizabeth Griscom, of Philadelphia. She later married a Philadelphia upholsterer and merchant named John Ross, and became his most valuable and skilled assistant in his work, as well as in the home. Her skill in choosing materials and using the needle was widely known, so it was natural that Betsy Ross should be chosen by the men who knew her to make the first flag. Legend says that she also designed it, but historians dispute this. At least she made the first flag designed from the resolution of the Continental Congress, adopted June 14, 1777, which read: "Resolved: that the flag of the thirteen United States be thirteen stripes alternate red and white; that the Union be thirteen stars, white on a blue field, representing a new constellation."

But a year and a half earlier General Washington had raised over his Cambridge, Massachusetts, camp a flag which had the thirteen stripes, although it had the Union Jack of the British flag in the corner. But this was raised on January 1, 1776, six months before the Declaration of Independence, while the Colonists still regarded themselves as Englishmen fighting for their rights. So we can really say that the first truly American flag was flown on New Year's Day.

American settlers first arrived in Texas on January 1, 1822, just eight years after the British had begun their siege of New Orleans in the War of 1812. In 1831 William Lloyd Garrison brought out the first issue of his famous anti-slavery paper, *The Liberator*, on January 1. Thirty-two years later, on January 1, 1863, Lincoln's Emancipation Proclamation went into effect, practically finishing what Garrison had started.

These are the outstanding associations of New Year's Day in American history, and show its interest and importance.—Harold Emery

3

The problem of civilization's future cannot be evaded. This is an age of crisis. Events are of global consequence: technical inventions place in men's hands power never known before; economic upheavals shatter so-called classic economic laws and demand a re-examination of the distribution of wealth; lands across the sea, once held as colonies or kept economically dependent on the nations of the West, have won political autonomy.

The future fills some men with dread. All they hold dear seems in danger. They have never distinguished between eternal values and the expression of these values in terms of bourgeois civilization; therefore they feel that they must defend the past from the assaults of the future. Others, on the contrary, trust the new forces unreservedly and believe that scientific progress and social transformations will produce an earthly paradise. We must ask ourselves what connection there is between Christian hope, which has for its object the heavenly city, and temporal hope, that which limits itself to the future well-being of the earthly city. It is of the essence of hope to hold a positive attitude in regard to time. This attitude, which seems so reasonable to modern man, the ancients would have found very strange. Time to them was an enemy

. . . the Bible completely reversed all values when it gave meaning to time and placed hope in the future. The man who knows the Bible thinks of time as the place where a divine plan is being shaped and he looks forward to the completion of this plan. Hope is, for him, this looking forward. Thus he avoids what seemed natural to the pagans—a nostalgia for the past. Jean Hering writes that "The Christian ideal is not the exiled princess longing to return; it is Abraham setting out towards an unknown land which God will show him." Ulysses, the hero of the ancients, after his years of wandering returns to his starting point and thus cancels time. Abraham knew no return. He left Ur of the Chaldees and never went back. He embarked on "the adventure of time," forgetting, as Saint Paul tells us, "what was behind so as to stretch forward to things that are ahead." Faith in the future was from the first the special message of the Bible.—Jean Danielou, "Hope and the Christian," *The Commonweal*

4

We cannot speak with any truth or realism about our faith in the future unless we understand the past.—Peter Marshall

5

Into our hands is given a New Year, to be used wisely or foolishly as we choose! Here is what one poet has the New Year ask:

I am the New Year—
All that I have I give with love unspoken.
All that I ask—you keep the faith unbroken!

Let us start the year knowing that we have a place in God's plan and the plan will suffer if we do not do our share in carrying it out. Moreover, our small lives can gain greatness by their connection with His great plan. Paul had a special call to serve, so have we. And we have the same source of power. Shall we not, then, enter upon this New Year realizing that into our hands is given the wealth of days and the power to make our lives just what we will? And shall we not make our goal "the measure of the stature of the fulness of Christ?" (Ephesians 4:13).—Cleland Boyd McAfee

6

How often we are admonished not to waste time. What an absurdity! We *can't* waste time, or spend it, or save it. It is like warning a fish in the ocean not to waste water. We have no influence at all on time, any more than we have on space. We are born in it; it surrounds us all. What we *can* waste—and do—is ourselves. The personal tragedy, the waste lies in what we *could* do with ourselves, but don't —the love we do not give; the efforts we do not make; the powers we do not use; the happiness we do not earn; the kindnesses we neglect to bestow; the noble thoughts and deeds that could be ours if only we realized *why* we are here.—Gerald Horton Bath, *Guideposts*

7

The person of tomorrow must have ability to live with himself. This assures inner strength to do what is right in material and human relationships. Its fruits are peace of mind and serenity of being.—Roger M. Kyes

8

"My voice shalt thou hear in the morning, O Lord;

In the morning will I direct my prayer unto thee, and will look up" (Psalm 5:3).

Rise up and pray, for another day
Awaits to welcome you.

We face the year
    God's way before us,
    God's strength to pilot us,
    God's might to uphold us,
    God's host to save us;
God's wisdom to guide us,
    From snares and evils;
God's eye to look before us,
    Seeing the temptations and
        vices;
God's hand to guard us
    From all who wish us ill;
God's Word to speak to us,
    Afar and near;
God's ear to hear us,
    Alone and in a multitude.
Rise up and sing, for another year
Awaits to welcome you.
—E. Paul Hovey, "A Prayer to Greet the Year," *Westminster Adult Bible Class*

9

That which is past and gone is irrevocable; wise men have enough to do with things present and to come. —Francis Bacon

10

. . . behind the dim unknown.
Standeth God within the shadow, keeping watch above his own.—James Russell Lowell

11

There are few principles less frequently realized than this: that we must begin to learn everything when there is no need to learn it, before the crisis comes. We must not wait till the needs come, for then it is too late.—Eustice Miles

12

We live in the present, we dream of the future, but we learn eternal truths from the past.—Madame Chiang Kai-Shek

13

That man is sure to win who can command the situation instead of allowing the situation to control him.—Hollis Burke Frissell

14

Lose this day loitering, 'twill be the same old story
Tomorrow, and the next day more dilatory.
Each indecision brings its own delays.
And days are lost lamenting o'er lost days.
What you can do, or think you can, begin it.
Boldness has genius, power and magic in it.—Goethe

15

Now God be thanked who has matched us with his hour.—Rupert Brooke

16

Around the corner of the street who can say what waits for us?—James Whitcomb Riley

17

So the New Year begins. It is not exactly what most of us would have wished or ordered a year ago! The world is still a scene of propaganda poses and threatening postures, like the "I did not!" "Yes you did too!" of our small children. . . . It would be easy to slump with head in hands and welcome the New Year saying: "It's a bad world. How could it be much worse?"

Or is it perhaps instead an unfinished earth where the New Year hands us the raw materials for more constructive changes than we have ever seen before? The New Year opens with fluid conditions. . . . Where will we have the stream of our life flow? Nothing is nailed down . . . what will we build with these rearranged materials? . . . raw materials from which we may fashion a good life. Help us welcome the New Year with its untold opportunities .and unexpected promises.—Donald S. Lamka

18

It may be true that I have much less to live on than I had a year ago, but it is certainly true that I have just as much to live for. The real values of life are unshaken and solid, a financial crisis can rob us of all that we have, but it cannot affect what we are.—Claiborne Johnson

19

The best preparation for a better life next year is a full, complete, harmonious, joyous life this year. Our beliefs in a rich future life are of little importance unless we coin them into a rich present life. Today should always be our most wonderful day.—Thomas Dreier

20

Whilst everything around me is ever-changing, ever-dying, I do dimly perceive that underlying all that change there is a living power that is changeless, that holds all together, that creates, dissolves, and re-creates. That power or spirit is God. . . . I see it as purely benevolent, for I can see that in the midst of untruth, truth persists; in the midst of darkness, light persists; in the midst of death, life persists. Hence, I gather that God is truth, light, and life. He is love. He is the supreme good. But He is no God who merely satisfies the intellect. God to be God must rule the heart and transform it.—Mahatma Gandhi

21

Having chosen our course, without guile, and with pure purpose, let us renew our trust in God, and go forward without fear and with manly hearts.—Abraham Lincoln

22

If you will do your best today, you will be able to do even better tomorrow.

23

Yesterday is yours no longer; tomorrow may never be yours; today is yours, and in the living present you may stretch forth to the things that are before.—Canon Farrar

24

Write it in your heart that every day is the best day in the year.—Ralph W. Emerson

25

At every moment of time we reach two ways—toward the past and toward the future. Today is always the day toward which we once looked forward, and of which we dreamed. Today is the day toward which we shall one day look back, and about which we shall muse.

New Year's Day more than any other is such a day, because we think of it as a turning point between the failures and faults of the past and the better and braver deeds of the future.—Harley H. Gill

26

What a mighty sum of events has been consummated; what a tide of passions and affections has flowed; what lives and deaths have alternately arrived; what destinies have been fixed forever! Once more our planet has completed one of those journeys in the heavens which perfect all the fruitful changes of its peopled surface and mete out the few stages of our existence; and every day, every hour of that progress, has in all her wide lands, in all her million hearts, left traces that eternity shall behold.—William Howitt, "New Year's Day"

27

To get the most out of the coming year we must put the most into it, and we put the most into it by living in a spirit of earnestness, doing with our might what our hands find to do, not trifling with the golden hours, but receiving each as a precious gift from God. Only such earnest purpose makes the day a blessing, insures progress from good to better, and causes us to live in eternity while we are in time.—James Freeman Clarke

28

The year begins; and all its pages are as blank as the silent years of the life of Jesus Christ. Let us begin it with high resolution; then let us take all its limitations, all its hindrances, its disappointments, its narrow and commonplace conditions, and meet them as the Master did in Nazareth, with patience, with obedience, putting ourselves in cheerful subjection, serving our apprenticeship. Who knows what opportunity may come to us this year? Let us live in great spirit, then we shall be ready for a great occasion. —George Hodges

29

Learn to live today—all the day through—it may be the last day. Dale Carnegie has stressed the importance of living in "daytight compartments" —one day at a time, one task at a time. It is important to live today for it will not return for a second try. If we miss its joy and zest we miss it forever.

A woman twenty-four years old was told that her husband, twenty-six years old, would soon die of an incurable disease. To be sure, this was a blow and caused a night of gloom to settle about this pair. After prayerful meditation they decided they would pack every hour of every day full of helpful service and joyous companionship. They were not careless of a single hour. They lived every day to its full in the face of death. By their wholesome, unselfish living they, according to the doctor's conclusion, added years to the young man's life.

Do we need to be shocked into seeing that so-called ordinary days are precious? Today is all we have. From sunup till sundown let us fill it with life. We take one another for granted. We let precious experiences, lovely relationships pass as ordinary and thus miss the joys with which they are packed.

See the boys on the vacant lot playing nine innings of baseball. They pack eternity into time. Nothing else exists. Life for them is there. We are to live for eternal values in the present. You will either have an enjoyable time with life or you will have a life of discontent, and the net result will depend upon your attitude. —Oliver G. Wilson, *The Wesleyan Methodist*

30

I would urge you to treat as more precious than gold that priceless treasure, time. Each new hour is a new opportunity for aspiration, for endeavor, and for achievement; for adding something to the world's wealth and to your own substance. Time, even in its smallest units of hours and minutes, is the raw material of all human achievement. Every grain of sand in the hourglass is a part of your life that, once gone, can never be called back again. Therefore, use every golden moment toward some useful purpose. And remember, when you waste time you are wasting life, your own!—*Windsor Press*

31

I will start anew this morning with a
  higher, fairer creed;
I will cease to stand complaining of
  my ruthless neighbor's greed;
I will cease to sit repining while my
  duty's call is clear;
I will waste no moment whining and
  my heart shall know no fear.

I will look sometimes about me for
  the things that merit praise;
I will search for hidden beauties that
  elude the grumbler's gaze.
I will try to find contentment in the
  paths that I must tread;
I will cease to have resentment when
  another moves ahead.
I will not be swayed by envy when my
  rival's strength is shown;
I will not deny his merit, but I'll strive
  to prove my own;
I will try to see the beauty spread
  before me, rain or shine;
I will cease to preach your duty, and
  be more concerned with mine.

32

Take time to work—
  It is the price of success.
Take time to think—
  It is the source of power.
Take time to play—
  It is the secret of perpetual youth.
Take time to read—
  It is the fountain of wisdom.
Take time to be friendly—
  It is the road to happiness.
Take time to laugh—
  It is the music of the soul.
Take time to dream—
  It is the road to greater vision.
Take time to give—
  The day is too short to be selfish.
Take time to love and be loved—
  It is the privilege of the gods.
        —Employment Counselor

33

God always gives us strength to bear our troubles day by day; but He never calculated on our piling troubles past and those to come on top of those today.—Elbert Hubbard

34

The past is a dead king who makes no peers, and rewards his living courtiers with no ribbons or stars; he has not a penny in his pocket.—John Ayscough, *Levia Pondera*

35

While bells are ringing midnight-clear
Three gifts I ask for this New Year:
Faith is the pilgrim staff I crave
To keep me strong, to keep me brave.
Hope is the candle's pinpoint star
To lead me on the path afar.
Love is the mantle I would wear—
Heart-warming garments lined with
     prayer.
Father God, with these priceless three
Enrich the days Thou sendest me!
—Marie Barton, "Prayer for the New Year," *War Cry*

36

Prepare and prevent instead of repair and repent.

37

You have not passed this way heretofore, so keep your eye on the Divine Guide.

38

A year of self-surrender will bring larger blessings than fourscore years of selfishness.

39

He who dwells in the past grows old before his time; he who lives in the future remains forever young.

40

All of life is either in the process of growth and development, or in the process of death and decay. There is no standing still.

41

You will open for yourself the doors of a better tomorrow if you greet each day with a deep sense of gratitude for being alive. Each day becomes better than the last for the person who feels grateful for the privilege of living. Any person who complains constantly is a poor person without a future, whereas the person is rich who gives thanks for being alive.

Every trial endured and every disappointment accepted in the right spirit make your soul nobler and stronger than it was before. A grief today may be so used that it makes your smile the kinder tomorrow. A loss today may be so used as to make you stronger tomorrow. You can so use what happens to you today to make your life better, richer, fuller, more complete when tomorrow comes.
—John H. Miller, *P E O Record*

42

Take all the swift advantage of the hours.—William Shakespeare

43

Let the New Year be a year of freedom from sin, a year of service, a year of trust in God, and it will be a happy year from first to last. It may be the hardest year we have known, but it will be the happiest.—J. M. Buckley

44

Toward the end of one of the busiest lives ever lived, H. G. Wells wrote: "Subordinate and everyday things surround me in an ever-growing jungle. My hours are choked with them; my thoughts are tattered by them. . . . The clock ticks on, the moments drip out and trickle, flow away as hours. . . . I am tormented by a desire for achievement that overruns my capacity."

Wells was setting standards impossibly high for most of us. The mass of mankind who think about the subject at all simply dismiss the Wellsian dilemma with the threadbare excuse "I'm too busy!" . . . But the "I'm too busy" alibi . . . is usually an unconscious confession of weakness, an attempt to excuse incapacity.—Fred De-Armond, "No Time To Live?" *The Rotarian*

45

"I don't have time" is not a valid excuse. "I don't know time" would be better. When a man comes to himself . . . he will know that time is what he makes of it.—*Notes from Fee*

46

Yesterday is a canceled check. Tomorrow is a promissory note. Today is the only cash you have—spend it wisely.

47

Time is the most valuable thing in life, and I don't want to waste it.—John Foster Dulles

48

Never look behind you. Something may be gaining on you.—Satchel Paige

49

To live is not enough; we must make life while living.—Earl F. Zeigler, *Westminster Adult Bible Class*

50

Man does not live by the clock alone.—Rollo May

51

Even if we knew nothing of calendars and new years we should still be wondering about beginnings, for we can see how trees grow from acorns, and acorns in turn grow on trees, but how did it all get started? Chicks are hatched from eggs, and the eggs are laid by hens, but which came first, the chicken or the egg? It is not so foolish a question as might at first be thought.

The Bible has the most satisfactory answer that ever came to man. At the very beginning, there was only God. The "beginning" began when God made everything that is. We can make things too—molding and shaping them from other things—but God made everything when there was nothing to mold or shape, and that is creation. Things did not just happen into being, nor did they always exist. They had their beginning in God's mind, and for God's purposes.—*Gates of Beauty*

52

True repentance has a double aspect; it looks upon things past with a weeping eye, and upon the future with a watchful eye.—Bishop South, *Rocky Mountain News*

53

Tomorrow is a stimulating word, for it intrigues the imagination. Tomorrow holds all the hopes and fears of the future. Hopes—hope for a better day, hope for success, hope for good health, hope for happiness. Fears—fear of the unknown, fear of uncertainty, fear of failure. . . . Some eighteen thousand American troops had been in combat with more than a hundred thousand Chinese Communists. A company of Marines, correspondents and photographers, tired and weary, cold and half frozen, had withdrawn from combat for a short rest period. A photographer asked a soldier if he could have anything he wanted at that exact moment, what he would want. He said, "I want tomorrow."—Charles L. Anspach, "Tomorrow," *Vital Speeches*

54

Widened horizons need not blind us to the near view.—John Deschner, *The Intercollegian*

55

Monotony is the law of nature. Look at the monotonous manner in which the sun rises. . . . The monotony of necessary occupations is exhilarating and life-giving.—Mahatma Gandhi

56

Today well-lived makes . . . every tomorrow a vision of Hope.

57

How fortunate we are that before we enter the New Year we first pass through Bethlehem, hear the Christmas angels "their great glad tidings tell," and lose our old fears in renewed faith.—*Gates of Beauty*

58

A golden day was yesterday,
Full fair to dream upon.
Oh, every joy filled yesterday.
But yesterday is gone.

Shall I dream of tomorrow,
A day that could become
As rich and fair as yesterday?
Tomorrow may not come.

Uncertain is the future.
Past dreams are vain. So how
Can I do aught but fully live
This day that I have now?
—M. E. Moore, "Now," *The Rotarian*

59

Anyone can carry his burden, however heavy, till nightfall. Anyone can do his work, however hard, for one day. Anyone can live sweetly, patiently, lovingly, purely, till the sun goes down. And this is all that life ever really means.—Charles B. Newcomb

60

A man has to live with himself, and he should see to it that he always has good company.—Charles Evans Hughes

61

This life was given to us that we might learn to expend it, thus adding to the appreciation of beauty and the enlargement of life itself. We keep living through the experiences of others. This has gone on for centuries, and the richness is what has flavored life for us all.—George Matthew Adams, Tacoma (Washington) *News Tribune*

62

Make use of life while you have it. Whether you have lived enough depends upon yourself, not on the number of your years.—Michel de Montaigne

63

To make a goal of happiness or comfort has never appealed to me.—Albert Einstein

64

When we have the courage to live one life instead of many, wear our real face instead of a mask, live the truth instead of a lie, our life with ourselves and with others becomes hallowed by a new quality of spirit. For no matter how hardened our hearts become, we all seek from life as much of serenity and gladness as day and night can give.—George Christian Anderson, *Your Life*

65

Even if I knew certainly the world would end tomorrow, I would plant an apple tree today.—Martin Luther

66

Some years ago a friend with philosophic leanings shouted outside my bedroom door, "Wake up, it's tomorrow!" At first this appeared as mere good humor, but later, the sense of it became apparent; I was indeed awakening to Yesterday's offspring christened "Tomorrow." This experience comes back to me now as I ponder Omar's line: "Yesterday this day's madness did prepare." Can there be any question about "this day's madness"? The evidence that argues "NO!" is too enormous to be more than sampled.—*Notes from Fee*

67

It is no great thing to live long, nor even to live forever; but it is a great thing to live well.—Augustine, *Sermons*

68

The sole purpose of life in time is to gain merit for life in eternity.—Augustine, *Letter 130*

69

A mistake is a friendly invitation to try again.

70

Anyone who is inclined to make a list of New Year's resolutions should realize that there is only one such resolution worth making and it can be made any day of the year. The chief trouble with most resolutions is that they are too negative and too puny. We decide that we will not indulge in some petty vice to which we have been accustomed, and we are left with an uncomfortable vacuum until the resolution has been broken.

Jesus offers a more positive approach to those who call Him Lord. It sounds simple enough: "Do what I tell you." Those who refuse are building for a fall.

A resolution to do what Jesus tells us is not quite as simple as it sounds. It requires thought and study. It cannot be kept without courage and a sacrificial spirit. Sometimes it will seem to be a difficult and impractical way of life, but only in such obedience is there assurance of the kind of character that can meet life's storms.—Donald F. Lomas, *Today*

71

The weakness of New Year resolutions is that they reach too far. They violate the principle that life, for the most part, has to be lived a day at a time. Good resolutions are hard enough to keep without needlessly making them harder. Where these resolutions are the beginning of new habits, it is better to make them *every* morning. It is easier to keep them for a day. If one fails fifty days during the year, the score is still 315 to 50. One stays on the winning side. How much better this is than to make a resolution for the year, and after the first lapse to say: "Well, that's out. One more resolution gone!" If we really mean business—every morning is a new beginning, not merely every New Year's Day.—Paul Calvin Payne, *Today*

72

As we grow older in life, years somehow seem to shorten and New Year's Day approaches with an ever-increasing tempo. The more mature we get, the more we realize that time is only relative; how we live means more than how long we live. Haply also we do not live by years, but by days. In His wisdom God does not show us all that lies ahead. So we enter a new year to live it day by day. What is past is past. Today we start anew, and what we do today will make our life for tomorrow. Chin up, shoulders straight, eyes agleam, let us salute the New Year, and each day let us follow more faithfully, more courageously, more daringly the lead of our great Captain who bids us follow Him. —William Thomson Hanzsche, *Today*

73

The main task of the New Year is to live it worthily. We must spend it somehow; when the end comes we will give back to God the last day, hour, minute, all used in some way. It is given to us to be lived and we could not escape the living of it even if we wished to escape it. But it can go back to God in shame or in glory. It can set God's purpose forward, or it can leave that purpose unserved save by His overruling. These decisions will protect us.

Let us resolve to make high choices as the year advances. We are always coming to the parting of the ways; "the high way and the low" keep opening before us; we take one or the other. All compromises land us at last in the lower way, because they involve our refusal to accept the rigors or the efforts of the higher. John Oxenham speaks the warning in his "Gadara, A.D. 31," describing the scene in which the crowd told our Lord to depart from them, after the demoniac was saved and the swine were lost:

And Christ went sadly.
He had wrought for them a sign
Of Love, and Hope, and Tenderness
  divine;
They wanted—swine.
Christ stands without *your* door and
  gently knocks;
But if your gold, or swine, the entrance
  blocks,
He forces no man's hold—He will de-
  part
And leave you to the treasures of your
  heart.

To be left to the treasures of our hearts and to find those treasures poor and mean! We build our treasuries out of our daily and decisive choices. Something high and fine—and diffi-cult—comes before us alongside something easy and pleasant—and less high —and we make our choice. We seldom mean it to be unworthy. We merely lack the heroic courage to hold to the high choice, so the year settles down upon a lower level of living. *Let us resolve to live gladly as the year advances.* It cannot be easy for some of us. All the surface roots of happiness may wither, but we are then thrown back upon the deep taproot of joy which is never cut. Gladness is not determined by surroundings nor by experiences from the environing world. Two men have the same experiences; one faces life with gloom and the other with joy. One man loses all faith in God when hard experiences come; another finds a deeper faith in such experiences. The victory may be as great as that of Coventry Patmore:

Thou sear'st my flesh, O Pain,
But brand'st for arduous peace my languid brain
And bright'nest my dull view,
Till I, for blessing, blessing give again.

Most of us have friends who live as gladly as this in the midst of pain. But sometimes the daily grind is harder to endure with joy than the sharp and cutting pain or sorrow. "Christianity is essentially a heroism" as von Hugel said. Only by the definite purpose to be heroic where no one looks to find a hero can we be sure of living the year gladly.

Let us resolve to live inspiringly as the year advances. The old year often ends in widespread depression and concern. . . . Courage is contagious when it is well founded. Pretended courage, mere whistling in the dark, may leave men in fear. But when in the midst of the shipwreck Paul renews his courage by commerce with God, then all the fearful sailors pluck up courage and take food for the new tasks. There is the inspiration of a deep confidence in the love and purpose of God, the confidence of our Lord facing the cross and yet speaking of peace. In behalf of that courage and confidence let us make high resolve. Sabatier said that "religion is a prayer for life." Each man's religion ought to become in some part an answer to the prayer of other men. Let this year witness it to be so in our own lives. Let men who touch us be inspired, as we ourselves are inspired in our contact with Christ.—Cleland Boyd McAfee, *The Presbyterian Magazine*

74

One of the greatest laborsaving inventions of today is tomorrow.—*Irish Digest*

75

God is never in a hurry. He's never too busy with one to care for another. —Ethel Banks

76

Do you remember the newspaper report about the eighteen-year-old girl who killed herself on New Year's Day? Before she died, she had written a letter telling of an agreement she had made with God, or fate, or something, the year before. "I agreed that if something did not happen in the year to make life worth living, I'd quit living. That wasn't asking too much, was it?" She had laid down her own conditions for life without attempting to understand those conditions which God had already written

into the nature of the universe.—
E. Paul Hovey, *Speakers' Illustrations for Special Days*, ed. by C. L. Wallis

77

A superintendent urging graduates to go on to college insisted that they should start and gave a simple illustration. A very rough road ran from the school to the town. It was a dark night. But the superintendent explained that one does not need a great searchlight shining all the way in order to walk the road safely. All one needs is a very small light shining one step ahead. When that step is taken the light moves up and reveals the next step. So it is with God's will. Most of us know what our very next step should be. Let us take that one, and then we will be delighted to see the Lord's light moving along with us.—Charles L. Allen, *Roads to Radiant Living*

78

I heard the Old Year talking, and he
    seemed to say to me,
"I am what men have made me—not
    what I hoped to be.
I did not bring the failures; my days
    were bright and new.
I was the time allotted—the work was
    man's to do.

"I am what others made me; I had no
    will or choice;
Through all the days of trial I was
    given not a voice.
If victory came, man earned it; his
    was the faith and power.
If sorrow came, God sent it; I fur-
    nished but the hour.

"I came here empty-handed—a year
    that was to be,

And what I am in passing, mankind
    has made of me;
I am their petty failures, their glory,
    their success;
I am their souls' advancement, their
    shame, and happiness.

"I was not born in evil or governed
    by the stars,
I brought to some high honors, to
    others ugly scars;
Only my days were numbered; I was
    the time for toil,
And each has reaped the harvest, as
    he has tilled the soil.

"I am what men have made me—not
    what I hoped to be,
And so shall be the New Year which
    soon shall follow me;
Our days are good or evil, as each man
    serves and strives,
For years are but the records on which
    men write their lives."

79

The year is closed, the record made,
The last deed done, the last word said,
The memory alone remains
Of all its joys, its griefs, its gains.
And now with purpose full and clear,
We turn to meet another year.
        —Robert Browning

80

As I set sail for another New Year,
May the winds be gentle, the weather
    clear—
And touching each Port, as I bear to
    the West
May I barter for Pearls, and give of my
    best.

Should storms lash the sail and waves
    sweep the deck,

May I trust the Wise Pilot through
    threatening wreck—
And should I debark, leaving cargoed
    regrets,
May I reach the last Port as the Eve-
    ning Star sets.
—Myra A. Wiggins, "Setting Sail,"
    P E O Record

81

The Moving Finger writes; and, hav-
    ing writ,
Moves on: nor all your Piety nor Wit
Shall lure it back to cancel half a Line,
Nor all your Tears wash out a Word
    of it.
—Omar Khayyám, "The Rubaiyat,"
    LXXI verse

UNIVERSAL WEEK OF PRAYER

82

True prayer is a bringing of our life
to God. The ancient worshiper
brought his sacrifice; the Christian
brings himself. It is a simple way of
praying which anyone can follow. We
may begin by counting up all the good
things of life which God has given us;
bread and work, strength of body and
daily help for living, friends and faith,
and, above all, God Himself as He
has come to us in Christ. And then
inevitably we end in thanksgiving.
We bring to God the sins and failures
of the day, not just in word or act,
but the failure of the spirit of trust
and truth and patience and love. That
prayer should end in a humble asking, and a humble but confident taking, of God's gracious forgiveness. We
bring to God our purposes, our ideals,
our ambitions. In His presence the
great is seen as little and that which we
have lightly passed over becomes great.
So we end by affirming a higher and
truer purpose and by dedicating our
life to God.—Harris Franklin Rall,
Prayer

83

There are various activities so closely
allied to prayer and worship that they
tend to become substitutes. There is
the sense of beauty, particularly the
lifting power of the beauty of nature
and of great music. Through these
channels men have often found God;
but not usually, if ever, until they
have found Him elsewhere and have
learned to make aesthetic exaltation
an aid to worship rather than a substitute for it. There is meditation—
honest self-examination or reflection
on some vital theme. This can be a
very fruitful part of prayer, but it is
not prayer unless it is centered in
God and His will. There is labor for
God and good causes, which ought to
be the fruit of prayer but too often
replaces it.—Georgia Harkness, *How
To Find Prayer More Meaningful*

84

Prayer is the power in a life which
enables one to grow in grace. We
marvel at the great pine trees that
grow on barren ledges of rock in the
high mountains. How do they survive? They have long roots running
down through the crevasses to life-
giving soil and moisture below. If
we seek the secret of victorious lives
about us, we will find life roots that
are reaching down to mysterious unseen sources of strength by means of
prayer.

85

Prayer is love raised to its greatest power; and the prayer of intercession is the noblest and most Christian kind of prayer because in it love—and imagination—reach their highest and widest range.—Robert J. McCracken, "What Happens When We Pray for Others?," *Reader's Digest*

86

The more you practice prayer, the less difficult you will find it to reach out for help in moments of extremity. Daily prayer provides the strength for daily tasks. It builds reserves of power for use in emergencies. In can banish fear. It will make your life fuller and richer than you would have believed possible. When you pray with utter confidence, your prayers will be answered.—William C. Taggart, "Your Prayers Are Answered," *American Magazine*

87

Besides "No" or "Yes," there is a third answer God very often gives when we pray. There are many ways of stating it, but I like to put it in the words that used to give me hope time and again when I asked my mother for some heart's desire. "We'll see," she'd say, "just be patient and do all you can about it, and then we'll see!"—Margaret Blair Johnstone, "There's No Unanswered Prayer," *Better Homes & Gardens*

88

God warms His hands at man's heart when he prays.—John Masefield

89

When we set ourselves to the work of collecting or re-collecting the scattered pieces of ourselves, we begin a task which, if carried to its natural conclusion, ultimately becomes prayer. —William Sadler, *The Practice of Psychiatry*

90

Wishing isn't prayer. Neither is mere resignation to what you believe to be God's will. Prayer is a definite act of the mind—a gesture by which the human spirit seeks out the spirit of the universe. In prayer you call upon the Infinite to help. Prayer is far less a thing "asked for" than it is a thing "done"—a reaching forth to link oneself to the sources of celestial power.— William C. Taggart, "Your Prayers Are Answered," *American Magazine*

91

There are times in the life of every man when he is driven into a quiet place to meditate, if not to pray. Jesus was no exception to this fact. He wanted to talk to God, but He also wanted God to talk to Him. . . . No one will ever know how much of the time Jesus spent in prayer was fellowship with God. Fellowship kept His heart very near the Father and His pulsating Heart. Fellowship is much more than just talking. Talk is not always a sign of friendship or fellowship. A quiet period is sometimes a good sign that two souls are knit together in love.—Guy Everton Tremaine, *The Prayer Life of Jesus*

92

A prayer can be beautiful without faith, but it cannot be effective without it. Faith cannot be seen in prayer, yet its lifting power is absent when faith is not there, and heaven is not moved nor is earth changed. Without faith a prayer has only form. Without faith a prayer has no heart or flame. The power of prayer does not rest in its beauty and form, but in its heart and beauty of spirit.—Guy Everton Tremaine, *The Prayer Life of Jesus*

93

If Jesus talked, thought, and felt in parables, He must also have prayed in parables. In other words, when He asked for physical and material blessings He must first have translated these needs into symbols of spiritual values and prayed not for the material facts but for the spiritual realities which these facts represented. . . . Seek spiritual values, and earthly things expressing those values will be given to you. Or, as Paul would put it: "Set your affections on things above, not on things on the earth."—Glenn Clark, *The Soul's Sincere Desire*

94

Prayer is the very sword of the Saints. —Maurice Goguel, *Life of Jesus,* trans. by Olive Wyon

95

I have lived to thank God that all of my prayers have not been answered. —Jean Ingelow

96

I was watching the craftsman turn out a table leg on his wood lathe. "It's beautiful!" I exclaimed. The man smiled and turned off the motor. "Now look," he said.

When the piece was no longer ro-

tating, I could see imperfections and rough places that the chisel had not yet smoothed out. Our present fast-moving life is a good deal like that. We become absorbed in the swift, endless round of things to be done and places to go and it is only when we stop for a while that we can get the true design of our lives.

That is one reason why prayer is so important. It enables us to turn off the motor for a little while and really examine our lives. With God we can then make plans to smooth out the rough places when life starts whirling again. For it is perhaps as true of life as of a piece of wood in the lathe stocks: It is shaped in the whirl of action, but only in a state of rest and quiet can an effective checkup be made.—Fletcher D. Slater, *Sunday Digest*

97

Here is the naturalness of Christian worship. First, we listen to God speak, then we give ourselves to Him and He Himself to us, in prayer and fellowship. It is the order of family worship; it is the order when you visit the sick; it is the order when you preach to win men for Christ—first, you carry the glad news to them; then, you lead them in confession and commitment of life. —*The Living Church,* ed. by H. W. Vaughan

98

Prayer is everlasting life. I live in proportion to my communion with God. Life is real when it is right with God. God's will for the common good does not come natural to me. Bluntly or subtly I want my own way. But my way, even when I get it, all too often hurts. I want more and something else. In prayer I learn to know God's community. That satisfies me. This community requires concern. When I accept this concern, to my great surprise, the cost of it gives satisfaction more and different from my own way. —Nels F. S. Ferre, *What Prayer Means to Me*

99

Remember that the Christian life cannot be lived without prayer.— Frederick M. Meek, *How To Pray*

100

Those who pray as Christ taught us to pray are never praying against each other; for they do not pray that their own will may be done, but God's, which they know to be better than their own for themselves and for all men. Such prayer is the outward reach of the spirit of worship.—William Temple, *The Hope of a New World*

101

Pray, and then start answering your prayer.—Deane Edwards

102

Prayer is a means of adding power to the strength we already possess. Sometimes we know what is right, but we lack the will power to do it.—Harry Thomas Stock

103

Prayer is not a substitute for work, thinking, watching, suffering or giving; prayer is a support for all other efforts. —George A. Buttrick

104

We must not suppose that reality in prayer is an experience which belongs only to saints and mystics. Prayer is not the exclusive right of preachers or of professional religious workers. Prayer is every man's opportunity and privilege.—Howard L. Stimmel, *Learning To Pray*

105

Prayer is the only form of revolt that remains upright.—Georges Bernanos

106

Prayer is part of the education of the human spirit. By prayer we come to know God and discover His plan for the world and for our own lives. In prayer we learn a great deal about ourselves, and one of the sources of our misery is that we do not know ourselves—we are fugitives from ourselves.—C. Irving Benson, *Finding God Through Prayer*

107

When you cannot pray as you would, pray as you can.—Dean Goulburn

108

Prayer gives us God. The very essence of prayer is communion with God. Our relationship to God is personal, not mechanical. Prayer is not just the opening of a valve, not some mechanical process by which power from a mysterious reservoir in heaven flows into our souls. Prayer is personal contact. The deepest, surest fact about prayer is that we find God, know God, learn to be at home with Him, and work with Him. How else can we get at the treasures of joy and peace and confidence that come from friendship? Friendship is not a gift, but a growth. God's relation to the soul is personal. It is friendship, love, sonship. This true, personal fellowship is not a sudden thing. It is the privilege of a growing friendship.—C. Irving Benson, *Finding God Through Prayer*

109

We readily admit that Jesus and all the genuine saints throughout history had spiritual power and that they had a deep prayer life. We believe that there must be some connection between their power and their life of prayer.—Sherwood Eddy

110

You can pray because you can desire. What you want in the presence of God is your prayer. You can pray because you can yearn. The longing of your heart when directed to your Father is your prayer. The soul's sincere desire is prayer.—Kirby Page, *How To Pray*

111

Prayer is the soul of religion, and failure there is not a superficial lack for the supply of which the spiritual life leisurely can wait. Failure in prayer is the loss of religion itself in its inward and dynamic aspect of fellowship with the Eternal. Only a theoretical deity is left to any man who has ceased to commune with God, and a theoretical deity saves no man from sin and disheartenment and fills no life with a sense of divine commission. Such vital consequences require a living God who actually deals with men.—Harry Emerson Fosdick, *The Meaning of Prayer*

112

Faith is fulfilled only in prayer. Prayer is at once faith's direct act and daily food, faith's venture and certitude. Faith without prayer is dead. "Speak to Him thou for He hears." By that speaking our hand, thrust into the unknown, is found and gripped by a Hand, and faith becomes certitude. Is there not a story of a man who saw little to inspire him in Thorvaldsen's statue of Christ, and of a child who said to him, "You must go close to it, sir. You must kneel down and look up into His face"? Alongside the road of endless argument and weary seeking there is a postern door that leads direct to God—the door of childlike prayer. We turn therefore to the best prayer, the prayer that Jesus taught. So we pray.—George A. Buttrick, *So We Believe, So We Pray*

113

Prayer is communion with God in the name of Jesus Christ, in which, alone or with others, we tell God of our love to Him, our sorrow for our sins, our thankfulness for His gifts, our desires for ourselves and others, and our dedication to His will.—*An Outline of the Christian Faith*

114

One who truly prays, prays not because he feels that he has to, or because he wants something. He prays because his heart is full of gratitude for life, love, and opportunity. Real prayer usually begins in a sense of gratitude. Prayer is just as much saying "thank you" as it is asking for God's help.—Harry Thomas Stock, *Young People's Topic*

115

A day of prayer may never be called as an escape into inactivity. It is a necessary part of Christian obedience to renounce evil and to repent before creative and redemptive prayer can be undertaken. [The Anglican Church in South Africa] therefore regards as hypocritical a corporate day of prayer so long as certain sponsoring churches have not openly denounced the primary evil causes of the present distress.—Archbishop Joost de Blank, of Cape Town, South Africa, *Newsweek*

116

The privilege of prayer to me is one of the most cherished possessions, because faith and experience alike convince me that God Himself sees and answers, and His answers I never venture to criticize. It is only my part to ask. If it were otherwise I would not dare to pray at all.—Wilfred Grenfell

117

There are three elements in prayer —the petition, the answer, and the acceptance of that answer. The first two are sure, the last depends upon the one who prays. One should pray knowing that he will be heard and that the Father will answer, and realizing that the answer depends upon his acceptance of it. The man with the withered hand had often prayed for healing. Jesus said to him, "Stretch forth thine hand. And he stretched it forth; and it was restored whole, like as the other." Christians should pray with hands outstretched, mind alert, and heart eager for the blessing that He is sure to bestow.—William F. Klein, *The Communicant Member*

118

Prayer begins in adoration. This is the starting point; God is God. However, He is not only the transcendent God; He is the loving Word spoken through Jesus as the Christ. We are called beyond adoration. He leads us into the mystery of other dimensions of prayer . . . adoration, looking toward the holiness of God, initiates a reflex by which we see ourselves in an entirely new light. This light discloses our own emptiness and fragmentariness, and our distance from the person we might be in and for God. Thus adoration leads to confession.—John B. Magee, *Reality and Prayer*

119

Prayer is the greatest thing in the world. It keeps us close to God. My own prayer has been most weak, wavering, inconstant; yet has been the best thing I have ever done.—Samuel Chapman Armstrong

120

Energy which but for prayer would be bound is by prayer set free and operates.—William James

121

Our moral strength comes to us not by thinking about it, but by living in the presence of God. It is plain fact—if we live with Christ, we shall grow like Him. A minister tells of seeing in a European gallery an old Greek statue of Apollo. He watched the crowds as they passed that model of physical perfection. If anyone paused to look at that statue almost invariably he would begin to straighten up. So if we live with Christ, test our judgments by His truth, our attitudes by His compassion, our idleness by His generous self-giving, without knowing it we, too, will begin to straighten up.

This means the habit of daily prayer. There is no substitute. If at the very beginning of each day we would look up into the face of our Father, seek His guidance for the day, test our plans for His approval, bring our personal and social responsibilities into His presence; and so undergirded at the beginning of the day often through its hours look to Him; and at the end of the day once again bring our burdens up to Him—we should grow in strength.—J. Harry Cotton, *The Power of God*

122

Pray in secret for this helps to make the prayer absolutely sincere. There need be no pretense when people are not seeing. Pretense before God is foolish for He looks into the heart. Pray in secret because God speaks to man in prayer with a "still, small voice" that cannot be heard unless the soul is still.—Hampton Adams, *Pray —Thy Kingdom Come*

123

Of course one can speak to God anywhere, but if you would come to pray with largest satisfaction, then pray habitually in one particular place.— Charles E. Jefferson, *How To Pray*

124

Our Lord is still hindered by small-scale local minds which cannot grasp the scope of His "Errand" or the size of His "Family." No wonder H. G. Wells said of Him: "He is too big for our small hearts." And no wonder we ask amiss when we pray only partial prayers about ridding ourselves of

spots and wrinkles, for like St. Augustine we answer each moving of the Spirit with an impatient postponement: "Anon! Anon! Presently! Presently!"—Margaret Applegarth, *Even As Christ Also Loved the Church*

125

Some years ago the Laymen's Missionary Inquiry made this appraisal: "We feel that the Christian view of life has a magnificence and glory of which its interpreters for the most part give little hint." The unsearchable riches of Christ to be carried to the world; someone less than the least doing the carrying! Yet devotion to unpopular causes made Jane Addams someone Chicago called "Mother Earth," so elemental was her warm concern for all mankind; Japanese slums and African jungles invested Kagawa and Schweitzer with enough of the everlasting mercy to prove to the rest of us that all the treasurable tendernesses wrapped up in Jesus Christ are reproducible, whenever a Christian gives himself to God in prayer, to create heaven on earth. Two old Latin proverbs and a line from a medieval mystic trace this development: "We perish from permitted things!" "We grow from our disgusts!" "Who rises from his prayers a better man, his prayer is answered." —Margaret Applegarth, *For This Cause I Bow My Knees*

126

Though one of the smallest books in the Old Testament, Habakkuk is one of the greatest. It is this third chapter that makes it great, for here Habakkuk is praying as God would have His children pray. Even though the Chaldeans came, even though famine was in store for the people, still Habakkuk affirmed that his trust in God would be unshaken. . . . Habakkuk knew God as both a sovereign and person. We must know God in just the same way. Our view about prayer is closely allied to our understanding about God. . . . Habakkuk was going to rejoice in God whether the Chaldean came or not, whether the crops were plentiful or there was famine in the land, because he had faith in God and honored God by putting his complete trust in Him. We too honor God when we hold that prayer does not violate His own natural laws.—*Universal Week of Prayer, 1948*

127

There is an "Archimedian" point outside the world which is the little chamber where a true suppliant prays in all sincerity, where he lifts the world off its hinges.—Søren Kierkegaard

128

Prayer changes things, but we must remember that sometimes God may give us the desire of our hearts, but send leanness into our souls. The discovery of oil in a certain part of Pennsylvania might serve as an illustration. Wells were originally dug for salt water in order to manufacture table salt. Oil, when it appeared, was a catastrophe. It is entirely possible that those who sunk the wells prayed that there might be a flowing gush of nice salt water and that they were terribly chagrined when oil began to flow which spoiled their salt water! Prayer could well have been offered for salt water and God in His bounty gave the

far greater riches of oil. This is so often true with His children. We may be praying for bread. If we insist on bread, He will give it to us, but what He really wants to give us is the magnificent boon of the bread of life.

129

The decree of the king . . . made not the slightest impression upon Daniel. This was not an opportunity for him to pray, ostentatiously, stubbornly showing his unwillingness to conform, it was a time to quietly continue his daily custom of praying. There is an understanding revelation of character in that little phrase "as he did aforetime." Daniel did not wait for a crisis in order to start praying. Deep distress comes before many a man cries unto God. It is scarcely being fair with God to wait until a dire extremity to call upon Him. Such a prayer is better than no prayer, for God honors every sincere prayer. However, there is something pitiful about people whose religion is useful only in a crisis. Daniel knew the glory of fellowship praying. In his prayer he did not ask for deliverance. The record simply states that he "gave thanks before his God." Daniel knew what it meant to walk and talk with God day by day. When the crisis came for him the fellowship with God was already established. . . . Daniel, like Jesus, did not hesitate to pray for himself. The record indicates however that Daniel was also praying for the king. He recognized that the king had been maneuvered by evil counselors into a wrong position. Daniel's prayer was not alone for himself, it was for his sovereign as well. He was a ruler who did not worship as Daniel worshiped, who did not believe in the Jehovah whom the prophet held dear. Daniel prayed for him nonetheless and knew that Jehovah, the God of all the earth, would do right to the king even as He would bring deliverance to the prophet in the den of lions.

130

Prayer is an offering up of ourselves to God, for things agreeable to His will, in the name of Christ, with confession of our sins, and thankful acknowledgment of His mercies.—Westminster Catechism

131

Prayer is the soul getting into contact with the God in whom it believes. —Harry Emerson Fosdick

132

Prayer is not conquering God's reluctance, but taking hold of God's willingness.—Phillips Brooks

133

We may witness for Christ through prayer. Strands of influence go out from us when we pray. Our prayer-thoughts may girdle the globe. . . . When Martin Niemöller was a prisoner, he was taken to see his aged father who was dying. The darkness of evil in the world had not blotted out the latter's hope. To the son, the dying father whispered: "All over the world people are praying and that gives me hope that things will not stay in this bad way."—Lloyd E. Foster, *The Dynamic Leadership of the Holy Spirit*

134

Not talk about prayer, but prayer itself—that is the thing! Our goal is not the outer court of preparation, but the inner sanctuary where we enter into creative communion with the living God.—Edward W. Bauman, *Intercessory Prayer*

135

Men *work* and pray for the things they really want—but just pray for the things they should want.

136

When you come to your great crisis and your own means are not enough to get by, and all you have learned points you only to doom, then pray for something you do *not* know; pray for a miracle! This is not a despairing cry. After all, miracles happen all the time. A miracle is not an exception to the laws of nature; it is a work of God within laws He knows, but beyond our comprehension. Spectacular miracles were pivotal men and events which have shaped history: Martin Luther at the Emperor's court, declaring that he believed with all his heart that salvation came from his own faith and not from the church; the Pilgrim Fathers with the germ of the American Commonwealth in their frail bark on the mountainous seas, sailing on unafraid. By what laws of human nature known at that time did *they* operate?

In order to pray for a miracle you must believe that a miracle can happen, and that your prayers will help bring it about. To pray for a miracle you must believe that humanity does not have to plod along in the same ruts century after century. You remind yourself that with God all things are possible.—Robert L. Eddy, "Pray for a Miracle," *The Pulpit*

137

Prayer . . . is the recovery of the soul's breathing.—Gerald Heard, *The Christian Century*

138

Prayer is a perfectly accurate instrument for grading the religious life of the soul. Did one only know how a man prays, and what he prays about, one would be able to see how much religion that man has. When a man, without any witnesses, speaks with his God, the soul stands unveiled before its Creator. What it has then to say shows quite distinctly how rich or how poor it is.—K. Girgensohn, *Addresses on the Christian Religion*

139

In praying to God we are praying to Him whose life we share as we pray, and whose life is shared not by us alone but by those for whom we pray. We do seem to have found the medium through which we may influence them aright—and that medium is God Himself. As we make our prayer in the power of the Spirit, "in the name of Christ," that same Spirit is quickened in the spirit of those we love and pray for, for "we are all members of One Body," and when "one member is glorified all the members rejoice with it."—Leonard Hodgson

140

By praying when we do *not* feel like it, we bring God not only the content of our prayer, but a disciplined spirit. We have kept our appointment with Him *against* inclination. We have displeased ourselves in order to please Him, and His pleasure is real indeed. —W. E. Sangster, *Teach Me To Pray*

141

We ought not to pray supposing that if only we pray hard enough we shall get whatever we ask for. Most of the bitterness of unanswered prayer comes from the assumption that God will juggle His universe to give us what we plead for if we plead long enough. On the other hand, many things can happen, both within and outside of the individual, in response to prayer without any setting aside of God's orderly processes.—Georgia Harkness, *Prayer and the Common Life*

142

Prayer is not bending God to my will, but it is a bringing of my will into conformity with God's will, so that His will may work in and through me. When you are in a small boat and you throw out a boathook to catch hold of the shore, do you pull the shore to yourself, or do you pull yourself to the shore? Prayer is not bending the universe to your will, making God a cosmic bellhop for your purposes, but prayer is cooperating with the purposes of God to do things you never dreamed you could do. The highest form of prayer is that of Jesus in Gethsemane: "Nevertheless, not my will, but thy will be done"—not "Thy will be borne" as we often translate it, but "Thy will be *done*"—a cooperating with an outgoing redemptive will that wills our highest.—E. Stanley Jones, *How To Pray*

143

Those who pray are the real light-bearers in any age.—George A. Buttrick, *Prayer*

144

The adoration of God is the beginning and the end of all our prayer, as it is of all our life.—John L. Casteel, *The Promise of Prayer*

145

At home, in my own house, there is no warmth or vigor in me, but in the church when the multitude is gathered together, a fire is kindled in my heart and it breaks its way through.—Martin Luther

146

In prayer a man should always unite himself with the community.—The Talmud

147

Prayer is an intensely personal matter but it is not individualistic. It is an expression of human solidarity, of spiritual fellowship within the body of Christ.—Olive Wyon

148

When Jesus swept clean the Temple at Jerusalem, He rededicated it as a "house of prayer for all nations." This the church should be. It is the center of the highest and most vital spiritual forces and the temple in which man's longing for Reality may be satisfied. All the ecclesiastical machinery, theologies, creeds, and rituals are properly means to that end. The church, the continuing incarnation of the body of Christ, has a function in creation which is not equaled by any other organization of life. That prime function is dependent upon the vitality with which the church prays and worships. From that praying, worshiping center flow those streams of life which are the church's ministry to the world.— John B. Magee, *Reality and Prayer*

149

Prayer is not merely an occasional impulse to which we respond when we are in trouble: prayer is a life attitude.—Walter A. Mueller, "The ABC's of Prayer," *United Church Herald*

150

We might call the basic steps the ABC's of prayer. The first is to begin with the attitude of appreciation for the blessings God has given and with adoration of God. A, then, is for appreciation.

B stands for barriers, the barriers in our lives that separate us from God. For if we are to come into real fellowship with God, we have to deal realistically with the barriers that separate us from God. They are attitudes of fear, guilt, anxiety, resentment, jealousy, dishonesty, impurity—the list is long and is made up of the unsurrendered areas of our lives where God is shut out. Many of us would like to have God as our friend and companion, but we want Him on our own terms. We pray as Augustine prayed when he was still a youth: "O God, make me pure, but not now."

The final step in the life of prayer is to fulfill the will of God, to commit ourselves to Him in all events of life that overtake us.

In the ABC's of prayer: A is for appreciation, B is for barriers and C is for commitment.—Walter A. Mueller, "The ABC's of Prayer," **United Church Herald**

151

Just going about is one of the handicaps that prevent us from achieving the best that is in us. Absence of purpose is perhaps one of the greatest sources of the tensions which are such marked phenomena of our times. A paradox of our day is that it seems as if half of the pharmaceutical companies manufacture pills that are intended to *tranquilize* us, while the other half makes *energizers* with which to speed up the tempo of our tension-weary and doubt-ridden lives.

Of course, pills are not the answer —we need to cultivate a prayer life, a spiritual outlook and a self-discipline to help control the tensions that prevent us from realizing *enduring values.* This is not to say that life does not require elasticity, for up to a point our lives are rich when we stretch them to their fullest extent. But aimlessness in life is self-defeating.

The need, of course, is for a faith that cannot be dimmed by tensions, weakened by doubts or shattered when a crisis portends. It is a faith that will dispel the clouds and symptoms of tension—and bring a cure. This is faith—faith in God—by which we may achieve what the Psalmist meant in the phrase, "The peace which passeth understanding."—Uretta A. Hinkhouse, "Enduring Values," *P E O Record*

152

Be not forgetful of prayer. Every time you pray, if your prayer is sincere, there will be new feeling and new meaning in it which will give fresh courage.—Fëdor Dostoevski

153

The fruit of the tree of knowledge had nothing to do with it. The Kingdom of Heaven is within the humblest mortal. Prayer is the key.

154

James wrote, "ask in faith, with no doubting" and revealed the technique of prayer most perfectly. A wavering petition bears no fruit. Approach God's throne boldly. Importunity is one secret. Pray without ceasing. That is, don't sign off when you stop speaking to God. Remain in an attitude of oneness and love and faith.

YOUTH WEEK

155

The Tried and the Untried

To build a world of brotherhood by the machinery of war;

To establish fellowship by feeding racial rancor—by keeping the Negro and immigrant in place;

To use force and violence in guaranteeing national security;

To dispose of the criminal by a prison system;

To put money first in the purpose of life;

To be a Christian without following Christ.

To build a friendly world by faith and understanding—to put love where there is now hate;

To lead the race toward a wiser, more just and merciful social order, where each individual is evaluated in terms of his true worth;

To fortify the nation by the armaments of faith and the power of love;

To give guidance to those who err and in time redeem the environment of every little child;

To work for the good of all—not for the gain of wealth;

To make an earnest trial of Jesus' Way of Life.—*Ecumenical Service for 1960*, United Christian Youth Movement

156

No one can live without values, especially if he is young. Perhaps the new generation realizes that ideals are necessary, but it no longer knows what to adhere to. The poll [of a French youth group] did not have any questions on religion . . . one of its serious omissions. But it was evident in going through most of the responses that we are dealing here with a youth without God, or without gods.

"If God is dead, and if no temporal faith succeeds in replacing Him, what will help man to live when he happens to fall into misfortune?" wrote one who replied. "The thing that young Frenchmen lack is to be caught up in some great collective adventure."—Robert Barrat, "French Youth in Profile," *Commonweal*

157

Youth is wonderful!

But we can spoil it or waste it. What's the hurry? What's the big rush? You'll never be eleven, or twelve, or thirteen, or any other teen year but once. Each day you can figure, "I have not passed this way before . . . and I will not pass this way again." Today is unique. Don't let its wonderful moments go by unnoticed—and unused.

I promise you something: you will grow ahead fast enough. The time will come when you can drive a car. When you can date unchaperoned. Marry. Earn a living. When you can wear spike-heeled shoes or a dinner jacket. But if you are only going to be happy when those times come, you will never be happy. Because then you will have the "tomorrow" habit.

I once knew a fellow who was "going to be happy" when he could drive a car. So that day came, but by then he was "going to be happy" when he could buy one. So he bought one. Then he was "going to be happy" when he could better it . . . by then the habit had a strong hold on him. He was always "going to be happy. . . ."

We don't go into whether it makes us a little ridiculous to be running around attempting to appear to be something we are not, because we should not make these changes based on what others will think of us. There would be no lasting value there. That's a "control" just like a spanking. But I'll tell you something. My friend, Bobby Morrow, says one of the reasons he won three gold medals at the Olympics is that he has never jumped the gun. Jumping the gun has penalties. Both you and I have seen some of the penalties paid by teen-agers who insist on living ahead of their physical or emotional or mental age and growth. At the worst, cars piled up. Girls' lives ruined. Boys in juvenile court. At the least, unbalanced lives, a lot of extra problems and discomfort.

You know, I think a lot of our worries and anxieties are rooted right here in this time goof, the inability to live today. And guilt, too—guilt if we haven't done today what today brought to us to do. You ask some depressed older fella, "What are you thinking of?" He says sadly, "My future." You say, "What makes your future so hopeless?" He replies, "My past!" Yet, like us, all that he has is today.

To guard against needless worry and anxiety, to overcome restlessness, impatience, and frustration, to be happy now and not waste a moment of our wonderful youth, I think we should all have written somewhere, on a locket, or in our minds, or on a sign in our room, *Jam Today!*—Pat Boone, *'Twixt Twelve and Twenty*

158

Youth and maturity are different phases of life, each with a special value. Youth is a period of growing, learning, experimenting. Youth is a delightful, exciting, questioning period of life, pulsing with excitement and full of discovery. But maturity brings qualities that youth cannot match. Youth cannot gain the wisdom that comes only with experience in living. Youthful creativity can seldom match the results achieved by talents that have had years in which to practice and ripen.—Lester and Irene David, "Let's Stop This Silly Worship of Youth!," *Everywoman's Family Circle*

159

We shall not build a Christian world in a day. But we are determined to be led by our faith and not our fears—

—to profit by the experiences of the past

　　—to become pioneers when experience fails

　　—to cast aside petty aims

　　—to lose ourselves in the great task at hand

—to seek a new heart and a new mind.

For us there is no alternative. We give ourselves—we invite others to join with us—Christian youth building a new world.—*Manual for the Community Call Committee,* United Christian Youth Movement

160

We are losing our Christianity because Christianity is a creed for heroes, while we are mainly harmless, good-natured little people who want everybody to have a good time.—Dean W. R. Inge

161

I am *you,* the youth of this church;
I am part of the story of youth who
　belong,
Youth who belong to the church, to
　whom the church belongs.
Youth who live in towns tucked in
　big cities, living on the same block;
Living in single small places where
　most youths live;
Tomkins Corners and Black Mountain,
Horseshoe Bend and Farmerville,
Willow Street and Morgan's Hill.
Never heard of them? Well . . .
Maybe they're too big for small talk
About who lives where on the map.
But they are you, and I am you,
And you are all of us.
Yes, I am you, and I have been called.
You are called!—Mildred B. Hahn,
"You Are Called," *International Journal of Religious Education*

162

Jenny Lind was described as a plain, undistinguished girl, but when she rose to sing her appearance was transfigured. The whole fire and dignity of her genius kindled a glory about her task, and the absorbed and mastered spirit shone. Similarly, it is said that those who listened to Webster's great oration on the Pilgrim Fathers remarked that the statesman's face made them think of a transparent bronze statue, brilliantly lighted from within, with the fire of the inward soul shining through the eyes and making the figure like animated radiance.

That is great mastery. Of the things that dominate men, is there anything finer than the passion of a great cause, the glow of a lofty principle, the authority of a splendid truth, the rapture of a great ideal, the thrill of a great commission?—*War Cry* (Canada)

163

We all played "cops and robbers" when we were children, but today's kids use "real" cops when they play cops and robbers.—Robert Culbertson

164

Help youth out of its confusion; never condemn it. While holding it up to its highest, always forgive it. Since you cannot live its life for it, you can only, after you have really done your duty by it, entrust it to God in utter compassion. There is joy in heaven when a tear of sorrow is shed in the presence of a truly understanding heart. And heaven will never weary of that joy.—Charles Malik, "A Rich Spiritual Climate," *YWCA Magazine*

165

Our sixteen-year-old Rosie was fussing at her twelve-year-old brother for lacking confidence around girls, but he set her back a notch. "You have

no idea," he said, "what a low opinion I have of myself. And how little I deserve it."—Burton Hillis, *Better Homes & Gardens*

166

A lack of a consuming goal because we are sitting on top of society affects our youth in that life has no meaning for them.—Howard Pierce Davis

167

You, at this moment, have the honor to belong to a generation whose lips are touched by fire. . . . The human race now passes through one of its great crises. New ideas, new issues— a new call for men to carry on the work of righteousness, of charity, of courage, of patience, and of loyalty— all these things have come and are daily coming to you.

When you are old . . . however memory brings back this moment to your minds, let it be able to say to you: That was a great moment. It was the beginning of a new era. . . . This world in its crisis called for volunteers, for men of faith in life, of patience in service, of charity, and of insight. I responded to the call however I could. I volunteered to give myself to my master—the cause of humane and brave living. I studied, I loved, I labored, unsparingly and hopefully, to be worthy of my generation.—Josiah Royce

168

Straight from the shoulder, have you found out who you are? Do you have any dreams? Do you have any ideals? One of my students told me it was the example of her grandmother that kept spurring her on. Has there been a person, a book, an event that has stirred you deeply? When you call on yourself is there anybody home? I like the title of Althea Gibson's book, *I Wanted To Be Somebody*. That would make a fitting motto for every member of this class. We all need the pull of an ideal. As you study history, I am sure you have been impressed by the compassion of an Abraham Lincoln, the energy of a Theodore Roosevelt, the intelligence of a Woodrow Wilson, the integrity of a Robert Taft, and the devotion of a John Foster Dulles.

Ambition, determination, responsibility, follow through—these cannot be measured and no one can give them to you. Mental tests often are deceptive. Your grades in the principal's office may and may not be a true index of your capacity. You may not have awakened yet. Some young men and women get into college without maturing. There is no greater joy for a teacher than to sit alongside a student who has finally awakened to his possibilities, one who finds he has a mind capable of great things. Be firm but patient with yourself. Make yourself count!

John Foster Dulles at the age of seven dreamed of being Secretary of State. Daniel Webster's father took home with him from a county fair a silk handkerchief with the Constitution printed on it. What an omen! Daniel Webster earned the title of "defender of the Constitution." No man has a greater battle than the conquest of himself; to liberate his God-given talents.—Lionel Crocker, "Straight from the Shoulder," *Vital Speeches*

169

While time lasts there will always be a future, and that future will hold both good and evil, since the world is made to that mingled pattern.—Dorothy L. Sayers, *Begin Here*

170

Public opinion is really private opinion which has been expressed and accorded a following. We ought to ask: "Who first expressed that opinion? Is his opinion likely to be basically a Christian viewpoint? Have we ever publicly expressed our honest opinions when we differed from the current public opinion?"

When someone appeals to you on the basis of "everybody does it," what is your reaction? To fall in line? Or do you think of the exceptions to that statement? This philosophy is based on a false generalization. The next time someone says, "Oh, everybody does it!," start counting the names of those people you know personally who do not do what you are being urged to do. . . . "Everybody does it" is the saying, and yet if that were really true, the habits of people would be identical. . . . If "everybody" did it, we should all be alike. . . . Paul in Romans 12 urged people not to conform but to be transformed (changed) from ways that were less than the best. Saying, "I can't be wrong, since everybody does it," would not give you a high grade in morals, or intelligence, or independence. Yet that is the basic principle of conduct for millions today. . . . They use other people, often people with a low moral standard, as judges of their conduct rather than God. . . .

If we base our practices on the idea that "everybody does it," we have lost our freedom in the pressure of the crowd. Paul had something to say about the freedom to do right: "For freedom Christ has set us free; stand fast therefore, and do not submit again to a yoke of slavery." Later he said to those "foolish Galatians": "You were running well; who hindered you from obeying the truth? This persuasion is not from him who called you."

The Christian's function is to set the standard for others, a higher standard than the world accepts. This is always an unpopular thing to do. But if the Christian does not do it, who will? Jesus does not ask us to do anything more difficult than He did, but He does expect our loyalty and courage. . . . Christians need not yield to the public opinion of "everybody does it." The power of God and the backing of a Christian Church stand ready to help.—E. Paul Hovey, "Everybody Does It!," *The Society Kit,* Vol. III

171

When a baby is born it is first limited by its crib; later it is confined to a room so that it will not hurt itself or the things about the home.

When the child enters school his limits are extended—but still the limits are quite well defined. The child knows where he cannot go. Limits are imposed by adults—his parents and the authorities in the school.

When he goes to college there are self-imposed limits. When one marries there are still other limits. And if, perchance, you get out beyond the limits, you may have to go back to the crib (jail?) to be re-educated.

But at the high-school level the limits are all too often rather vague. It is here that many young people get into trouble. The limits have never been adequately defined and they have not been mature enough to impose adequate limits on themselves. Young people often want adults to say "no" to save face, or because they do not want to take the responsibility for their decisions.

If authority is too strict and confining, they cannot grow; if it is too lenient, bedlam is the result.—Robert Culbertson

172

Do not let any girl, no matter how sweet, tell you what to do with your life. Do not think they won't try to! In *The Caine Mutiny* by Herman Wouk there is a tender letter from a father to his son. The father admonishes his son, "Son, you can afford to sell almost everything else in life, but do not bargain away the right to do the thing you want to in life. . . ." Preach, teach, farm, sell— do anything you want to do. Choose a girl who will be in tune with your dreams. Those of us who teach can testify that our work has been made more pleasant and easier because we have had wives who have believed that teaching was the most wonderful thing in the world. Mark my words! If you let any girl choose what you are going to spend the next forty years doing, you will be the most miserable of men. —Lionel Crocker, *Vital Speeches*

173

A Spanish proverb runs, "Take it, and pay for it." Take it! Take what? The present, this day of increasing opportunities and responsibilities—but if you take it, you must pay for it with study, with spiritual dedication and with sacrificial activity.—Henry H. Bagger

LINCOLN'S BIRTHDAY

174

The Creed of Abraham Lincoln

I believe in God, the Almighty Ruler of Nations, our great and good and merciful Maker, our Father in Heaven, who notes the fall of a sparrow and numbers the hairs of our heads.

I believe in His Eternal Truth and Justice.

I recognize the sublime truth announced in the Holy Scriptures and proven by all history that those nations only are blest whose God is the Lord.

I believe that it is the duty of nations as well as of men to own their dependence upon the overruling power of God, and to invoke the influence of His Holy Spirit; to confess their sins and transgressions in humble sorrow, yet with assured hope that genuine repentance will lead to mercy and pardon.

I believe that it is meet and right to recognize and confess the presence of the Almighty Father equally in our triumphs and in those sorrows which we may justly fear are a punishment inflicted upon us for our presumptuous sins to the needful end of our reformation.

I believe that the Bible is the best gift which God has ever given to men; all the good from the Saviour of the world is communicated to us through this Book.

I believe the will of God prevails. Without Him, all human reliance is vain. Without the assistance of that Divine Being I cannot succeed; with that assistance, I cannot fail.

Being a humble instrument in the hands of our Heavenly Father, I desire that all my works and acts may be according to His will; and that it may be so, I give thanks to the Almighty, and seek His aid.

I have a solemn oath registered in Heaven to finish the work I am in, in full view of my responsibility to my God, with malice toward none; with charity for all; with firmness in the right as God gives me to see the right, commending those who love me as to His care, as I hope in their prayers they will commend me. I look through the help of God to a joyous meeting with many loved ones gone before.— Quoted in *The Defender*

175

A mother with her young daughter walked one evening past the old Lincoln home in Springfield. Lights were shining through the window. The mother told her daughter about Lincoln and explained that this was the house where he lived before he went to Washington to be president. The girl looked up and said: "Mr. Lincoln forgot to put out the light when he went away."

The child did not realize the profound truth suggested by her words. Lincoln has long been gone, but his light will always continue to shine. He forgot to put it out.—Walter Dudley Cavert, *Ours Is the Faith*

176

I don't think much of a man who is not wiser today than he was yesterday. —Abraham Lincoln

177

Let the people know the truth and the country is safe.—Abraham Lincoln

178

What constitutes the bulwark of our own liberty and independence? It is not our frowning battlements, our bristling seacoasts. . . . Our reliance is in the love of liberty which God has planted in us. Our defense is in the spirit which prizes liberty, in all lands everywhere.—Abraham Lincoln

179

Abraham Lincoln Harris is asking Superior Court to change his name to Al Harris. Lincoln may have been a great president, he said, but he's made life miserable for his namesake, who is greatly embarrassed by such nicknames as Rail Splitter, Emancipator and President.—*AP* report

180

I remember a good story when I hear it, but I never invented anything original; I am only a retail dealer.—Abraham Lincoln

181

The world has never had a good definition of the word liberty, and the American people, just now, are much in want of one.—Abraham Lincoln

182

Let us have faith that right makes might; and in that faith let us to the end dare to do our duty as we understand it.—Abraham Lincoln

183

Abraham Lincoln was born in a log cabin in Kentucky, February 12, 1809. His elementary education was obtained by the light of the fireplace. He worked at the hardest labor as farm hand and railsplitter. In 1834 he was elected to the Illinois Legislature where he served for eight years. He became an able lawyer. In 1846 he was elected to Congress. Later efforts to become a United States Senator ended in defeat. He was elected President of the United States in 1860 and reëlected in 1864. On April 14, 1865, he was shot by an assassin and died the next day. Many people consider Abraham Lincoln the greatest man of the nineteenth century. He rose from lowly beginnings to the highest office; led our Republic through a crisis that might have destroyed it; and left a mighty heritage of kindliness, idealism, and political wisdom.

184

A significant thing about Lincoln is that our interest in him is not limited to the years that he served as President. Perhaps more than in the case of any other great character, we honor him in his private life. The incidental matters in his life are well-known. They remind us with mighty emphasis that it is Lincoln the man that calls forth our veneration, rather than Lincoln the President. We see him in the White House, pacing the floor in the wee small hours of the night bearing the burdens of a nation and talking with God; we note the letter he wrote to a mother who lost five sons in the war; we note the human interest features in connection with his conferences with diplomats, royalty, and statesmen; we retell the stories he told in the times of stress and strain, as he said, to relieve his own pent-up feelings and to keep his nerves intact. It was the manhood of the man that arose above all officialdom and formality. He was a man before he was a president. That saved him to humanity after he was laid low by the assassin's bullet. That served as the basis for the homage paid him by the whole world and by succeeding generations. That saved him to us as Abraham Lincoln, the man.—*Religious Telescope*

185

Abraham Lincoln was a big, unwieldy kind of man whose dreams and hopes and principles were always bursting out of the nicely ordered boundaries of faction, party and nationality.

One of the shrewdest of partisans, Lincoln always used party methods to advance larger-than-party goals. One of the most zealous of patriots, he consistently elevated patriotism to the high plane of holding aloft the torch of principle for all men of all nations.

These essential traits of Abraham Lincoln are worthy of remembrance at any time, and especially so during the season of speeches in his memory.

All manner of speeches are made in the name of Abraham Lincoln. That, too, is a tribute to him, for his shoulders were broad enough to bear all the little, clattering creeds and "pitches" that surrounded him when he lived and surround his memory still.

But ordinary citizens in the United States and around the world must pause now and then amid the bursts of oratory to remember the central truth of Abraham Lincoln—that he was a man of principle whose principles stand yet for all men of all nations.

He fought the cruelest, hardest kind of war for unity. He fought to shape the hardest kind of peace for justice. He went down through the valley of the shadow so that this nation, "or any nation, so conceived and so dedicated, can long endure."

And when those who speak for segments and splinters and factions promote causes for narrow interests in the name of Abraham Lincoln, it is well to remember that this is not Lincoln speaking. He could see beyond his own preferences, his own party and the boundaries of his own nation to feel the pulse of all mankind.

"Thanks to all: for the great republic—for the principle it lives by and keeps alive—for man's vast future—thanks to all."

That is Lincoln speaking, with his head high and his eyes forward toward "man's vast future."—William Johnston, editorial in Lewiston, Idaho *Morning Tribune*

186

Lincoln's indebtedness to the Bible is obvious and beyond dispute. He read it in his boyhood and its influence over him increased with the years. In his public addresses he quoted from the Bible more often than from any other book, and this was the smallest part of his debt to it. The Bible influenced his literary style, which indeed was modeled on the writings of the great prophets of Israel, as is especially evident in his deeply moving Second Inaugural, which reads like a leaf from Isaiah. And more, the Bible gave direction to his thought. To an extent probably unparalleled among modern statesmen, Abraham Lincoln thought in terms of Biblical ideas and convictions.

He was, moreover, a man of prayer, and this without apology or self-consciousness. He did not hesitate to request the prayers of others or to acknowledge that he himself prayed. Prayer for him was a necessity, and it never occurred to him to conceal the fact. He spoke of seeking divine guidance and aid as though it were altogether the most natural and reasonable thing to do.—Ernest Fremont Tittle, *The Methodist Layman*

187

Lincoln was often a lonely man. Under the surface of his native humor there flowed a current of sadness. His great heart was often lonely, and, knowing that the Bible contained help for the sorrowful, he would frequently turn to this Book of comfort to find what human friends could not give. He had early discovered that the Bible was a dependable guide. It was the one to lean upon in the dark days of public service.—Ernest Lloyd, "Lincoln's Debt to the Bible"

188

Religion gave to Lincoln a sense of proportion. He could, and sometimes did, get excited over matters of importance (he worried a good deal over the conduct of the war), but never over trivialities. . . .

Also, religion gave to Abraham Lincoln a sure sense of direction. It qualified him for the task of statesmanship, which, according to William Ewart Gladstone, is that of discovering "where Almighty God is going during the next fifty years." Evidence of Lincoln's sense of direction is to be found in much that he said and did, but in this connection consider especially the dramatic and controversial speech in which he said: "A house divided against itself cannot stand. I believe this government cannot endure permanently half slave and half free." . . . he submitted this speech to a dozen or more of his political friends, and they, almost without exception, condemned it as rash and potentially ruinous . . . but Lincoln stood his ground. Give a man to see, as Lincoln saw, the demands of eternal truth and right, and he will come to possess one of the prime qualifications for statesmanship.

Religion made Abraham Lincoln a righteous man and completely delivered him from the spirit of self-righteousness. He was never smug, never self-complacent, never harsh in his judgments upon others. . . .

Religion delivered him from the spirit of self-righteousness, and so from hate, malice and vindictiveness. It purged him of all uncharitableness and filled him with the spirit of understanding and compassion. Those are merciful, and those alone, who know themselves to be in need of mercy. Only a man who himself felt the need of a divine forgiveness and healing could have uttered those immortal closing words of the Second Inaugural: "With malice toward none; with charity for all."

Religion enabled Abraham Lincoln

to rise above self. He was possessed of a towering ambition; he wanted to be president. The taste of it was in his mouth, as he once frankly confessed. And more, he wanted to go down in history as a great man, to be remembered and revered by future generations. Yet he was capable of amazing self-subordination . . . but he wanted above all to be a humble instrument in the hands of his Heavenly Father to work out His great purposes. And in Abraham Lincoln the saying came alive: "He that humbleth himself shall be exalted."—Ernest Fremont Tittle, *The Methodist Layman*

189

Abraham Lincoln's greatening ideals of government affairs included the belief that God is and that He is a rewarder of them who seek after Him. His religion has been the subject of innumerable controversies, some of them acrimonious and withal, unwarranted.

Mr. Lincoln often referred to the precepts of Christianity; what is more important, he practiced them.—Edgar DeWitt Jones, *Social Progress*

190

No hero in American history is more honored and revered than Abraham Lincoln. His common touch, the stories of his gentle but penetrating wit, the simple and beautiful eloquence of his speeches, have assured him a place in American history that is secure and unique. Washington is called the father of his country and Lincoln is sometimes called its savior.

Adamant and unswerving in time of peril, he was generous once the victory was won. He proposed terms for reconstructing the South which were intended to help "bind up the nation's wounds," but his untimely death at the hands of an assassin changed all that. Instead of a policy of "malice toward none," the vengeful factions in the Northern states insisted on punishing the South and years of bitterness resulted.

In times of great peril America has always produced leaders who could summon up the courage of all the people to meet the test. Lincoln was such a leader. Yet he was a simple man who could find the time to stop and discuss with a small girl whether his appearance might be improved by a beard. In the rush of affairs of state he found time to write to Mrs. Bixby, bereaved by the reported death of her five sons, a letter which is a masterpiece of simplicity, sincerity and sympathy.

Lincoln once remarked that God must have loved the common people because he made so many of them. Lincoln loved them too, and even when he had risen to uncommon heights he thought of himself as one of them. God loved the common people indeed when he made Abraham Lincoln one of their number.—Rapid City (South Dakota) *Daily Journal*

191

I feel how weak and fruitless must be any word of mine which should attempt to beguile you from the grief of a loss so overwhelming. But I cannot refrain from tendering you the consolation that may be found in the thanks of the republic they died to save. I pray that our Heavenly Father may assuage the anguish of your bereavement, and leave you only the cherished memory of the loved and lost, and the solemn pride that must be yours to have laid so costly a sacrifice upon the altar of freedom. —Abraham Lincoln, to a mother whose five sons died in battle.

192

I have been driven many times to my knees by the overwhelming conviction that I had nowhere else to go. My own wisdom, and that of all about me, seemed insufficient for the day.—Abraham Lincoln

193

This particular paragraph from a speech by Mr. Lincoln at the outset of the Civil War contains what I should call the quintessence of his political principles:

"This is essentially a people's contest. . . . It is a struggle for maintaining in the world that form and substance of government whose leading object is to elevate the condition of men—to lift artificial weights from the shoulders, to clear the paths of laudable pursuits for all, to afford all an unfettered start and a fair chance in the race of life. Yielding to partisan and temporary departure from necessity, this after all is the leading object of the government for whose existence we contend."

Here are four mighty affirmations of a political creed truly Lincolnian. They are worthy of much pondering since they are fundamental in the life of a republic.

First: "To elevate the condition of men." This is basic democracy. It is applied Christianity also. In the synagogue of his home town Jesus selected a passage from the prophet Isaiah and applied the same to himself. . . . "He anointed me to preach good tidings to the poor. . . ." Here Lincoln affirms that it is the object of such a government as ours to better conditions of living. . . .

Second: "To lift artificial weights from the shoulders." The word "artificial" is used here with discrimination. Consider the artificial burdens that rest heavily on drooping shoulders— unjust systems of taxation, iniquitous tariffs, unfair and discriminating legislation . . . it is the high business of a government by the people and for the people to remove . . . burdens. . . .

Third: "To clear the paths of laudable pursuits for all." A democracy must be interested in clearing paths, blazing highways, cutting channels that the spirit of the people, their hopes and dreams may find free course, and be fruitful.

Fourth: "To afford all an unfettered start and a fair chance in the race of life." The first few years of life practically settle destiny, and "an unfettered start" would mean wholesome food, adequate shelter and clothing. It would mean education. It would mean every man's opportunity. Mr. Lincoln knew from experience how hard it is to rise above the level of one's environment. He knew that slavery was wrong, and averred that no man, however good, is good enough to own another human being.—Edgar DeWitt Jones, *Social Progress*

RACE RELATIONS DAY

194

It is the most ordinary, everyday sense which makes us see to it that "Poison" labels are kept pasted on the bottles of dangerous chemicals we all need on the shelves of our medicine closets. Iodine, for instance, although it is an excellent disinfectant, would be the death of a child who took a drink of it. We know very well that such labels must be renewed if they fade or become unreadable.

In exactly the same way a constant repetition is needed of the label "Poison" on all forms of mass prejudice, on racial injustices, on making an individual suffer for something he doesn't do, or is not, because some of his group have done it or been it.

They are all poisons—some slow and insinuating and gradual, some lightning-swift like a rattlesnake's bite. And every variety—slow or swift, mildly sickening or quickly fatal—should be labeled in our minds, "Poison," so that we recognize it as dangerous the instant we see or hear it.

When we see somebody incautiously step out towards a piece of ice on a sidewalk on which we have seen others slip and fall, we shout to him, "Look out! Danger!" We should train ourselves to have the same reaction of shocked alarm when we hear somebody voice one of those horridly mild-sounding conversational expressions of prejudice: Well, he's this or that. What would you expect?

Civilized people have advanced so far in understanding as to feel discomfort on hearing such phrases. But the discomfort is not yet great enough, in most cases, to match the discomfort of answering boldly in a good loud voice, "Such talk is dangerous. Words like that grease the slide down which it is mighty easy to slip to hellishly iniquitous acts."

One of the difficulties is that we get tired of the necessary repetition of the warnings against racial discrimination, but we have the cheering hope that they may not always be needed. A good many warnings of the past can be laid aside, because we have outgrown the practices they labeled as dangerous.

We can get rid forever of all this talk about resisting racial discrimination—by stopping it. When American citizens, men and women, are judged not by the group to which they belong but by their individual personalities, and admitted on this same obviously American principle to theaters, hotels, schools, hospitals, graduate schools, and the like, we can stop this tiresome hammer-hammer-hammer on the theme that unjust exclusion of one is "Poison" for us all.—Dorothy Canfield Fisher, *Advance*

195

Since we use the term "colored" for the Negro race, I would suggest that the Negro use the term "colorless" for the White race. "A group of colored and colorless got together for a meeting."—Harry Golden, *The Carolina Israelite*

196

If you will protest courageously, and yet with dignity and Christian love, when the history books are written in future generations, the historians will have to pause and say, "There lived a great people—a black people—who injected new meaning and dignity into the veins of civilizations."—Martin Luther King, Jr.

197

Seven weeks after a would-be assassin sent two bullets crashing into his head, South Africa's Prime Minister Hendrik F. Verwoerd made his first public speech. . . . At the Jubilee celebrating the Union of South Africa's fiftieth anniversary, he declared: "A great white nation must be developed here . . . [in which the whites remain] the guardian of the black men." He also warned that "a black dictatorship" was spreading over Africa and urged that English-speaking whites unite with Afrikaans-speaking whites "for their own survival."

At the very time that Verwoerd was speaking, Dr. Joost de Blank, Anglican Archbishop of Cape Town, led 10,000 multiracial marchers through the city's streets to the beat of muffled drums. Later, the marchers made a mass declaration of principle, protesting against South Africa's "direst poverty," lack of civil liberties, and "the injustice of racial discrimination."

As one gesture toward such protests, the government released 154 political prisoners. Verwoerd himself added another gesture. To symbolize South Africa's desire to remain at peace with the rest of the world, he tossed a white dove into the air. The bird fluttered down to the ground and refused to fly.—*Newsweek*

198

[The] awareness of another's existence in a nodding acquaintance may provide casual information and deliver us from the total loneliness of abject isolation. [But] such a relationship does little toward relieving the world's pain or increasing its joy; toward outlawing social evils or creating conditions that will bring wholesome community life to birth; toward banishing ignorance, prejudice, ill will and in their place nuturing health of body, mind, and spirit.

These blessings of the body and the spirit require the cooperating labors of all men. In so far as we refuse to labor together we reject the blessings that are promised those who work together for good. If we would sincerely pray together for the coming Kingdom we must work together for its realization.

Our common enemies at home and abroad are of such strength and power that only by working together can we claim any possibility of success. Our opportunities are so wide that only our common labor can match them. Many hands joined in the task make lighter work and also happier hearts. Let those who have stronger hands bear the heavier burden, but let us all share the task. We can work together. We should work together in Christ's name.—Bishop Lloyd C. Wicke, *Together*

199

In nine cases out of ten what goes by the name of tolerance is really apathy. There are too many easygoing Americans who are up in arms against nothing because they have no fixed standards of right and wrong. They do not come out positively and wholeheartedly on the side of anything because, unlike their fathers, they have no robust convictions. Tolerance is a virtue, but it is not the supreme virtue.—Robert J. McCracken

200

There is no such thing as Negro education—only education. I want my people to prepare themselves bravely for life, not because they are Negroes, but because they are men.—Mary M. Bethune, *Time*

201

I have come to the point where I can embrace all humanity—not just the people of my race or another race. I just love people.—Mary M. Bethune *Time*

202

The fact that racial and religious prejudice should, in any form, exist in a great democracy is an incredible mockery of the very word "democracy." It should be considered in the light of a personal disgrace to every citizen of that same democracy—a disgrace as shocking and as tragic as that of the discovery that a near and dear member of one's family has become a hardened criminal.

For prejudice is a crime. It is a crime against the democratic ideal, a crime against the teachings of Christianity, Judaism, and the other great religions, a crime against human decency, and a crime against just plain common sense. Furthermore, it is a crime for which every American citizen, directly or indirectly, is responsible, if not for its inception, at least for the continuance of its presence.

We are responsible because of our apathy in sidestepping the issue, because of our outmoded given-time-it-will-cure-itself attitude, because of our kidding ourselves with the preposterous fable that it is a special problem to be solved by the special persons involved. The problem is our problem, and as long as prejudice exists in our land we are the persons affected.

The solving of it must be done by us all—each and every man, woman, and child of this nation, of every walk of life, and of every race, creed, or color. It must be solved by our actions, by our words, and by our thinking. And if we and our children are to survive as living creatures worthy of the name of human beings, it must be solved, not in a theoretical future, not tomorrow, but now!—Cornelia Otis Skinner, *Advance*

203

Hate is a prolonged form of suicide.—Schiller

204

Are they a minority through choice; or a forced minority?

205

Fortunately for serious minds, a bias recognized is a bias sterilized.—A. Eustace Haydon

206

An optimist is a person who sees a green light everywhere. The pessimist sees only the red stop light. But the truly wise person is color-blind.—Albert Schweitzer, *Look*

207

Men can make no peace with any exclusion or discrimination within the body of Christ. So long as there is a single congregation of Christ's flock in which a son or man is unaccepted because of his earthly difference of social status or race, there is an offense against sovereignty among the King's own people. "Offenses must come," states the Bible, "but woe unto him by whom they come."—Bishop Angus Dun

208

It is unfair to laugh at the segregationists for the inflexibility of their creed. Inflexibility is all they have.— Editorial, "The Fervor of the Faithful," *The Nation*

209

Prejudice is a state of mind, a disposition unfavorable to certain persons, which may or may not find outlet in hostile behavior.—Michael Banton, *White and Colored*

210

The Christian religion is color-blind. —Timothy O'Hara

211

Brotherhood lives in the Christian love and concern of one person for another. We cannot be Christians in our separateness. . . . This brotherhood includes all nations and races, for Christ suffered and triumphed for all men. This brotherhood is not yet accomplished, but the churches are called upon to lead the world and to pledge their loyalty to the community that is being born.—D. Elton Trueblood, *Race Relations Sunday Message, 1950,* National Council of Churches

WASHINGTON'S BIRTHDAY

212

Washington, the brave, the wise, the good . . . valiant without ambition, discreet without fear, confident without presumption. In disaster, calm; in success, moderate; in all, himself. The hero, the patriot . . . the friend of mankind, who, when he had won all, renounced all, and sought in the bosom of his family and of nature, retirement; and in the hope of religion, immortality.—Inscription at Mount Vernon

213

When George Washington fell heir to Mt. Vernon, he was twenty years old. The next twenty years of his life were spent in the social whirl enjoying the freedom and power of his new wealth. He followed the social pattern and joined the church, later becoming a vestryman. This new influence in his life made him want to become something more than a social drifter. On his fortieth birthday he went out on the vast lawn of Mt. Vernon at a point overlooking a wide expanse of the Potomac River. Here, alone, he meditated, dreamed, planned and perhaps prayed. He gave himself to God. In that environment he pledged his life to his Country, a life not to be sacrificed, but a life to be fully lived in service. George had been touched by the Holy Spirit. His start was humble, as an adjutant in one of the five military districts of Virginia. By living his first moment with God, he was able to live other moments with Him, and through these experiences

George Washington was guided to international immortality in the service of his fellow men.

214

If Washington had a favorite book of the Bible, it probably was Micah, for he quoted from that book more generally than from any other. A quotation from the sixth chapter and the eighth verse of that book is contained in his prayer, which he sent as a circular letter to the governors of the thirteen states on June 8, 1783, shortly before relinquishing his command of the Army. The letter contains this appeal:

"I now make it my earnest prayer that God would have you, and the state over which you preside, in His holy protection; that He would incline the hearts of the citizens to cultivate a spirit of subordination and obedience to the government; to entertain a brotherly affection and love for one another, for their fellow citizens of the United States at large and particularly for their brethren who have served in the field; and finally that He would graciously be pleased to dispose us all to do justice, to love mercy, and to demean ourselves with charity and humility, and a pacific temper of mind, which were characteristics of the Divine Author of our blessed religion, and without an humble imitation of whose example in these things, we can never hope to be a happy nation."

215

George Washington was a First American; first President of the United States, first in peace, first in war, first in the hearts of his countrymen. He set a standard of quality for American citizenship that has not been surpassed since his birth.

We have had great men, heroic generals, fine citizens, but none of quite Washington's quality, the quality of character that made him the beloved, admired leader of the people. It was this quality that shone through every action from childhood, when he destroyed his father's cherry tree and truthfully confessed his wrongdoing, up to maturity, when, in the triumph of victory, he set aside the proffered crown and retired to his peaceful home.

Washington was eager for life and enjoyed every good thing it brought him, but he never clutched it. It flowed through his open hands as clean as when it entered and as freely. He loved gayety, but when, as often happened in his life, he was called to duty, he could lay it aside cheerfully and shoulder the task to its completion. He loved his home, he cherished the things he had planted there, the memories that sanctified it, but he could live through the bitter winter of Valley Forge, sharing the hardships of his men, cheering them on with words of hope for a victory certain to come. He was a practical hardheaded businessman; yet, when the Colonial Cause was at its lowest depths, Washington could go apart in the woods, kneel in the snow and beseech God to aid him, to aid a suffering and oppressed people, and know his prayer answered.

He was, we are told, a man of impatient temper, but how patient he was when he listened to a Congress wrangling about the money the Army had to have or disband; and with what patient wisdom he persuaded the Congress to hold on, to have faith, to give their all in Freedom's cause.

The victory won, he was once more summoned to his country's aid, to lead his people out of the welter and confusion that follows a great war's end. He became our first president, the statesman to whom his country's need was his opportunity for service.

Today . . . we feel the spirit of Washington leading us, forcing us toward the ideals of truth, honor and justice that he set in us at the beginning. His spirit is the conscience of the United States. It is speaking today and we are listening.—Angelo Patri

216

Labor to keep alive in your breast that little spark of celestial fire called Conscience.—George Washington

217

We can have little hope of the blessings of heaven on our arms, if we insult it by our impiety and folly.—George Washington

218

It is impossible to rightly govern the world without God and the Bible.—George Washington

219

A gentleman of one of the first fortunes upon the continent . . . sacrificing his ease, and hazarding all in the cause of his country.—John Adams

220

The father of his country.—Francis Bailey.

221

His memory will be adored while liberty shall have votaries, his name will triumph over time and will in future ages assume its just station among the most celebrated worthies of the world.—Thomas Jefferson

222

The character and the service of this gentleman are sufficient to put all those men call kings to shame. While they are receiving from the sweat and labors of mankind prodigality of pay to which neither their abilities nor their services can entitle them, he is rendering every service in his power, and refusing every pecuniary reward. He accepted no pay as commander-in-chief; he accepts none as President of the United States.—Thomas Paine

223

America has furnished to the world the character of Washington. And if our American institutions have done nothing else that alone would have entitled them to the respect of mankind.—Daniel Webster

224

Washington is the mightiest name on earth—long since mightiest in the cause of civil liberty; still mightiest in moral reformation. On that name a eulogy is expected. Let none attempt it. In solemn awe pronounce the name and in its naked, deathless splendor leave it shining on.—Abraham Lincoln

225

No gilded dome swells from the roof to catch the morning or evening beam; but the love and gratitude of United America settle upon it in one eternal sunshine. From beneath that humble roof went forth the intrepid and unselfish warrior, the magistrate who knew no glory but his country's good; to that he returned happiest, when his work was done. There he lived in noble simplicity, there he dies in glory and peace. While it stands, the latest generation of the grateful children of America will make this pilgrimage to it as to a shrine; and when it shall fall, if fall it must, the memory and the name of Washington shall shed an eternal glory on the spot.—Edward Everett

BROTHERHOOD WEEK

226

Brotherhood—Believe it! Defined as a willingness to give to others every right and dignity we claim for ourselves, brotherhood is essential to the fulfillment and perpetuation of American democracy. Until that conviction controls the thinking of our citizens, democracy is not safe. So long as any minority among us is not free, all of us are threatened. That belief is fundamental.

Brotherhood—Live it! That injunction finds us where we dwell. It reaches into our schools, our churches, our community organizations. Every denial of brotherhood anywhere menaces its establishment everywhere. It is our contention that the world-wide acceptance of brotherhood as the rule of life for nations is essential to permanent peace. . . . What we do in our own country speaks more loudly to the world than anything we can say.

Brotherhood—Support it! That is, spread brotherhood. It is necessary, but not sufficient, to believe brotherhood and to live it as persons and citizens. We must proclaim it, be its advocates. Brotherhood has many adversaries. Selfishness, prejudice, ignorance, are divisive. They disrupt the human family, drive and hold its members apart. We must educate for brotherhood in every community in the land. We must establish conditions within which brotherhood is possible. The friends of brotherhood must seek each other out and put their heads together. We must campaign for brotherhood. For the fight for brotherhood is never completely won. There is no surcease to this war. Strategy and tactics must be adapted to conditions .as we find and face them. All of us—together!—National Conference of Christians and Jews

227

The inevitable result of clear Christian thinking proves that there is no possible way in which the Christian can justify the racial discriminations which are the common experience of the daily lives of black people in particular and other races in some measure. . . . There is no possible way of reconciling with the profession of God the personal reaction of exclusion which many of us once had or still have toward these people of other races, whom we oftentimes piously call children of one Father.

This means specifically that there are no areas in the common life of men and women on this earth where a person is to be excluded from any relationship because of the color of skin, the shape of features, or any other characteristic by which we are aware of so-called racial strains. It would be dishonest thinking if we did not face the fact that our civilization, which bears the label Christian, is a long way from accepting this implication of the gospel in the first place, to say nothing of practicing it in the last. We must face two facts: the uncompromising principle of our Christian profession and the unprincipled practice of our daily living.

Far more than being a Negro problem, the problem of color in America is a white problem. Men once fought to free slaves. The problem today is whether we can free ourselves from slavery; slavery to the customs and the persistent attitudes which permit those patterns of conduct to continue.—Allan Knight Chalmers, *The New York Times*

228

There was a poor Presbyterian family living up the road and some of the kindhearted ladies of the church took pity on them and sent the family a big box of secondhand clothing for the children. But for the next three weeks none of the children appeared at Sunday services. The minister and the elders of the church were concerned. They made a personal inquiry and the mother said that the children looked so handsome in the clothes she decided to send them over to the Episcopal Church.

Jews do not have this kind of opportunity. Because of their lack of numbers in most towns there is just one temple, and no matter how high a Jew goes along the rungs of the middle-class ladder, he still has *one* temple. He must suffer it out. He must do it the hard way. If he is really a heavy donor, he will be invited to the big gifts dinner where he will be called upon to announce his pledge. Or if he does not have that much money, he can send his wife to the Women's Luncheon and everyone knows what the minimum contribution is. Or failing that, he can always become "active" and "involved"; just plain "active" and "involved." Ah, if we only had an Episcopal Church!—Harry L. Golden, *The Carolina Israelite*

229

When all is said and done, the rule of brotherhood remains as the indispensable prerequisite to success in the kind of national life for which we strive. Each man must work for himself, and unless he so works no outside help can avail him; but each man must remember also that he is indeed his brother's keeper, and that while no man who refuses to walk can be carried with advantage to himself or anyone else, yet that each at times stumbles or halts, that each at times needs to have the helping hand outstretched to him. To be permanently effective, aid must always take the form of helping a man to help himself; and we can all best help ourselves by joining together in the work that is of common interest to all.—Theodore Roosevelt

230

It is our duty to make sure that, big as this country is, there is no room in it for racial or religious intolerance. —Franklin D. Roosevelt

231

Within us we have a hope which always walks in front of our present narrow experiences. It is the undying faith in the Infinite in us. It will never accept any of our disabilities as a permanent fact. It sets no limits to its own scope, and it dares to assert that man has oneness with God, and its world dreams become true every day. —Rabindranath Tagore

232

Across the wild dance and mad whirl of this tired world, we catch the song of faith, and we send its sure triumphant note back over the boundless domain of apparent hostility to man. If God is for us, who is against us? We believe that the sovereign things in the universe are God's mind, God's heart, and God's character. We believe that the sovereign values in time are not physical magnitude and power, but truth, love, and good will expressed in service. Above the heavens is the glory of God. Above the heavens in life and in death is the value of man.—George Gordon

233

Five-year-old Patrick and Dennis McBride, who have become accustomed to being called "the twins," made a startling discovery at kindergarten recently. Rushing home excitedly, they shouted: "Hey, Mom! Do you know what we found out today? We're brothers!"

234

Men exist for the sake of one another. Teach them then or bear with them.—Marcus Aurelius, *Meditations*

235

What is brotherhood? Brotherhood is giving to others the rights you want to keep for yourself . . . giving to the individual in another group the same dignity, the same full appreciation that you want to have yourself.— Everett R. Clinchy

236

If you really believe in the brotherhood of man, and you want to come into its fold, you've got to let everyone else in too.—Oscar Hammerstein II

237

Let us remember that all American citizens are brothers of a common country, and should dwell together in the bonds of fraternal feeling.—Abraham Lincoln

238

The Talmud explains how the site for King Solomon's Temple was selected. A father left a field to his two sons. They plowed together, planted together, cultivated together, harvested together, and when the harvest was completed they divided it equally. The one took his share of the harvest to his home at one end of the field, and the other took his share to his home at the other end.

At night the brother at one end of the field began to ask himself the question, "Was that a fair division of the harvest?" And he came to the conclusion that it was not, for, said he to himself, "I have no one dependent upon me. My brother has a wife and two sons dependent upon him. It was a very selfish thing of me to take a half of that harvest." So he went into his storehouse and threw all the sheaves that he could carry over his shoulder and started across the field toward his brother's home.

That same night, at the other end of the field, the same question had arisen in the other brother's mind. He too had asked himself, "Was that a fair division of the harvest?" He too decided that it had not been.

To understand his reasoning, one must understand the Jewish idea that responsibility for the care of aged parents devolved upon the children. Consequently, he who had children, particularly male children, was blessed because he was thereby assured of security in his old age. This second brother reasoned, "I have these two fine sons who will look after me in my old age. My brother has no one to look after him. Surely it was very selfish of me to take half of the harvest." And so he too went into his storehouse and threw all the sheaves that he could carry over his shoulder and started across the field.

They met midway. Each, sensing the thought that had been in the mind of the other, dropped his sheaves, and they embraced with tears coursing down their cheeks. And the Talmud says that on that spot, consecrated with the tears of true brotherhood, they erected the Temple of Solomon.

Note that they were not asking the question, "Did I get all that was coming to me?" They were asking, "Did my brother get what he was entitled to receive?" This concern about our brothers is a part of the ability to say "We."—Matthew W. Hill, *National Parent-Teacher*

239

Looking through the wrong end of a telescope is an injustice to the astronomer, to the telescope, and to the stars; likewise, looking at our neighbor's faults instead of his attributes gives us an incorrect conception of ourselves, our neighbor, and our God.—William A. Ward, Tulsa *Herald*

240

If there's a stranger in your neighborhood today, better check up on him: he may need a friend. If he's still a stranger tomorrow, better check up on your neighborhood.—Burton Hillis, *Better Homes & Gardens*

241

The more mind we have, the more original men do we discover there are. Common people find no difference between men.—Pascal, *Pensées*

242

He is not well bred who cannot bear ill breeding in others.—Benjamin Franklin

243

The law cannot make you love your neighbor, but the law can make it much more difficult for you to express your hate.—Neil Lawson, *Look*

244

No one can have more peace than his neighbor will allow him.—Chinese proverb

245

Only reasoned argument . . . can overthrow ignorance and prejudice.—Allan Nevins

246

One language builds a fence. Two languages can construct a gate.—Boyd A. Martin

247

Tolerance implies a respect for another person, not because he is wrong or even because he is right, but because he is human.—John Cogley, "A Word for Tolerance," *Commonweal*

248

Animals are such agreeable friends; they ask no questions, pass no criticism.—George Eliot

249

Is thy heart right, as my heart is with thine? Dost thou love and serve God? It is enough. I give thee the right hand of fellowship.—John Wesley

250

If I only had one wish, I wouldn't waste it on wishing I could see. I'd wish instead that everyone could understand one another and how a person feels inside.—A twelve-year-old boy, blind since birth, *McCall's*

251

We talk a lot about our various denominations and during the papal elections someone remarked, "The Cardinals are electing a new pope in Rome."

"My goodness," the other responded, "I do hope they won't elect another Catholic."

252

The best way to keep your friends is not to give them away!—Wilson Mizner

253

If I wanted to punish an enemy, it should be by fastening on him the trouble of constantly hating somebody.—Hannah More

254

No one is so rich that he does not need another's help; no one so poor as not to be useful in some way to his fellow man; and the disposition to ask assistance from others with confidence, and to grant it with kindness, is part of our very nature.—Pope Leo XIII

255

For one human being to love another; that is perhaps the hardest of all our tasks, the ultimate, the last test and proof, the work for which all other work is but preparation.—Rainer Maria Rilke, *Letters to a Young Poet*

256

It is only the souls that do not love that go empty in this world.—R. H. Benson, *The History of Richard Raynal Solitary*

257

The heart sometimes finds out things that reason cannot.—R. H. Benson, *Lord of the World*

258

It is to the credit of human nature that, except where its selfishness is brought into play, it loves more readily than it hates.—Nathaniel Hawthorne

259

To the mind of Christ, love of man was an essential part of the fundamental law of religion, without which no man can truly love God.

When Jesus stated the "great commandment in the law,"—"Thou shalt love the Lord thy God with all thy heart and with all thy soul, and with all thy mind,"—He added a second, "Thou shalt love thy neighbor as thyself."—Harry F. Henry

260

Understanding can be a sword that cuts two ways; it may lessen personal antagonism and increase ideological antagonism. Something like this is happening in the current attempts of a number of Catholics to. gain new insights into Protestantism, both in its historical and in its contemporary manifestations.—Daniel J. Callahan, *Commonweal*

261

Human unity, like human peace, is correlative—cannot be achieved by any one master stroke. It cannot be accomplished by sudden and spectacular "change." It must be a growth, not an instantaneous realization. It must be built up through the hard labor of decisions, great and small. The growth of this vast body of decision, among mankind as a whole, corresponds to the growth that each decision works in the life of the individual person.—John LaFarge, *An American Amen*

262

He who cannot forgive others breaks the bridge over which he must pass himself, for every man has need to be forgiven.—George Herbert

263

The mind of the bigot is like the pupil of the eye; the more light you pour upon it, the more it will contract.—Oliver Wendell Holmes

264

Not in a day nor in a year have men grasped what Jesus meant when He told them to love their neighbors as themselves. We have not grasped His meaning yet, but little by little the horizons of our minds have widened. Let us be thankful for those who have made the first discoveries in the meaning of Christian brotherhood, and let us give ourselves to following in their train.—John Irwin

265

When brother clasps the hand of brother, a new courage and strength is established through their unity. The strong hand sustains the weak, the weak strengthens the strong through its needs, and Christians are bound together by sharing the vision, the faith, the longing, the hope, the conflict, the peril, and finally the joy which comes at the end of toil and gloom. "Brother clasps the hand of brother" and together they step fearless into the building of a world made pleasant and beautiful because all men live together in unity. This is a persistent vision. It is the vision of Jesus.

Each human hand, consciously or unconsciously, is reaching for a human hand. Brotherhood is not equality or likeness in all things, but a giving and receiving of that which each has. "Two are better than one; . . . For if they fall, the one will lift up his fellow; but woe to him that is alone when he falleth; for he hath not another to help him up."

There is the story of a fisherman in a small boat, spending many summer hours fishing near the private dock of a summer home on a lake. The owner was sometimes annoyed by the man's constant presence. Why must he always fish in his waters? Then came the day when the little girl of the family, left alone for a few minutes on the dock, fell into the deep water. It was the persistent fisherman who, jumping quickly from his boat, saved the life of the drowning child.

In the brief span of a day's life, there is a constant flow of giving and receiving. From dawn to dark, and through the night, life as we know it here in the United States is constantly dependent on the mental or physical giving of some human soul, near or far. Added to this is the constant spiritual benefit in human relationships we so often underestimate or fail to recognize.—Mrs. John Hastie Brown, *Come Before His Presence*

266

Little Carley . . . granddaughter of the late Bishop Adna W. Leonard, had been taken by her father for a visit to New York. The most impressive experience of all was a trip to the Statue of Liberty and the long climb up inside. That night she could not sleep. When her father asked her what the trouble was, she replied, "Daddy, I'm thinking of the big lady with the lamp standing out there all alone. She must get awfully tired. Don't you think somebody ought to help her hold up that lamp?"

Yes, somebody—millions of somebodies—need to help her hold aloft that lamp of freedom. Who shall these somebodies be? They must be above all men and women of faith. Of faith in God, yes; but also faith in active good will and justice. They must be plain people with an honest faith in each other and with a continued faith in religious freedom.—Charles M. Crowe, *Sermons for Special Days*

LENT

267

I am Lent (from the old Teutonic word, "Lenz," meaning "Spring").

I continue forty days just preceding Easter.

I emphasize the words of Jesus: "If any man will come after me, let him deny himself, and take up his cross, and follow me."

I am an appropriate time for heart-searching in the light of the purity and the self-effacement of Jesus Christ.

I help people to renew holy vows.

I call Christian people, who have grown careless about Kingdom matters, back to the path of fidelity.

I remind the church of its great redemptive mission in the world.

I call upon those who have sinned to acknowledge, lament, and turn away from their evil ways.

I make people more alert to detect temptation and the snares of wickedness.

I face every Christian with the deeper meaning of the cross.

I awaken the careless, encourage the faint-hearted, and confirm the faith of those who begin to doubt.

I call attention to the great burden of sin which the human race carries.

I remind the church of the unfailing mercy and loving-kindness of God.

I bring Christian people face to face with the mysterious and majestic fact of God's redemption offered through Jesus Christ.

I set forth the truth that man, living in time, belongs to eternity.— Norman E. Richardson, *Central Truths of the Christian Youth Movement*

268

Most Lenten practices, with the terms used to designate them, date from pre-Christian times . . . in southern Germany . . . the first Sunday of Lent is called *Brandsonntag* or "Fire Sunday," because torches were lit at that time as part of the campaign against frost and cold. Then, as spring approached, the people celebrated "winter's burial," a custom which persists today in the "burning of Judas" on Holy Saturday.

Lent traditionally is a fast of forty days, not including Sundays, in token and remembrance of Jesus' fast in the wilderness. As a result, for centuries, Shrove Tuesday or Mardi Gras (fat Tuesday)—the day before Lent begins —has been a time in Latin countries of great merrymaking and carnival— the latter, a word derived from the Latin, *carne vale,* or "farewell to meat." "Shrove," on the other hand, is an old English word meaning "confession," and there the day was given over to a more solemn preparation for Lent.

Faithful Roman Catholics appear on Ash Wednesday, the first day of Lent, with a mark of ashes on their foreheads in the form of a cross to signify the beginning of fasting and self-denial which, according to strict rule, continues until the Saturday before Easter. Since the period of penitence and fasting extends through forty days, its observance was formerly called "quarantine," from which has evolved our modern use of the term to denote the separation from human contact of anyone with an infectious disease.

Not many know how our common pretzel got its start, and will be astonished perhaps to learn that it began in high honor as a certain kind of bread made of a special dough and shaped in the form of two arms crossed in prayer. These queerly contrived but religiously significant biscuits were called *bracellae* or "little arms," and were eaten as a reminder that Lent is a season of penitence and devotion. The Germans translated the word into *brezel* or *pretzel,* the earliest picture of which may be seen in a manuscript from the fifth century in the Vatican. Whenever we see or buy pretzels hereafter, we may possibly remember the spiritual posture for which these bits of food once stood.

Another special item of food which has remained with us to this day is the traditional "hot cross bun," sold only during Lent. In Germany and Scandinavia, these buns are filled with a paste of almonds, sugar and rosewater called *marchpane*—"Tuesday's bread." The significance of the cross is obvious but it is not generally known that many people in Europe still make the sign of the cross with the knife on a loaf of bread before cutting it.

The term Maundy Thursday, which is being employed increasingly in Protestant circles to commemorate the night when Jesus was betrayed, comes from the word *mandatum,* meaning "commandment."

This day of Holy Week is known in German-speaking countries as Green Thursday or *Grundonnerstag,* which probably goes back to the old German word *grunen,* "to mourn," rather than to any color reference, although it may refer to the green vestments that were worn in the thirteenth century for the mass said on that day.

The traditional term in England was Shere Thursday, meaning "sheer" or "clean." A survival of this anniversary of the washing-of-the-feet is seen in the ceremony at Westminster Abbey when the King or Queen distributes "Maundy Money" to poor subjects.

The liturgical Roman Catholic title of what we call Good Friday is "Friday of the Preparation," in Latin, *Feria sexta in Parasceve.* The word *parasceve* is, however, of Greek derivation and was used by the Jews in Christ's time to denote the day of preparation for the Sabbath. The early church applied the named *Pasch,* from the Hebrew *pesach* or "passover," both to Good Friday and Easter Sunday. From this, of course, come the terms "passion" and "passiontide," as applied, for example to Bach's *St. John Passion* and *St. Matthew Passion.* There are actually hundreds of items, some deeply serious, some superstitious, others happily whimsical, which belong in the richly varied catalogue of Lenten lore.—Elsa Kruuse, "The Human Side of Lent," *Advance*

269

Addition is written into our words Lent and Lenten. Lenten is a shortened form of lengthen. The days are lengthened now; the sun's welcome stay with us is extended each day; his strength is increased.

And it is the addition of the light which compels the subtraction called housecleaning. The added intensity of the light shows us things that were tolerable only in the dark days. The light has been added, and things which the housekeeper could endure in the gray and smoggy hours of winter she will not tolerate in the searching radiance of the longer days. . . .

This is judgment by sunlight. This is the significance of all spring cleaning. There is a word in our New Testament which is translated "sincere." The word is thought to be made up out of the words "sunlight" and "judgment" (II Corinthians 2:17). Sincerity is allowing ourselves to be judged by the sunshine. We are sincere when we have been tested by the light—Christ's light. . . . We must take our acts, our thoughts, our affections . . . into the light of Christ's presence. Are they fit . . . in the sight of men and of angels?—George Arthur Frantz, *Morning Morning*

270

A real Lent for us is welcoming Christ for lengthened hours. It means lengthening the time we spend with our Bibles. It means lengthened time spent in prayer. It means lengthening the time we spend caring for God's other children. . . . You mind the addition, and Christ will help you with the subtraction.—George Arthur Frantz, *Morning Morning*

271

Lent may be a time of reconsideration, a time in which we re-examine the foundations of life and reconnoiter the field of our human activity. The Lenten season should remind us that man does not live by bread alone, that there is a vertical as well as a horizontal aspect to life. . . . Lent should help to make clearer the absolute claims of God upon us. . . . It is in the losing of life that we come to possess the abundant life. Emerson said that we forget ourselves into immortality. Only as you negate yourself, blot self out, crucify self, act as if self did not count, do you come to participate in fullness of being. Christ died that they that live might no longer live unto themselves. . . . Our world again needs turning upside down. Lent challenges us to face Calvary. The way of self is the way of death; the way of the cross is the way of life. God forbid that I should glory save in the cross.

272

These many centuries the call of the cross, like the call of the morning, has drawn men from the darkness and the dead works of night to the glorious light and the activities of a new day, filling their lives with faith, hope and love.

273

Lent is that season of the church year set aside for the lighting of inner fires.

274

The Lenten season means an honest effort on the part of adults to place spiritual things first in the lives of children and in their homes. Parents cannot expect children to get out of Lent what fathers and mothers do not put into it.

275

Lent is both a Christian cue and a clue. The cue may be taken from the church calendar, but the clues are taken from the gospel and the need of our lives. I suspect we are less likely to miss the Lenten cue if we make use of its clues.—James Willis Lenhart, "It's About Time," *Advance*

276

Jesus planned His entry into Jerusalem on Palm Sunday, not to arouse the populace to a frenzied demonstration, but as His last solemn appeal to be received as Saviour and Lord. The multitude, however, saw in Jesus the popular hero of their national dreams, and nothing more, and the very tumult of their cheers moved Him to tears at their blindness of heart. The tears of Jesus, not the hosannas of the throng, should claim our prayerful thought on Palm Sunday. Jesus wept over a people who saw in Him only a popular prophet, not a heaven-sent Redeemer. They stood to cheer Him as He rode by. They did not kneel to surrender their hearts to Him in repentance and in faith. That was the tragedy of Palm Sunday.—Walter Barlow, *Today*

277

Characteristic of many of the mighty rulers of history have been their pride and arrogance, their ostentatious display of power and riches. As a consequence, they were generally more feared than loved by the rank and file of their subjects.

In sharp contrast to such sovereigns of the world stands the Ruler of them all, the King of kings and Lord of lords. Palm Sunday was the day He chose to permit the people to hail Him and proclaim Him the Son of David, their King. But with His entry into Jerusalem, there was no pomp and circumstance; only the acclaim of the people and the children, who in their enthusiasm spread their garments before Him.

Riding the humblest of animals, He moves on in majestic humility, accepting the homage and praise of the festival throng. All through the following week this blending of majesty and humility is constantly in evidence. Consistently He mingles with the common people. At night He retires to a modest home in Bethany. But with majestic indignation and righteous vehemence, He cleanses the temple of those who were making it a den of thieves.

In Gethsemane He accepts His Father's will as an obedient child. But moments later, when He confronts those who have come to arrest Him, a flash of his majesty, revealed in His calm words and perhaps in His authoritative voice and general bearing, causes them all to fall back in confusion.

Appearing a bound prisoner before both the high priest and the Roman Governor, He maintains a majestic calm and silence more eloquent than words. When He does speak, He confounds His judges and the court. When the day on which He died is drawing to a close, the Centurion, presiding at the crucifixion, declares, "Truly this was the Son of God."

WORLD DAY OF PRAYER

278

Make me gentle, Lord, and kind;
 Honest, frugal, pure of mind;
Patient, humble, meek and mild;
 Trustful as a little child.

Make me earnest, Lord, and strong;
 Just and faithful; foe of wrong;
Slow to anger; friend of all;
 Swift to answer duty's call.

—Huldah L. Winsted, "A Prayer," *North Dakota—Land of the Sky and Other Poems*

279

In our prayers we expect to communicate our panic to God instead of seeking His calm for us.—Bishop J. W. Lord, *Upper Room Pulpit*

280

Prayer is the chief agency and activity whereby men align themselves with God's purpose. Prayer does not consist in battering the walls of heaven for personal benefits or the success of our plans. Rather is it the committing of ourselves for the carrying out of His purposes. It is a telephone call to headquarters for orders. It is not bending God's will to ours, but our will to God's. In prayer, we tap vast reservoirs of spiritual power whereby God can find fuller entrance into the hearts of men.—G. Ashton Oldham

281

Too many of our prayers begin, "Now I lay me down to sleep." A man's size prayer runs more like this: "Now I get me up to wake; I pray the Lord my soul to shake."

282

Prayer is a rising up and a drawing near to God in mind, and in heart, and in spirit.—Alexander Whyte

283

Prayer is the breath of heaven breathing through the life of man.

284

It is our privilege to pray boldly. It is often said, "Beggars must not be choosers." But here is a place where beggars may be choosers. And beggars we are when we come before the Throne of Grace—otherwise, "grace is no more grace." Nevertheless, because grace is grace, the beggar-petitioner may come, find acceptance, ask and ask boldly.

Sir Walter Raleigh once made a request of the Queen and she petulantly answered, "Raleigh, when will you leave off begging?" Sir Walter replied, "When your Majesty leaves off giving." And his request was granted. But the God of all grace never grows weary of our asking and never rebukes us for coming.—Henry W. Frost

285

Prayer is the atmosphere in which all Christian virtues grow to perfection.

286

How often we hurry into the day without our armor on—without asking God to give us wisdom and courage to face the trials we may have to meet! If we honestly asked ourselves, "Do I really expect God to keep me from sin this day?" would our answer expose our lack of faith in God? Each day begun and lived without faith must end with the cry in the seventh chapter of Romans: "O wretched man that I am!" Each day begun and lived in faith will end with the victorious cry of the eighth chapter: "We are more than conquerors through him. . . ." These two chapters in Romans show us two ways of facing life. In the seventh chapter the word "I" occurs more than thirty times—the Holy Spirit is not mentioned once. In the eighth chapter the "I" is almost gone—it occurs only twice—and the Holy Spirit is mentioned sixteen times!

Our Master taught His disciples to seek His help when He taught them to pray, "Lead us not into temptation, but deliver us from evil." If we truly pray and ask His help, temptations can be overcome. The Christian must have on his full armor if he is to stand against the wiles of the devil.—E. Paul Hovey, *The Upper Room*

287

A common petition in our prayers is to ask God to bless us. . . . What do we really mean when we ask God to lay His blessing upon us? . . . How many times have we prayed for the blessing of God when what we actually wanted was for God to bless choices we had made without consulting Him? . . . How can we expect God to approve a decision in which His judgment was never asked, His preferences never considered? . . .

One day a boy asked his pastor to

pray for him in a financial matter. Solemnly he said, "If I can get enough people to pray for me I can make this thing work." His pastor asked what he proposed to do with his profits. The boy explained he intended to go into a business involving a serious moral question.

"How can you expect God to bless you when the thing you propose is morally wrong?" his pastor asked. The boy replied, "If a man can't expect God to help him, what is there to religion?" This implies that God is like an errand boy, expected to help without asking questions. One of the important lessons every Christian must learn is that some of God's blessings are accompanied by unpleasant circumstances.

Skill is never achieved except at the cost of serious work. Character is never fashioned except at the cost of strict, sometimes painful, discipline. Some of the rarest virtues in life are attained only by way of pain. If God sends pain in answer to our prayer for a blessing, are we to regard it as affliction?

There is an Old Testament tale involving Jacob which illustrates our point. He found himself wrestling with an unknown antagonist. Suspecting that he was dealing with God, he exclaimed, "I will not let you go until you bless me." And from that hour to the end of his life he walked as a lame man. But he achieved immortality!

When we ask God to bless us we are never able to specify the form in which the blessing may come. It often appears as a misfortune, or even as a tragedy. But God's blessing is there. Making it easy for us is not always God's way of blessing. God's greatest favors can come in heavy loads that make us strong; baffling situations that make us cautious; profound questions that compel us to think, and suffering that constrains us to seek His presence.—Roy L. Smith, "When Does God Bless Us?," *Together*

288

Faith and experience alike convince me that God Himself sees and answers, and His answers I never venture to criticize. In the quiet of the home, in the heat of life and strife, in the face of death, the privilege of speech with God is inestimable.—Wilfred Grenfell

289

In an age which places so much emphasis on personality, we cannot afford to neglect the practice of prayer . . . communion with God can . . . make you winsome and attractive. . . . "What you are inside shows in your face," says the famous artist, Norman Rockwell. "Your eyes sooner or later become the mirror of your soul." Rockwell . . . finds it difficult to paint individuals who have lost their faith or who never had any. "I could sketch the outline of their faces, but the inner glow that gives them character would be missing."

Henry James wrote a story called "Roderick Hudson" in which a young artist left home and led a dissipated life in Rome. His mother never ceased to pray for him. . . . At last she decided to visit her son. The artist looked at her in surprise and said, "What has happened to your face, Mother; it has changed its expression." "Your mother has prayed a great deal," she replied. The artist son said, "Well, it makes a good face. It puts fine lines in it." "Moses did not know that the skin of his face shone because he had been talking with God" (Exodus 34:29).—Walter D. Cavert, *Ours Is the Faith*

290

Archibald MacLeish has a play called "Panic." It depicts a woman standing in a crowd at Times Square, New York, reading a news bulletin which announces the closing of the nation's banks and predicts unemployment and suffering. Knowing it meant that countless people might go hungry while she ate her own food, she exclaimed prayerfully, "Forgive us our daily bread." It is a prayer every American Christian might well make as he recalls that millions of God's children in other countries never have enough to eat.—Walter D. Cavert, *Ours Is the Faith*

GOOD FRIDAY

291

I am the cross.

I am the symbol of the vicarious suffering of Jesus Christ.

I am the emblem of God's costly love in seeking to save mankind from sin.

I am Christ's final acceptance of and submission to the will of the Father.

I am a demonstration of the utter iniquity and moral perversity of sin.

I am the burden of sorrow and suffering which sin places upon those who share Christ's passion to rid the world of sin.

I show how ethically blind religious fanatics can be.

I am the God-given assurance of the ultimate victory over sin.

I can become a source of comfort, resignation, and fortitude for those who are the victims of aggressive evil.

I demonstrate the possibility of man's willingness to give his life for the welfare of others.

I give drawing power to the gospel.

I am the utmost effort of evil to frustrate God's plan of redemption.

I justify the attitudes of gratitude, loyal devotion, and worship, toward Jesus Christ.

I am the turning point in the religious history of mankind.

I provide a way by which those who have been guilty of wrongdoing may establish fellowship with the God of righteousness.—Norman E. Richardson, *Central Truths of the Christian Youth Movement*

292

The cross is unique, intrinsic, fundamental in Christianity. The cross is the symbol of Christian truth. It stands for the reality of realities—eternal God, Father of all mankind. It reveals the essential nature of God—love.

That this love is revolutionary in technique, redemptive in purpose, creative in potency and eternal in validity was most convincingly demonstrated by the Cross of Jesus Christ.

Love is longsuffering, selfless, sacrificial in service, does not judge others lightly but trusts in His righteousness. Love is humble, penitent, forgiving, reconciliatory, peacemaking and does not condemn but leaves vengeance to the wrath of God. Love resists hatred with mercy, matches violence with compassion, overcomes evil with good. This is the spirit of the victorious cross.

Peoples come and go in an endless procession, empires rise and fall, but the cross stands towering above the wrecks of time radiant in a light prophetic of the new heaven and the new earth.

In the fellowship of the cross lies humanity's hope. To be a Christian is to belong to this fellowship.—Hachiro Yuasa, "The Fellowship of the Cross," *The Missionary Herald*

293

Carl F. Lueg, writing in *The Upper Room*, described a group of college students who were having their pictures taken with the guest speaker after a religious meeting. The photographer arranged them around a big cross which had been erected on the platform. Trying to create the appearance of group action, he said to them: "Be adusting the cross." All too often that is exactly what Christians do. Because we cannot face the staggering demands the Cross of Christ lays upon us, we adjust it to our own ideas.—Walter Dudley Cavert, *Ours Is the Faith*

294

This was the world which executed the Life subsequent generations until this hour revere as the best earth has seen. And plainly it is the world in which we still live. All these forces are present and active in our society: religious intolerance, commercial privilege, political expediency, pleasure-loving irresponsibility, unfaithfulness, the mob mind, militarism, public apathy.—Henry Sloane Coffin, "The Meaning of the Cross"

295

Christianity is a religion of sacrifice. The cross is not only the symbol but also the secret of its power.—Don D. Tullis

296

A cross on a mission church altar has two holes in it. Once it had been a crucifix. But the woman who had owned it came to see that she must worship a risen rather than a dead Christ and gave it to the church.—Richard K. Smith

297

The cross is "I" crossed out.

298

Had Jesus stopped even a little way short of the cross, He could never have inspired the Church to be the Church, He could never have qualified as the world's redeemer, He could never have escorted His followers through the martyrdom that awaited them.

Every man who faces an extreme situation has cause for thanksgiving. God has assigned him to play against the top.—Roy L. Smith, "Play Against the Top," *Together*

299

We bring the atoms of sin to the cross where they are smashed.

300

The craze to get something for nothing is upon the American public. . . . In a Boston store a large crucifix was placed in the display window with a sign: "This beautiful crucifix on easy terms." One wondered if that storekeeper had any idea of the incongruity, almost sacrilege, of the phrase he had used: a cross that could be purchased on easy terms! We know that a cross can never be purchased cheaply. You just don't take up any kind of cross on easy terms. . . . The worth-while things of life—the birth of a child, the building of a family unit, the evolution of love through travail and pain, a war to win everlasting peace—these things, too, are not available to us on easy terms. . . . Even God had to take the hard way to prove His love and holiness.—O. W. Bell, *Together*

301

Excessive display of religious symbols is a form of hypocrisy which hurts rather than helps the church. Institutions tend to become formalized and ofttimes symbols become more important than what they symbolize. . . . It happens when we install crosses all over; on the altar, to be sure, but also on doors and doorknobs, on steeples, in windows, on pew ends, on hymnbooks, in light fixtures—everywhere. Such use of the cross is no substitute for carrying it. . . .

In a sense it is a form of hypocrisy. We would do better to display it less and practice it more. We would certainly lose some members. Our income would shrink markedly. But our effectiveness would be vastly augmented.

And possibly we might be instrumental in saving ourselves and our society.—Stanley U. North

302

Without the cross we will never know the real way to meet our difficulties. In our day we have seen the destruction of much we thought was good and the breakdown of moral ideals. Our Christian faith gives us all the necessary equipment in the cross to meet all these disappointments.—Paul Deane Hill

303

Let us look at the cross and then into our own hearts.

304

In the cross is salvation, in the cross is life; in the cross is strength of mind, in the cross joy of spirit. Take up therefore thy cross and follow Jesus. He went before bearing His cross; that thou also mayest bear thy cross. If thou be partaker of His suffering, thou shalt be also of His glory.

305

There is only a comma in the Apostles' Creed to fill the gap between Jesus' birth and His death; ". . . born of the Virgin Mary, suffered under Pontius Pilate. . . ." Strange, isn't it, that His life is taken care of by a comma! What a comma it is! Nearly everyone wants to be remembered for something he has done. We identify most people by some particular accomplishment. But wherein was Jesus a success? What did He do other than lead a life that led directly to His death? . . . Is the Apostles' Creed right in stressing the birth, death, and resurrection of Jesus as being of primary significance for our faith? It is obvious that if it were not for His life, the birth, death, and resurrection would be meaningless. But on the other hand, every attempt to understand Jesus that does not seek first to understand *who He is,* fails. When we call Him the "Man of Galilee" in preference to the "Son of Man" we do not come closer to Him; instead, we find ourselves farther away. To try to see Jesus from our human point of view is not to see Him at all. Because Jesus is who He is, the events of His life, His teachings, and His deeds are authoritative for us—not the other way round. What Jesus did on earth did not make Him a Son of God, and neither can we make ourselves sons of God by doing the same. . . . If we ignore who Jesus was, and concentrate merely on His earthly ministry, it is impossible for us, for instance, to understand why He was crucified. Certainly the cross could have been avoided easily. Nevertheless, He walked directly and knowingly to the cross. It is almost as if Jesus understood that His life was a "comma," a pause between, when God came to men.—*The Lord of Christian Faith and Life* (revised)

306

The physical darkness described in the Bible during the hours of the crucifixion of Jesus was only the symbol of the spiritual darkness in which the people were living. Even in the darkest hour of the crucifixion the "Unquenchable Light" was shining. To most Christians the darkest hour was when Christ uttered the cry, "My God, my God, why hast thou forsaken me?" but others assert it was the time when all His disciples forsook Him, leaving Him alone. But whichever was the darkest moment, there was never a time when the Unquenchable Light did not shine from the cross. The Son of God died an undeserved death that through His sacrifice many might attain an undeserved eternal life.— Lorell Weiss

307

The revelation which we have in Christ is that of a God who can be known, trusted, and loved. The great purpose of His coming was to make peace between man and God. Heathen religions are based on the idea of reconciling God to man; hence their altars, many with dark and bloody rites. The Gospel of Christ declares that God is reconciled to man, and now offers man the opportunity of being reconciled to Him.

Only the cross could bring about such a reconciliation. With His arms outstretched on the cross, Christ lays hold upon man and brings him to God.

308

During World War II there was a wonderful Russian nun, Mother Maria. She lived in Paris under the Nazis and did her best to relieve the suffering, not only of the Catholics but of the Jews under persecution. But one day, when the Nazis were lining up the Jewish girls in her convent school to take them off to the execution chambers, one high-school girl was so frightened that Mother Maria took off her nun's habit, quickly put over her head the yellow scarf of the Jew and said gently: "I'll go for you; I'll take your place." And Mother Maria died as a Jew. You see, there is such a thing in this world as suffering in behalf of others. Christianity says that God suffers that way too. This is the meaning of the Cross. Christ went in our place.—Harry H. Kruener, *Specifically to Youth*

309

The cross of Christ radiates a power that transforms life as light dispels darkness. It is a power that creates in human hearts a new disposition to build brotherhood, a power that dams up the destructive energies of passion and hatred and lust and converts them into love and service and sacrifice.— R. S. Dougherty

310

The cross may be made into a doctrine; it was prepared by Jesus as a discipline. . . . Jesus did not walk one way Himself and propose another for the disciples, but invited them to His experience if they wished His attainment. Jesus nowhere commanded that one cling to his cross; He everywhere commanded that one carry his cross; and out of this daily crucifixion has been born the most beautiful sainthood from St. Paul to St. Francis, from à Kempis to George Herbert.— Ian Maclaren

311

The cross marks the Great Divide in human history. It also marks the Great Divide in any person's life. The world has been different since that hour when Jesus bore His cross. Human lives have been different from the hour when they began to bear their cross and live for Him.

312

God's will is God's power in action. Since God's will is wise, he who obeys it and walks in it is sure to be blessed. Since His will is good, the man who lives by it is seeking his own true welfare. Since God's will expresses His power, he is strong who walks in it.

In Gethsemane Christ was confronted with the ultimate will of God— the cross. His strong, yet sensitive human nature shrank from the prospect of a shameful, agonizing death on the accursed tree. Still there was God's holy and perfect will. "On to the cross," was its unalterable decree.

Christ had subjected Himself to the will of the Father. His deepest conviction was that the will of God was good and must be done. Hence His three times repeated prayer, "Not my will, but thine." His strength lay in His complete trust in the holy and perfect will of God.

God, our Father in Christ, speak to us through the cross of Thy well-beloved Son. Grant that through Him we may find strength daily to walk in obedience to Thy perfect will.

313

The cross speaks of death. To all the world it proclaims the death of "Jesus of Nazareth, King of the Jews." Around the world the cross confronts men with the simple message, "The Son of God died on the accursed tree. The lamb of God, bearing the sin of the world, died on the cross that He might bring "life and immortality to light."

The cross speaks of life. To Christ it was the gateway to life in glory.

Whoever in faith accepts for himself the atoning sacrifice of Christ on the cross "shall not perish, but have everlasting life."

Even as Christ died on the cross that in Him all men might have life, so the humble believer in Christ "dies daily to sin" but lives again in "newness of life." As all nature dies in the fall of the year only to break forth to new life in the spring, so he who puts away the old finds strength in the cross to live the new life in Christ.

314

The cross is the supreme symbol of our Christian faith. The Apostle Paul said that bewildered Jews had found the cross a stumbling block. Greeks with their pagan culture found in it foolishness but those who had found the "New Way" of life in Christ found in the cross the wisdom and power of God.

How can anyone tie up in his thinking the idea of a God of infinite love and the need for an instrument of torture and death? Certainly Jesus' supreme picture of the nature of God has no cross in it. He told us of a wayward son who, after he had violated most of the commandments, "came to himself" and said, "I will arise and go to my father." It was not necessary for anyone to die to appease the anger of that father. He was yearning for the homecoming of his son and he rushed forth with welcome and forgiveness while the son was "yet a great way off."

Why then a cross? Jesus climaxed His ministry with His teaching, "Greater love hath no man than this, that a man lay down his life for his friend." His whole life and His death were alike a revelation of God's infinite love for humanity, a love that would pay the supreme price for friends or children. When people commence to understand that love, then Jesus, by His death, becomes their atonement or, as some people pronounce it, their at-onement; it draws them into oneness with their heavenly Father. They commence to sing Isaac Watts's hymn:

When I survey the wondrous cross
On which the Prince of Glory died,
My richest gain I count but loss
And pour contempt on all my pride.
Were the whole realm of nature mine,
That were a present far too small,
Love so amazing, so divine.
Demands my soul, my life, my all.
—I. B. Wood, *Rapid City* (South Dakota) *Journal*

315

To those who had undertaken to lead Christ to the cross He said, "This is your hour, and the power of darkness." Reporting the tragedy on Calvary the Evangelist says, "When the sixth hour was come, there was darkness over the whole land until the ninth hour." As the Son of God was dying, light seemed to be passing from the face of the earth. Still the Christian Church resolutely lifts up its voice and sings of the cross,

All the light of sacred story
Gathers round its head sublime.

In a day of history when the powers of darkness very definitely are having "their hour," the only Light that brings a ray of hope to groping mankind is that which shines out from

Calvary. . . . Into the hearts of men, into the homes of the lowly and the rich it sends its warm cheering message, "Walk in the light and it shall lead you through this world of bewildering darkness and perplexity into the peace and certainty of His glorious presence."

316

No story has been told with more concise fullness than that of the Passion Week and Last Day of our Lord's earthly life. Its significance, however, has never been fully measured by human minds.

At one time, its human side stands out most clearly. We can see that death on the cross was the inevitable close to such a life as Christ's. We know that if any man sets himself to confront moral evil, that moral evil will prey upon him as a wolf attacks its victim. The course of events runs toward a natural issue. The envy of the Pharisees, the hatred of the Sadducees, the craft of the High Priest, the treachery of Judas—all worked together for evil to Him who was God's beloved.

But if we read the story again, if we look at it in the light of the comments of the Word of God, we shall see the working of another Hand. We will see that it was God the Father who sacrificed His Son. We will hear the prophet say, "It pleased the Lord to bruise him; he hath put him to grief" (Isaiah 53:10). We will hear the Apostle proclaim, "Him, being delivered by the determinate counsel and foreknowledge of God, ye have taken, and by wicked hands have crucified and slain" (Acts 2:23). We will hear Christ's own quiet voice saying

in the midst of it all, "Thou couldest have no power at all against me, except it were given thee from above" (John 19:11). We will find ourselves standing before the deepest mystery which has been revealed to man, a mystery deeper than that of the Incarnation, more difficult to understand than the miracle of the Resurrection —the truth set down in the words, "He [that] spared not his own Son, but delivered him up for us all . . ." (Romans 8:32). Yes, God the Father was at the Cross of Christ His Son. He knew what was taking place.

317

"A parable of the beautifying of disaster" the Niagara River was called some years ago by the late William T. Ellis: "The Niagara River is not one of the great rivers of the world. Running from Lake Erie to Lake Ontario, it is only a few miles long. But what makes the river significant is that at Niagara Falls there is a tragedy in the channel—a break in the even flow of the stream, so that the waters make a stupendous leap into the gorge below. As they are shattered and bruised on the rocks beneath the falls, however, there is cast up into the sunlight the exquisite rainbow of the Niagara, which even kings and queens come from the ends of the earth to see."

Life is like that. We may go along for years in a contented flow of experience. Our health is good. We have our friends, our work, our faith. But suddenly there comes an unexpected tragedy—a war, a depression, a breakdown in health, the loss of a loved one, or maybe even a moral disaster. We have to make a blind leap of faith into an overwhelming abyss of suffering. Completely shattered on the cruel rocks of reality, our emotions are churned into a seething foam of bewilderment. But out of our distresses there is cast up into the sunlight of God's love a rainbow of penitence, hope, and trust—a radiance in the midst of our tears—so that what could have been our ruin is transformed into a glorious Christian testimony.

That is what was accomplished by our Lord Jesus Christ. He beautified disaster. Death had been up to that time an unrelieved tragedy. But ever since Calvary and Easter, the Christian believer has been able to trace the rainbow through the rain, and know "the promise is not vain, that morn shall tearless be."—Edwin T. Dahlberg, "Rainbow Over Calvary," *National Council Outlook*

318

In the light of His life we will recognize men put the wrong person on the cross. That person should have been I. Arnold Bruce Come has said, "In Jesus Christ God confronts man so that, on the one hand, man stands convicted of sin, but, on the other, he simultaneously hears the offer of merciful forgiveness." When we willingly experience the historical Jesus Christ thus in our lives, then we begin to know God.—Kenneth Beall, *Prophetic Realism*

319

We believe that Jesus humbled Himself, becoming obedient even unto death, yea the death of the cross.
We believe that He went out, bearing the cross for Himself unto the place called The Place of a Skull.
We believe that there they crucified Him, and the malefactors, one on the right hand and the other on the left.
We believe that we are reconciled in one body unto God through the cross.
We believe that then hath the stumbling block of the cross been done away.
We believe that unto us who are saved the cross is the power of God.
We believe that Jesus is the author and perfecter of our faith, who for the joy that was set before Him endured the cross, despising the shame, and hath sat down at the right hand of the throne of God.
We believe that we ought not to glory, save in the cross of our Lord Jesus Christ.
We believe that if any man would come after Him, he must deny himself, and take up his cross daily, and follow Him.
          —A Creed in the Cross

320

There are three accepted ways by which man's identity may be established: by *fingerprints*, by *blood tests*, and by his *name*.

Criminals are required by detectives and police to submit to a fingerprint test. Babies who have been mixed in a hospital ward, in order to be restored to their rightful parents, are submitted to a blood test. Friends writing from far away are recognized by the name test.

Jesus tells us that He came to save "sinners." He tells us that unless we turn and become as little children we are not worthy to enter the Kingdom of Heaven. Finally He calls us friends.

Doubters will find their doubts swept away when they see the *nail prints* in His hands. Sinners will find their sins washed away by the *blood* shed on Calvary. Believers will find their prayers are answered when they ask in His *Name*.

These, then, are the three great mysteries in the Christian religion: the Cross, the Blood, the Name. One meets them all on Golgotha hill. All are means of identifying Christ. All are means of interpreting Christ. All are means of salvation through Christ.

"If any man will come after me, let him deny himself, and take up his *cross,* and follow me" (Matthew 16:24). "The *blood* of Jesus Christ . . . cleanseth us from all sin" (I John 1:7). "And whatsoever ye shall ask in my *name,* that will I do, that the Father may be glorified in the Son" (John 14:13).

If one truly has been redeemed by the blood, and truly knows that Name that is above every name in heaven and on earth, and then brings his entire being into harmony with Jesus, immediately Jesus is in his midst, and all his prayers are answered. But how can this redemption be achieved, how can this miracle of answered prayer come to pass? These questions can be answered only by considering these three mysteries of Jesus: the Cross, the Blood, and the Name.—Glenn Clark, *The Three Mysteries of Jesus*

321

We have not truly borne a cross when we have simply endured it; but only when we have taken it and have changed it from a burden into a victory.—G. Pitt Beers

322

Our contemplation in Holy Week of the dying form of Christ on the cross should remind us of His companionship with ourselves in suffering. We call to mind the 22nd Psalm, which Charles Spurgeon refers to as a "photograph of our Lord's saddest hours, the record of His dying words, the lachrymatory of His last tears, the memorial of His expiring joys." How deeply does this Psalm reflect all that is darkest in human experience!

Our Christian faith has not swerved from having its center in the cross of Christ. And when we look again at that cross we get a new and deeper sense of fellowship with Christ. Christ is open to those who carry crosses in His name. We drink the same cup that was drunk by our Lord. The cross tells us that Christ has not merely entered into the fellowship of human suffering, but has taken upon Himself the burden of human sin. The cross is a symbol of the atonement, of the companionship with Christ in suffering and victory. Out of all the thought and controversy over the atonement one element stands sure, and that is the element of satisfaction. Satisfaction could only be achieved through Christ's voluntary obedience. He accepted death freely, following His Father's will; His death was a result of His unconquerable love.

Christ makes religion consist in fellowship with God and obedience to His will, and Christ is our true High Priest because He shared our human life and knew it from the inside. In Hebrews 5:7 we are told that, in agony, when He prayed with "strong crying and tears" to be saved from death,

His prayer was granted, but He refused the deliverance in order that He might submit Himself utterly to His Father's will. Here is an emphasis in the Passion Story which ought to be placed in the foreground. Shakespeare's Iago, for once speaking the truth, says of Desdemona: "She is of so free, so kind, so apt, so blessed a disposition, she holds it a vice in her goodness not to do more than she is requested." So the spirit of the cross is well said to consist of Christ's having done what no one could possibly have demanded.

The cross also is a symbol of the salvation wrought by Christ, a salvation we should not neglect. He saved us from sin. In this connection William Ellery Channing wrote: "Jesus came to be the emancipator of the oppressed conscience; to break the power of the passions; to redeem and seat on the throne of human nature the moral power; to give new life and range to the law of duty; to present a glorious ideal of goodness and greatness, so that the mind may aspire after a lofty rectitude, such as worldly morality, drawn from prudence and utility and seeking chiefly security and comfort, never dreamed of."

Also He saved us from enslavement to superstition, prejudice, and passion; from selfishness, and from the tyranny of the whole material creation. We are impressed that the death on the cross was a voluntary act. Christ offered Himself as priest and victim both. The eternal nature of God came out on Calvary. Here supremely God was in Christ reconciling the world unto Himself. When God determined to save men He took home to Himself, in the person of His Son, the agony and the curse and the cost of sin, and by bearing them suppressed them for ever. It was therefore eternal redemption, an act in which the Eternal Trinity participated; the manifestation in time of an eternal fact of the divine nature.
—Walton M. Rankin, "The Wondrous Cross," *Monday Morning*

323

Who are the candidates for the divine forgiveness implored and certainly secured by this prayer of our Lord?

Not Pilate. There is a sense, of course, in which he knew not what he did. But there is another sense in which he knew too well. It was a realization of guilt that made him wash his hands. He knew that he had been false to the Roman ideal of justice. He knew that, for fear of a riot with its untoward influence on his career, he had delivered an innocent man to his death.

Not the people. There is, again, a sense in which they knew not what they did. But "Hosanna to the son of David" and "Crucify him, crucify him" made guilty bedfellows on their now silent lips. Never before in the history of the world had sheep consented to the crucifixion of their shepherd.

Not the rulers. We must say, again, that there is a sense in which the rulers knew not what they did. They did not know because they did not understand the nature of their professed religion. If the members of the Sanhedrin had been crucified that day no better inscription could have been erected over their crosses than the words of Jesus, "They say, and do not." It was of the rulers that Jesus said: "Wherefore ye witness to yourselves, that ye are son of them that slew the prophets. Fill ye up then the measure of your fathers." No, He did not mean the unrepentant rulers when He prayed, "Father, forgive them; for they know not what they do."

It was the Roman soldiers. They did not know what they did. All they knew was to obey orders. "Theirs not to reason why." Theirs but to do and kill. "And when they came unto the place which is called the skull, there they crucified him. . . . And Jesus said, Father, forgive them; for they know not what they do." It was the soldiers who knew not what they did when they turned the carpenter's hammer and nails against Jesus.

These unwitting soldiers, condemned by society to a brutish life, are of the vast company of those who live in "the times of ignorance . . . [which] God overlooked." God forgave them for Jesus' sake.—Harold McAfee Robinson, *Mr. Valiant-for-Truth*

324

We go to Calvary to learn how we may be forgiven, and to learn how to forgive others, to intercede on their behalf, to join the noble band of intercessors.—S. J. Reid, *The Seven Windows*

325

Forgiveness is the gateway by which the cross becomes inward. When we accept forgiveness from anybody, we open our hearts to that person's love. The initial contact of the cross of Christ with those whom it reaches is by way of offering the forgiveness of God to those who admit their personal responsibility for the event.—Charles Duell Kean, *The Inward Cross*

326

Hard is the lesson of forgiving those who despitefully use us. But there is no better place to learn it than here at the cross of Jesus. It is here, at the cross, that Ralph Connor makes his Paul Gaspard learn that lesson in its deepest meaning and overcome the bitterness in his soul over the wrongs suffered by himself, by his father, and by his mother. He learned a portion of the lesson at his mother's knee as he conned the Bible lesson of seventy times seven. He learned a little more of it from the lips of his savage foster-mother, as she died in the depths of the Canadian woods. But he learned it best at the communion table, in remembering the death of Jesus. Listen to the story from *The Gaspards of Pinecroft*, as Paul tells a friend how he was able to forgive the man who had wronged him:

"I will tell you . . . why I was able to keep my hands off him today, and perhaps some day forgive him. . . . That's my mother's chair you are sitting in, and this is her Bible. I am going to read you her last lesson to me. . . . 'Father, forgive them, for they know not what they do.' God knows . . . I have not yet arrived at that mountain peak. For seven years it has seemed utterly beyond me. But tonight I glimpse it far up in the clouds. Here my mother learned to forgive; here my father found forgiveness; and here I begin to feel how much I need to be forgiven."

Yes, we learn that lesson best as we sit at the foot of the cross and hear Jesus say again, "Father, forgive them;

for they know not what they do."—William C. Skeath, *His Last Words*

327

Jesus had very real grievances—the rulers had opposed Him and plotted His death, His disciples had betrayed Him, and people had chosen sorry Barabbas over Him, His trial had been unjust, He had been mocked, cursed and spit upon, His friends had deserted Him. But when He prays for the forgiveness of "them" He means all of them. There is no bitterness in His heart. In a beautiful act of charity, He even excuses them and seeks to remove their guilt by saying they do not know what they do. This is surely a time for each of us to throw the blanket of love and forgiveness over those who have done us wrong—to wipe the slate clean by extending our own forgiveness and seeking even for those who have wronged us the forgiveness of the Father.—Charles L. Allen, *Roads to Radiant Living*

328

On Golgotha there was a dialogue between two criminals and Jesus. One of the condemned, twisted by his hatred of society and of himself, railed at the guiltless victim beside him. The other had been moved by this strange encounter with the Man whom he knew to be the victim of judicial murder. The dialogue concerning sin and responsibility and the future proceeds. But to the response the divine mystery seems to make through Christ, the penitent thief makes his own response: "Jesus, remember me. . . ." Still through the Man on the cross comes the divine assurance, "Today you will be with me in Paradise."—David A. MacLennan, *Entrusted with the Gospel*

329

Jesus was a neighbor to the thief on the cross. That is, He was conscious of his need and did something about it. Imagine, even with His last breath of life almost gone, He gave to the dying thief. Oh, the thoughtfulness of His love.

But how else could a penitent one advance into light? Unless someone stretch out a helping hand and lead him? Unless one who knew the way to the light made the way clear for another? A man, a human being, a child of God, had appealed to Him for help. Jesus had the answer and gave it. He was suffering Himself, but not too much to help one suffering more. He was thoughtful of this miserable man. Here was a man literally *in extremis,* lost, everything gone, honor, home, and now life itself beginning to flicker. "What lies beyond this moment of ending?" . . . Jesus drew him up and out of his present condition, his present state of mind, when He said: "Today shalt thou be with me in Paradise." —James W. Kennedy, *Advance into Light*

330

This was a prayer of faith. In fact I think a more daring faith is hardly to be found in the Bible or out of it. He did not pray, "Remember me *if* thou comest in thy kingdom," but "Remember me *when* thou comest." . . . This prayer received an answer. . . . Our Lord gave to this dying outlaw certain assurances that are as precious to us as they were to the man.

—Clovis G. Chappell, *The Seven Words*

331

The cross had won its first victory. The first step in any moral realignment then or now is for goodness to get wrongness on its side. Goodness has usually to suffer, and often to suffer long and bitterly, before it can get wrongness on its side. . . . Because the malefactor was on Jesus' side, Jesus bestowed upon him the victor's reward: "Thou shalt be with me. . . ."
—Gaius Glenn Atkins, *From the Cross*

332

Many of the prophets had shrunk back from the voice of divine commission . . . but no . . . attempted excuse, evasion, or hesitation marked the reply of Mary . . . to that decree, announced by Gabriel . . . that she was to be the mother of the long-expected Messiah . . . and in Moffatt's translation we catch something of the glow and wonder of her spirit—not the submissive surrender of, "Be it unto me according to thy word," of the King James Version, but rather the eager acceptance of a life's vocation, "I am here to serve the Lord." "To serve the Lord"—how many times did Mary have to repeat these words of dedication? . . . Jesus did not forget the lonely figure . . . in tender solicitude Love speaks from the cross: "Woman, behold thy son!"—Leslie Badham, *Love Speaks from the Cross*

333

Jesus knew that part of the pain of bereavement is to be no longer needed by some other person for whom one has a unique responsibility, to whom one is tied not only by affection but also by practical duties. Life without functional ties, by which the respect people have for each other is given practical expression in the routine affairs of home and business and community, is life without meaning. But in the deeper sense, while we recognize that there are no real substitutes to take the place fully of those we have lost, the family pattern of the Kingdom of God means the turning of our sense of personal loss outward so as to transform it into brotherly service to others. . . . So Jesus gave to Mary and to John the responsibility of making a home for each other. Since He would no longer need the ministrations of either of them, they would find themselves wanted and useful in serving each other instead.— Charles Duell Kean, *The Inward Cross*

334

Even as He is suffering the agony of death He has a word of compassion and concern for one whom He loves. In the midst of more pain than it seems anyone could bear He still is anxious about the needs and well-being of another. Here is a rebuke to selfishness, a shame for hardheartedness. It reveals that we ourselves are living at our very best when we can turn away from our own sorrows and disappointments and seek to meet a need in a weaker life.—Charles L. Allen, *Roads to Radiant Living*

335

Out of the word emerges the value of a real friend's help. Jesus trusted John with a most sacred and most precious charge. The cross will test our friendships, whether they are good or evil, whether their influences are upward or downward.—S. J. Reid, *The Seven Windows*

336

No one dying with the words of a Psalm upon his lips has lost his faith in God!—Martin Dibelius

337

Jesus may have thought that God had forsaken Him, but He held fast to God. It was still, in that nadir hour, "My God, my God—why?" His despair was still undergirded by faith. He could not resolve the situation but He knew that there was reason in it and for it, though He could not see the reason. He clung to "my" and "why" when everything else seemed lost; "my" in personal relationship with His Father, "why" in His confidence that the whole issue in which He was involved was morally right even though He could not see it either steadily or victoriously or as a whole. It is always out of such steadfast faith that the dawn of moral understanding arises. . . . Faith will not surrender—it will still say, "My God." —Gaius Glenn Atkins, *From the Cross*

338

Happy the soul that in such circumstances can fall back with certainty on the promises of the Scriptures; that can find steadiness and hope in the thought of the unbroken witness of the worshiping church, and that, above all, can look to Him who for our sake endured the cross, despising the shame, and is now set down at the right hand of the throne of God.—Leslie Badham, *Love Speaks from the Cross*

339

Jesus used the faith of Israel to bridge the gulf of isolation between Himself and God, and Himself and His fellow man. Psalm 22 is a Day of Atonement psalm, when the solidarity of Israel is dramatized by the penitence of every Israelite. On the Day of Atonement, every loyal and pious Jew beats his breast and takes upon himself moral responsibility for the suffering of his people. His own personal experience is made to be the bearer of the destiny of Israel, and his own personal hope to focus the general expectation of his nation. The liturgical expression of the mood is in these words: "My God, my God, look upon me; why hast thou forsaken me? why hast thou put me from thee, and art so far from me and the voice of my complaint?"

This cry from the cross was both the deepest and most poignant expression of Jesus' own personal need and at the same time a description of faith's answer. . . . These words from the cross are an identification through faith with God's purposes for man.— Charles Duell Kean, *The Inward Cross*

340

Lord Halifax, then Baron Irwin, when he was appointed to India as viceroy, arrived there on Good Friday. Instead of courting all the pomp with which the viceroy should have been welcomed, he slipped away to a church for three hours of worship. There were those who thought that the Indian officials would resent this putting of worship ahead of "official ceremony," but it was this devotion to his God which more than anything else gave the Mahatma confidence in him as an official at a time when such confidence meant much to the British Empire.

How much more confidence might there be around the world today if the leaders of nations would display such fidelity to God? Yet can I expect more of the great in the nation than I expect of myself? Have I allowed really important things to interfere with my keeping of the holy day?—George S. Bancroft, *Today*

341

Jesus Christ cannot do anything for us without the law of the cross. We might as well expect electricity to light our house without wires or lamps, as to expect Him to save us from our perils without the spirit and the fact of sacrifice.—John A. Marquis

342

The Gospels report no sickness in that vigorous body. But they do report weariness and pain. Weariness He knew, reaching a desperate climax when His ever-willing spirit could no longer force His exhausted body to bear up against the weight of the cross. His flesh failed Him on the Via Dolorosa. Pain He knew, from the sharp intrusions of the thorns into His forehead, through the keener lacerations of His hands and feet by the nails, into the long agony of the whole crucifixion experience. That experience was "excruciating." On this physical agony our Lord made but one comment, "I thirst." But that one comment makes Him the great Companion of all those from whose compressed lips pain forces its toll of words.

It is a commentary on the extreme selfishness of our lives that we require an experience of pain to awaken us to the sufferings of others. In that we lay ourselves open to the anger of Jesus. For it was precisely "the insensibility of the Jews to human suffering, exhibited in a tendency to put ritual integrity above humanity, [which] filled Jesus with indignant anger." But when we have been once aroused by our own experience of pain, however inconsequential in itself, we see human history as that

Ocean of Time, whose waters of deep woe
Are brackish with the salt of human tears!

Then it is that we find in Jesus a Great Companion, and because a Great Companion, a Great Saviour. For, as Dr. Warfield writes, "When we observe Him exhibiting the movements of our human emotions, we are gazing upon the very process of our salvation; every manifestation of the truth of our Lord's humanity is an exhibition of the reality of our redemption."—Harold McAfee Robinson, *Mr. Valiant-for-Truth*

343

Here is represented the physical price that Christ paid—the cost of something grand and glorious. There are no short cuts to the things that really matter. And, also, it represents His very deep thirst for God just now. In the midst of suffering even He who was so close is drawn even closer to the Father. Not always is that so. A sorrow makes us either bitter or better. But for those who will see and feel, God is closer in times of deep sorrow than at any other time.—Charles L. Allen, *Roads to Radiant Living*

344

"I thirst" (John 19:28).

Can it be Jesus who uttered these words? Yes, for His death was real, as His life was real. The author of the Gospel of John insists upon the utter reality of Jesus' life and death, from the beginning to the end of his book. Christ was no God in disguise, traveling the earth incognito, a phantom or a transient epiphany of the deity (as in the tales of the pagan gods)—one who could not suffer because He was divine. The Gospel of John is deeply and steadily concerned to assert and to vindicate the truth that Jesus' human life was real.—Frederick C. Grant, *Christ's Victory and Ours*

345

Was His cry, "It is finished," only the acknowledgment that all was over? That man is incapable of a better life in the Kingdom of God? Or perhaps not even worth saving for such a life? Let him relapse into the animal state from which he has lately emerged . . . man is not fit to live!

No, we can never think that Jesus died in despair—or "of a broken heart," as some have said. He was dying in victory, not defeat. He foresaw, if anyone ever did, that future which is more real than the past, more real than the present; that future which draws events forward, magnetically and by an irresistible attraction, as the purpose of God. . . . "It is finished"—these can only mean that the whole course of His life has reached its end; His work is done; His victory won. . . . The rest God will attend to, in His good time. History will bear Him out. The seed is planted, and the harvest is sure. . . . "It is finished"; the redemption is accomplished.—Frederick C. Grant, *Christ's Victory and Ours*

346

"It is finished." The understanding of these words of Jesus brings final victory of God-self over human-self for others and for us. He held to His faith in God's way as the only way, to the very end. Jesus had faith in what He had done, or rather what God had been able to accomplish through Him.

"It is finished. . . ." Did this not mean that the ladder between heaven and earth, between God and Man, which Jesus the carpenter came to fashion, was finished?

Within He must have felt and fashioned His feelings into spoken words for His ears alone: "Completion at last—my part of the task is done. What I have lived will endure, for 'The stone which the builders, the unbelievers, rejected has become the chief cornerstone.'" He was indeed a workman who needed not to be ashamed of any of His work.—James W. Kennedy, *Advance into Light*

347

We are not surprised to find that Jesus closed His life with a prayer. His whole life had been an abiding in God, an at-one-ness with Him. Nor was His final prayer a form of words put together in a crisis. It was a prayer that was familiar. The mind had traveled its thought before. He had known it since childhood. It was taken from a book that enshrined the poetry and piety of His people—the book of Psalms. Now from the treasury of devotion Jesus chose the thirty-first psalm, an old testimony of faith, which spoke of God as a rock and a fortress, which proclaimed His power to preserve the souls of the faithful, and which included some words that Jesus felt were ideally suited to bring His life to a close. "Into thine hand I commit my spirit."—Leslie Badham, *Love Speaks from the Cross*

348

He reigns a king, upon the tree! And that is the very oldest impression of all. Mark has it—and I think an often disregarded variant reading of some of the manuscripts really belongs in his text (you can find it in the margin): "And when the centurion who stood there saw that he thus died with a great shout, he said, 'Truly this man was a Son of God.'" It was the shout of victory—He had won. Something was defeated, and the victor uttered His cry of victory, and died.—Frederick C. Grant, *Christ's Victory and Ours*

349

Jesus has finished His life with its stupendous task, and is facing death, a death especially abhorrent in that it was being experienced for the sins of others. But He is facing that death with the certain knowledge that the same God is lord of life and death, that the God who could guide the life of the psalmist could also accept the life which had completed its tasks. So Jesus is like the child who has completed his task, and has brought it to his father for approval.—William C. Skeath, *His Last Words*

350

"Into thy hands." This final word of Jesus brings completion of faith for others, completion of faith for us. Faith in Him leads us at last to trust. We yield our all to Him because we believe what He said about God and life as true. "Into thy hands. . . ."

Here is perfect assurance. This is what we mean by "leaning on the everlasting arms." . . . Watch a child jump from a high place into his father's waiting arms. Here is absolute trust, dependence without any qualifications or any equivocation. Jesus went to the cross with God's arms around Him. He allowed revilement, humiliation, torture to be heaped upon Him because He trusted God to lead Him in safety at last to His appointed Haven.—James W. Kennedy, *Advance into Light*

EASTER

351

I am Easter.

I am the anniversary of the resurrection of Jesus Christ.

I am celebrated on the first Sunday after the full moon that occurs on the vernal Equinox of any of the twenty-eight days thereafter.

I am appropriately celebrated in the morning, and with spring flowers, brilliant music, and an exhilarating challenge to faith.

I have held the world in astonishment for nineteen hundred years.

I am a source of dependable knowledge and confident assurance concerning eternal life.

I take away fear of the grave.

I ease the anguish and bereavement of those who part with loved ones.

I am a necessary part of the gospel of salvation by faith in Jesus Christ.

I am the source of assurance that there is no end to the life that is identified with the living Christ.

I generate a spirit of hope which, more than argumentation, causes people to believe in immortality.

I challenge the world to know Jesus and the power of His resurrection.—Norman E. Richardson, *Central Truths of the Christian Youth Movement*

352

Tolstoy, the Russian writer, tells of a peasant in Crimea who was forced to stay at the plow on Easter Day. Unable to attend church and to burn a votive candle there, he fastened a candle to the handle of his plow and kept it lighted while he turned the furrows. His work, which had seemed a great hardship, thus became a sacrament. It was made holy and joyous by the presence of God. He plowed the field with a good spirit, and the work was done with care and thoroughness.—*Pathways of Prayer*

353

Thomas Wolfe in *Look Homeward, Angel* has the hero write about his brother Ben. They were as close and intimate as two brothers can be and, when Ben died, his brother wrote this: "We can believe in the nothingness of life, we can believe in the nothingness of death and the nothingness of life after death, but who can believe in the nothingness of Ben?" There's the rub! Who can? Somehow people who have been drawn into any sort of intimate relationship with Jesus, whether it was in those years when His friends gathered together with Him in Galilee, or whether it is now—people who have

had any kind of experience like that cannot believe in the nothingness of Jesus. As we pursue this relationship with Jesus, this is what happens. The larger life keeps breaking into our little corners. He brings it with Him, so to speak. We may live in one room, but there is the window open toward the unbroken seas of life beyond.—Theodore P. Ferris, "The Easter Frame of Mind," *Pulpit Preaching*

354

The *Saturday Review* had a striking cartoon during the time that the annual marathon race was being held in Boston. The race, of course, takes its name from the famous long-distance run of Pheidippides after the Greeks defeated the Persians at Marathon. He ran twenty-five miles to carry the news to Athens and collapsed as he gasped out the word, "Victory." The cartoon showed a runner carrying a torch who reaches a group of people eagerly awaiting him only to say, "I have forgotten the message."

The story suggests a truth of which the Christian Church continually needs to be reminded. Every Christian is entrusted with a great message about the revelation of God's love in Christ and the victory won by Christ in His death and resurrection. Church people, as they rush about breathlessly in their hurry over other matters, often forget to tell the story they are supposed to deliver.—Walter Dudley Cavert, *Ours Is the Faith*

355

Easter can be an uncomfortable holiday, for the serious-minded. The pagan in us can enjoy the rite of spring, the new clothes on the street, the fresh smells in the air. But to the average church-going American, Easter is the climax of the Christian Year and its meaning cannot be tamed or diluted. If we think about Christ's resurrection at all, we are face to face with the most basic questions a man can ask himself, the questions about his nature and destiny and the meaning of his life.—"Why Are We Here?," editorial in *Life*

356

Pilate had assigned men of steel at the request of the priesthood to make sure that there would be no disturbance. The first night and the day following the entombment passed without incident. The second night moved well past midnight. All remained quiet. Evil, so it seemed, had conquered. If only the victory of Jesus' foes could last through sunrise! But it didn't. God moved in to win the day. No array of force stopped Him. Righteousness struck terror into the hearts of those who aligned themselves with wickedness. The rugged guards trembled and became like dead men.—Thomas F. Chilcote, Jr., *Daily Bible Lessons*

357

Christians had lost all fear of death. Since, therefore, the fear of death is mother of all fear, when it has been destroyed, all other forms of fear are thereby vanquished.—John Sutherland Bonnell, *Heaven and Hell*

358

One of the first ladies of the American theater . . . was the late Gertrude Lawrence. One of her most famous roles was Anna in "The King and I."

. . . Her husband, Richard Stoddard Aldrich, wrote her life story in the book *Gertrude Lawrence as Mrs. A.* Speaking of her interior life, Mr. Aldrich reported her saying: "I've always wanted something to hang on to. Something to make me know that all this does include heaven too. You see, I don't know how to pray alone."

How human and how honest was that confession! Who doesn't want "something to hang on to"—something to make us know that "all this does include heaven too"? You and I need . . . invisible means of support. This is what God gives.

Easter is the festival of this glorious gift. . . . Easter is God's assurance, not only that we have "something to hang on to," but that "all this does include heaven too."—David A. MacLennan, *Making the Most of Your Best*

359

The impact of Jesus' crucifixion was shattering. Some of the disciples fled the city. Others gathered together—but behind locked doors, as they so candidly tell us, because they were afraid that they would be crucified too.

And then came the world-shaking experience that Jesus who had been dead was no longer dead. They knew that He was alive and with them. They could not always describe just how He appeared to them. Sometimes they felt that they must not touch Him, while at other times He was so earthy that they could offer Him boiled fish. But that He was alive and in their midst, they had no doubt. This faith transformed them from people who were scared to death into people who were willing to go the length and breadth of the Roman Empire, proclaiming that God was victor over sin and death, and that they could be in constant relationship with a risen Lord.

There is a monastic order today called "The Community of the Resurrection." It would be a good name for the whole church.—Robert McAfee Brown, *The Significance of the Church*

360

Without the language of eternity we seek vainly to make life significant. Herbert Farmer reminds us that when Leonidas called on the Spartans to die at Thermopylae he did not say to them, "I am inclined to think and doubtless on consideration you will agree with me, that on the whole Spartan civilization is preferable to Persian." He cried, "Sparta forever." In Britain's crisis, with the Empire threatening to crumble, Churchill made one of the strongest appeals when he said, "Let us therefore brace ourselves to our duties, and so bear ourselves, that, if the British Empire and its Commonwealth last for a thousand years, men will say, 'This was their finest hour.'" Life has little meaning if all that we cherish seems to be destroyed in the span of a few short years. It has still less significance if those who serve nobly and unselfishly among us are swallowed up in death. The resurrection makes all the difference between apparent defeat and radiant triumph. What is the validity of Paul's claim? He had talked with men who had seen the risen Lord. They were men with differing temperaments. If some were mystic souls, some too, like Thomas, were hard-

headed men of reality. John might have dreamed that he had seen the Spirit of Christ return, but not Peter, who looked after his own welfare when dreams came tumbling to earth. Added to the witness of these were hundreds of others who were sure of it. The men who had seen Christ were possessed of a certainty so universal as not to be doubted or so compelling as not to be denied. . . . So the end is the beginning. Compelling faith in the good news begins at the end of the earthly pilgrimage of Christ where one meets the Risen Lord.—K. Morgan Edwards, *Shepherds*

361

Easter is one of the most confusing days in all the world. But when all is said and done, Easter is Christ's greatest contribution to the human race. All down through the ages mankind has wondered, "Is there a life beyond death?" There are many who say, "No, man is like any other animal of the field, here today and gone tomorrow." The wisest men of all the centuries have asked, "Isn't there something beyond death?" All are trying to reach out for some hope of something, but man needs something tangible. Man needs proof. We are a pragmatic people.

This proof is held in the story of Jesus. He went out into a world which was very skeptical and He taught as no man ever has. His lessons have never been duplicated. Every brilliant man has studied the words this Man spoke. They have found that when the words are obeyed there is peace and justice. When the words are forgotten, there is bloodshed and destruction.

Jesus said, in effect, "If you want

to know what God is like, look into My eyes and follow Me day by day." Some believed, most people doubted, and that is true today. Jesus died as any other man dies, only His was a horrible death on the cross. He was put in a tomb which was sealed. His disciples scattered. Then He came back to them. Their faith also came back to them and they began a march across the centuries which has never ceased. Christianity suddenly bloomed out of the womb of an empty tomb.

Easter, the resurrection of Christ, is God's answer to the question, "If a man dies, will he live again?"—Frank Warren

362

The great Easter truth is not that we are to live newly after death—that is not the great thing—but that we are to be new here and now by the power of the resurrection; not so much that we are to live forever as that we are to, and may, live nobly now because we are to live forever.— Phillips Brooks

363

The greatest obstacle to belief in immortality is the fear of death. When this fear is removed, men are free to enjoy eternal life. . . . When men have faith in the Kingdom of God, they are released into a radiant assurance that death cannot separate them from Eternal Love.—Walter G. Muelder

364

The plant that seems to suffer and die with the winter frost becomes the new bloom of the spring; the seed buried and rotted in the ground grows to beautiful flower or grain; the caterpillar that painfully abandons its shell becomes the beautiful butterfly. The babe that is born of another's pain— even of her death—may become a growing creature of happiness and joy.

365

E. Stanley Jones suggests that if there is no life after this life—no conservation of energy and of the values created by man's living—then the universe does not make sense, in fact it makes nonsense! In no place in the universe does Dr. Jones—nor any scientist—see values wasted, and he cannot believe there is waste of human personality.

366

The simplest meaning of Easter is that we are living in a world in which God has the last word. On Friday night it appeared as if evil were the master of life. The holiest and most lovable One who had ever lived was dead and in His tomb—crucified by the order of a tyrant without either scruples or regrets. He who had raised the highest hopes among men had died by the most shameful means. A cross, two nails, a jeering mob of debauched souls, and a quick thrust of a spear had ended it all. Those hours when His voice was stilled and His hands were quiet were the blackest through which the race has ever lived. If Caesar could put an end to Jesus then no man could ever dare aspire or hope again. Hope, in such a world, could be nothing better than a mockery. Then came Easter morning and the glorious word: "He is Risen!" And evil's triumph was at an end. Since that hour when Mary in the garden first discovered the staggering fact of victory, no man whose heart was pure and whose labors were honest has ever had reason to fear or despair if he believed in the resurrection. It is the assurance to all the godly that their faith is not in vain.

367

My risen Lord, I feel Thy strong protection;
I see Thee stand among the graves
today;
I am the Way, the Life, the Resurrection, I hear Thee say.
And all the burdens I have carried
sadly
Grow light as blossoms on an April
day;
My cross becomes a staff, I journey
gladly
This Easter day.

—Author unknown

368

"He is risen" is the message of Easter. It is a simple message. Yet it carries with it a most tremendous implication for life. Christ the Lord is alive! He is alive today and is doing mighty things. In Him there is life and hope, for from Him flows love and power and mercy greater than man in his feeble way can imagine.

"He is risen" is the message of Easter. It is a message that gives promise not just of an old life somehow renewed, but a new life, a resurrected life. His promise of life eternal, made a reality by His resurrection, is evident in the lives of a vast multitude of human beings who have walked with Him in faith, who have caught hold of the compelling power of a radiant Christian experience.

"He is risen" is the message of Easter. It is a simple message in which there is hope for the whole world.—Eugene Carson Blake

369

The resurrection cannot be tamed or tethered by any utilitarian test. It is a vast watershed in human history, or it is nothing. It cannot be tested for truth; it is the test of lesser truths. No light can be thrown on it; its own light blinds the investigator. It does not compel belief; it resists it. But once accepted as fact, it tells more about the universe, about history, and about man's state and fate than all the mountains of other facts in the human accumulation.—Editorial in *Life*

370

The Epistle to the Hebrews has as its theme "the excellency of Christ" and its key word is the word "better." Jesus is a better representative of God than the angels, a better lawgiver than Moses, a better king than David, a better high priest than Aaron. If Abraham had faith, Isaac gentleness, Jacob initiative, Christ had even more of all three. Was Barnabas generous, was Luke philanthropic, and John the Baptist unselfish? Then Christ exceeded each one in his own particular excellency.

In our Lord we discover humanity at its highest as well as the fullness of God in human form. As pure white light is the composite of all the colored lights of the rainbow, the composite Christ contains all the colorful characteristics of all the other sons of men. As all the colors of the rainbow superimposed in proper intensity one upon the other produce white light, the placing together of the highest characteristics of all the Biblical saints gives us a fair picture of the composite Christ. Take the purity of Mary, the guilelessness of Nathanael, the fearlessness of Stephen, the simplicity of John, the moral earnestness of Hezekiah, the patience of Job, and much more, and we have a fair picture of the character of this great Son of Man whom we acknowledge as well to be the Son of God.—Jarvis Scobey Morris, *Follow Me*

371

Walter Rauschenbusch put it wisely and well when he said that a great task demands a great faith. To live a great life a man needs a great cause to which he can surrender, something divinely large and engrossing for which he can live and, if need be, die. A great religious faith will lift him out of his narrow grooves and make him the inspired instrument of the universal will of God. Perhaps as we come to Easter and hear the familiar story of Christ's triumph, His death and His resurrection, we feel a certain inspiration—that we really are lifted up to proclaim the universal will of God. Dr. James Martin warns that we must recognize a difference between a conviction that the resurrection took place and a faith in the risen Christ, and illustrates it with the story of Blondin, a famous tightrope walker, who on one occasion carried a man across a tightrope stretched perilously above an admiring crowd. In the forefront of the crowd was a boy, gazing at the feat in open-mouthed wonderment. Blondin noticed the lad and said to him: "Do you believe that I could carry you across that tightrope?" The boy replied, "I'm sure you could." "Well, then," said Blondin, "Jump up and I will do so." But this was a different affair, and the boy refused.

Similarly, it is not enough to believe that Jesus has risen and is alive today. Faith involves taking a further step, the taking of which will depend on that belief, but which will carry a man far beyond it, and mean the committing of himself in complete confidence to the living Christ. Here is the secret of Jesus' expectation: that we will do great things; not in our own strength, but through faith in Him. By our own strength we can never climb the heights which we envision, but within us we have the capacity to respond to the love of God through Christ, through which we are lifted up. The Lord is risen indeed! We know it is true, for we have witnessed fear-tormented men transformed, like Peter. The Lord is risen indeed!—Archie H. Hook, *The Congregational Way*

372

No one can prove immortality. The church does not claim to do so. To prove immortality one would have to experience immortality and that is impossible. What the Christian Church claims is that immortality is a reasonable hope. A belief in personal survival is a matter of faith. But it should be noted that a denial of immortality is also a matter of faith. We must choose which faith is more reasonable. It is more reasonable to believe in continuance of life after death than to deny it. If the soul perishes with the body, then this life has no meaning whatsoever. Man's highest reasoning leads us to a belief in immortality. Certainly it would seem that the soul is as indestructible as matter or energy. The justice of God, the unfulfilled desires of men, and the witness of Christ Himself point in the same direction. Christ believed in immortality, He taught it and accepted a future life as naturally as His physical life on earth. The Christian Church was built on this daring hope, and I repudiate the idea that it was founded on a falsehood. Extinction of the soul at death makes all things meaningless.

The immortality of the soul carries with it the clear implication that human life has dignity and is of infinite worth. Christianity has always taught the sacredness of the individual and Christian civilization has nourished it. We are always fighting to safeguard life and to protect it in every way. One of the most appalling aspects of communism, with its material, atheistic philosophy, is its utter disregard for the individual. A man counts as nothing; the state is all in all. Thus those who are under such a regime must live in fear. They never know when the blow will strike and they will be imprisoned or liquidated. Millions are destroyed, nations are conquered; violence is glorified no matter what the cost in human life may be. What a travesty! Immortality, as Robert Louis Stevenson has said, implies "the immortal value of life." . . . If man is immortal, then eternity has already begun. We need not be concerned with the nature of death itself. The soul knows no death. What we need to realize is that our eternal life started when we were born. As Wordsworth has said, "Heaven lies about us in our infancy." This being true, we ought to start now to practice immortality. We should cast off those things which have no abiding worth. . . . As we move toward Easter, let us rejoice in its message of triumph and of hope. . . . Our souls are of infinite worth. We must continue to grow. We must take the initial steps in the great adventure *now*.—Alfred Grant Walton, "Faith in Our Time"

373

It is a happy circumstance that Easter comes to remind us that "the things that are seen are temporary, but the things that are unseen are lasting." You can build your life on what won't endure if you like, forgetting the forever and the values that last; Caiphas did, and Pilate and Herod. We are doing it now in personal life, in political affairs, and in international relations. We are indulging in what somebody has called "crisis behavior," with nothing of the forever in it. But Easter condemns us and events are betraying us because a crisis in personal or social affairs makes no change in the abiding values by which we are judged. Indeed,

. . . the slow watches of the night
Not less belong to God.

The open tomb of Easter dawn keeps saying . . . "Don't forget the forever." But at the moment we are immersed in the immediate, having lost our sense of the infinite.—Harold Blake Walker, *Specialty Salesman*

374

What is eternal life? Sometimes in the New Testament it is spoken of in the present tense as something to be had now; at other times it is thrown into the future, is something that still lies ahead of us. For it is both. It begins here and now. And one can know and live it in this world. But it comes to its fullness only in the other life. As Percy Gardner put it, eternal life is spoken of not strictly in the present, or in the future, but rather in "the mystic tense." As Christ describes it here (John 17:3), it means and is to know God as He really is; and all that flows from that. For to take in what God is, to grasp something of His unselfishness, His generosity, His patience, His humility, must give one a new standard of measurement, a new scale of values; a new idea of how life should be used. And with that one must begin to try to live it in that fashion. That is eternal life. It is to live after God's way, as life is lived in the eternities.—Arthur John Gossip, *The Interpreter's Bible*

375

To a hilltop in Galilee the eleven more or less faithful apostles returned after the arrest, trial and crucifixion of Jesus in Jerusalem. The excitement of those last days had given way to a mixed mood of disappointment, expectancy, confusion and hope. He who had been their leader, more than that, the very center of their lives over the months and years they had followed Him, was no longer with them in the intimacy to which they had grown accustomed. He had died. The worst had happened. His enemies had triumphed and, although they could recall much that He had said to try to prepare them for their loss, they had found themselves unprepared. How could they carry on with Jesus dead?

But some had seen Him. They recounted again and again Peter's report of the empty tomb, the stone rolled away, and that of Cleopas's supper at Emmaus, and the testimony of the two Marys. Was He then not dead after all.

Some of the eleven were sure that Jesus had risen, but how can anyone be sure of a miracle? Others had begun to doubt the reality of their whole experience. It was too good to be true. But the memory of Jesus was sufficient to keep them together. Despite disappointment and confusion, hope and expectancy drew them north to Galilee where some of their number said He would meet with them. No one was sure, all of them doubted. But all of them hoped enough in the face of their own unbelief to climb the familiar green hill to meet Him if He would come to them.

And He came. It is very simply stated in St. Matthew's Gospel. There He was. They saw Him again. One would think that this would be enough. They saw Him. One would think that it would be proof enough, incontrovertible evidence enough, so that no longer would any of the eleven have any further reason to be dismayed.

But the account reads "and when they saw him, they worshiped him; but some doubted." Even when they saw Him alive again, some doubted, all were not sure.

This seems to be the characteristic response of almost all to the Easter and post-Easter appearances of Jesus to His disciples. One would suppose that this resurrection would be treated either as fact or fantasy. Yes, He is alive; no, no, He is still dead. But the response of the disciples as recounted in the Gospels is not a simple dialectic between yes, I believe or no, I disbelieve. The Easter dialectic is not simple choice between dead leader and living leader, between unbelief and belief.

No, the Easter dialectic is between worship and doubt, and this is different. The resurrection cannot be treated as an *item* of faith. You worship the risen Lord or you doubt. Even to have seen Him standing solidly on the green grass of a familiar Galilean hilltop is not enough unless you were ready to fall down and worship Him as the Son of God, the Lord of life and death. . . . Jesus is either what the church has proclaimed Him to be, God and Saviour, or else He is dead. And the response to God is always worship. The alternative to doubtful opinion is not strong opinion. It is the devotion of all of oneself to the everlasting and eternal Lord.— Eugene Carson Blake, *National Council Outlook*

376

The doctrine of the resurrection must be sharply distinguished from philosophical speculations concerning the survival of the soul after death. The story of the New Testament is not about a good man grossly misunderstood by his contemporaries who suffered a martyr's fate but whose teaching and example continued to be an inspiration to his disciples, enhanced by their conviction that he was still alive with God. It was, on the contrary, a recital and interpretation of momentous events centering in Jesus Christ in which God was declared to have overcome the powers of darkness and to have decisively triumphed over the last enemy, death. Herein lies hope. "He was destined before the foundation of the world but was made manifest at the end of the times for your sake. Through him you have confidence in God, who raised him from the dead and gave him glory, so that your faith and hope are in God." The impact of the resurrection upon those who preached it was not that by it evidence had been given for the soul's survival; on the contrary, the inference is that apart from God's act death would be an agonizing finality. Hope is born when the believer sees that, as God raised Jesus Christ from the dead, so He will raise also all those who belong to Him.

The resurrection which disclosed the glory of God also restored Jesus Christ to His disciples in a dimension of existence inexpressibly new. Jesus, who was raised from the dead, was the same person they had known and loved before the atrocity of the cross shattered their hopes, but who was discerned now with a wonder which compelled worship. The same, but not the same. Both sides of this equation were true and equally important. That this was so is attested by the act of the disciples in choosing a successor to Judas—he must have been with the company of Jesus from the time of his baptism and also a witness of the resurrection. The re-apprehension of Jesus was the recognition of Him as exalted by God to be Lord of all.—Paul S. Wright, "A Living Hope," *McCormick Speaking*

WHITSUNDAY (PENTECOST)

377

I am Whitsunday.

I was first constituted on the day known to history as Pentecost.

I am the spiritual birthday of the Christian Church.

I am the anniversary of an occasion when a company of religious people made vital contact with a supernatural power.

I remind the church that it was launched by a group of laymen who, with courageous certainty, mapped out a course of witnessing.

I bring to mind the effectiveness of the simple gospel that is true to the historic facts.

I point to the fact that the straightforward testimony of those who speak from experience is an effective means of winning converts.

I witnessed the emotional transformation of a gathering of socially discredited and uninfluential men.

I emphasize the incongruity of fear, timidity, and embarrassing self-consciousness as characteristics of Christians.

I suggest the value of quiet times of devotional meditation.

I rescue religion from the slough of doubt and uncertainty and baptize it with victory-achieving power.

I constituted Christianity a world power, with a genius for transcending racial, national, and other social barriers.

I reassure the church, annually, of the facts that faith generates energy and that confidence fosters enthusiasm.

I validate the divine promise that, in the midst of those who follow Jesus Christ, there will abide a spirit of comfort and a dependable guide into ever-enlarging bodies of truth.

I foster the conviction that the gospel, when advocated by men who are clothed with the spirit of truth, is irresistible.—Norman E. Richardson, *Central Truths of the Christian Youth Movement*

378

In thinking of Pentecost we naturally turn to the Book of the Acts where we read of the movement of the Spirit that led to the emergence of the Christian Church. But we shall appreciate its significance more fully as we first turn to the story of Babel (Genesis 11:1-9) as a picture of the human condition that the Spirit at Pentecost overcomes.

The account of the tower of Babel is a fascinating illustration of . . . man's proud assumption that he can, without any reference to God and His will, build a civilization that shall "reach to heaven." It drives home the point that all such self-assertive and self-centered efforts end at last in chaos. . . .

We usually refer to the Biblical story only in terms of "the tower" of Babel, but the narrative in Genesis speaks of men as building "a city and a tower." The "city" is a symbol of men in their associated life, as the "tower" is a symbol of their vaulting ambition. The Babel of the story was the primitive parallel of our modern metropolis with its skyscrapers. The word "Babel," of course, is a play on words, suggests Babylon, the proud city. . . . The people who set out to build "the city and the tower" of Babel said, "Let us make a name for ourselves!" . . . In Babel man was putting himself in the place of God. . . . Over against this Babel, which comes from man's ignoring God and rebelling against His will, stands the reality of Pentecost. Pentecost affirms that there is a Holy Spirit in the world which can overcome man's self-centeredness and his consequent estrangement from both God and his fellows. The Spirit at Pentecost brings into being a new kind of community, a *koinonia* which is centered around the mission of the living Christ. This community, the church, is not something merely of man's devising, like Babel, but is a way of fulfilling the will of God . . . *Koinonia* in the New Testament is the experience of those who know themselves bound together not by their own gregarious impulses, but by their common relation to Christ. As Dietrich Bonhoeffer . . . put it, our community with each other as Christians "consists solely in what Christ has done for both of us." This means that the fellowship which the Spirit creates may be a fellowship with people with whom, on the level of merely human preferences, we might prefer not to have any fellowship at all. It is only as we find, in our common relation to Christ, a oneness so deep that the natural difference of culture, class, sect, race, and nation no longer divide. . . . So Pentecost marks not only the beginning of the church as an organized society, but also the recognition of its unity. Since there is only one Lord, from whom the Spirit comes, there is only one Body of Christ's people . . . that there is a basic oneness of the Christian community is a reality which Pentecost never allows us to forget.—Samuel McCrea Cavert, "The Meaning of Pentecost," *National Council Outlook*

379

Fourscore and seven generations ago, the Apostles brought forth on another continent a new fellowship, conceived in the liberty of redeemed men, and dedicated to the proposition that all men are created for redemption.

Now—and always—we are engaged in a great, global war, testing whether this fellowship, or any congregation thereof, is worthy to endure.

We are met on one small battlefield of that war. We have come to dedicate our common endeavor as a living testimony for Him who gave His life that we might live. It is altogether fitting and proper that we should do this.

But in a larger sense we cannot dedicate, we cannot consecrate, we cannot hallow this endeavor. God's only Son, who died and lives, having conquered death has consecrated it far above our poor power to add or detract.

The world will little note, nor long remember, what we might do (today); but it must never forget what He did in A.D. 33.

It is for us, His soldiers, therefore to be dedicated to the ongoing work which He, who ever goes before us, has so clearly commanded.

It is for us also to be dedicated to the task at hand:

That from our living Lord we take increased devotion;

That we here highly resolve that He shall not have died in vain;

That this congregation, under God, shall have a new breadth of service;

And that the church of Christ, led by Christ, striving for Christ, shall advance in all the earth.—John R. Bodo, "A Paraphrase of Lincoln's Gettysburg Address," *Presbyterian Life*

380

The Acts of the Apostles in our New Testament is a forthright recital of some amazing results from the living and preaching of Spirit-filled men. Except for the help that came from divine sources, the church would never have survived its many adversities.

The failure of the modern church to give proper instruction in the matter of the Holy Spirit has resulted in a generation of powerless Christians —men and women unable to hold out against the intense pressures of temptation, opposition, ridicule, and loneliness.

The major problem in every Christian life is the achievement of power. There is scarcely a day when we do not stand in dire need of spiritual reinforcements. The pressures of modern life are so insistent, so sinister, that nothing less than divine aid enables us to measure up to the demands that inevitably will be made upon us.

"I do not know why I should have caved in," said one young mother. "Now that it is all over, I have a feeling that I was actually unclean. I had no intention of doing anything wrong. I guess I was just swept off my feet by the crowd. But I am so ashamed."

In the midst of a social situation concerning which she had been warned, she had surrendered to the pressure of her associates and indulged in behavior that was to her, as she remembered it, repulsive. And the most hopeful aspect of the situation was that she was ashamed. But her shame was helpless to alter the past. Her soul had been required of her and she had foolishly squandered it!

Perhaps the most serious step she had taken was to deliberately compromise with her conscience. She deliberately did that which she had long believed to be wrong. Then with the sense of guilt upon her soul, she found her soul's strength ebbing away. No person, feeling guilty, ever feels strong at the same time. After that it was inevitable that she would do more wrong. And she did, with highly disastrous results that left scars on her soul.

She caved in because she had not stood guard over her own soul, her own sense of right, her own inner citadel of conscience. In the face of temptation she was without the power that comes with the approval of the Holy Spirit. Shakespeare put it: "Conscience does make cowards of us all." But it is much more than cowardice that follows upon an accusing conscience. It is powerlessness—Roy L. Smith, "When Power Seeps Away," *Together*

381

Almost unconsciously we use the language of the family in speaking of the church and its message. God is our Father. We are sons of God. We are brothers of one another. Why is it that this vocabulary comes so naturally to the lips of Christians when they speak of life in the church?

For one thing, the image of the family suggests the nature of the ties which bind members of the church together. These are not the same kind of ties which one assumes when he becomes a member of a social organization, a fraternity, or a club. One does not become a member of the family of God simply by making up his mind to join it. The New Testament speaks of Christians as "born again" and "newborn babes." Just as one comes into his natural family by the process of birth, so one comes into the household of God by the "new birth" or the "birth from on high." It is the gift of God. As we shall see, infant baptism symbolizes our entrance into the family of God.

In this family, men are no longer "strangers and sojourners." The differences of color, nationality, and social condition which divide men in the world do not obtain in the Father's household. A private in the British army refused to kneel when he came to the altar with the Duke of Wellington for Holy Communion. The great general is reported to have said, "Kneel, young man, for in God's eyes all men are alike and common."

We note another fact about this family. Those who belong to it do the will of God. They are not gathered together simply to enjoy one another's company. What binds them together is their relationship to God. As Jesus described this relationship, it involved an obedient response to the gospel. —Roger Hazelton and Robert V. Moss, Jr., *The Church's Life*

382

In the last resort it is for Christ's sake and His Kingdom's that we love men; it is in His power that we believe in the new humanity. The unity of the church has this for its goal and its ground.—Peter T. Forsyth

383

The church with no great anguish on its heart has no great music on its lips.—Karl Barth

384

A church serves as a home for the family of God . . . a church also is a temple in which God is to be worshiped. . . . It is a holy building and should be reverenced. . . . It is also a school in which spiritual things are studied and learned. . . . It should be a workshop for the things of God. . . . Church members should work together toward the salvation of souls and the general uplift of the community and for the advancement of the Kingdom.—Ralph M. Riggs

385

One task of the church is national resurrection in all lands. She is the instrument of God for His purposes. Unless a new spirit is given to the world, civilization may break itself upon the rocks of greed and hate and selfishness. The church can become and is increasingly becoming the center of all the forces of hope and righteousness. She is meant to be the new life, bringing this country and every country to realize its true destiny under God.

386

It is absurd, when a man takes Holy Orders, to say, as we usually do, that he is "going into the church." He cannot do that, because he is there already; all baptized people are "in" the church; they are the church.— Dorothy Sayers, *Begin Here*

387

We are prone to say that the church of today needs an outpouring of the Spirit. The truth of the matter is that the Spirit *has been given* to the church. The church *has* the power to perform its mission in the world. The sad fact is that it has not often enough laid hold upon that power so readily available. The restless mood, which is so characteristic of the present time, is evidence that the church needs to lay hold upon the Holy Spirit for power to perform its task in this day, as the early church did in the day of its strength.

388

We can't hold an abstraction which we call civilization responsible for its own defects. We can't blame an institution called the state when things go wrong. Responsibility goes back to the men and women whose corporate thought and action constitute civilization. The state is the collective life, the collective action, of individual citizens who compose it. Neither can we call to account an institution called the church, and blame that for neglecting its obligations to God. The church does not exist apart from its members. The church is just the corporate life, the corporate will, of a group of individuals. When we talk about what the church has failed to do and what it ought to do, we are too often talking about abstractions. We would do better to deal with hard facts and individuals. Someone is to blame, and amendment must begin there. Responsibility is always personal.—*The Free Methodist*

389

William James once said: "Men habitually use only a small part of the powers which they possess." We are surrounded by power in various forms and sometimes we are not aware of it. A story such as Mark Twain's *The Connecticut Yankee in King Arthur's Court* reminds us of the powers which men discover from time to time which in reality have been in existence all the time.

Electric power has been in existence all the time although primitive man was not aware of it. Steam power could have been available long before Watts sat watching the tea kettle, but mankind in general was ignorant of this fact. The same is true of our more recently discovered power in the atom. The power was there, but it was unused. We are surrounded by other forms of power much of which is either unused or unknown.

One such neglected power is spiritual power. We are often amazed at some people. They possess powers of understanding, of good will, of love, of being kind, just and the like. They are victorious in situations which defeat others. Their lives are filled with power which other lives seem to lack. Why does not everyone have this power? It is not because the power fails to exist; rather because some never have learned to possess it and make use of it. . . . Pentecost Sunday [is] the birthday of the church. The story is related in the Book of the Acts. Jesus prepared His followers after the resurrection when they questioned Him about the restoration of His Kingdom. In His reply he said: "You are to be given *power* when the Holy Spirit has come to you. You will be witnesses to me, not only in Jerusalem . . . but to the very ends of the earth!" The story of Pentecost is the story of the reception of that power. The writer of the Gospel according to John had said: "Wherever men did accept him he gave them the power to become the sons of God." He gave them the power, and that power oft unused and often unknown is all about us.

The inventor has to study and examine if he is to put power to use. Prayer is largely the means by which spiritual power is made available and useable in our lives. When the little group of disciples gathered in Jerusalem after the resurrection, "with one accord they devoted themselves to prayer." After Pentecost they devoted themselves to "teaching and fellowship and prayers." Before and during every crisis, there was prayer. All through the stirring story of the birth of the Christian Church, prayer was the channel by which the power of God came into the life and fellowship of the newborn church.—E. Paul Hovey, "Prayer as Power"

390

Faith is, in the Christian tradition, the pre-requisite to baptism and the bestowal of grace; it is the key to the entrance into the church; it is the most fundamental of the virtues, the first and most basic contact of the soul with God, as well as the divinely infused faculty by which the supernatural realities of God's redemptive plan are known. The concept of faith in a Christian theology will be warp and woof of all its teaching on one after another essential doctrine.—Leonard F. X. Mayhew, "Concept of Faith," *Commonweal*

391

The world is too strong for a divided church.—Bishop Charles H. Brent

392

The man who does not habitually worship is but a pair of spectacles behind which there is no eye.—Thomas Carlyle

393

There is a difference between making an organization go and creating an atmosphere in which an organism can grow. We would not have the pressures we have if we were not a growing church. As we grow we have tensions in the world.—Herman Klahr

394

Somehow we must understand and appreciate the divine nature of the church. Too often we have thought of the church only as a building or place of worship, or a group of people. This is to cheapen it. Rather, "the church is not just a human organization. It did not call itself into being; it was called. God spoke and acted in history, and the church as we view it in action is simply man's response to the mighty acts of God." That Church is inseparably in the world in which we live and must be related to it. This creates an inevitable tension for the church. But it can never deny it. In that secular world, it must "always seek to exert its influence upon the world, the whole world, witnessing with the intent of redeeming." You and I are the church. May we by the grace of God be redeeming witnesses to the incarnation.—Jack L. Zerwas, *The Presbyterian Pilot*

395

A society without its radicals is a dead society, just as a church without its saints is a blighted church. They—the nonconformists of every age—do not need us; we need them to remind us of uncomfortable truths, to rebuke our slothfulness and ease. When we dishonor them, we dishonor ourselves. If we imprison them, we set shackles of mediocrity upon our own spirits. (Nonconformists) . . . may go to prison in any age, and they will go cheerfully, because they will still be free. But who then will deliver us? The rights of nonconformity are an index to the free society's well-being. We curtail these rights at our own great peril.—"The Rights of Nonconformity," editorial in *Commonweal*

396

The Holy Spirit is not an influence, but a Person—one of the three Persons of the Godhead. As such, He possesses all the attributes of personality. He is a Friend whom we can come to know and to love.

We learn to know Him rather slowly, however, for He deliberately and modestly submerges Himself in Christ. It is His specific work to point us to Jesus, to glorify Him, to bring Him and His words to our remembrance, to woo us and lead us to Him. The Helper might be compared to a spotlight, ever focused on Jesus, so that we are not aware of the spotlight itself, but of that One who stands in the center of its brilliance.—Peter and Catherine Marshall, *Today*

397

I am the church.

I am the institutional embodiment of the gospel, the body of Christ.

I am a social group in which the Kingdom of God is demonstrated.

I am the organized guardian over personalities seeking to discover and to do the will of God.

I make possible the exchange of pleasant and character-building social experiences.

I am the corporate witness to the truth that points out for every man and community the true way of life.

I stimulate and purify cultural interests.

I conserve the achievements of prophets, mystics, and social reformers.

I am the home base of far-flung missionary endeavors.

I safeguard the use of the holy sacraments and the exposition of the Word of God.

I teach old and young the language with which they can express religious sentiments and aspirations.

I guarantee the integrity and historic continuity of the religion of Jesus Christ.

I enlarge the spiritual horizons of knowledge, devotion, and service.

I maintain sanctuaries of worship.

I generate courage to resist unrighteousness in industry, politics and social relations.—Norman E. Richardson, *Central Truths of the Christian Youth Movement*

398

How shall we know when we do have the Holy Spirit? We shall know because sooner or later, in His own way and His own time, He will manifest His presence to us. We may have to wait patiently for this. We can never go faster than grace. The Helper is a Person, however, and any person dwelling with us will inevitably reveal Himself by His ways, deeds, words, or personality traits.

We should guard against expecting a highly emotional or dramatic experience at the moment of our baptism with the Holy Spirit. To some it does come that way, but on the whole God is not fond of spectacular ways or exhibitionism. His most wonderful works are performed silently. No trumpets herald the dawn. No bugles announce the opening of a rosebud. The Spirit, Jesus said, comes to our hearts as the wind. We know not "whence it comes or whither it goes."—Peter and Catherine Marshall, *Today*

399

On this day of Pentecost we remember the gift of the Holy Spirit and the power that it brought to the church. It came following the prayers of the early church leaders.

This spiritual power can be ours today, if we will but pray. Prayer is the passage of divine energy into the lives of mankind. By prayer we are able to obey the revealed will of God, and carry burdens laid upon us, discharge tasks presented to us, respond to challenges sounded to us, welcome opportunities which beckon to us and resist the temptations assailing us. Only through prayer can we achieve that complete harmony of body, mind and spirit which gives us unshakable spiritual strength. Prayer brings us the power to become the sons and daughters of Almighty God and to

live as they ought to live.—E. Paul Hovey

400

The early church was separating itself as a new creation. It was not just more of the same, but a new thing. It had to be freed of Judaism. God had done a fresh and new deed. God had called them to a future, a new destiny.—Paul S. Wright

401

At Pentecost the disciples left the security of the Upper Room and preached at great risk to themselves. That is the way of self-giving love, the Christian way. Comfort and happiness are dangerous goals. The chief end in the law of life is to maintain life, but the way of Christ is that love is greater than life, Life with a capital "L."—Kenneth G. Beall

402

From discouragement to confidence, from paralysis to creative living, from worry about our own problems to a vision of God active in His world— what would we not give if that change could come in our day? Where shall we look for the compelling proof of God's active presence that wrought the miracle of Pentecost? . . . Let us lift up our eyes and look at God at work in His world. Let us take fresh heart as we realize that if we will, we may be part of the great company of Christians in every land going forward together, following the call of the Spirit which came on that first Pentecost.—Mrs. John D. Hayes, *Advance*

403

How many of those present in church at Easter returned . . . seven weeks later? Does it matter? Why the concern about Whitsunday? Well . . . why the concern about Easter? And why the concern about Christmas? Do people attend church at these two seasons merely to maintain contact? Or, is it because the church has somehow put across the idea that there is really something special about these two occasions? And if so, what is that importance? Christmas, probably most would say, stands for the Saviour's birth and Easter for the assurance of immortality. Salvation—immortality: is this what we are holding out to vigorous men and women? "Join the church of Jesus Christ and be saved. Be assured of a future life"? This was far from being Jesus' own interpretation of His significance for busy people. He put it like this—"Follow me and I will make you become fishers of men." And He added later, "Whoever does not bear his own cross and come after me, cannot be my disciple." Jesus saved men to serve and to "walk in newness of life."

It is for this busy life of service under His guidance as Lord that Whitsunday stands. Whitsunday is Pentecost. And Pentecost is the day of the church's "coming of age." It is a birthday—not as some have thought, *the* birthday—of the Christian Church. That church must look for its first birthday back into the remote past when God first called forth a people of His own possession. Since that day the church has had many birthdays. But it has had but one birthday (Pentecost) when it came of age and realized its moral responsibility to become the witness of Jesus Christ before a pagan world (Acts 1:8). It was on this day that Jesus' living and

lively Spirit first filled His new Body with energy and zeal to go forth into the world and achieve. Whitsunday, then, is the truly reformed or evangelical Sunday in the religious calendar. It is the day of the Evangel and its proclamation, the day for every member of the church to search his own heart and to ask whether he is doing his bit as a follower of Jesus Christ. . . . The sermon and the worshiper's heart can be selfish at Christmas and Easter. Neither may be so at Whitsunday!—John Wick Bowman, *Prophetic Realism*

404

Do you remember how it was at Pentecost, when people stood around watching these first Christian disciples whom they saw plainly were gripped with a strange new power? They said, "These men are filled with new wine, they are drunk." "Not so," said Peter, "it's just nine o'clock in the morning. We are not filled with new wine. We are filled with new Life. We are under the influence of a new Spirit." And as it happened to them, it has happened again and again as the new Life in Christ has possessed every successive generation—and it can happen to you. —J. Wallace Hamilton, *Ride the Wild Horses*

405

It is perhaps the experience of all of us that it is easier to capture the spirit of Christmas or Easter than that of Pentecost. Why should it be so? Why is it easier to sing joyously "To us is born a blessed Child," and, "Christ the Lord is risen again," than to sing in praise of the coming of the Holy Spirit?

The reason is this: We more readily rejoice in the works of God outside of ourselves, than in those He works in our hearts. All the while the message deals with what Christ has done, "Christ for us"; we can easily imagine that we have a share in it, even though our hearts remain untouched.

The situation is quite different when the message concerns the work of the Holy Spirit within us, such as regeneration, conversion, renewal of the mind, or the fact that salvation cannot be attained except as a result of the work of the Holy Spirit.

The names given the Holy Spirit suggest why man does not readily rejoice in the message concerning His work. He is called the "Comforter" and "Spirit of Truth." But he only who is troubled and anxious will rejoice in the Comforter. He only who stands accused of his own heart senses the blessing of having the Spirit of Truth as his advocate where his salvation is concerned. When sin and sorrow beset us in full earnest, all confidence in self vanishes. From our hearts we confess, "I believe that I cannot of my own reason or strength believe in Christ my Lord or come to Him. . . ." But thanks and praise be to God, who has promised us the Holy Spirit. He can and will work in our hearts the salvation which we of ourselves never can achieve in part or in its entirety.

406

One needs only to read the story of Jesus' arrest to find out how terribly afraid the disciples were that night. As Matthew told it, ". . . all the disciples forsook him and fled." Even Peter's courage disappeared, and he thrice denied that he had ever known the Galilaean.

On the Day of Pentecost, seven weeks after the crucifixion, we find the disciples before a feast day crowd, bluntly accusing their hearers of common guilt in crucifying the Messiah. They stood proclaiming that Jesus Christ, the Messiah, had risen from the dead—a proclamation they knew would cause their arrest by the authorities who had sought to rid themselves of Jesus once and for all.

Such a transformation in a group of men seems impossible to us. In fact, it could come to pass by no human means, but only, the record states powerfully, in its simplicity, as they were filled with the Spirit. Once they had cowered in fear; now they risked death in order to witness. How many of us dare even to risk "offending" our unbelieving friends by "making too much of a to-do" about our religion? How great is our need to be Spirit-filled!

Transformations in the early church were not limited to the disciples. Consider the people to whom Peter preached, whom he charged with the guilt of the crucifixion. Moved by the Spirit, "they were cut to the heart, and said to Peter and the rest of the apostles, 'Brethren, what shall we do?' " Peter called them to repent and be baptized, and day by day enemies of God became sons of God.

This can occur only as we can admit we are inexcusably guilty, without justification . . . once we repent, this confession is good news that we no longer have to maintain a false image of ourselves as good people in order to be acceptable. God has accepted us as we are.

The first converts were Jews, reared in an exclusive, patriarchal society. As the realization grew that all men, Jew and non-Jew, are sinners, loved and sought by God, the early church was enabled to reach out even to the once-hated Gentile. Not a few outstanding converts were women. . . .

In this same way, prejudices crumble today. When we know God through Christ and are able to accept ourselves as we are, redeemed though sinful, we no longer have to build ourselves up by insisting that we are superior to other people. The Holy Spirit removes the barriers of guilt and cowardice that render us unable to know or serve God. He removes the barriers of false pride that separate us from our brothers. His is the power of reconciliation.—Sara Wescoat, *Discovery*

CHRISTIAN EDUCATION DAY

407

Happiness is beneficial for the body, but it is grief that develops the powers of the mind.—Marcel Proust

408

Christian education seeks so to touch the learner's life that it may become his purpose to do the will of God. It seeks to bring every person more fully into the church, to help him find strength in its fellowship and joy in its work.—Paul Vieth, *The Church School*

409

"The purpose of the classroom is not to inform but to transform." This statement appeared in a bulletin from a university. As I pondered the implications of this statement, it said a great deal to me not only regarding public school education but also about church school teaching. In the church school classroom it is not enough to inform persons *about* God, Jesus Christ, the church, and the Christian way of life. That information is needed, of course, but the way in which the information is shared must be such that the informing becomes transforming. Transformation means change. The church school . . . becomes a place where changes of personality can occur, a place for transforming.—Patricia Risdon, *Church School Worker*

410

What we have tried to do, in the academies and out of them, is to sustain a Christian morality based on a non-Christian, even anti-Christian, philosophy of life. Morally, we have tried to be Christians; intellectually, we have been Freudians, behaviorists, pragmatists, materialists of one variety or another, determinists—and sometimes all at the same time. Christianity, as a thing of the mind, an intellectual commitment, a philosophy of life, has been neglected when it has not been altogether abolished from the intellectual centers of the nation. And in the course of time, we have begun to act as Freudians, behaviorists, pragmatists and materialists of one kind or another might be expected to act. We have resisted everything but logic.

Now I would not like to be misunderstood. I am not opposed to learning the truths that Freud left us. I am not opposed to the knowledge the behavioral sciences have to offer. I am not supercilious about the uses of pragmatism. Our problem is not that new learning was developed; our problem is that these new insights and discoveries have not been integrated with the Christian intellectual tradition. Christian scholars have not done their work as it might have been done.

That work was twofold: one, to show the relevance of Christian thought to the world in which these new discoveries were dominant: two, to show the relevance of these new discoveries to Christianity itself. Most young intellectuals, in the absence of this effort, felt that they were called upon to make a choice between, say, the truths of Freud or the truths of Christianity, the findings of the behaviorists or the Christian philosophy of man. Most of them, as a matter of fact, chose the truths which were dominant in the universities. But the dilemma was an unnecessary one, and if Christian scholars were doing their work well, they would have seen that it was false. The "young intellectuals" I speak of are no longer young, of course. And though they may have managed throughout their lives to sustain a traditional Christian moral heritage by the simple process of good will, the next generation insists on consistency between thought and action.— John Cogley, "The Search for Morals," *Commonweal*

411

The past is the only ground on which a human being can stand.— George N. Shuster, *Education and Moral Wisdom*

412

All who are concerned about leading others into the fullness of the Christian life will first be concerned about their own spiritual enrichment. They will seek by personal study of the Word of God and by regular periods of prayer to become spiritually equipped for this important service.

A verse to ponder is Ezra 7:10, "For Ezra had prepared his heart to seek the law of the Lord, and to do it, and to teach. . . ." It will be recalled that Ezra was the leader of a large party of exiles who returned from Babylon to the Holy Land. Upon arriving in Jerusalem, he found that the people had disregarded the sacred laws of God. He saw his task at once. He instituted many reforms, revised the Law of God, and established public worship with the reading of the Scriptures.

Ezra was a leader and an educator. Under his guidance the reading and expounding of the Word of God became a regular practice. Under his leadership the Scriptures came with the force of a new revelation and wrought wonders in the life of the nation. And this can and perhaps is happening today in our world. . . . Christ expects every follower to be also a teacher and a leader. He demands that those who attach themselves to Him shall not remain static, but shall make progress so that they may be able to impart the Christian faith to others. The name by which the followers were first addressed was "disciples," which means "learners."— *Monday Morning*

413

In Europe, America and elsewhere religious thought is returning hopefully to the Bible. The Bible has ever proven its authority when men have turned to it in times of crisis or calamity. It does not yield its deepest secrets when approached in a faithless or negative attitude. But when men reverently and lovingly turn to it as the Word of God, or to discover honestly if it be the Word of God, the search is rewarding and deeply satisfying.

It was belief in the authority of the Bible which gave rise to the Reformation principle of universal education. This principle was brought to the new world by our founding fathers. Why, then, should Christian education desert the very attitude which gave rise to the American system of public education?—Harold C. Mason, *Abiding Values in Christian Education*

414

The ideal of every good teacher . . . is maximum participation of all members of the group or class through the medium of the discussion technique. This does not mean a pooling of all mental vacuums in an endless round of talk but rather an interchange of ideas and experiences growing out of given situations. . . . The teacher must be prepared to interrupt at the right time with the needed information, question or suggestion. The teacher is the guide, not the general who commands and gives orders. Authoritarian methods cannot be used . . . democratic procedure is absolutely essential.—E. E. Schwarztrauber

415

An almost everlasting monument is . . . carved out of solid rock at Mount Rushmore in the Black Hills of South Dakota. There, on a bleak and barren moutain, Gutzon Borglum began carving out the features of four great Americans—Washington, Lincoln, Jefferson and Theodore Roosevelt. He died before the work was finished, but his son carried on. He and his son have done a great work. They have transformed the face of a mountain, making it into the likeness of four great men.

Much greater is that work which is being carried on wherever Christ is redeeming the lives of men. He takes hard, unyielding hearts and minds, and by His grace fashions them into the image of His own glorious likeness. He takes men who were "dead" in their trespasses and sins and makes them alive. He is the infinite sculptor, saying to weak, sinful, finite men, "Ye therefore shall be perfect, as your heavenly Father is perfect."

God has called a multitude of men and women to share with Him in this work. Christian witnesses throughout the church are co-workers with Christ in the task, which is at once more thrilling and more difficult, more immediate, and more everlasting than any other in which man can ever engage. Men too become sculptors of the spirit as they work with Christ. It is true in the making of souls as George Eliot said about Stradivari and the making of violins: "He could not make Antonio Stradivari's violins without Antonio."

The sculptors of the spirit are many. Parents begin the process, with evidence of their handiwork enduring for good or ill through all eternity. . . . Partners are . . . all who are engaged in that process which is called Christian education.—Report of the Board of Christian Education, 1945

416

A few summers ago my little daughter and I were walking from our cottage to the shore for our afternoon swim. It was a hot summer day and the sun beat upon the cement walks. We were barefoot and the heat of the pavement hurt my little girl's feet. It was not long before she came running to me almost in tears. Then, as she clung to me, we walked on a few more steps and she looked up at me in wonder and said, "Why, Mommie, it doesn't hurt any more when I walk in your shadow!"

I knew then, as I had before, that I must teach her to walk in the shadow of her Master. There are requirements for the traveler on life's Christian highways, and they must be carefully observed and consistently carried out. Nowhere was Jesus more explicit than in His instruction about the plan that leads to the life whose goodness is abiding and indestructible. He said, "Do this, and, you will live." I want my children, more than anything else in this world, to learn to walk in His shadow.—Eleanor Stone Roberts, "A Parent Speaks," *Monday Morning*

417

To live is to grow. Nobody ever quite succeeds in growing up. His bones may stop growing, but if his mind, or his spirit, or his will stops growing, he is in that moment beginning to die. To grow is to develop, increase, expand, advance, reproduce. The purpose of life is to grow. The Christian's purpose is to grow in grace.
—Gilbert F. Close, Jr., *Today*

418

Thou, Christ,
Didst take a lump of clay like this,
Cold, moist, and gray,
And, placing it upon a blind man's eyes,
Restored his sight,
And brought him paradise.

O Christ,
Guide thou these hands.
Shaping and molding,
Help them to feel the Master's touch and strength
As through these fingers flows a living warmth
Into each mass and line,
Until from out this dust,
Kept moist with tears,
Shall grow the pulsing vision of my heart.

Then shall this be, that men,
Heads bare,
Shall look upon its form
And see thee, Christ, in beauty standing there.

—Eda O. Borseth, "The Sculptor Prayed," *If I Be His Disciple*

419

The teacher cannot hope that anything can happen to the child that he is not willing to have happen to himself. He cannot hope to bring the child under a discipline that he is not willing to accept for himself. . . . He cannot hope that the child will desire to see Christ come alive in his own life if he cannot sense that Christ is alive in the life of the teacher. He cannot believe that the Bible will seem to the child to be worth studying if it is only a textbook to the teacher.

He cannot believe that the child will find the living truth hidden in the Scripture if the teacher is more concerned about Bible facts . . . than he is about the redeeming Word of life. —Dorothy Arnim and Herman J. Sweet, *Together We Grow*

420

We have come on a generation of teaching that simply holds before men various truths and says to them, "Reach your hand into the basket and take your choice." I know the reason for this. It encourages men to think for themselves and to be able to say, "This truth is mine." This method of teaching, however, can be as false in its refusal to share the deepest and the truest that generations have known as the other method which sought merely to cram undigested truth into the mouths of gullible students. In an endeavor to adapt truth to life, we have forgotten that life must be brought to God through Jesus Christ. —Harrison Ray Anderson, *God's Way*

421

Going to school to Jesus must have been very interesting. You never knew where the class would be held, or what would turn up. Sometimes you would be off in the woods for days. Sometimes you would be on the street corner, another time out in a boat, and another, in the home of a friend. —*Gates of Beauty*

422

Human reason is weak, and may be deceived, but true faith cannot be deceived.—Thomas à Kempis

423

Wisdom precedes, religion follows; for the knowledge of God comes first, His worship is the result of knowledge. —Lactantius, *Divine Institutes*

424

This spiritual universe is responsive to feelings rather than intellect. The unfeeling man, no matter how brilliant, is a thoroughly sick soul. And I submit that in the education of children and adolescent youth, nothing should enter the curriculum that tends to produce unfeeling callousness.— Dorothy Thompson, "A Question of Value," *Ladies' Home Journal*

425

Everything of importance to life and policy arises out of feelings. The education of the feelings is no less important than the education of the intellect. If we are to have science, we must have art, music, poetry, literature, manners, deportment, instinctual "good behavior," or society is a jungle. —Dorothy Thompson, "A Question of Value," *Ladies' Home Journal*

426

Do we settle the religious problems of the child or sigh with relief when another child asks a question that changes the subject?—Ethel Smither

427

Superstition is the cruelest thing in the world. Faith is to live in the sun. Superstition is to sit in darkness.— Katherine T. Hinkson, *The House of Foxes*

428

Happy is the child
  Whose teachers guide by love.
And not by authority.

For the teacher who is feared
  More than he is loved,
Can neither guide nor teach effectively
  But increases rebellion of spirit;

For love rules the heart,
  But fear hardens the mind.

—E. Paul Hovey, "A Beatitude,"
Pilgrim Elementary Teacher

429

If the truth be mighty, and God all-powerful, His children need not fear that disaster will follow freedom of thought.—François de Fénelon

430

There seems to be a fresh need to examine the career of the human self in the modern world, with his religious development especially in mind.—Lewis Joseph Sherrill, *The Struggle of the Soul*

431

One Sunday morning, a little girl came home from Sunday school clutching a small pamphlet. Her daddy asked her what she had in her hand. "Oh," said the little girl, "it's a commercial from heaven."—Arthur L. Kasser

432

Christian nurture is not content, but direction; it is not a set of facts, but a set of attitudes. These attitudes are in the framework of a total philosophy of life. . . . Christian nurture is not a thing outside ourselves that we learn about; it is a way of doing things, a way of looking at things, and a way of getting ourselves set to get things done.—Herbert N. Allen, *Church School Worker*

433

You've heard it said that "Christianity is only one generation from extinction" . . . and it's true! It has been true since the disciples of Jesus carried the gospel to the first generation of Christians. . . . Christianity has been communicated down through the centuries from person to person. . . . This process of teaching Christ is Christian education.

The light of our faith sometimes has flickered and nearly failed. Yet, through the darkness, dedicated men and women of each generation have carried the light—have told the good news of Christ—to the next generation. Today, thanks to their devotion, we experience the joy of Christian living.

In all critical moments in history, each generation has the solemn obligation—the glorious opportunity—to communicate the gospel of Christ to the next.—William A. Morrison

434

There is a story about the son of a famous sculptor who, trying to follow in his father's footsteps, toiled away in a garret, trying to create a masterpiece in stone. But this unknown boy did not possess his father's skill as a workman. He handled his tools awkwardly; he made mistakes as he used his hammer and chisel. He could never seem to visualize the result of a deft stroke here or there; nor could he seem to see where he had left an ungraceful curve on the stone. Often at the close of a day's work he would stop in disgust. Then, all alone, the famous father would come to the garret and, with the touch of a master, give the stone the needed shaping by skillful use of the chisel.

The son never knew what his father was doing; he would come back to his work marveling at how well he had done the day before and would set to work with new vigor.

How like that boy is the Christian teacher! The tools of teaching are badly handled, mistakes are made, the vision of the future is overlooked, and the lives of pupils are often ungracefully molded; because of this the teacher becomes greatly discouraged. And yet these leaders are helping the Master to shape boys and girls, men and women, into the pattern of Jesus. Though they be crude workmen, the Master, without their knowledge, does touch their work, and in later years men say, "Surely the Master has been here and influenced the lives of these people!"

Men were like that in Jesus' day. Recall the story of the Mount of Transfiguration. The disciples who remained in the valley tried in a blundering way to heal a boy—and failed. It was necessary for Jesus to go over their work and make him whole. The discouraged teacher is comforted by the fact that some of the apostles were comparatively obscure, inferior men and yet, with the unseen touch of the Master, were able to accomplish "greater things than these." The great teachers of Jesus' day, like Gamaliel, did not become the leaders in the Christian movement; our Lord had to look elsewhere for helpers and teachers. Today it is not always possible to enlist the best teachers to carry on the work of the church. But even the least may be useful as a witness for Christ. To be a witness of Christian fact is the main business of a church school teacher. It does not take a great man to make a good witness. Witnessing, plus the unseen touch of the Master, produces the masterpiece.

Because the master does touch up the teacher's work does not mean that the teacher need go unprepared and trust that a masterpiece will be the result. Rather, he needs to work to the best of his ability, leaving as few spots as possible to be touched up. Many who stop attending church school and have never been of any influence in building the Kingdom of God might truthfully say, "My Sunday school teachers didn't even try."

Whatever man's part of the work may be, it should be done as a part of God's work. One understands why so many masterpieces of music came from the brain and pen of Johann Sebastian Bach when one knows that at the top of every page of a new musical composition Bach wrote, "To the glory of God," and at the finish inscribed, "With the help of Christ."

No Christian teacher can take his task lightly. The sincere teacher is influenced by the thought that long after he is gone his handiwork will be on display in the lives of those he has touched or failed to touch. A teacher never knows whether his lesson falls on barren or on fertile soil. Therefore, the Christian teacher tries to find better ways to witness and to bring the mysteries of God to his pupils, praying with humility that the Master will come and touch up the unfinished spots.—E. Paul Hovey, "The Master Has Been Here," *Westminster Uniform Lesson Teacher*

435

I would like to propose a new degree, MTC, "more than conquerors." The ills of life are not to be explained, or escaped, or endured with bitterness. They are to be transmuted into mature, fruitful living. . . . What is the technique for becoming "more than conqueror"? In "Damn Yankees," that lively play about the New York Yankees, rings this bracing line, "You've got to have heart—miles and miles and miles of heart!" We cannot win in sport or in daily living without backbone.

But it takes more than virility. Paul gives the secret, "through him who loved us."—William R. Leslie, *Together*

436

Primitive religion . . . was utilitarian. It was a magic way of getting rain, raising crops, winning wars, and defeating the ghostly hordes of demons. But when the understanding of spiritual life deepened and primitive dreads were a little lifted, men began to play with religion. They rejoiced in the Lord, sang songs, and danced before the Lord, built beautiful temples to the Lord, held celebrations of festival and thanksgiving, and like the Hebrew psalmist, went up to the sanctuary and kept holyday. That is to say, they were religious, not because they had to be, but because they loved it.—Harry Emerson Fosdick, "Living for the Fun of It," *Reader's Digest*

437

Does your teaching task thrill you the longer you teach? It ought to. Teaching is one of the most marvelous opportunities given to human beings; by it they can share with one another the things that are essential to life. Animals do little or no teaching. Their activities are governed by instincts. Domesticated animals have been taught by man, but they do not teach one another—at least, not much.

Human beings must be teachers. The natural instincts of the human being do not provide much that gets him anywhere in the world. When taught, he may achieve marvelous results with his body, mind, and spirit. To teachers, therefore, falls the task of developing in human beings understanding, love, and other virtues and characteristics.

Teaching, therefore, ought to be thrilling. It may be tiring, but it need not be irksome. To have the opportunity of leading another to appreciate the glory of God and His handiwork, and to teach such a one to have communion with the great God Himself, should be enough to stimulate every fiber of your being. You have no doubt read the story of Anne Sullivan Macy's efforts to bring knowledge to Helen Keller. Finally Miss Keller perceived. Through her finger tips she learned of God, and she rejoiced. The story is thrilling. And yet, each of us who teaches is in a comparable way opening the minds and hearts of children, youth, or adults to the same knowledge. Our task is to make God known and loved. God will seek our pupils even as we teach them to seek Him. When their spirits meet, there will be fellowship. What a goal—to teach so that we may bring others into fellowship with the great God of the universe!—Editorial in *Westminster Uniform Lesson Teacher*

438

If a son says he no longer believes in the Christian religion, what is the only convincing reply? It is (for the parent) to live like a Christian.—William Lyon Phelps

439

We are molded and remolded by those who love us; and though the love may pass, we are nevertheless their work for good or bad.—François Mauriac

440

How many parents would attempt to teach Latin or mathematics with no preparation, who answer questions of religion and theology without a moment's thought?

441

The most futile mental pattern of all is regret; the most inspiring is faith.—James J. O'Reilly, *Your Life*

442

Our goal must be no lesser goal than that which Jesus and the apostles had before them. We teach so that through our teaching God may work in the hearts of those whom we teach to make of them disciples wholly committed to His gospel, with an understanding of it, and with a personal faith that will enable them to bear convincing witness to it in word and action in the midst of an unbelieving world.

We teach young children and youths and adults that by the grace of God they may grow up into the full life and faith of His church, and may find their life's fulfillment in being members of the very body of Christ and sharers in His mission.—James D. Smart, *The Teaching Ministry of the Church*

443

It is the task of Christian education to furnish imaginations with the story of salvation so that it may become a part of each individual's own history, absorbed into the context of his own particular life, be he young or older, rich or poor, from East or West. The church's best efforts are needed in the development of the great art of such teaching.

This art, like all true art, is embedded in life. Such teaching cannot be merely descriptive of something that happened long ago. It must be expressive now of the meaning of those historic events in the life of today's community, the community of which the pupils are a part, the Holy Spirit being interpreter and guide.—Hulda Niebuhr, *McCormick Speaking*

444

Keep your eyes on everything, but keep your fingers out. Young people just getting started frequently overdo this. A leader has to work with people, and if you are forever checking on trivial points, you irritate those who can do the work for you. If you want to be a leader, you have to act like one before your peers will accept you. There's nothing magical or mystical about the process. Anyone can be a leader who is willing to pay the price.

445

Though I teach with the skill of the
    greatest of teachers,
And have not love,
I am become a thing for mere display,

A discordant note in my School of Religion.

Though I am an artist in story, music and drama,

And though I have the keenest understanding of modern theories

Regarding democratic processes;

Though I have all faith so as to overcome the most stubborn obstacles to progress

And have not love,

It profiteth me nothing.

Though I give all my time and my resources to teaching,

And though I consume my strength in overwork,

Yet have not love,

It profiteth me nothing.

Love suffereth patiently and is kind,

Love knoweth neither envy nor jealously of other teachers,

Love is herself teachable;

Is not boastful of success;

Doth not behave unbecomingly when new methods are proposed.

Seeketh not to exploit the child for personal prestige;

Is not easily overwrought;

Doth not brood over slights;

Rejoiceth in that which is genuine and true.

Love patiently beareth discouragement.

She trusteth the best in children, hopeth for the best.

And confidently waiteth for the best to conquer.

Love never faileth,

Whether there be liberal or conservative theologies, they shall be changed;

Whether there be differing schools of psychology, they shall be reconstructed;

Whether there be variant ideals of education, they shall be reconceived.

For we know but little and we teach but imperfectly.

When that which is better is discovered, that which is surpassed should be discontinued.

When I was but a child in my own character achievement

I spoke as a child,

I felt as a child and I thought in childish patterns.

Now that I am striving for a religion worthy of my years,

I should put away the prejudices of the childish.

Even yet I see as through a darkened mirror.

Some day I shall see clearly,

Now I know but in fragments;'

Then I shall know fully, even as fully as I am known.

Now abideth faith, hope and love, these three, and the greatest of these is love.

CHRISTIAN COLLEGE DAY

446

Christians in every college and university are called to act as a creative minority which dares to speak the truth in love. In our institutions of higher education, much of the failure to engage in fruitful and creative cross-disciplinary and intra-disciplinary discussion arises precisely out of the unwillingness and inability to live beyond the edge of one's knowledge. This, in turn, is one aspect of our deeper failure to admit the significance of the fact of sin in the life of the mind.

We have a witness to deliver at the point of ends and values. It is most distressing to realize how little impact is made on the average college and university campus by the followers of Jesus Christ. Is this impotence due to a basic misconception of the way in which the witness is best made?

Our witness is no mere addendum, something extra to be tacked on to the academic structure of the college or university. The need is not primarily for more and better Bible courses, or for the addition of more courses in religion, or for the addition of a college chaplain.

The task is to evangelize the life of the college and university for Christ at all the points where their own nature is most seriously jeopardized. . . . Evangelization will take place when Christians . . . demonstrate effectively in the sphere of voluntary religious life and thought on campus the power of that new community which they call the church of Christ.—Arthur R. McKay, *McCormick Speaking*

447

I like small colleges that nestle
  In quiet little towns
And seem to offer something more
  Than credits, caps and gowns,
I like small classes filled with friends
  Who have a smile for me.
I don't like profs who know me as
  Row thirty-one, seat three.

    —*The Southern Union News*

448

It is one of the noblest duties of a university to advance knowledge and to diffuse it not merely among those who can attend daily lectures—but far and wide.—Daniel Coit Gilman

449

Our university is a place of the mind, and the mind is an activity, not a repository. In this spirit we invite students to come and learn with us.—Dean Robert Hoopes

450

From our forebears who in less propitious times have taught and labored and hoped here, we have inherited a priceless trust which will be fostered until, as the Arabs say, the stars grow old, the sun grows cold, and the leaves of the judgment book unfold.—Abbott Lawrence Lowell

451

If we acknowledge that ideas are more important than matter, that what man has thought is of vastly more significance than the material wealth he has amassed, our task becomes all the more clear. It is then of compelling importance that our effort in the struggle for men's minds shall receive our best and full measure of devotion. It is in this area that the Christian college can make a lasting and unique contribution.—Homer Cunningham, *Whitworth College Bulletin*

452

Tell me today what the philosopher thinks, the university professor expounds, the schoolmaster teaches, the scholar publishes in his treatises and textbooks, and I shall prophesy the conduct of individuals, the ethics of businessmen, the schemes of political leaders, the plans of economists, the pleadings of lawyers, the decisions of judges, the legislation of lawmakers, the treaties of diplomats, and the decisions of state a generation hence.

453

We must make certain that among the many competing interpretations [in institutions of learning] the Christian view of man is given an articulate and intellectually vigorous presentation.—Truman B. Douglass

454

Education and training, or at least its rewards, it was thought, could be effortlessly acquired, without the grueling labor involved in mastering any subject, or the dedication needed to push out into new ground. We are discovering that America is entering a period of great national stress and of unlimited international rivalry, without adequate resources of trained and responsible men at all levels. That discovery has already led to an uproar, directed at educational institutions all the way from top to bottom. It has not died down.

Each successive realization that the quality of American life and American intellectual effort must be far tougher, far better disciplined and far more productive will bring more criticism of our educational system, from parents to graduate faculties.—Adolf A. Berle, Jr., *Vital Speeches*

455

Most Americans realize that the greatest values come not from personal pleasure or profit, but from contributions made to the community, the country, and the progress of humanity. They know quite well that education comes ahead of transient luxuries. They know that the running gear of business is justified not by its profit, but because it meets human needs. Profit is essential, but secondary. . . . They want business that does not organize waste at consumers' expense, and they understand quite well that "planned obsolescence" is either cheating or waste, or both. In other words, they want an organization of affairs that realizes instead of violates their value system.—Adolf A. Berle, Jr., *Vital Speeches*

456

The church college exists because our fathers saw the vital connection between faith and learning. The contemporary church must recapture this vision.—Gaylord M. Couchman

457

Ideas are the merchandise of education, and every worthwhile educational institution must provide and guard the conditions for breeding them.—*Dakota Wesleyan University Bulletin*

458

Universities give to the young in their impressionable years the bond of a lofty purpose shared, of a great corporate life whose links will not be loosed until they die.—John Masefield

459

The serious truth of the matter is that you [the alumni] are the distilled essence of the university, for you are its product and the basis for its reputation. If anything lasting is to be achieved by us as a community of scholars, it must in most instances be reflected in you. If we are to win intellectual victories or make cultural advances, it must be through your good offices and your belief in our mission.—Samuel B. Gould

460

Many years ago a young man from western Pennsylvania decided that he wanted to go to Princeton because he had been deeply impressed by what he had heard of its president. He took the examination and failed, but before returning to his home decided that he would try to see President McCosh. . . . Mr. McCosh came to the door. The young man told him that he had planned to enter Princeton and had not been able to meet the requirements, but before going home wished to thank him for what he had learned there. McCosh asked what he had learned.

The young man replied, "How little I know."

"Mon, we will take ye," McCosh answered. "Ye are two years ahead of the rest of them."—Thomas Dreier, *Your Life*

461

A college waves an invitation to join the human race.—Joseph Sittler

462

Unquestionably the younger generation makes some grave mistakes. For example, it learns things much too readily from the older generation.—Burton Hillis, *Better Homes & Gardens*

463

It has been said that an educated man has a sharp axe in his hand, and an uneducated man a dull one. I would say that the purpose of a college education is to sharpen the axe to its keenest edge.—Nathaniel Butler

464

The church-related colleges know that knowledge without the spirit of service is dangerous. They are not afraid of advancing science. They understand that, as a tool in the hands of those guided by a right spirit, knowledge is strength for good works. They realize that the skills that go with knowledge can be applied where they count, so that love of their fellows will bear fruit in deeds that are really useful.—Arthur H. Compton, *The Christian Advocate*

465

Only when people in positions of leadership in the professions, in business, in government, in the laboring world, realize that they have a call to "full-time Christian service" equally with the minister can there be much hope of a Christian victory in the world of today. Only when people in these lay positions apply their united intelligence to the solution of the problems of the world in accordance with the mind of Christ can secularism be finally defeated.—Robert D. Bulkley, *About the Christian College*

466

All liberal education is an adventure in humility. In the final adventure of the liberal mind, the true follower learns the wisdom of humility. He first loses his life and then he finds it again. Surrendering himself to God, he receives from Him the return of infinite love—flooding every portion of his life till there is a new light upon the land and on every human face, and in his own heart a peace the world cannot give. This is the final humility, and it is the crown of intellect.—Howard Lowry, *Presbyterian Life*

NATIONAL FAMILY WEEK

467

I should like to feel that, in every American family, some place is made for an expression of our gratitude to Almighty God, and for a frank acknowledgment of our faith that He can supply that additional strength which, for these trying times, is so sorely needed.—Dwight D. Eisenhower

468

Nothing outside of home can take the place of home. The school is an invaluable adjunct to the home, but it is a wretched substitute for it. The family relation is the most fundamental, the most important of all relations. —Theodore Roosevelt

469

The life of the state rests and must ever rest upon the life of the family and the neighborhood.—Theodore Roosevelt

470

I think a man and woman should choose each other for life, for the simple reason that a long life with all its accidents is barely enough for a man and a woman to understand each other; and to understand is to love. The man who understands one woman is qualified to understand pretty well everything.—J. B. Yeats

471

The first few rounds are easy in prize fighting and in matrimony. It's staying power that counts.—Tommy Burns

472

The Christian home is the Master's workshop where the processes of character molding are silently, lovingly, faithfully and successfully carried on. —Lord Houghton

473

For wives of all ages: Wiles are preferable to wails.—Marcelene Cox, *Ladies' Home Journal*

474

Everyone either belongs to a home or else wants to belong. Everyone either looks back on a happy home which gave security and understanding of life or else sadly, perhaps even resentfully and bitterly, recalls the opposite. As a result the warp and woof of life are woven around the pattern of our home.

How very much then we need Christian homes—homes from which will flow "rivers of living water" in deeply spiritual lives.—H. W. Sutherland, "Foundations of the Christian Home," *His*

475

Life consists of relationships. At first examination these appear to be a million and one in variety. Only a few are basic, possibly five in all: husband and wife, parent and child, master and servant, teacher and pupil, friend and friend. Of these the first two are fundamental and entirely within the family. The others relate the individuals within the family to the rest of society. Yet even these exist in embryo within the home in childhood days. Thus the family is a complete training ground for the roles that an individual may occupy later in society. Indeed, the meaning the child discovers within these roles in the home will be the meaning he brings to them as an adult. Thus the family is the fundamental building block of society.—H. W. Sutherland, "Foundations of the Christian Home," *His*

476

Nowhere is selfishness seen more clearly than in the home. Therefore if it is not dealt with here, it is not really dealt with anywhere. Yet selfishness is but the expression of self-centeredness which is at the heart of sin. If we profess to love God and yet our home betrays that we really love ourselves first, where are we? Our selfishness may be glossed over in public but not at home . . . honesty is a first requirement for reality, for spiritual growth.—H. W. Sutherland, "Foundations of the Christian Home," *His*

477

The Christian family is . . . a building block of the new society, the church.—H. W. Sutherland

478

We are all human beings and we will always make mistakes. The best we can do is to replace bigger mistakes with smaller mistakes.—Alfred Adler

479

That was a nice wedding we attended, and I liked best what the bridegroom's father told him as he kissed his new daughter-in-law: "Everything you have is hers now, Son. But there's one thing I want you to keep: keep that light shining in her eyes."—Burton Hillis, *Better Homes & Gardens*

480

A marriage that had never been a partnership in good times could hardly be expected to run smoothly when things went bad.—James F. Brown, "We Learned How To Live," *Redbook*

481

All children are angels and every house is heaven when they are asleep.—Imogene Fey, *Your Life*

482

Judge Camille Kelley has spent more than twenty years in salvaging children from society's scrap heap. Out of her experiences with 45,000 children who were brought before her, she observed, "The child's richest heritage is a well-ordered home. If every child had such an opportunity, delinquency would fade from court records. There would be no need for juvenile courts and juvenile judges." Then she added sadly, "But all children do not live in houses and all houses are not homes." That is the painful truth.—John S. Bonnell, "Power of the Home," *P E O Record*

483

When a wandering boy finds himself, then all roads lead to Home.—Marcelene Cox, *Ladies' Home Journal*

484

In dismay a father said to me, "I feel I'm a complete stranger to my daughter who is in high school. We cannot talk to each other any more. I'm simply appalled."

Do you remember the Scripture in the second chapter of Luke which reads: "But they, supposing him to have been in the company, went a day's journey; and they sought him among their kinsfolk and acquaintance." Mary and Joseph had assumed that their Son Jesus was among the group of pilgrims returning from the festival at Jerusalem. They were wrong. They had gone on without Him.

It is so easy to assume that our children are with us; that they are growing emotionally and spiritually, thinking in the same realm as we are. We take it for granted that they are accepting the moral values and ideals which we have, and in general keeping abreast of us as we move toward the goals which we have established.

Then comes the rude awakening—what we have assumed to be true may not be so at all. Our youngsters may awaken us to the fact that we and they are literally miles apart. . . .

In developing religion in the home, the important thing is the spirit which dominates all relationships. If religious teaching is to be effective, it must be part of the normal pattern of living. As someone has aptly expressed it, "The problem is not one of teaching religion; it is one of making the family religious." In other words, religion is not taught, it is caught.

The religious family learns also that it cannot isolate itself or insulate itself and remain complete and retain its strength. As it witnesses its beliefs to the world, it gains spiritual strength for itself. . . . Families which are genuinely stable and secure within themselves do more than spiritually nourish their own members—they build a Christian world. As parents, we assume a tremendous responsibility for the world. But this is only a by-product of the great responsibility in being worthy parents.

Therefore, daily we must do that which Mary and Joseph did—*find out if our children are with us.* If not, it is necessary immediately to retrace our steps, reunite our family, and travel life's road together. We cannot ask to be discharged from this responsibility until our children are ready to travel alone and begin families of their own. Even then it is essential for their sakes and for ours that we still keep our faith strong and our witness vital; for surely when we reach heaven's gate, we will be asked, "Are your children with you?"—Edgar J. Helms, *Are Your Children with You?*

485

Parents are like editors. The planning for a new child is not unlike planning for a new issue of a magazine. The blue pencil must be used frequently and a rough draft worked on until it becomes presentable copy. —John W. Cook

486

We are fond of saying, in an unexamined platitude, that children are the hope of the race. We forget that the guidance of children is still entrusted to adults. There would be real hope if children and parents together would daily pray.—George A. Buttrick, *Prayer*

487

A boy asked his father a question and was told to "ask your mother." The boy commented, "Oh, skip it. I don't want to know that much about it."

488

Toward him who slaves in house and garden
My feeling now begins to harden:
He gives my prodding spouse too ample
A weapon with his good example!
—Luke Neely, *The Wall Street Journal*

489

A small boy was trying very hard to lift a heavy stone. His father, happening by and noting the son's failure, said to him, "Are you using all your strength?" "Yes, I am," the boy exclaimed impatiently. "No," the father replied, "you are not. You haven't asked me to help."

490

James Lee Ellenwood in his book, "There's No Place Like Home," reminds us that the average family is the most illogical grouping of all human associations—young and old, big and little, with a host of interests, hobbies, and varied capacities. What could God have been thinking of when He created families?

God in His infinite wisdom knew that if we were all the same, we'd be very narrow and that if we could get along only with our own kind, our characters would be very flabby indeed.

The whirlpool of variety that is the average family is God's laboratory for teaching us appreciation for others, mercy, forgiveness, courage, and love. As Bishop Oxnam has said, "Home is where the ultimates become intimate."
—Elizabeth and William Genne

491

Obedience insures greatness, whilst disobedience leads to repulse. Whosoever possesseth the qualities of righteousness placeth his head on the threshold of obedience.—Saadi

492

Parents need guidance in religious training of their children as they need a doctor's advice on the physical problems.—Ethel Smither

493

As a parent or teacher we hold a child's assets in trust. If we hold them too long the result is that the child's growth in responsibility is curtailed and he is immature. If we release them too soon the child is not ready and rebels at responsibility and this also results in immaturity.—Robert Rhay

494

Our local child psychologist says one trouble with children is they all have mothers and fathers, but some of them do not have parents.—Marcelene Cox, *Ladies' Home Journal*

495

Home is a place where we can learn by making a mistake and still not be defeated. It is a place of the second chance.—James Rathbum

496

In the home, children learn what to want and respect.—Adlai Stevenson

497

If we are to make a mature adjustment to life, we must be able to give and receive love.—Anna Trego Hunter, *Ladies' Home Journal*

498

When a baby is born, he is completely dependent upon his parents. From then until the child is completely out of the home, his parents have the problem of helping him become independent.

The parent who fails to establish controls and restrictions early is doing the child a tremendous disservice. The problem is made worse if you don't say "no." However, it will slow him down very seriously in his development if you say "no" too often.

It is an exceedingly difficult problem to know at any stage how much liberty to give to a child. You have to give him, as he grows, more and more freedom so he is ready to step into the world when he reaches maturity.—Myrick Pullen, Jr., M.D.

499

The only social security any able man needs is a good place to work, a good place to worship, and a good home to love.—James J. O'Reilly, *Your Life*

500

The church is the family of God. It is seen in miniature in each family. The impulse which sends us to worship together as a church should send us to worship together as a family.—John Ferguson, *Christian Faith for Today*

501

In a "what-is-life" conversation across the fence the other day, Bill Norman offered a brave definition of success. A man is a success, he said, when he actually can believe he is the sort of man his mother thinks he is and his mother-in-law hopes he will become.—Burton Hillis, *Better Homes & Gardens*

502

Advice to young girls: Select the man whose wife will be able to make him succeed.—Marcelene Cox, *Ladies' Home Journal*

503

The goal in marriage is not to think alike, but to think together.—Robert C. Dodds, *Two Together*

504

Marriage is the alliance of two people, one of whom never remembers birthdays and the other never forgets them.—Ogden Nash

505

When Anatole France was a boy, he read a book on the saints and was impressed by the story of Simeon Stylites who showed his holiness by living on top of a pillar. Young Anatole decided to imitate the saint. With boyish ingenuity he made a pillar by putting a chair on the kitchen table. Then he began to sit. His mother, however, was not in sympathy with his method of attaining sainthood. Before it was time to get supper, she made him climb down from his perch and pull the chair after him. He said, "I perceive it is a very difficult thing to be a saint while living with your family." True indeed! It is never easy to be a Christian at home, but this is the acid test of our religion.—Walter Dudley Cavert, *Ours Is the Faith*

506

Having a Christian home means far more than a houseful of nice people who treat each other fairly kindly and who go to church fairly regularly. It means a home where Christ is known and loved and served; where children come to know Him through their parents; where Christian training of children is placed ahead of the social ambition of the mother and the business ambition of the father; where the father is determined to carry on his business in conformity with the mind of Christ; where both father and mother are determined to make their social life conform to high Christian ideals; and where eyes see far horizons of a world to be won for Christ.—Paul Calvin Payne

507

Success in matrimony depends not on marrying the first person who comes along, but on marrying the right person first.—Marcelene Cox, *Ladies' Home Journal*

508

There is no spectacle on earth more appealing than that of a beautiful woman in the act of cooking dinner for someone she loves.—Thomas Wolfe

509

A man's home can be his hassle.—Dwain A. Bass

510

A newspaper once reported a wedding in the following succinct and ominous paragraph:

"Bob and Madeline were married on October 20, thus terminating a friendship that first began way back in junior high school."

The fact is that many a marriage has indeed terminated a beautiful friendship. The inescapable intimacies of marriage can introduce intolerable strains into the relationship between a man and a woman. Especially where two people are rigidly inflexible or somberly determined to have their own way, friendship can be weakened or destroyed.—Robert C. Dodds, *Two Together*

511

While some girls stay single—
And choose that lot—
Nearly all of them
Would rather knot.
—Kay Owens, "Ladies' Choice," *Ladies' Home Journal*

512

The home is, after all, the most vital social unit in any democracy. It influences the actions of all society. But goodness must not only be cultivated in the home, it must be carried forth beyond its doors.—James Keller, *You Can Change the World*

513

The best home temperature is maintained by warm hearts rather than hot heads.—Burton Hillis, *Better Homes & Gardens*

514

Overheard the neighborhood kiddie-car set talking about the origin of babies. One lad said the doctor brought him. A four-year-old girl assured her pals she was purchased in a store. But a third little charmer said, "My parents were too poor to buy me, I was home-made."—Burton Hillis, *Better Homes & Gardens*

515

Mitch Miller, the bearded record man, describes his parental connections with his own three teen-agers this way: "We keep 'em on a rubber band. It stretches out real far—far enough to give them a sense of freedom. But when the kids need it, that rubber band can snap fast."—"Living with People," *McCall's*

516

He that flies from his own family has far to travel.—Latin proverb

517

Win the family for Christian living and the world is won.—Nels F. S. Ferre

518

One of the nicest symbols of the entire marriage service is the act of joining hands. It portrays, in simple sign language, the warm truth about Christian love. Probably your court-ship began when you first held hands, and it has been a symbol of your being together ever since. But had you ever thought how much the open hand, held out in love, can mean? A closed fist suggests the extreme opposite of love—self-defensiveness and readiness to hurt. A hand held back reveals a person who is afraid to give his love away, who wants to protect himself against possible mistreatment. But a hand held out in open love is ready to trust, to suffer, to be hurt, and to give itself away. When two people, in a dramatic service of divine worship, extend open and defenseless hands and clasp them together, they are showing to God and to the world their readiness to learn from each other the mysterious penetration of real love.—Robert C. Dodds, *Two Together*

519

As a Kiwanis president, I have found that a club and a family are much alike. The head man of each raps his gavel, sounds off impressively, issues some orders, is listened to attentively, after which the members go right ahead and do as they darn well please.—Oren Arnold, *Bluebook*

520

We find that our faith is not a burden but a guiding light that frees us from the hazards created by thoughtless living. We do not need to accept everything that society suggests as good. Our function as a family is to weigh and measure against the promise and demand of our faith.

Our approach must be positive. We are not necessarily *against* things that everybody is doing, but we are *for* those things our faith says are good.—Helen and Myron Wicks, "Our Faith Can Make Us Free," *Christian Home*

521

No nation has ever prospered in which family life was not held sacred.—Dean William Inge

522

"We need more courtesy, more ladies and gentlemen, in our homes," our pastor counseled us at Family Night dinner. "You can be refined in any language—but not *with* any language."—James J. O'Reilly, *Your Life*

523

Togetherness has been nicely and variously described as belonging without possessiveness, as love and understanding, as a reverence for God and the dignity of man, as working jointly without destroying individual initiative. But may I suggest that just once in a while, when our very young children tell us how much more they know than we know, togetherness can also refer to an almost lost art—the coming together of the adult hand and the juvenile backside?—Editorial in *McCall's*

524

No grandparent knows his true strength of character until he has silently witnessed his grandchild being disciplined for the first time.—Marcelene Cox, *Ladies' Home Journal*

525

The first step in disciplining a child is to discipline oneself.—Marcelene Cox, *Ladies' Home Journal*

526

When I haven't helped with a single task,
My wife isn't one bit vexed
Until it occurs to me to ask,
"What can I do for you next?"
—Thomas Usk, "Line of Least Assistance," *The Rotarian*

527

The magic of first love is our ignorance that it can ever end.—Disraeli

528

Kindness is the golden chain by which society is bound together.—Goethe

529

From the time he is two, and perhaps before, a baby is learning many words, the vocabulary of the world. At the same time, *and never any later*, he should be learning the heavenly vocabulary.—J. R. Lumb

530

We desire to build our home on love, self-forgetful and God-centered.

We desire to grow in fellowship with God, and to share that fellowship with our children.

We desire to take our part, and to encourage our children to take theirs, in the life of the church, that the message of Christ may come to our generation with sincerity and strength.

We desire to be honest in our dealings with each other, our children, and all people.

We desire to face fearlessly all intellectual problems, and to answer our children's questions truthfully and constructively.

We desire to seek counsel from persons and books on problems that are beyond our ability to solve alone.

We desire to cultivate for ourselves and our children friendships with all sorts and conditions of men, knowing that only in this way can God's family come true.

We desire to think and act courageously in all moral situations, and to help our children make habitual for themselves Christian ways of living.

We desire to play our full part in the bringing in of God's Kingdom and the doing of His will in the world, and to help our children to share in this work as their rightful heritage.

We desire to encourage in our children the fullest development of their personalities, that each may be the best he can be, unlimited by our preconceived ambitions.
—*Ideals for Christian Parents*

531

Certainly we must encourage our son and daughter to do their best, but it must be *their* best. We have to be careful in helping them set their goals. If too high they are discouraged, if too low they are not challenged. But above all we must help them, the home and church working together, to build a Christian scale of values; so that they will not put first success as measured by possessions, power, position.—W. Taliaferro Thompson, *Adventures in Parenthood*

532

The best way for a child to learn to fear God is to know a real Christian. The best way for a child to learn to pray is to live with a father and mother who know a life of friendship with God, and who truly pray.—Pestalozzi

533

Our Father in Heaven, who are the guide of parents and the guardian of children, help us to learn that reverence for Thee is the beginning of wisdom. Humble us with a sense of Thy greatness and hearten us with confidence in Thy goodness.

Keep us faithful, O God, to the ideals of the noblest who have gone before us. Dedicate us to develop our dreams for those who come after us.

Lead us where we may see life's largest possibilities and keep us from stopping beside the second best. Illumine our insights with love that we may bring out the best in others and consecrate our wills that we may give our best to others. For Thy Kingdom's sake we ask it. Amen.—Ralph W. Sockman, *Parent's Magazine*

534

It is the little annoyances which may grow into mighty storms if they are not brought under control of love. Since even within a family there are marked differences in personality, there are sure to be many irritations in the course of a year. How may we meet this test of recurrent irritations?

Love will meet the test. Love will find a way to remove the source of annoyance in many cases. An irritating habit in another may be corrected if it is pointed out *lovingly*.

But even when the irritation continues, the law of love works. You may rise above it on the wings of love and prayer. Fill your mind with love for God, and you will be surprised how your exasperation dissolves. Try it! You can win over your irritations—with the help of Christ.—Arthur L. Miller, *Today*

535

The Christian faith is a personal matter. However, the way we think affects the way we act, and our actions affect the lives of others. In Colossians 3:18—4:1 the home is the center of attention. Husbands, wives, children, parents, and servants all come in for some very practical advice. Each person in the home has an obligation to every other person. So much depends upon attitudes of one to the other.

In the Oriental home the father is very much the head of the household. He is the one who takes care of all the members of his household, looking after both their physical and spiritual needs. The wife is not considered equal to her husband. A word of warning was therefore needed for both husband and wife.

Many Oriental homes had servants who became almost like members of the family. Paul was making an appeal for the Christian attitude on the part of both the servant and the master. Paul here lifts the two-way relationship between servant and master to a higher plane of living by relating both of them to Christ. Both servant and master have a higher Master.—Maurice D. Bone, *Today*

536

When the young mothers brought their children to Jesus, they sought His blessing for their children. When the mother of James and John nudged her grown sons toward Him, it was for quite another purpose. She wanted political privilege for them, special favors in Christ's Kingdom, which she evidently did not understand. She earned Jesus' rebuke and explanation:

His Kingdom featured humility, not promotion.

The folly of parents who push their children ahead to excel in everything possible is seldom as well-intentioned as they themselves think. The psychiatrist for a school system in a large American city states that many of the maladjusted children in its schools have come from privileged homes where they are urged to surpass other children.

There ought to be a bill of rights for children. They can be dealt unchristian treatment by those who love them most. About such children, George Bernard Shaw once wrote that "their condition is that which adults recognize as the most miserable and dangerous politically possible for themselves; namely, the condition of slavery."—John Charles Wynn, *Today*

537

Leland Foster Wood says, "The world is constantly being fashioned and refashioned in our homes." This is clearly shown in Cornelius's household. The observance of family prayer met with favor in God's sight. It helped to show Peter that Christianity belonged to the world instead of just to the Jews. Family prayer was the cause of an entire household's being baptized into the Christian faith.—Frederick E. Udlock, *Today*

538

Family commotion means life. People are growing up, learning to live together. Prayer can help to prevent our getting on one another's nerves. The church, a symbol of both peace and power, is to millions of families the larger "family" from which come comfort, friendship, and faith.—Editorial in *National Council Outlook*

539

"Guard well thy words," says Mabel Haskell, "how else can thou be master of thyself? Well-poised and courteous speech can make thee King among thy fellows."

A teacher was having a great deal of difficulty in securing proper registration data from a small girl. The child apparently did not know her father's name. Finally in desperation the teacher asked, "What does your mother call him?"

The youngster promptly replied, "She doesn't call him anything—she likes him."—E. Paul Hovey

540

Let us now renew our vows to God and dedicate our lives to Him again:

Let all *fathers* stand and recite: "As for me and my house we will serve the Lord."

Let all *mothers* stand beside their husbands and recite: "Beloved, let us love one another; for love is of God; and every one that loveth is born of God and knoweth God."

Let all *children* stand beside their parents and recite: "May we be like Jesus, who grew in wisdom and stature and in favor with God and man."

Let the *entire family* recite: "May the Spirit itself bear witness with our spirit that we are the children of God."

Our Lord Jesus Christ said: "But ye shall receive power when the Holy Spirit is come upon you, and ye shall be witnesses unto me, both in Jerusalem, and in all Judea, and in Samaria, and unto the uttermost part of the earth." Amen.—"A Family Dedication," *Agricultural Missions Bulletin*

541

Home—a world of strife shut out, a world of love shut in.

Home—a place where the small are great, and the great are small.

Home—the father's kingdom, the mother's world, and the child's paradise.

Home—the place where we grumble the most and are treated the best.

Home—the center of our affection, round which our heart's best wishes twine.

Home—the place where our stomachs get three square meals a day and our hearts a thousand.—Charles M. Crowe, *Sermons for Special Days*

542

If more people could get a divorce from themselves, they might live happily with someone else.—Joseph Fort Newton

543

I have not been able to find a single useful institution which has not been founded by either an intensely religious man or by the son of a praying father or a praying mother. I have made this statement before the Chambers of Commerce of all the largest cities of the country, and have asked them to bring forward a case that is an exception to this rule. Thus far, I have not heard of a single case.—Roger Babson

MOTHER'S DAY (FESTIVAL OF THE CHRISTIAN HOME)

544

Somehow, Mother's Day is a little different from other holidays and special occasions. Christmas has a deep religious meaning, as has Easter. But too many of us look upon Christmas merely as a time to get and give a lot of presents, and on Easter as a day for wearing new clothes or hunting a few hidden eggs.

Other holidays usually mean a day of freedom from work, a chance to eat a lot, or shoot off firecrackers, or watch a parade, or to have some sort of celebration for our own special pleasure and enjoyment. But on Mother's Day we are unselfish. We think of somebody besides ourselves. It is a day set aside to express to our mothers the love and honor and respect which we hold for them. We don't decorate the house or march behind a band or hold a gay party. We simply give Mother flowers or some other gift, and try to make her realize a little of what she means to us.

545

A mother is not a person to lean on, but a person to make leaning unnecessary.—Dorothy Canfield Fisher, *Her Son's Wife*

546

A small child received an "A" on her essay about mothers: "A mother," she wrote, "is the one who takes care of the children and gets their meals, and if she's not there when you come home from school, you wouldn't know how to get your dinner and you wouldn't feel like eating it anyhow."

547

A mother does not need to be briefed regarding her attitude toward her child. That attitude would make a good neighborhood, a good city, a good world.

548

If the youth of today receives proper instruction at the knees of its parents, aware of a sacred place in the home, in the future we will not have to number the criminals sought in the millions.—J. Edgar Hoover.

549

A mother is a maker, a mender, a moderator, and a teacher. She makes boxer pants and chocolate pudding, law and sometimes order, threats, promises, and rabbit suits. She makes horses' heads from paper bags, little suits from big ones, new dresses from old ones, sun-suits from kitchen curtains, small balloons from popped ones, stew from nothing whatever. She makes peanut butter and jelly sandwiches, more peanut butter and jelly sandwiches, and peace when possible. A mother is a maker and a mender. A mother mends broken dishes and broken hearts, trouser knees, hurt noses and hurt feelings, trouser knees, torn jackets and torn fingers. She mends old sheets, old rosebushes, old baby dolls, and brand new trouser knees. A mother is a maker, a mender and a moderator. She is a moderator in times of war—civil war, verbal war, insurrection, minor skirmishes, attacks from the enemy; in times of strife, in times of injustice, in times of temper, in times of hair-pulling.

A mother is a maker, a mender, a moderator, and a teacher. She teaches how to button buttons and how to say a prayer. She teaches how to hold a knife and fork, how to hang up clothes so they sometimes stay hung, how to sit still in church. She can teach a love of books and of music— she can even turn child hearts to God. But almost never can she teach how to close a door without a bang or how to come in without bringing mud. A mother can count. She counts calories and blessings, pennies and children's heads in the car. But she never counts sheep! A mother is immune to surprise—whether it be a glass of water in her desk drawer, the cat sleeping on fresh sheets in the linen cupboard, worms in trouser pockets, good report cards, bad report cards, split foreheads, split knees, split infinitives. Nothing really surprises her.

But sometimes a mother reaches despair. The dryer won't dry when all the clothes are washed and wet. The baby bites the cat's tail and is scratched for it. Three-year-old dumps the tinker-toys by the front door when you expect the minister to call. The baby screams for attention—soothing medications must be halted while mother sprints to a relentless doorbell. There stand two neighbor children to report, "Your baby is crying." Six-year-old after forty-five minutes cannot spell "what." Eight-year-old dashes in to say he forgot, but it is his turn to take the cookies to his meeting today. Fingerprints all over the house loom suddenly vivid. The ragged edge of the rug seems suddenly dreadful. Three-year-old won't go out. The cat won't come in. The gelatin won't jell. The sun won't shine. The stew sticks and the pudding boils over while the phone rings on and on. And with it and above it and through it all comes, "Mommy, come and see . . . Mommy, come and see," incessantly, monotonously, unendingly, from three-year-old. Mother leans chin on broom handle and mutters, "Next time I'll raise chickens, Lord. Children are too much." Then ten-year-old crashes in —rough and ready, all boy—to confide, "Mommy, at Cub Scout meeting we had to list the five things most precious to us, and I did: One—God; two—love; three—America; four—babies; five—sunsets."

Suddenly the baby's eyes seem very blue, six-year-old recites from memory the entire 23rd Psalm which is better than spelling "what," fingerprints retreat again, Daddy walks in. Really, life could not be richer. It is a glory never to be bartered.—"Dear Lord, keep the chickens. I'll carry on for now. And thank you—from the bottom of my heart."—Jeanne Merrihew Lofgren, "Motherhood," *P E O Record*

550

Henry James wrote the life of Charles W. Eliot, Harvard's great president. He tells of the birth of the little fellow. The new child carried an ugly birthmark that covered most of the right side of his face down to the mouth. His mother understood the significance from the beginning. She could not lean over the helpless baby without gazing at the scar on his face and reflecting that she school herself not to notice it. "That Eliot became an aloof personality is not to be wondered at," said a cousin of Eliot's. You must realize when a boy, he was hooted off the Boston Commons because of his face. From the beginning, mothers have said, "It is my son." This mother could say it with growing pride as the years passed and honor followed honor. The great educator, who become internationally known, had not failed her.

551

Mother, the dream that you have for the little lives God has entrusted to your hands can come true if it is God's will and you help to shape it in love and Christian ideals. . . . True mother's love is in miniature a form of the love of God. How vital and important it is for every mother to know God intimately.—Wilbur W. Morgan

552

When I remember how your love was
there
Before I came, a living, breathing
thing,
Into this world of sorrow, doubt and
care,
And how you sheltered me 'neath
brooding wing,
I cannot but give thanks on bended
knee
To Him who all this heavenly love
creates.
Through you it came from Him, our
Lord, to me.
In your dark eyes, a wealth of kind-
ness lies.
On your white head, the burnished
silver gleams,
And from your face a heavenly bright-
ness beams
That oft has helped the sick and fallen
to rise

And little ones into your lap to creep,
For, in your arms, what infant could
not sleep?
—Lillian E. Rogers, *P E O Record*

553

There is an enduring tenderness in the love of a mother to a son that transcends all other affections of the heart! It is neither to be chilled by selfishness, nor daunted by danger, nor weakened by worthlessness, nor stifled by ingratitude. She will sacrifice every comfort to his convenience; she will surrender every pleasure to his enjoyment; she will glory in his fame and exult in his prosperity. And if misfortune overtake him, he will be the dearer to her because of the misfortune; and if disgrace settle upon his name, she will still love and cherish him in spite of his disgrace; and if all the world beside cast him off she will be all the world to him.—Washington Irving

554

Mother-love is a wonderful and precious thing for which we should daily give thanks to God. When mother-love is enriched by Christian-love, the blessing is even more wonderful. The extension of mother-love is the Christian home.

555

His mother had just returned from the hospital. She had been away for such a long time, at least it seemed long to her little boy. But now she was at home again, and he was beside himself with excitement. As soon as he could put his thoughts into words, he exclaimed, "Mother, you're just like glue!" At first she did not understand what he meant by such an odd expression. But he continued, "I mean that you hold us together. When you are gone, we just fall apart. Sister lives in one place, Buddy somewhere else, and Daddy and I get along by ourselves. You're just the stuff that keeps us together."

In his own way, the child had paid a high tribute to the mother who keeps the family together. As she supplies the affection and care that make a contented home, each mother is strengthening the individuals within her own circle as well as in the nation. —Earl E. Chanley, *The Secret Place*

556

The mother's heart is the child's schoolroom.—Henry Ward Beecher

557

He is bare of news who speaks ill of his mother.—Irish proverb

558

A space-age mother needs to keep her feet on the ground and her heart in the heavens. The man in the moon will never replace the man in the home with a dedicated mother working with him to raise a Christian family.

The answer is to put our thoughts and deeds in the right orbit. "Seek ye first the kingdom of God and his righteousness, and all these things shall be added unto you." The home that is in orbit around the Lord Jesus Christ will never fail in the countdown.—Mrs. Herman E. Eberhardt

559

Mighty is the force of motherhood. It transforms all things by its vital heat; it turns timidity into fierce courage and dreadless defiance into tremulous submission; it turns thoughtlessness into foresight and yet stills all anxiety into calm content; it makes selfishness become self-denial and gives even to hard vanity the glance of admiring love.—George Eliot

560

Most of all the other beautiful things in life come by twos and threes, by dozens and hundreds. Plenty of roses, stars, sunsets, rainbows, brothers and sisters, aunts and cousins, but only one mother in the whole world. —Kate Douglas Wiggins

561

May has become a symbol to honor the magic name of mother. Most of us remember and cherish the memories of the simple faith of childhood which sent us into the magic of mother's arms for protection, or to receive the magic of a kiss to brush away into childish dreams with the soft, but magic, lullabies. However magic these memories are, the greatest magic in the name of mother is her relationship as a co-creator with God. Motherhood becomes a part of God's infinite plan for man. With it comes the grave responsibility of nurture and development of that little life for God. How marvelous that God's plan has designed that we "are workers together with Him," and the responsibility of life becomes one of community interest. We do not live unto ourselves alone. We have a responsibility to each other. . . . The problems of one mother must necessarily become a concern to every other mother. No child can be entirely safe until all are safe. There is more than magic in "organized mother-love"; there is strength and courage.—Mrs. Herman Stanley, *The Union Signal*

562

If a mother is forced to cut too many corners, she may find herself going around in circles.—Marcelene Cox, *Ladies' Home Journal*

563

No man is really old until his mother stops worrying about him.— William Ryan

564

Who is best taught? He who has first learned from his mother.—The Talmud

565

Maternal love: a miraculous substance which God multiplies as He divides it.—Victor Hugo

566

When Mother, in sheer exasperation
Is tempted to hand in her resignation,
What adds to her gloom
Is not knowing to whom!
—May Richstone, "On the Spot," *Better Homes & Gardens*

567

A mother's hardest to forgive.
Life is the fruit she longs to hand you,
Ripe on a plate. And while you live,
Relentlessly she understands you.
—Phyllis McGinley, "The Adversary"
The New Yorker

568

What makes a mother great? Is it her experience in the valley of the shadow of death in giving birth to her child? Or because of her physical duties in caring for her own? No, for these are normal and routine to all mothers, and not all are great.

The source of greatness is the right development of that which is spiritual. No mother is or can be great who does not strive constantly to keep her spirit and will in tune and submission to the eternal and perfect Spirit and will of God.

Samuel achieved much because Hannah prayed. Augustine was saved because his mother, Monica, constantly brought him to the throne of God in prayer. Abraham Lincoln attributed his success to his mother, whose contribution was of the spirit. These sons were great because God was so vital to their mothers.

True greatness for each of us is to be found in the realm of the spirit.— Frederick E. Udlock, *Today*

569

In enumerating good people, we must admit that the mother is certainly more indubitably righteous than the father. She is, in fact, the symbol of absolute devotion. Father D'Arcy may be right in regarding the feminine principle in life as closer to the realm of grace than the masculine. The ages of Madonna worship are an explication of this fact. The Madonna who was worshiped in the Middle Ages was as frequently the human mother with the genial smile for her baby as she was the Mother of God.

Now we Protestants, not having Madonna worship, have invented Mother's Day, a kind of sentimentalized version of Madonna worship. No one can question, in other words, the righteousness of a good mother. Yet a dean of one of our universities has declared that, among the problems that children face, the most serious are mother problems and when psychiatrists analyze the root of these problems they come to the conclusion that the poor mothers can make so many mistakes. They may be tempted to be too permissive or too possessive or too dominating; the flaws in motherhood are, in short, many. . . . Are not all the symbols of the Kingdom taken from the family? Yet the Lord was very critical of the family: "Whoso loveth father and mother more than me is not worthy of me.". . . There are flaws in fatherhood and motherhood but the ascetic elimination of fathers and mothers is not the answer. We must live our lives as individuals, as fathers, as mothers, and as families, trying to be as just and righteous as possible, but we must also recognize that absolute purity is not possible for us and that the grasp after it, involving the veiling of the flaw within our hearts, usually creates a final evil rather than a final good. Let us not fool ourselves. Let us be responsible and just but also know that our final peace is the peace that comes from God's forgiveness.—Reinhold Neibuhr, "From Diagnosis to Cure," *Advance*

570

The cross was heavy on the shoulder of Jesus as they drove Him out past the city wall. And when at last the abominable thing was placed, of what did watching Mary think? She could remember sunny Galilee; she could recall that yesterday when the Boy played with the other boys at Nazareth; but did not the darkness and the silence take her back to the stable of Bethlehem? And within her did there not well up in anguish the heartbreaking minor of that cradle song? "Now you are mine, all mine. . . ." (And Christ on His cross!)

This is the irony of motherhood, a love that cares for but cannot finally take care of its own.

Evidently there is a strain of motherhood in each one of us. Have you never endured the moment when you would have gone to a rescue but could not? . . . Perhaps it is a loved one who is far away, and between him and you are sea dangers or city dangers or dangers of the highroad. What can you do? Nothing . . . remember Mary, who saw the Jesus whom she loved crucified—and could not save Him. . . .

The way of motherhood to many may seem tragic (to care, and not be able to protect!), but we survey the events only between birth and death, while God has all eternity to show His meanings and His issues. . . . There comes, in God's eternity, a day of gladness, a day of victory, and unfading day, for those who, in spite of all its costs, have allowed themselves the experience of such selfless love as filled the heart of Mary.

If you do not know this to be true, you had better look no longer at humanity, its poverty, disease, and ignorance. The sight can only be discouraging. . . . Best turn your eyes aside . . . you are not equipped redemptively; you have not wherewith to supply mankind with the first essential faith.

But if you know the universe is only the minister of God, your Father, and that God's love must one day make prevail all of your love that accords with His; if you know that in a just cause for which men have given all they had and seemingly in vain, the failures are only battles lost in a war not lost nor to be lost; if you are aware that humanity, when it escapes your care, falls not into stark cosmic neglect but into the hands of God; then you are armed for the warfare of reality. Then we need you! Then we desperately need you. Come in and help us! You stand with Mary. Stand with us: before all other things we need your faith!—Douglas Horton, *Taking a City*

MEMORIAL DAY

571

Once more the day is here when we
  remember those
Who, loving life, responded to their
  country's call,
Who turned their backs on ease, and
  gave their all.
  These we remember.
Their readiness to risk, to take a
  chance,
The courage and the valour they dis-
  played,
The blood they shed, the lives they
  gave,
  We will remember.
The long and weary hours they spent
On land, on sea and in the air,
The deadly combats which they fought,
  We will remember.
For the hardships they endured,
For the pain and anguish suffered,
For the loneliness they bore,
  We thank them.
For resisting vile temptations,
For defending truth and right,

For upholding justice, linked with
  mercy,
  We honor them.
The noble cause for which they bled
  and died,
The cherished freedom, honor, they
  secured,
These ever we shall treasure and pre-
  serve.
  We will remember.

572

Memories are expensive things; you pay for them with a chunk of your life. —Roy Ringo Program

573

It is good to remember and our loveliest memories are our bequest to ourselves. It was so in the experience of O'oka, a Japanese soldier. He had been fighting in the Philippines and, after the struggle, he wrote a letter home. He described how a young Yank carelessly stood up in his fox-hole to present a perfect target. O'oka took aim with his rifle, but he did not pull the trigger. He watched the Yank, wondering about him. Then he wrote, "I, a father, smiled to myself after-wards, thinking of the mother in America whose son's life I had spared."

War is bitter and cruel, but shining through the agony and the hurt of it was the memory of a generous impulse, and a Japanese father found comfort and satisfaction in the memory of his compassion. Perhaps there were a hundred other times when O'oka was cruel, but he is richly blessed by the priceless memory of a lad who lived because he stayed his hand.—Harold Blake Walker, "At Your Best," *Specialty Salesman*

574

A distinguished British statesman noted thoughtfully that when he looked back over his past, with the good and the bad in it, he began to understand the truth of the proverb, "You can become strongest in your weakest place." It is so. Moses put the matter aptly when he admonished his troubled people to "Remember all the experiences through which the Lord your God has led you." Our memories, when God is in them, are priceless. Indeed, the better the memories, the finer our tomorrows will be, and the stronger we will be in our weakest places.—Harold Blake Walker, "At Your Best," *Specialty Salesman*

575

There is no greater tribute we could pay to America's war dead than to find the road to peace.—Richard M. Nixon

576

The American people delight in memories and we are fit to entertain great hopes only as we cherish great memories.—George A. Gordon

577

Why is there such a difference between an event we can never forget and an event we shall always remember?—Marcelene Cox, *Ladies' Home Journal*

578

There is a voice in the soul of every human being in America that cries out to be free. America has answered that voice. These stones cry out, "To you we throw the torch; be it yours to hold high." On Memorial Day the stones cry out to us, "Life is not a gamble; we pay highly and dearly for the best things in this world and for our freedom." How long will it take us to realize that this universe did not just happen? We must live and let live in this generation.—Paul Deane Hill

579

At Thine altar, O God, we remember the heroism of men and fortitude of women in our times of trial—those who endured with valor, those who suffered with patience, and those who gave all, even the sweet blood of youth, for a better day.

God of mercy, let us not by carelessness or indifference be guilty of the worst of all sacrileges—the waste of sacrifice.

God of justice, make us just in mind and spirit, that the kingdoms of the world may become the kingdom of justice.

We pray not for a peace of ease, but for the peace of righteousness and good will, and the moral love that fulfills itself in fellowship. Comfort Thou Thy people and guide our groping humanity out of chaos into brotherhood. Enlighten our darkness; let ignorance, oppression and envy cease, and heaven and earth be joined in praise of the Prince of Peace. Amen.—Joseph Fort Newton, *Advance*

580

In times of stress and difficulty, recollection of our finest hours always is a source of hope and courage. Arnold Toynbee felt the truth when he noted that in the East End of London during the Second World War, when large areas of the city were being destroyed by bombardment from the air, people whose homes were being blasted began to show a curious interest in monuments. In peacetime the same people were quite indifferent to memorials to the great servants and leaders of the nation. But when their lives were threatened they became interested in the greatness in their past. They found hope in it.

So in your own life you find courage in remembering the minor monuments you fashioned in your past. The moment when you sacrificed your own desires on the altar of another's good becomes a source of strength. The days gone by when life seemed to be breaking out in Spring and you felt as if you were walking on air come flooding back to lift you above despair. The hour when you took disappointment in stride and pushed on to at least a little triumph becomes a resource.—Harold Blake Walker, *Specialty Salesman*

581

Is it enough to think today
Of all our brave, then put away
The thought until a year has sped?
Is this full honor for our dead?

Is it enough to sing a song
And deck a grave; and all year long
Forget the brave who died that we
Might keep our great land proud and
  free?

Full service needs a greater toll—
That we who live give heart and soul
To keep the land they died to save,
And be ourselves, in turn, the brave!
—Annette Wynne, "Memorial Day"

582

The brave die never, though they sleep
  in dust;
  Their courage nerves a thousand
    living men,
Who seize and carry on the sacred
  trust,
  And win their noble victories o'er
    again.
                    —Minot J. Savage

583

A monument's dimensions should be determined by the importance to civilization of the events commemorated. We are not here trying to carve an epic, portray a moonlight scene, or write a sonnet; neither are we dealing with mystery or tragedy, but rather with the constructive and the dramatic moments or crises in our amazing history. We are coolheadedly, clear-mindedly, setting down a few crucial, epochal facts regarding the accomplishments of the old world radicals who shook the shackles of oppression from their light feet and fled despotism to people a continent; who built an empire and rewrote the philosophy of freedom and compelled the world to accept its wiser, happier, forms of government.

We believe the dimensions of national heartbeats are greater than village impulses, greater than city demands, greater than state dreams or ambitions. Therefore we believe a nation's memorial should, like Washington, Jefferson, Lincoln, and Roosevelt, have a serenity, a nobility, a power that reflects the gods who inspired them. . . .

I want somewhere in America . . . a few feet of stone that bears witness

... of the great things we accomplished as a nation, placed so high it won't pay to pull it down for lesser purposes ... carved high, as close to heaven as we can. ... Then breathe a prayer that these records will endure until the wind and the rain alone shall wash them away.—Gutzon Borglum

CHILDREN'S DAY

584

How would you like to form a new club? I know you belong to a number of groups now, that you enjoy a great deal. The society that I am thinking of is a little different but I think you would enjoy being a member of it.

It is the Society of the Kindly Tongue. Most of your friends are doing the best they know or are able to do; and if only we spoke kindly to the best in them out of the best in us we would be and have a lot more and better friends.

We are all anxious to live and make the most of the life we live. So we might take the word "live" for a password.

When we think of words it reminds some of us about the spelling of them. And some of us who aren't such good spellers wish we lived way back before they had spelling rules and spelled a word just any way they liked. I suppose there is only one right way to spell our password "live" and yet when you were learning to spell, in some words you got just one letter wrong and sometimes that wrong word was in some way related to the word you were trying to spell.

Let's look at our password. If we should change just one letter in it what would happen? For instance, let's leave out the letter "v" and what do we have? The word "lie." That is wrong spelling which we really do do. For if we do not tell the truth we are "living" a "lie."

Now let's try it another way. Suppose we change the letter "i" to "o" and we have the word "love." If we live our life in the spirit of Jesus—of love —we are true members of the Society of the Kindly Tongue. Jesus would have spelled it that way if He had been a member of the Society, and if we think about it He looks as though He were the Founder of the Society. When we join how are we going to live up to our password? Spelling it "lie" or "love?"—E. Paul Hovey

585

Polly looked down at the writing pad on her lap and read over to herself what she had written: " 'Our Father, who art in heaven'—that means God up in the sky."

Polly frowned. She leaned back among the cushions and let her eyes travel up to the top branches of the tallest tree, up to the thick gray clouds. . . .

Where is heaven? wondered Polly. Where is God? And suddenly she crumpled up the paper on which she had written.

"Where is heaven?" Polly asked her father a few minutes later. He was busy at his workbench in the cellar. He stopped working and looked down at Polly.

"Heaven?" he said, "Well, some people think heaven is up in the sky."

"I know," said Polly.

"And some people think heaven is a place we go to when we die."

Polly nodded again. "Like grandmother," she said.

"Yes. But you know what I think?" went on father. "I believe heaven isn't only a place where people are with God *after* they die. We don't have to wait till we die to go to heaven. I think we can be in heaven right now."

"You mean, when we're happy?" asked Polly.

"It's more than being happy," said father. "When Jesus said 'Our Father, who art in heaven,' I think He meant that heaven is wherever God is."

"But that's everywhere," said Polly.

"Yes," said father, seriously. "That's everywhere."

"But," argued Polly, "there are lots of places where heaven isn't."

Father stood without answering for a moment. Then suddenly he reached up and turned off the light over the bench.

"Is the light still here, Polly?" he asked.

"No," said Polly.

"Isn't it?" asked father. He turned it on again.

"It *could* be here," said Polly. "But it wasn't."

"Exactly," said father. "Heaven could be ours, anywhere, everywhere. We are the ones who stop it and keep it from being here."

Polly looked puzzled.

"It's like this," her father said. "When all of us in this family remember how God wants us to live together, it's as though the light were on. Then we're thoughtful of each other, and helpful and unselfish. But when we forget and hurt each other, or some-one holds a grudge, then it is as though the light had gone out. . . ."

That night, just before she turned out her light, Polly pulled her pad and pencil to her. "Our Father, who art in heaven," she wrote. "That means heaven is wherever God is. And wherever people are loving God and trying to do what He wants them to, then that's heaven, right there."—Florence M. Taylor, *Thine Is the Glory*

586

Simple things are often most profound. The remarks of a five-year-old can be more significant than the deliberations of scholars. So the great commandment to love God and our neighbors as ourselves is simple, but how profound in its implications, its complications, and His expectations for our living!—Gilbert F. Close, Jr., *Today*

587

I've been finding out that mules are a lot like people or people are a lot like mules, in some respects. In a 1,660 mile trip by muleback in Brazil with a pack train, I've noticed that every mule in the "Tropa" wants to be first. Now some places it is possible for them to run and dispute for first place. . . . But there are places where orderly single file is absolutely necessary. . . . Imagine my surprise to see one especially alert mule, carrying a heavy cargo, start to pass another loaded pack mule going down a steep, narrow pass. If she had slipped over the edge, she would have fallen several hundred yards into the river below. How that mule managed to pass the other and to take the lead, I don't know, but she did it very cleverly. I thought: "One day that won't turn out so well." And it didn't.

We approached a steep climb on a short cut, where trees had been felled to open a path over a low, but abrupt, cliff. Arriving at the foot of the climb, the guide called to the same alert pack mule, which was in front, to halt, as he dismounted to take the trunks off the pack animals to carry them on his back up the steep bank. The mule stopped, but seeing out of the corner of her eye that the guide was coming, and not wanting man or beast in front of her, she started up the embankment. About halfway up, one of the trunks caught on a stump. The mule was thrown sideways, lost her footing, and went rolling down— trunks, pack saddle, and all—till she finally stopped at the foot of the hill, wedged against a tree. There we pulled her out, unhurt, but greatly surprised to find herself in last place after all. That should have been a lesson to her, but being a mule, I am afraid she won't learn too much by experience. . . . That's where people have the advantage.—Robert Lodwick, *Westminster Uniform Lesson Teacher*

588

The child is surrounded by so much authority, so much school, so much dignity, so much law, that it would have to break down under the weight of all these restraints if it were not saved from such a fate by meeting with a friend.—Dr. Wilhelm Stekel

589

It seems impossible that children should ever grow to be men, and drag the heavy artillery along the dusty road of life.—Henry W. Longfellow

590

I remember seeing a picture of an old man addressing a small boy. "How old are you?" "Well, if you go by what Mama says, I'm five. But if you go by the fun I've had, I'm 'most 100."— William Lyon Phelps

591

A child tells in the street what its father and mother say at home.—The Talmud

592

If your basic attitude is one of loving-kindness, you may yell at children and even cuff them around a bit without doing any real harm.—Dr. Smiley Blanton

593

They dwell and flourish in their own natures, preternaturally practical and crafty pygmies in the world of dull and tyrannous giants into which it has pleased God to call them.— Walter de la Mare

594

The real child does not confuse fact and fiction. He simply likes fiction. He acts it, because he cannot as yet write it or even read it; but he never allows his moral sanity to be clouded by it. To him no two things could possibly be more totally contrary than playing at robbers and stealing sweets. —G. K. Chesterton

595

I wonder if we who have grown up will ever know on this side of the grave how much we owe to children, who seem, but only seem, to owe us so much.—Bishop Francis C. Kelley

596

The only trouble with all the new theories about bringing up children is that it leaves the job just as hard as ever.—Heywood Broun

597

One of the best things about a very little child is that he never thanks you for doing things for him—he is so sure you wanted to.—Maurice Horspool

598

We of this self-conscious, incredulous generation sentimentalize our children, analyze our children, think we are endowed with a special capacity to sympathize and identify ourselves with children. And the result is that we are not more childlike, but our children are less childlike.—Francis Thompson

599

He who helps a child helps humanity with an immediateness which no other help given to a human creature in any other stage of life can possibly give again.—Phillips Brooks

600

We are always too busy for our children. We never give them the time or interest they deserve. We lavish gifts upon them; but the most precious gift—our personal association, which means so much to them—we give grudgingly and throw it away on those who care for it so little.—Mark Twain

601

All the little ones of our time are collectively the children of us adults of the time, and entitled to our general care.—Thomas Hardy

602

Happy the child that has for friend an old, sympathetic, encouraging mind, one eager to develop, slow to rebuke or discourage.—Arthur Brisbane

603

A fairly bright boy is far more intelligent and far better company than the average adult.—J. B. Haldane

604

While avoiding the extreme of over-strictness, father will avoid the other extreme of being too lenient.

Children want and need kind yet firm control for the sake of their own security. Although it sounds like a flat contradiction, children do not want to do everything that they want to do.

A little eight-year-old girl proved this to her parents when she came home from school with this complaint, "We had a substitute teacher today. She let us do just anything we wanted to do, and we didn't like her."

Children want good, firm, fair discipline and they thrive on it. Children who do not have it are unhappy and they become handicapped in their personalities.—Grant and Ruth Stoltzfus, "Father and His Family," *The Defender*

605

Art Linkletter asked a six-year-old boy, "What is your favorite Bible story?" The boy said, "The Three

Bears." Art then asked what the story taught. The boy replied, "That you should eat before you go out."—"House Party" program

606

One man told me: "I let my children act as my conscience. If they behave badly or are troubled, I inquire into myself. For I know that somehow I have failed them, something is not operating in me that should be. In some part of myself I am being irreligious without knowing it." I admired his concept greatly and asked him if it works. "It has never failed," he told me. "My young ones are an infallible guide on how I am relating to God at any given moment."

If you stop to think that statement over for a short while you may realize how deeply religious this man must be, how instinctive and intuitive a real belief in God is. For was it not Christ, Himself, who said: "And a little child shall lead them?"—James F. Fifield, Jr., *The Single Path*

607

The capacity for happiness is the most valuable trait parents should nurture in their children.—Charles Wertenbaker

608

The only moral lesson which is suited for a child—the most important lesson for every time of life—is this: "Never hurt anybody."—Rousseau

COMMENCEMENT

609

At commencement time a friend of some years standing said it was nostalgic to go to class reunions—that when you saw the many changes and realized that others saw the same in you, it was very depressing.

But suppose she saw no change, no sign of growth, no evidence of dreams fulfilled, no hint of heavy responsibility, no proofs of valuable service to humanity, no line of care for the next generation, no deep furrows where some, bolder than the rest, had attempted to help solve the world problems. Suppose the class were the same jolly, fun-loving, sports-minded individuals of college days, with little responsibility for others—that *would* be depressing.

It is hard to name the value of maturity. We might not call it beauty unless beauty of character, beauty of service, beauty of accomplishment. Perhaps charm would be a better word —the charm of maturity, of doing something worthwhile.

Thomas Moore, who has given us in verse the classical example of life-long devotion to "all those endearing young charms," is equally devoted to what he calls "the dear ruin," which we would prefer to call the charm of maturity.

Let us rejoice that there are changes, that there are values in maturity not shared by the charms of youth.—Ada Simpson Sherwood, *The Union Signal*

610

There is more adventure alive in the world today than there ever was, plenty of unexplored places. Adventure is there waiting for any man with the courage to go and find it. But you'll never discover it by looking at the calendar—and counting yourself to death.—Louis L'Amour

611

Your plan for work and happiness should be big, imaginative and daring. Strike out boldly for the things you honestly want more than anything else in the world. The mistake is to put your sights too low, not to raise them too high. The definite, faraway goal will supercharge your whole body and spirit; it will awaken your mind and creative imagination, and put meaning into otherwise lowly, step-by-step tasks you must go through in order to attain your final success.—Henry J. Kaiser

612

We live in an age of "popularity contests." Were such a contest to be held for certain words and the ideas they represent, my guess is that the word "love" would win hands down— although what it stood for would be as uncertain as most candidates for public favor! "Peace" would probably rank next; "happiness" would be a close third; "freedom" and "security" would race neck and neck even as they do in the minds of men; 'way down the list surely would be "obedience."

Yet "obedience" is essential to the implementation of faith, to the fulfillment of hope, to the experience of love, to the service of truth, to the possession of peace, to the bringing into being of unity, to the enjoyment of freedom. . . . Obedience is the essence of faith. "By faith Abraham when

he was called to go out . . . obeyed. . . ." The obedience of Abraham revealed the quality of his faith in God. God promises Abraham a land and a people, neither of which Abraham can come to possess save as he puts his faith in action—the promises are fulfilled in exact measure as Abraham obeys in faith. There is an implicit "authority" in every "covenant-relationship." If I proclaim my faith in the credit system, then that faith requires me to pay my bills. Lip service is worse than useless here; lip service without bill paying is a denial of faith. So it is in the parent-child relationship. No child ever develops a real faith in his father and mother apart from giving his parents obedience. The child will never come to know his parents to be trustworthy until he obeys them— not always understanding the reason "why"—because the proof the child wants lies on the other side of his obedience. His safety and his character alike depend upon his obedience in faith. . . . So it is with getting an education. The promised land of a cultivated mind and an understanding heart come only as the result of obedience—in going to school, in being taught, in an imposed self-discipline. . . . Obedience remains essential to faith because it is the bridge over which the soul journeys from faith to the experience which justifies faith. The sequence of life is faith, then obedience, then knowledge. Abraham went out in the first instance, "not knowing whither he went." Christ "learned obedience by the things which he suffered." Surely part of the redemptive suffering of Jesus Christ (humanly speaking) was His "not knowing" the ultimate character of the victory until

the dawn of a glorious Easter Day!—
Ganse Little, *Seminary Chimes*

613

Down the ages the capacity to antici-
pate and to discount bad ideas and
the capacity to sense in advance and
to appropriate good ideas, without
waiting for events to indicate their
badness or their goodness, has been
considered the supreme achievement
of man as a thinking animal. When
the Lord of ancient Israel was searching for the most withering rebuke and
the most devastating penalty he could
lay upon a recreant people, he asked
that they be robbed of the capacity
to see and to understand. "Make the
heart of this people fat," He cried,
"and make their ears heavy, and shut
their eyes; lest they see with their
eyes, and hear with their ears, and
understand with their heart, and be
healed."

From Isaiah to Bernard Shaw this
belief that insight and understanding
are the Godlike gifts has held . . .
in the Epilogue of *Saint Joan* is this
scene:

It was twenty-five years after the
burning of the Maid. The curtain
rises on the bed-chamber of King
Charles VII of France, who, at the
opening of the play, was the none-too-
bright Dauphin. The spirits of those
who played a part in the trial and
burning at the stake of Joan were
entering the King's chamber. Among
them was an old rector, formerly a
chaplain to the Cardinal of Winches-
ter, a little deaf and a little daft. He
had gone somewhat crazy from brooding over the burning of Joan, but
insisted that the sight of that burning
had saved him.

"Well, you see," he said, "I did a
very cruel thing once because I did
not know what cruelty was like. I
had not seen it, you know. That is
the great thing: you must see it. And
then you are redeemed and saved."

"Were not the sufferings of our
Lord Christ enough for you?" asked
the Bishop.

"No," said the old rector. "Oh no,
not at all. I had seen them in pictures,
and read of them in books, and been
greatly moved by them, as I thought.
But it was no use. It was not our
Lord that redeemed me, but a young
woman whom I saw recently actually
burnt to death. It was dreadful. But it
saved me. I have been a different man
ever since."

Poor old priest, driven astray in
his wits by the haunting memory of his
youthful inability to see what cruelty
is like without watching a maid burn
slowly to death at the hands of her
executioners, a man who had to wait
for events to educate his judgments!

The Bishop of Beauvais looked at
him pityingly and, with infinite pathos
in his voice, cried out, "Must then a
Christ perish in torment in every age
to save those that have no imagination?". . . The Godlike gifts of insight and understanding . . . will be
needed in the days ahead.—Glenn
Frank, "If the Young Can But See"

614

As the late Al Smith used to say,
"Let us look at the record." We may
start with Ralph Waldo Emerson. I
choose him not only because his name
is familiar to you but also because
he is a comfortable time away from
us. The sage of Concord lived over
a hundred years ago. Despite differ-

ences in our ages, he clearly ranks as a forefather, both to you and to me. Further, he was a philosopher who found honor in his own country, and in his own day and generation. His credentials as a spokesman are, therefore, well authenticated.

In 1837 appears this passage in his journal: "Society has played out its last stroke. It is checkmated. Young men have no hope. Adults stand like day laborers, idle in the streets. None calleth us to labor. The present generation is bankrupt of principles and hope, as of property."

Admittedly, that passage was written during an economic depression. That heightens its validity as evidence in our present inquiry. The point at issue is precisely whether in times of stress men of earlier days felt defeated and frustrated, or whether, on the other hand, they were buoyed amid a sea of troubles by an undaunted optimism. No one by any stretch of imagination would regard that entry as reflecting a serene faith in automatic progress. His word was dramatic: society, he asserted, is checkmated. Youth, he declared, are without hope.

Let us take another example—1844 —after that depression of which Emerson spoke was over. Henry H. Ellsworth, first United States Commissioner of Patents, was a respected and influential figure in his day, a fair choice as a spokesman for thoughtful men. He was aware of progress. "The advancement of the arts, from year to year, taxes our credulity, and seems to presage the arrival of that period when human improvement must end." That has not the hard, bitter pessimism that characterized Emerson's statement some years earlier, but it

has no buoyant expectation of a golden age toward which America was marching with confident stride. Indeed, it was seriously suggested that in a few years the patent office should be closed. Gadgets would be developed, a better mousetrap for instance, but the vital inventions would all have been discovered, and it would not be worthwhile to maintain a government agency to register the trivia that remained to be invented.—Henry M. Wriston, "Dawn Will Break," *Vital Speeches*

615

The smartest person is not the one quickest to see through a thing, but to see a thing through.—Adam Walters

616

How many ideas go unexplored because people lack the courage to fail? —Wilbur M. McFeely

617

The commencement speaker represents the continuation of a barbaric custom that has no basis in logic. If the spate of oratory that inundates our educational institutions during the month of June could be transformed into rain for Southern California, we should all be happily awash or waterlogged.—Samuel B. Gould

618

The challenge of the hour is one in which we face adversity for the first time in our history. We face a moral and spiritual adversity within our own borders, brought on by a general slackening of will, a general tendency to countenance cupidity and applaud cunning, a general distrust of intellectual pursuits and those who pursue them, each a general vagueness as to national purpose and resolve. We have learned to distrust the intangible, to fear the nonconformist, to worship the material.—Samuel B. Gould

619

To many, not just the colleges but the whole Western world has for some time seemed adrift with little sense of purposeful direction, lacking deeply held conviction, wandering along with no more stirring thought in the minds of most men than desire for diversion, personal comfort and safety.—Nathan M. Pusey

620

Violence is not only that of pistols and fists; that of the pen is more dangerous.—Japan's Premier, Nobusuke Kishi

621

Power is a dangerous thing to handle, even in religion.—Joseph R. Sizoo, *Preaching Unashamed*

622

He who raises his head above the heads of others will sooner or later be decapitated.

623

It's the hardest thing in the world to accept a pinch of success and leave it that way.—Marlon Brando, *Redbook*

624

What you do for yourself may start you up in the world. But from there on up, it's what you do for others.— Burton Hillis, *Better Homes & Gardens*

625

In the Pacific off Vancouver Island, there is a stretch of water known as "The Zone of Silence." Because this area is acoustically dead, no sound can penetrate it. And since no siren or bell warns ships of dangerous reefs, the ocean floor is studded with wrecks.

The world of ideas and events also has its "Zone of Silence." Here, too, everything is hushed, and unknown dangers lurk beneath the surface.— Advertisement for *The Reporter* Magazine

626

Abraham Lincoln is one of our greatest national heroes. We are constantly being reminded of his greatness. One fact that will continue to make the Lincoln story grow forever more important is his great perseverance and his rise through and over countless failures. He lost many more elections than he won. His whole life was besieged with tragedy. And death, which would seem to be the final great failure, has only accentuated his victories. Haven't you at one time or another heard a person say, "Be thankful for your failures"? Perhaps you thought, "That's fine for him to say, but he obviously doesn't know my problems.". . . One of the real keys to success is how we handle and overcome our failures. Each fall brings us one step nearer success. Thomas Edison failed ten thousand times. But he's famous for one great feat. We will not remember Edison for his failures, but if he had quit any one of the ten thousand times he failed, we would be years behind times today. . . . Lost battles do not lose a war, if our cause is just and our spirit strong.

The first three letters of "triumph" are t-r-i. If we do this, failures will have less and less effect on our attitude, and we will succeed. Show me a champion, and I'll show you a man who has failed more times than anyone in the race. But a champion thinks success, and he must have success. Defeat isn't bitter if you don't swallow it.—Ben K. O'Dell, "Success or Failure?," *Specialty Salesman*

627

We measure greatness by the distance between the dream and the failure. We all fail. None of us matches the dream.—William Faulkner

628

"The bigger your head gets son," my wise old dad used to warn me, "the easier it'll be to fill your shoes."—James J. O'Reilly, *Your Life*

629

Straight from the shoulder, may I tell you of the physical problems that confront your older brothers and sisters in college. There are many, but I shall mention only three that must be met head on and conquered or they will be the victors. We live in an alcoholic society. You must come to terms with that society. Alcohol is the nation's number one social problem. I hope your home, your school, your church have fortified you to meet the challenge of alcohol. Number two problem is the TV set. Our students call it the idiot box. You can waste your time watching trash put out for thirteen-year-olds. Killing time by watching TV twaddle is mental suicide. TV has flunked more college students than all the tough professors put together. And the third conflict you must come to terms with is the automobile. Do you want a car or do you want a career?—Lionel Crocker, *Vital Speeches*

630

Nothing is so hard that it does not yield to that which is harder.—Bernard, *On Consideration*

631

Mistakes happen so easily, why do you have to help them along?

632

In a lifetime everybody needs. Some get and some do not.—"Wagon Train"

633

In the earlier years of my life I studied the peculiarities of others. Lately I am studying my own.—Ed W. Howe

634

Life proceeds at an uneven pace, in jerks and spurts, like growing plants and children. It rushes headlong for a while and then it seems to stop. It is not unlike a river, tearing through a narrow channel over shoals and treacherous rocks, and then abruptly spreading out into a placid stream, ripples slowly on its way—or, trapped in an eddy near the shore, may actually flow backwards for a time.

It is good that there are eddies—periods in which there is nothing to remember, when the picture is blurred by the softness of the colors, when the sunshine is not bright and the shadows are not black—when nothing happens. But of course something is happening all the same, but so gently and persuasively that one is unaware of it. Life does not really stop, though now and again it rests upon its oars—preparing perhaps for fresh acceleration. —Martin Flavin, *Journey in the Dark*

635

All American universities should have a college of life in which students would learn to:

Express yourself—your best self. . . . I would plead for a new emphasis on a high psychiatry. I would prove . . . that the loss to personality development through suppression of the good urges in us has been vastly more damaging than has the inhibition of the bad.

Attach yourself—to a cause bigger than yourself. "What's in it for me?" has become a question so primary in our time that its virus is crippling our world and producing a generation of moral and spiritual pigmies.

Lose yourself—in someone other than yourself. Anyone preparing to make a life needs to know that when we concern ourselves with others, putting self into the background, some surprising imprisoned splendors come out—as surprising often to us as they are to others.—Clarence W. Hall

636

One of the things that gets us down is that we form distorted pictures of things that affect us. When a friend slights us, intentional or otherwise, we are in danger of considering all friends unworthy of our confidence. When we fail at some undertaking— singing a solo, driving a car, applying for a job—we often go home, and in a mental state approaching despair, assert, "I'm no good; I'll not try again.". . . Life is not made up of a single event, but a long series of occurrences. Failure today may be the preparation needed for tomorrow's effort. Rewards come from difficulties surmounted. No achievement is the apex of success. Always there are more mountains to climb and more precipices to get over. Don't lose life's perspective; keep things properly related. If you must be overwhelmed, let it be in an ocean not in a bathtub. . . . We may long for the good old days . . . and miss the challenge of this our day. There is no road to yesterday. Today is our opportunity, our responsibility. This is a frightening age because men hold not life in true perspective. We have looked at things and are confused, frightened. Take a look at God—supreme, just, holy, good. Nothing is too hard for Him. Out of the welter and maze and degradation of this generation, Christ is gathering a band . . . of people. . . .—Oliver G. Wilson, *The Wesleyan Methodist*

637

Speaking on a text from Romans, ". . . be not overcome of evil, but overcome evil with good," Yale President, Dr. A. Whitney Griswold, told the graduates: "If appeasing our enemies is not the answer, neither is hating them. . . . Somewhere between the extremes of appeasement and hate there is a place for courage and strength to express themselves in magnanimity and charity, and this is the place we must find." There are many reasons why, as Dr. Griswold says, hate is not the answer. One of them is as profound as it is obvious, and being both it is often overlooked: men do not hate unless they also fear. In fact, it is probable that men do not hate until they have first begun to fear. And fear, says the beloved disciple, "hath torment"—for the one who is afraid. Robert Graves has said:

Hate is a fear and fear is rot
That cankers root and fruit alike:
Fight cleanly, then, hate not, fear not.
Strike with no madness when you
    strike.

Hating is not only painful: it is inefficient. Professional soldiers have learned that ages ago. . . . It is not too soon for youth just leaving college to start thinking about it.—*Christian Science Monitor*

638

In the conditions of modern life the rule is absolute, the race which does not value trained intelligence is doomed. Not all your heroism, not all your social charm, not all your wit, not all your victories on land or at sea, can move back the finger of fate. Today we maintain ourselves. Tomorrow science will have moved forward yet one more step, and there will be no appeal from the judgment which will then be pronounced on the uneducated.—Alfred North Whitehead, *The Aims of Education*

639

There is a crying need for people who take open eyes and open minds out with them into the society which they will share and help to transform. —Adlai Stevenson

640

No amount of pay ever made a good soldier, a good teacher, a good artist, or a good workman.—John Ruskin

641

We have but to change the point of view and the greatest action looks mean.—William M. Thackeray

642

There are many paths to the top of a mountain, but the view is always the same.—Chinese proverb

643

The first great rule of life is to put up with things.—Baltasar Gracian

644

Thinking without learning makes one flighty, and learning without thinking is a disaster.—Confucius

645

The first proof of a well-ordered mind is to be able to pause and linger within itself.—Seneca

646

There are several indigenous American platitudes, none of which describes reality. Among these platitudes, now grown to the proportion of myths, are "Think"; "Does it sell flour?"; "It is later than you think"; and "The great wisdom of the world comes from taxi drivers." But the biggest hoax of all these platitudes is the cliché, "Anyone can be replaced."

If there were an ounce of truth in this statement, life would spin itself out pretty stupidly.

The psychological force that the statement creates is engendered among the great mass who look hopefully toward an equality of mediocrity, helplessness, lack of initiative, and stupidity. It is for this reason that men of talent are usually pacificists. A war culture is a great leveller and makes everyone more or less alike. The tremendous acceptance of Fascism, Nazism and Communism in our generation is partly explained by the fact that these systems are extensions of the war culture into the everyday milieu. These systems effectively eliminate intellectual competition and everyone thinks that it will be share and share alike. The decisions are made for the docile elsewhere and the fellow who never had an idea in his head becomes a captain.

Mediocrity breeds in a crisis. All too often politicians and demagogues perpetuate the crisis for the sole purpose of maintaining their jobs. And their power.

As far as we know, man is the only animal with a memory. No animal fights for its young with the scratching, tearing loyalty of the female Adirondack bobcat. But once the baby bobcat is weaned, the mother goes about her business and the new bobcat shifts for itself. It is forgotten.

Not with man. We remember, and because we remember we know that there are too many who can never be replaced and who will never be replaced—Mozart, Shakespeare, Beethoven, Thomas Jefferson. There are thousands of others. And, of course, there are your own father and your mother and your loved ones.—Harry L. Golden, *The Carolina Israelite*

647

The error of the past is the success of the future. A mistake is evidence that someone tried to do something. If we will only admit our mistakes, we will grow thereby.—*Megiddo Message*

648

Knowledge does not necessarily indicate wisdom. There is an unprecedented emphasis upon learning and accumulating knowledge in our day. Yet, in spite of all that, all sorts of organized crime and corruption continue to exist in our society and politics. Certainly this would not indicate wisdom. Knowledge which excludes God is not wisdom. Of all who do not reckon with the true God in their living, the Lord Himself says such a person is a fool. There must be respect and reverence for God in all of our plans and purposes in life . . . knowledge is never enough alone. Whatever knowledge you acquire must be applied to life so as to honor God. —Paul R. Daneker

649

In Joshua 14:8-13, Caleb asked for a mountain inhabited by giants, which he sought for his people. "Who wants a mountain?" Mountains are going for the asking. Do not be content with marbles—take the mountain. Too many people are seeking the easy way and every mountain is an inspiration. Hard work is the open door to greatness. The world needs faith, courage, and patience. There is a premium on men and women who will walk on the high road with God. The faith, courage and patience of Caleb were important, but the most important of his virtues was his faith that godliness is eternal. He dared to possess a mountain, which eventually became the Holy Land, because he believed.—John E. Besant

650

William Herndon, law partner of Abraham Lincoln said: "Mr. Lincoln read *less* and thought *more* than any man in his sphere in America."—*Time*

651

Millions of persons in this corrupt world still ask, *Is it right?* They are the ones who seldom get into the papers. We must admit, however, the frequency of the questions, *Can I get by with it?* and *Will it work?* . . . From kindergarten to college commencement many students work harder just to get by than they would have to work to learn. For the habit of learning makes learning easier as time goes on, while the habit of limiting learning to barely enough to get by breeds difficulties and complications that trap the student in his own net.

Mrs. Franklin D. Roosevelt, speaking to a ninth-grade English class, admonished them: "Don't try to just get by. The future will require all to develop ourselves to the best quality, the best capacity. Nobody can do this for you. Do your best, do it wherever you are, and you will find your influence will grow." Mrs. Roosevelt said the love of life is too strong for us to destroy the world, although we know how. But, she admitted, young people face a difficult as well as an exciting time. Then she flung her challenge: "I think we have an opportunity to do for the world what the early people who established America did for this country. If we can show that we are able to live here with our differences of race and religion, we can demonstrate that the world can live together too."

This gigantic job can never be accomplished on mere "get by" knowledge; it is going to demand the wisdom of the ages. And the beginning of wisdom is the realization that we do not learn a thing just to answer today's question or to pass next month's test. Whatever we actually learn can be used over and over all through life. When the question of getting by applies to education, it means doing the very least possible. . . . The home, where education really begins, must take the first step in proving that merely getting by doesn't work. The task of education is to help each individual find his own purpose in life and to inspire him with the feeling of responsibility necessary to accomplish that purpose, without sacrificing others on the way to his goal.—Emma Kidd Hulbert, "Getting By," *The Union Signal*

652

The graduate's royal road should be marked with a star, a song, a book, and love.—Frank F. Warren

653

Selfishness and anger become stumbling blocks, truth and faith become steppingstones. Look up to Christ that your lives may be steppingstones. It is your decision—no one else can make it for you.—Robert M. Chamness

654

In the free world the individual has the opportunity of exploring the frontiers of knowledge as far as his ability will carry him, or he can sit back and let the opportunity be seized by others. Each will find his own frontier in the search for truth. The choice is strictly up to the individual. There are more frontiers today than ever before, but this fact is meaningless if the individual has not the ability to get along with others. Not only in the scientific field but in all fields of endeavor, teamwork is essential.—Kenneth E. Hungerford

655

Your educational opportunities have provided values, standards and vision which have given a purpose to your life beyond vocational skills and social adjustment. To achieve the richest values and regards from the total college educational experience an individual must be expected to exhibit a real sense of personal responsibility for what is happening to him. While it is the obligation of institutions such as this to instill in their students the proper attitude toward growth and learning and creativity which will in turn shape our society, we are fully aware that the primary responsibility for learning and growth must rest with the individual.—Donald R. Theophilus

656

The hope of conquering failure and being completely successful in life is foremost in the hopes of the individuals of the world.—Linwood Laughy

657

Success is as obsolete as a buttonhook. Once the great American dream, it has slowly wheeled around to become the great American bugbear. The fashionable thing is to cry down success as neurotic in origin, selfish in pursuit, doomed to disappointment in the end. You can say these things openly in good company and be considered wise and prudent; but more often this attitude is not stated, it's insinuated. . . .

In reality there is no such thing as abstract success, there is only your individual success, or mine, or somebody else's. It is not necessary for a prime minister to be a cook, nor the other way around; but each can be successful. Success isn't a time or a substance waiting for us to catch up to it; it's what we do, day by day, minute by minute, with our capacities. It is the realization and utilization of capacities. If we don't use them, nobody else will—or can. . . .

People today sneer at success as "corny" but want security. Yet what is security except a limited kind of guaranteed success, an insurance against failure? . . . This dilute ambition for a subsistence success, cushioned against both triumph and adversity, overlooks the fact that maximum security is a term applied to prisons. It is not enough for free human beings to hold on to what they've got; something in ourselves impels us to make, produce, try, do. If we take the view that whatever falls on us like a coconut is justifiable and good but whatever we have to strive for is somehow unnatural, the human spirit is stillborn. Success isn't a monster that consumes our talents; it is the art of living with those talents— and living implies continuity, progression, evolution. The very word "succeed" means one thing following another. Success isn't a single peak of achievement, it's a whole mountain range. Each pinnacle scaled leads on to others, and that's precisely why it captivates the mind; it presents endless possibilities and the mind is at home in such a landscape. A vigorous mind craves activity, just as a vigorous body does; but both can be taught to be fearful, lazy, even to misfunction. . . .

Success is not a kind of overindulgence. It's an investment of the self in being fully what it is capable of becoming. The alternative is to go through life a pseudo-self, never completely realized, vaguely dissatisfied without enough wholeness even to know what's missing.

If the search for success is native to man, why are we dragging our feet? How does a campaign of anti-achievement get started? The philosopher Santayana gave one answer when he wrote, "Man has a prejudice against himself." The human creature has two natures: a longing for daring and a hunger for safety. We need: success tempered by awareness that devoid of human values it is cold, sterile, dead; and human values disciplined to understand that only hard work has brought man out from witchcraft and protozoic dark. . . .

Competition is a dirty word when it implies only getting ahead of others. But success is getting ahead of where we were yesterday. "Mediocre" means literally halfway up, middling. It doesn't mean I'm not as good as somebody else; it means I'm not as good

as I could be, and no amount of leveling off—whether up or down—can change that. There is still myself to reckon with. . . .

Success is the culmination of endeavor, whether it is directed toward achieving an atomic chain reaction or making a dress; digging up ancient cities or learning to ski. . .

Success isn't a perennial holiday, nor does it always look pretty. It is dedication to purpose and lifelong attention to that ideal. . . .

If success is fleeting, so is life in a sense; and that doesn't mean either one was never worth having. To say, "I don't care to succeed," is really to say, "I don't expect anything," which is avoiding defeat by being defeated before you start. Young people sometimes talk to me about their chances of becoming writers, and I have found a useful query to put is this: Have you any idea what the chances are against you? If the question depresses them, they had better choose another field. If they shrug it off, there may be a remote hope. If they pause, discuss it, and then maintain that, odds or no odds, they want to write, the whole world of possibility exists for them. . . .

Success is expectancy plus responsibility. It is much needed at all levels and it is intrinsic to success that it won't leave you at one level. If you succeed at whatever you're doing today, the reward will be more to do tomorrow. In success there is no place to stop and some people find this disquieting. But the definition of succeeding—one thing following the next —is a pretty good working definition of life, and even of infinity. The other way is to fold one's hands and give up and become something less than man.—Michael Drury, "Success, Good or Bad?," *Glamour*

658

It is time that the grand old colonial adage, "Beaten paths are for beaten men," be dusted off and placed before American youth. The fact is, the greater the responsibility and duty the less the security. After all, every man in a battle fleet knows exactly what he must do except the Admiral who must give the command. To him comes the agony of responsibility in constantly reviewing the calculated risks. Chance—and therefore insecurity —is the heavy price of command. Chance means challenge. A person who refuses the challenge of life has died without living.—James A. Farley, "What I Believe," *The Atlantic*

659

Symbolic terms of life:

. . . the treadmill, the sense that life has no meaning, a monotonous routine repetition;
. . . the saga, the exalting of distinctly human qualities and the heroism of the common life but bound essentially by the human horizon;
. . . the pilgrimage, wherein life is related not only to nature and to humanity but also to God, who transcends nature and humanity.—Frances Helen Mains, *YWCA Magazine*

660

We adhere, as though to a raft, to those ideas which represent our understanding.—John Kenneth Galbraith, *The Affluent Society*

661

Much of life lies through trackless wilderness, through forest and over mountain, into cloud and through darkness. Sometimes—not often—we catch glimpses of the Delectable Mountains. Sometimes our way lies through pleasant places, but not always, and we shall go astray if we test our path merely by its superficial pleasure.— John Ferguson, *Christian Faith for Today*

662

I warn of Stupidity, Timidity, Bad Luck and Bad Timing. All you have to do is avoid these four elements in your life and the rest is easy.—Eric Sevareid, *Saturday Evening Post*

663

There are two events over which we have little control, birth and death, but we can enjoy the interval between.— George Santayana

664

Habits actually control a life. The only way to become master of one's career is to form such habits as will guarantee the fulfillment of one's deepest wish. A good habit will fight a moral battle for the individual and win the victory before he is conscious that he has been in danger, while on the other hand, evil habits may carry him to defeat even when he tries desperately to hold his own.—Arlo Ayres Brown, *Problems of Christian Living*

665

During World War II drift bombs were dropped at sea to give a point from which the navigator of a plane could reckon his direction.

Amelia Earhart, famous woman flyer, was 300 miles off her course when last heard from on her fatal flight.

It was found that she had left her drift bombs in her hotel room, having taken them there for safekeeping the night before her departure. Forgetting them, she failed to have a mark from which to determine her course.

666

Moral education is impossible apart from the habitual vision of greatness. . . . We are at the threshold of a democratic age, and it remains to be determined whether the equality of man is to be realized on a high level or a low level. There was never a time in which it was more essential to hold before young people the vision of greatness.—Alfred North Whitehead

667

The major events that determine the future have already happened, and irrevocably.—Peter Drucker

668

With willing hand and open mind, the future will be greater than the most fantastic story you can ever write —you will always underrate it.— Charles Kettering

669

I cannot give you the formula for success, but I can give you the formula for failure—which is: Try to please everybody.—Herbert Bayard Swope

670

To fail is human and there is no assurance of victory to anyone. But what matters in the end is that the battle for good was fought whatever the dangers, and even in situations in which to worldly wisdom failure is certain, simply because conscience, the consciousness of one's duty, has said; "None the less—fight." Where there is no such will to fight, the will that thinks no longer of life and will hear nothing of "failure," there Satan .has definitely won.—Gerhard Ritter, "The German Resistance," *New Republic*

671

Overheard my neighbor's college-age boy whining around the house about his personal shortcomings, failures and frustrations. When his dad had enough of it, he gently but firmly said, "Son, all in the world you need is a swift kick in the seat of your can'ts."—Burton Hillis, *Better Homes & Gardens*

672

Life is a race and you have to press forward to the reward; few finally achieve the reward of life's race. You have to have a vital godliness, for the battle is bitter and the victory is to the strong. Life isn't a waltz through a bed of rose petals, it's a struggle that will call on every bit of manhood and womanhood in you to go onward and upward.—Roland Hegstad

673

How good it is to desire a little and to have a little more than enough.

674

The game of life is like a game of cards: the chief credit goes, not to the man who wins, but to the one who plays a poor hand well.—Josh Billings

675

Count on luck, expect it. But—be ready for it or it will not serve you.— James A. Walker

FLAG DAY

676

Everyone knows that the American flag is honored not for what it is— a bit of bunting—but for what it represents, yet many of us too often forget that it does not represent the same thing to all of us. To the veteran of the old Rainbow Division it symbolizes glory on the battlefield, but to the immigrant it is more apt to symbolize the security of peace; to the skeptic it represents the right to dissent, but to many others it represents the power of the majority; to the business leader it may represent the thing he calls "free enterprise," but to the investor it means protection against unbridled capitalism. If there were such a thing as the "American Way of Life," that is what the flag would represent to everybody, but there is no such thing. What we sometimes call the American way of life is really the sum of all the different ways in which Americans live and think and work and worship, not always compatibly but always under the same flag. There is only one thing we all have in common, and that is our diversity.

To honor the flag is considered a requirement of patriotism, but patriotism, again, is a hard thing to define. Is a Jehovah's Witness not patriotic if he refuses to salute the colors in a schoolyard because his religion tells him not to? Would he be a better patriot if he were to submit to restrictions upon his freedom of worship in disregard of the guarantees in the Constitution which that flag represents? Love of one's country probably is the best simple definition of the word patriotism, but when one attempts to discern what love of country is, he finds a multitude of answers and some of the answers conflict. It is partly love of place—of the earth, the sidewalks, trees and rivers of his country—and it is partly love of institutions—the social, political and economic foundations of his country's life. And to a greater or lesser degree, depending upon the individual, it is the love of the ideas which seem to him to form the moral basis of his country's laws and customs. All of these attachments in sum make up that thing we call patriotism. Isn't it strange, then, that some of those who have most fiercely attacked American institutions and national ideas have been our greatest patriots?

There is nothing holy about the American flag, or about the soil, the institutions and the ideas it represents. We are a nation under God, but so is every other country also a nation under God; it would be impossible to believe in one God and feel otherwise. Predominantly, we profess to be a nation of Christians and Jews. As such, we cannot claim in any undertaking that God is on the side of the United States and consider the claim a mark of patriotism. Patriotism is not religion, and those who make it so deny their highest obligations.

Patriotism is not nationalism, either, although a great many of us seem to think it is. Love of one's own country does not mean hatred of the rest of the world and its people. In our time, as a matter of fact, it is the internationalist who sees beyond the borders and thinks beyond the seas who serves his country well and is therefore the better patriot.

Patriotism does not consist of reverence for the flag, but the true patriot will honor the flag today and every day in many constructive ways.

How? Simply by honoring and defending those great, broad principles which the scrap of bunting represents. Has a man been unjustly convicted? The flag is honored when justice is done. Has somebody's freedom to worship been infringed? The flag is honored by the man who complains about it. Has a reputation been ruined in the hysteria of pseudo-patriotism? The flag is honored by the patriot who restores reason. Has a minority been unfairly treated? He honors the flag who risks his own comfort and position to defend the right.

There is, in other words, no easy way to honor the American flag, and there never has been. That is why it needs honoring on Flag Day.—L. H., *Lewiston* (Idaho) *Morning Tribune*

677

This flag means more than associations and reward. It is the symbol of our national unity, our national endeavor, our national aspiration. It tells you of the struggle for independence, of union preserved, of liberty and union one and inseparable, of the sacrifices of brave men and women to whom the ideals and honor of this nation have been dearer than life.

It means America first; it means an undivided allegiance. It means America united, strong and efficient, equal to her tasks. It means that you cannot be saved by the valor and devotion of your ancestors, that to each generation comes its patriotic duty; and that upon your willingness to sacrifice and endure as those before you have sacrificed and endured rests the national hope.

It speaks of equal rights; of the inspiration of free institutions exemplified and vindicated; of liberty under law intelligently conceived and impartially administered.

There is not a thread in it but scorns self-indulgence, weakness, and rapacity. It is eloquent of our community interests, outweighing all divergencies of opinion, and of our common destiny.—Charles Evans Hughes

678

A thoughtful mind, when it sees a nation's flag, sees not the flag, but the nation itself. And whatever may be its symbols, its insignia, he reads chiefly in the flag the government, the principles, the truths, the history, that belongs to the nation that sets it forth. The American flag has been a symbol of liberty and men rejoiced in it.

The stars upon it were like the bright morning stars of God, and the stripes upon it were beams of morning light. As at early dawn the stars shine forth even while it grows light and then as the sun advances the light breaks into banks and streaming lines of color, the glowing red and intense white striving together and ribbing the horizon with bars effulgent; so, on the American flag, stars and beams of many-colored light shine out together. And wherever this flag comes and men behold it they see in its sacred emblazonry no embattled castles or insignia of imperial authority; they see the symbols of light as in the banner of dawn.—Henry Ward Beecher

679

A patriotic American is a man who is not niggardly and selfish in the things that he enjoys that make for human liberty and the rights of man. He wants to share them with the whole world, and he is never so proud of the great flag under which he lives as when it comes to mean to other people as well as to himself a symbol of hope and liberty. I would be ashamed of that flag if it ever did anything outside America that we would not permit it to do inside America. —Woodrow Wilson

680

If yonder flag, hanging in graceful folds, could find expression, it might say to the world, "I had my birth in Philadelpiha; my stripes of red and white and field of blue and thirteen stars were first kissed by Pennsylvania sunlight. I was the first to reach the top of your tower on Independence Hall; I was first to point out from whence came the music of your Liberty Bell; I led the vanguard of the Continental Army from Valley Forge to Yorktown; I festooned the capitols of every state until, instead of thirteen, I display fifty; I first blushed in protest against slavery in my native Keystone State; the lilies of France once floating over Fort Duquesne were lowered to the lion of St. George floating over Fort Pitt, but both gave way to me when the wind from the free Alleghenies unfurled my colors above the waters of the Ohio, at the town of Pittsburgh; I led your conquering armies from Vera Cruz to the City of Mexico; I was trailed in the dust, but rose again to feel the loyal grasp of Lincoln and Grant, I was flown on the Normandy beaches and returned with MacArthur to the Philippines, I was raised at Iwo Jima, to give inspiration to the millions of men and women who loved the country and the cause for which I stood, and today I float in peace and in glory over every capital in this broad land, and I stand for liberty, for the noblest ambitions of humanity, and for peace through the world and for the dignity and honor and protection of all who love liberty and equality, and who claim the sheltering protection which I have always given."

681

That flag and I are twins. We cannot be parted in life or in death; so long as we can float we shall float together; if we must sink, we shall go down as one.—John Paul Jones

682

During the whole history of America our flag has been the flag of a *country*, not the personal standard of a king or of an emperor. It stands, and it has stood for us as the symbol of an abstract idea, not as the sign of the power of any ruler. It is, and it has been, a national flag, not a personal standard.

This is by no means the case with the flags of other and of older nations. —Edward S. Holden, *Our Country's Flag*

683

A flag is a symbol that stands for [a people and a nation] just as the cross stands for Christianity. How is it that the symbol of the cross really represents Christianity to our thoughts, not merely to our eyes? How is it that a flag, which is nothing more than a bit of colored cloth to our touch or to our sight, really comes to stand for the idea of our country?

Symbols stand close to man and interpret great ideas to him. They enable his feeble imagination to maintain a grasp on vast abstractions like the idea of religion, or of country. Two bits of stick crossed and held aloft have sustained the fainting heart of many a Christian martyr in the presence of the savage beasts of the arena; and the sight of his country's flag has nerved the arm of many a soldier in extremest stress and trial.

A true and complete history of the flags of the world—of national symbols —would be nothing less than a history of the aspirations of men and nations, and of the institutions that they have devised to obtain the object of their hopes and to preserve intact what they have conquered.—Edward S. Holden, *Our Country's Flag*

684

We will have no government standard but our own, and will accept no other flag than the glorious Stars and Stripes.—William McKinley

685

[The flag] is the banner of dawn. It means liberty; and the galley slave, the poor oppressed conscript, the down-trodden creature of foreign despotism, sees in the American flag that very promise and production of God: "The people which sat in darkness, saw a great light; and to them which sat in the region and shadow of death, light is sprung up."

In 1777, within a few days of one year after the Declaration of Independence, the Congress of the colonies in the confederated states assembled and ordained this glorious national flag which we now hold and defend, and advanced it full high before God and all men as the flag of liberty. It was no holiday flag gorgeously emblazoned for gayety or vanity. It was a solemn national symbol. . . .

Our flag carries American ideas, American history, and American feelings. Beginning with the colonies, and coming down to our time, in its sacred heraldry, in its glorious insignia, it had gathered and stored chiefly this supreme idea: *Divine right of liberty in man.* Every color means liberty; every thread means liberty; every form of star and beam or stripe of light means liberty; not lawlessness, not license; but organized, institutional liberty—liberty through law, and laws for liberty!

It is not a painted rag. It is a whole national history. It is the Constitution. It is the Government. It is the free people that stand in government on the Constitution.—Henry Ward Beecher

FATHER'S DAY

686

Father's Day, which is observed the third Sunday of June, was not the brain child of a group of disgruntled fathers who resented the attention given to mothers. According to the National Father's Day Committee, a volunteer organization of notables from every walk of life united to promote better father-child understanding. Father's Day was launched on June 19, 1910, three years before the first official Mother's Day.

Mrs. John Bruce Dodd of Spokane, Washington, suggested the idea to honor her father, William Smart, a veteran of the War between the States, who reared his six motherless children on an eastern Washington farm.

William Jennings Bryan was one of the first to give endorsement to Mrs. Dodd's plan, and James Whitcomb Riley wrote, "My heart is with you in this great work." In 1924, President Calvin Coolidge was the first Chief Executive to recommend national observance of Father's Day.

Father's Day is dedicated to the building of good citizenship at home and in the home.

687

Heavenly Father, I give thee thanks for my earthly father, who has been a type of Thee in His love and concern, and has helped to point me to Thee. I thank Thee for his unassuming virtues and integrity, and I ask help of Thee to follow in his footsteps. Help me to remember that the speeded-up techniques of this electronic, atomic age have by no means suspended the need for manly men, that in fact the need is increased. Help me, therefore, dear God, to respect my father and the good, tried ways in which he has walked, and to walk in them beside him. I thank Thee for my father and for our relationship. Bless him and my mother, and, if it be Thy will, give them length of days. In Thy name. Amen.—Grace Helen Davis, "A Prayer for Father's Day," *Forward*

688

I hope you'll have your father's smile,
 Your father's brow and eyes,
So I will always find him near,
 Clothed in an infant's guise.

And since you are a love made flesh,
 This is my constant prayer,
That he will search your face and find
 A little of me there.
—"A Mother's Song to a New Baby"

689

Every day is Father's Day in the household where one and all have come to know that family happiness is not alone in giving and getting but also in forgiving and forgetting . . . there are no hurts unshared, no blessings undivided . . . there come, impulsively and gladly, the little precious gifts; a touch of hands in passing, sweet evidence of trust unquestioned; a bit of praise unasked; a tender kiss at nighttime . . . and where, from hearts by love united, a prayer goes up at twilight: of gratitude for dreams come true, of thanks for one another.
—Burton Hillis, *Better Homes & Gardens*

690

Several TV programs depict father as being almost as dumb as his teen-age children consider him.

691

Fathers are the great gift-givers of the world.—Mrs. John Bruce Dodd, founder of Father's Day

692

When is a Father just "Dad?" H. C. Chatfield answers this question this way: If he's wealthy and prominent, and you stand in awe of him, call him "Father." If he sits in his shirt-sleeves and suspenders at ball games and picnics, call him "Pop." If he tills the land or labors in overalls, call him "Pa." If he wheels the baby carriage and carries bundles meekly, call him "Papa," with the accent on the first syllable. If he belongs to a literary circle and writes cultured papers, call him "Papa," with the accent on the last syllable. If, however, he makes a pal of you when you're good, and is too wise to let you pull the wool over his loving eyes when you're not; if, moreover, you're sure no one else you know has quite so fine a father, you may call him "Dad."

693

There is a growing solidarity within the American family; we can see clear signs of the domestication of husbands and fathers. They are becoming home-bound creatures who help.—Bishop Hazen G. Werner

694

Listen, son, I am saying this as you lie asleep, one little paw crumpled under your cheek and the blond curls stickily wet on your damp forehead. I have stolen into your room alone. Just a few minutes ago, as I sat reading my paper in the library, a stifling wave of remorse swept over me. Guiltily I came to your bedside.

These are the things I was thinking, son: I had been cross to you. I scolded you as you were dressing for school because you merely gave your face a dab with a towel. I took you to task for not cleaning your shoes. I called out angrily when you threw some of your things on the floor.

At breakfast I found fault, too. You spilled things. You gulped down your food. You put your elbows on the table. You spread butter too thick on your bread. And as you started off to play and I made for my train, you turned and waved a hand and called, "Goodby, Daddy!" and I frowned and said in reply, "Hold your shoulders back!"

Then it began all over again in the late afternoon. As I came up the road I spied you, down on your knees, playing marbles. There were holes in your stockings. I humiliated you before your boy friends by marching you ahead of me to the house. Stockings were expensive and if you had to buy them you would be more careful! Imagine that, son, from a father!

Do you remember, later, when I was reading in the library, how you came in, timidly, with a sort of hurt look in your eyes? When I glanced up over my paper, impatient at the interruption, you hesitated at the door. "What is it you want?" I snapped.

You said nothing, but ran across in one tempestuous plunge and threw your arms around my neck and kissed me, and your small arms tightened with an affection that God had set blooming in your heart and which even neglect could not wither. And then you were gone, pattering up the stairs.

Well, son, it was shortly afterward that my paper slipped from my hands and a terrible sickening fear came over me. What has habit been doing to me? The habit of finding fault, of reprimanding—this was my reward to you for being a boy. It was not that I did not love you; it was that I expected too much of youth. It was measuring you by the yardstick of my own years.

And there was so much that was good and fine and true in your character. The little heart of you was as big as the dawn itself over the wide hills. This was shown by your spontaneous impulse to rush in and kiss me good-night. Nothing else matters tonight, son. I have come to your bedside in the darkness, and I have knelt there, ashamed!

It is a feeble atonement; I know you would not understand these things if I told them to you during your waking hours. But tomorrow I will be a real daddy! I will chum with you and suffer when you suffer and laugh when you laugh. I will bite my tongue when impatient words come. I will keep saying as if it were a ritual, "He is nothing but a boy—a little boy!"

I am afraid I have visualized you as a man. Yet as I see you now, son, crumpled and weary in your cot, I see that you are still a baby. Yesterday you were in your mother's arms, your head on her shoulder. I have asked too much, too much.—W. Livingston Larned, *Westminster Adult Bible Class*

695

I do not know of a better shrine before which a father or mother may kneel or stand than that of a sleeping child. I do not know of a holier place, a temple where one is more likely to come into closer touch with all that is infinitely good, where one may come nearer to seeing and feeling God. From that shrine come matins of love and laughter, of trust and cheer to bless the new day; and before that shrine should fall our soft vespers, our grateful benedictions for the night. At the cot of a sleeping babe all man-made ranks and inequalities are ironed out, and all mankind kneels reverently before the living image of the Creator. To understand a child, to go back and grow up sympathetically with it, to hold its love and confidences, to be accepted by it without fear or restraint as a companion and playmate, is just about the greatest good fortune that can come to any man or woman in this world—and, perhaps, in any other world, for all we know.

And I am passing this confession along to the fathers who may be privileged to read it, and for the benefit of the little fellers—the growing, earth-blessing little Jimmies and Marys of this good world of ours.—Justice W. McEachren (an addition to W. L. Larned's "Father Forgets"), *Together*

696

The finest praise a son may know
. . . Is when his father's words bestow
. . . A high approval of the ways . . .
He acts and soulful pride displays
. . . In how his son has met the test
. . . And given of his very best . . .
I think that Jesus must have known
. . . Joy when God claimed Him as His own . . . And said He did His Father please . . . Does your father hear such words as these?—Julien C. Hyer, *Pasadena Star-News*

697

The father needs to take stock of himself, and like David of old, stop and think on his way. Fatherhood must be the greatest thing in the world since God reveals Himself in this highest and most sacred of all relationships. God has manifested Himself as supreme, as the Creator of all things, but the best of all is the revelation of Himself as Father, and as such He is the source and imparter of life.—R. S. Beal, *The Defender*

698

The head man of any family, like the head man of any business, holds importance only so long as he isn't unduly impressed with it.—Oren Arnold, *Bluebook*

699

Dad. . . . The Provider of the Household—The Head of the House —The Father of the Family—The Priest of the Home. Did you know you were all of these things, Dad? Or did you think you were just that man around the house?—*The Upper Room Press*

700

A certain young man had two sons. The younger of them said to his father: "Father, give me the portion of thy time and thy attention and thy companionship and thy counsel which falleth to me." So he divided unto them his living—in that he paid the boys' bills, and sent them to a select preparatory school, to dancing school, to college, and tried to believe that he was doing his full duty to his boys. Not many days after, the father gathered all his interests and aspirations and ambitions, and took his journey into a far country, into a land of stocks, bonds and securities and other things that do not interest a boy. There he wasted his precious opportunity of being a friend to his own son.

When he had spent the very best of his life and had gained money, but had failed to find satisfaction, there arose a mighty famine in his heart; and he began to be in want of sympathy and real companionship. He joined one of the clubs of that country, and they elected him chairman of the house committee, and president of the club and sent him to Congress. He would have satisfied himself with the husks that other men did eat, and no man gave unto him any real friendship. But when he came to himself he said: "How many of my acquaintances have boys whom they understand and who understand them, who talk about and associate with their boys and seem perfectly happy in the comradeship of their sons—and I perish here with heart-hunger? I will arise and go to my son—and will say unto him: 'Son, I have sinned against heaven and in thy sight; I am no more worthy to be called thy father. Make me as one of thy acquaintances.' " He arose and came to his son. But while he was yet afar off, his son saw him and was moved with astonishment, and instead of running and falling on his neck, he drew back and was ill at ease. The father said unto him: "Son, I have sinned against heaven and in thy sight; I am no more worthy to be called thy father. Forgive me now and let me be your friend."

But the son said: "Not so. I wish it were possible, but it is too late. There was a time when I wanted to know things, when I wanted companionship and counsel, but you were too busy. I received the information and received the companionship, but I got the wrong kind; and now, alas, I am a wreck in soul and body, and there is nothing you can do." It was too late.—Douglas D. Tiffany, *The Idaho Challenge*

701

Sometimes fathers try to hide their real feelings.

A soldier with a limp and a bandaged arm got off the coach. A small gray-haired woman ran toward him, followed by a big man who kept up with her by merely walking fast. She embraced the boy. The father moved closer and said, "I'm glad to see you, son." Not much more was said until they reached home and the boy was in the kitchen with his mother.

"You know, Mom, I get a belt out of Pa," he said. "Did you notice him at the station? No dramatics. No frog in his throat like a lot of men would have. 'Course, you understand, I know he likes me—I mean he probably loves me—but what I mean is you'll never catch Pop losing his head. Boy, he's got ice water in his veins. What a general he would have made!"

"Son," his mother said, "he loves you very much. I know."

"Sure, I know, too. Say, where is Pop?"

"He's outside. You better run in and see how we've fixed your room." The boy left, and she went out the back door. She knew where her husband would be. She looked through the crack of the woodshed door. He was on his knees, and the big chopping block was his altar.

"I want to thank you, God," the big man was saying. "I asked you, God, to give me a break and let him come out all right, though I knew then I didn't have any more right to ask than anybody else. But he's back now,

and he will be all right, and so I want to thank you, God. I want to thank you very much. Amen."

He rose slowly, and the woman returned to her kitchen. The boy came back saying: "The room looks swell. Say, where did Pop go?"

"He'll be right in," his mother said. "There was something he had to do." —Michael Griffin, in *This Week* Magazine

702

Dad, do you remember. . . .

The thrill of reeling in that six-pound bass? Or putting for that important eagle? Or hitting that perfect Texas leaguer? Or owning that first car? Or getting that unexpected promotion?

Well, such thrills are nothing to be compared with the deep satisfaction of teaching your child about God. It is strange many fathers leave this to the church school or even to the mother alone. When you take time to go fishing with your boy, or drive your daughter on an errand, an unexpected moment of closeness will come when you may talk together of the God in whom you believe.—"Dad," *The Upper Room*

703

Every father can teach Christian principles:

He teaches Kindness—by being thoughtful and gracious even at home.

He teaches Patience—by being gentle and understanding over and over.

He teaches Honesty—by keeping his promises to his family even when it costs.

He teaches Courage—by living unafraid, with faith, in all circumstances.

He teaches Justice—by being fair and dealing equally with everyone.

No one so effectively teaches the Bible truths as the parent who strives to live by its principles and to guide his children in its precepts.—"Dad," *The Upper Room*

INDEPENDENCE DAY

704

I am the Nation.

I was born on July 4, 1776, and the Declaration of Independence is my birth certificate. The bloodlines of the world run in my veins, because I offered freedom to the oppressed. I am many things, and many people. I am the Nation.

I am 180 million living souls—and the ghost of millions who have lived and died for me.

I am Nathan Hale and Paul Revere. I stood at Lexington and fired the shot heard around the world. I am Washington, Jefferson and Patrick Henry. I am John Paul Jones, the Green Mountain Boys, and Davy Crockett. I am Lee and Grant, and Abe Lincoln.

I remember the Alamo, the Maine and Pearl Harbor. When freedom called, I answered and stayed until it was over, over there. I left my heroic dead in Flanders Fields, on the rock of Corregidor, and on the bleak slopes of Korea.

I am the Brooklyn Bridge, the wheat lands of Kansas, and the granite hills of Vermont. I am the coal fields of the Virginias and Pennsylvania, the fertile lands of the West, the Golden Gate and the Grand Canyon. I am Independence Hall, the *Monitor* and the *Merrimac*.

I am big. I sprawl from the Atlantic into the Pacific, three million square miles throbbing with industry. I am more than five million farms. I am forest, field, mountain and desert. I am quiet villages—and cities that never sleep.

You can look at me and see Ben Franklin walking down the streets of Philadelphia with his bread loaf under his arm. You can see Betsy Ross with her needle. You can see the lights of Christmas, and hear the strains of Auld Lang Syne as the calendar turns.

I am Babe Ruth and the World Series. I am 169,000 schools and colleges, and 250,000 churches where my people worship God as they think best. I am a ballot dropped in a box, the roar of a crowd in a stadium, and the voice of a choir in a cathedral. I am an editorial in a newspaper, and a letter to a congressman.

I am Eli Whitney and Stephen Foster. I am Tom Edison, Albert Einstein and Billy Graham. I am Horace Greeley, Will Rogers, and the Wright brothers. I am George Washington Carver, Daniel Webster and Jonas Salk.

I am Longfellow, Harriet Beecher Stowe, Walt Whitman and Thomas Paine.

Yes, I am the Nation, and these are the things that I am. I was conceived in freedom and, God willing, in freedom I will spend the rest of my days.

May I possess always the integrity, the courage and the strength to keep myself unshackled, to remain a citadel of freedom and a beacon of hope to the world.

This is my wish, my goal, my prayer on July the 4th. . . .
—Advertisement of Norfolk and Western Railway, *Newsweek*

705

We must first have faith in God before we can enjoy the blessing of liberty, for God is the author of liberty. Our failure to fight for the preservation of that liberty is a crime, the punishment for which is servitude.— J. Howard Pew

706

We were born a nation dedicated to liberty, and we have become a nation dedicated to equality. Liberty and equality are diametric opposites. Where men are free, they will not be equal, and where men are equal, they are not free.

Our national purpose should be to practice and to preach one doctrine, and one doctrine only: the importance of the individual, his development through self-reliance, and his encouragement through rewards proportionate to his achievement.—Carleton Putnam, *Life*

707

We have lost sight of ultimates. Students today have no concept of the meaning of the phrase "all men are created equal." They have no understanding that our founding fathers were deadly serious when they said that they were founding this nation on belief in a Supreme Being to whom they appealed for the defense of these rights.

We seem now to be in a headlong flight in our scientific work from a belief in God. We do not seem to realize that this abandons goals and guarantees of liberty. Inalienable rights, after all, are absolute rights, and absolute rights can only be justified by an appeal to an absolute standard.—George F. Carter, *Life*

708

We have allowed the aspects of individuality and responsibility in the idea of freedom to be eroded away. We refer to security as freedom, while in fact the two ideas are in opposition to each other.

When we are secure in the satisfaction of our bodily needs, we are "free from want"; when we are secure from unbridled force we are "free from fear." This is not freedom.

Freedom connotes a right to pursue happiness in your own way. Freedom lives with nonconformity. Freedom recognizes no limits save the extent of your reach. Being free in a free society imposes the responsibility to recognize the freedom of others. This is the basis of a society that is not well-ordered, but divinely ordained.

History has proved that the creative mind, which can soar beyond the boundaries of existing knowledge, is nurtured in freedom.

Both profound insight and common sense lead inevitably to the conclusion that the world of the twenty-first century will need creative genius in its leadership. . . . Such leadership must come from the ranks of the free.

Americans will die for freedom. We must also heed the warning of our forefathers that it can be destroyed by slow attrition unless we are eternally vigilant to protect it.—Gov. William F. Quinn, of Hawaii, *Vital Speeches*

709

The men who won our independence and laid the foundations of the American nation were devoted patriots but they were, too, men of the world. They were children of the Enlightenment. Reason taught them that all men were brothers, that purely national distinctions were artificial, that there existed a great community of arts and letters and philosophy and science cutting across and transcending mere national boundaries. . . . The nationalism of the eighteenth century did not rest on a narrow base but on a broad one. It did not find nourishment in fear and suspicion but in faith and confidence. Perhaps one reason for the decline in statemanship is that we have hemmed our potential statesmen in, we have denied them tolerant and spacious ideas.—Henry Steel Commager, quoted by Paul Goodman in *Mademoiselle*

710

The United States was not always characterized by great power or prosperity. The continuous thread in our history has to do rather with a philosophy of government, with the way in which government is related to fundamental beliefs about the nature of man. The founders of the United States invented and adapted devices for applying certain beliefs to government, but they did not invent the beliefs themselves. These had been developed by the West for more than 2,000 years. They include what many peoples of the world today consider a peculiar way of relating the idea of order to the idea of freedom.

Men are bound, in a sense, by the order established by their Creator, "The laws of Nature and of Nature's God." But men are also free to search for meanings and applications of those laws and are even free to disregard them—at their peril. Out of this paradox of bound and free comes an idea of morality that applies to governments as well as to individuals. Government need not be weak, but it ought to be limited. It may not, ultimately, determine what is "right." It is, instead, held responsible for building and maintaining situations of order in which men are allowed to engage in the pursuit of happiness, meaning the free choice of right. Governments, like men, have the power to do what is wrong—and the people are responsible for what government does in their name. That moral bond is the basis of democracy, and it is symbolized in the Declaration of Independence by the phrase "sacred honor."—Max Ways, "The Confused Image America Presents," *Life*

711

Liberty is like a sharp knife. But it may be held in the hands of a doctor or the hands of a convict.

712

Courage is rare and admired. Throughout all history few have been the men who have stood forthrightly and without flinching upon their convictions. An ancient example is the three Hebrew children, Meshach, Shadrach and Abednego, who refused to worship the image that Nebuchadnezzar had set up. The penalty for failure to bow down and worship that image was death in a fiery furnace. When these men refused, they were hauled before the tyrant. Hear their ringing, defiant and uncompromising words: "Our God whom we serve is able to deliver us from the burning fiery furnace, and he will deliver us out of thine hand, O king. But if not, be it known unto thee, O King, that we will not serve thy gods, nor worship the golden image which thou hast set up" (Daniel 3:17,18).

These men defied a horrible death rather than compromise with their consciences. They spoke in unequivocal words whose meaning could not be misunderstood. They stand out in sharp contrast to the compromisers and equivocators who try to please everybody by endeavoring to be neutral or sympathetic with all points of view on every issue that arises.

Another excellent example of men of integrity, convictions and courage was that of the signers of the Declaration of Independence. They defied the strongest nation on earth. They did not even know they would be supported by a majority of their countrymen. They knew for certain that many of the colonists would not support them.

The Declaration of Independence was not vague or uncertain. It could not be explained away. It did not hint or equivocate. It was plain, unadulterated treason punishable by death. The men who signed it knew for a certainty that they were placing their property, their families and their lives in the gravest danger. Nevertheless, they walked boldly to the table and signed that great document. Their courage gave us our great country and all that it has meant to civilization and the well-being of mankind. No wonder men place a high value upon courage. It is not only rare. It is constructive. Without it there would be little advance in economics, science, government, culture, or art.

An untold number of men have paid with their lives because they had the courage of their convictions. To these men we owe most of the progress that has taken place in this world. A long line of martyrs has gone to the stake, the gallows, and the lions, rather than to sully their honor, renounce their God or stultify the truth as they saw it. It would be a good moral discipline for all of us to stand in our imagination with Martin Luther before the august council and see if we could find it in our hearts to say, "Here I stand, I can do no other, God help me"; or to face Nebuchadnezzar and the fiery furnace and defy him with the words "We will not." And coming closer home, how many of us would have risked all to sign our names to the immortal Declaration of Independence?—Howard E. Kershner, *Christian Economics*

713

If you cherish an undying love of civil and religious liberty, and mean to enjoy them yourselves, and to transmit them to your children and to your children's children, then you will be worthy descendants of those who landed from stormy seas on the Rock of Plymouth.—Daniel Webster

714

Liberty is the one thing you cannot have unless you are willing to give it to others.—William Allen White

715

It is by the goodness of God that in our country we have these three unspeakably precious things: freedom of speech, freedom of conscience—and the prudence never to practice either of them.—Mark Twain

716

The moment a nation ceases to rest heavily upon God it turns the hands of the clock back to savagery. Religion is the bulwark of freedom.—Joseph Sizoo, *On Guard*

717

Life must have meaning. But there can be no ultimate meaning in life without freedom. And freedom must be illusory, dangerous, in the absence of inner disciplines. The freedom that produces nothing more than means, power, and affluence can more easily wreck than fulfill a person or a society. Freedom, to be useful, must be disciplined and ordered by a believable and inner conviction that life has meaning, purpose, and aims far beyond the mere piling up of goods and services.

718

Our greatest strength in America is our freedom to say what we want, to laugh at and criticize ourselves. If we stop that, or think it's subversive, then we become like Russia, where they don't have freedom.—Mort Sahl

719

The greatest freedom man has is his freedom to discipline himself.—Bernard Baruch

720

The love of liberty is the love of others; the love of power is the love of ourselves.—William Hazlitt, *The Rotarian*

721

Freedom is not a gift which can be enjoyed save by those who show themselve worthy of it. In this world no privilege can be permanently appropriated by men who have not the power and the will successfully to assume the responsibility of using it aright. . . . Freedom thus conceived is a constructive force, which enables an intelligent and good man to do better things than he could do without it; which is in its essence the substitution of self-restraint for external restraint—the substitution of a form of restraint which promotes progress for the form which retards it. This is the right view to take of freedom; but it can only be taken if there is a full recognition of the close connection between liberty and responsibility in every domain of human thought and action.—Theodore Roosevelt

722

No one shall ever convince me that freedom can be destroyed by any power other than its own failure to live with freedom's own inspiring standards of conduct.—Henry P. Cain

723

The saint and the radical (and they are often one and the same) share a common, ironic destiny; honored by posterity, they are usually persecuted during their lifetimes. Joan of Arc was burned at the stake; Henry David Thoreau was imprisoned. We honor the saint and we honor the radical—dead; alive we find them too uncomfortable for our tribute.—"The Rights of Nonconformity," editoral in *Commonweal*

724

Liberty is the state in which a man is not subject to coercion by the arbitrary will of another or others.—F. A. Hayek, *Newsweek*

725

Dr. Tom Dooley tells of interviewing a citizen of Red China and hearing through the interpreter that the man was not free to choose when he ate, when he went to bed, when he went to work. The interpreter added, "He does not have the freedom of *when*."

726

True liberty shows itself to best advantage in protecting the rights of others, and especially of minorities.— Theodore Roosevelt

727

Freedom, which we usually think of as a desirable thing, becomes for most of us a burden at some times in our lives. Just the endless decisions which must be made become burdensome. When these decisions are complicated by uncertainty about what is right, or by conflicts between what we want to do and what we ought to do, most of us would like to escape from freedom.

We can see this very human tendency written large when a whole nation gives up its freedom to follow a dictator. We see it in our own lives when we "follow the crowd" rather than make our own choices and stand by them. We even see attempts to escape from freedom through religion when we look for rules or laws of the church which will make decisions for us. (This is very alluring, because then we have someone else to blame if things do not work out well.) Some of us try to escape freedom, when presented with a choice, by not choosing. But even this act is a choice and will affect us and our future.

All through history men have, like Job, complained about God and His ways with us. The chief complaint is often against the burden of freedom. We say, "Why didn't God make us in such a way that we couldn't do wrong? Then we'd have the kind of a world He and we want." Of course, God could have made us this way. But He didn't. Evidently something was more important to Him than our obedience, or a well-ordered world. Our faith tells us that this something was love—the free response of a free being. . . . We cannot escape the burden of freedom, for God created us free.—Cynthia Wedel, *The Glorious Liberty*

728

Guizot once asked James Russell Lowell, "How long do you think the American Republic will endure?" And Lowell replied, "So long as the ideas of its founding fathers continue to be dominant."—Edward L. R. Elson, *America's Spiritual Recovery*

729

If some great Power would agree to make me think always what is true and do what is right on condition of being turned into a sort of clock, I would instantly close with the bargain. The only freedom I care about is the freedom to do right; the freedom to do wrong I am ready to part with. —Thomas Henry Huxley

730

Almost all of us have had more freedom than we cared to use.—O. Meredith Wilson

731

Security, it would seem, comes in several brands. For example, in . . . prison people are very "secure," some of them for life. The government looks after their creature needs, fixes their teeth, feeds, clothes, boards them. The folks up there worry no more about making a living, or meeting other problems of life. Most people, fortunately, don't value total security that much. They want security, but they want freedom, too . . . people in prison won security, and lost their liberty, because they never learned a fundamental truth, namely, that real freedom, real liberty also carries certain obligations, one of which is responsibility. Without personal responsibility, and accountability, there can be no real freedom, no liberty, and precious little else we value in life. . . . Security, like character or personality, cannot be conferred on any man. It belongs to those who have earned it, by producing things people need. Any other kind is a delusion and a sham.—Vollie Tripp, "Security vs. Liberty"

732

Is life so dear or peace so sweet as to be purchased at the price of chains and slavery? Forbid. . . . —Patrick Henry

733

Liberty is the one thing you can't have unless you give it to others and democracy means not I am as good as you are, but rather you are as good as I am. As it is true that eternal vigilance is the price of liberty, so it is true that those who expect to reap the blessings of freedom must, like all men, undergo the fatigues of supporting it; and no man is worth his salt who is not ready at all times to risk his body, to risk his well-being, to risk his life, in a great cause. Liberty will not descend to the people, the people must raise themselves to liberty. It is a blessing that must be earned before it can be enjoyed. And our country has liberty without license, and authority without despotism. The sacred rights of mankind are not to be rummaged for among old parchments or rusty records. They are written as with a sunbeam in the whole volume of human destiny by the hand of divinity itself, and can never be erased or obscured by mortal power. Liberty lies in the hearts of men and women. When it dies there, no constitution, no law, no court can save it. The spirit of liberty is the spirit which seeks to understand the minds of other men and women. The spirit of liberty remembers that not even a sparrow falls to earth unheeded. The spirit of liberty is the spirit of Him who, nearly two thousand years ago, taught mankind that lesson it has never learned, but has never quite forgotten: that there may be a kingdom where the least shall be heard and considered side by side with the greatest.—Marian Anderson (based on William Allen White, Theodore Parker, Thomas Paine, Theodore Roosevelt, Alexander Hamilton, Benjamin Franklin, Cardinal Gibbons and Judge Learned Hand), presented on TV

734

The distinguishing feature of our American government system is the freedom of the individual; it is quite as important to prevent his being oppressed by many men as it is to save him from the tyranny of one.—Theodore Roosevelt

735

We are all familiar with the adage that tells us that the price of liberty is eternal vigilance. This is the minimum price . . . freedom has always been one of the most costly of man's wants. To him who is denied it, through involuntary servitude or any other device, it is a priceless objective. To him who enjoys it, it is a priceless possession, one whose original value does not depreciate with age or use. But between what we might call kinetic freedom and potential freedom, there is this difference; kinetic freedom, however valuable, is not an end in itself. Once we have won it, it is no longer the mere fact or condition of freedom, but the use to which we put it, that counts.

We may expand the four freedoms many times but we can find no room for such as freedom of idleness or freedom of ignorance. In this direction freedom soon loses itself in license. . . . Vigilance is not enough; it can serve tyrants as well as the defenders of freedom. In the service of freedom, it is imperative that we know what to be vigilant about. . . . The reason why vigilance . . . miscarried is plain. Much of it was uninformed vigilance; the watchful eye in the empty head . . . through the uncritical use of tactics it sometimes honored that enemy by imitation . . . and gave credence to the . . . doctrine . . . that the end justifies the means . . . by allowing itself to become committed to one enemy . . . freedom allowed other enemies . . . such as ignorance to gain ground. . . . Ignorance is the arch enemy of freedom . . . none of it need have happened, if vigilance had been properly informed.—Alfred Whitney Griswold, "Freedom and Education," *Commonweal*

736

A century that began with Lenin, Sun Yat-sen, Gandhi and Wilson was certain to be shaped by ideas. The struggle for the minds of men has now become sharp and clamorous. That struggle can and will be won by those nations east, south, north and west who genuinely subscribe to the four principles laid down at Bandung, and who are now prepared to work together to give those principles substance in world affairs . . . in the present day challenge of East to West and West to East. May we accept it together with the passionate conviction of free men determined to remain free and to make freedom meaningful.

As General Carlos Romulo said our success "will be measured not by what we do for ourselves but by what we do for the whole human community." "Is freedom fully achieved," asked Romulo, "when the national banner rises over the seat of government, the foreign ruler goes, the power passes into the hands of our new leaders? Is the struggle for national independence the struggle to substitute a local oligarchy for the foreign oligarchy?" Gandhi, years before, had said it differently, "Merely to replace the white sahibs with brown sahibs was to get rid of the tiger but to keep the tiger's nature."—Chester Bowles, *Vital Speeches*

737

Freedom has been defined as the opportunity for self-discipline. Should we persistently fail to discipline ourselves, eventually there will be increasing pressure on government to redress the failure. By that process freedom will step by step disappear. No subject on the domestic scene should more attract the concern of the friends of American working men and women and of free business enterprise than the forces . . . that threaten a steady depreciation of the value of our money. —Dwight D. Eisenhower

738

Freedom is nothing in the world but the opportunity for self-discipline. —Georges Clemenceau

739

The price of liberty is more than eternal vigilance. The price of liberty, like the price of everything else we prize, is vigilance translated into action, starting now. Not fearful and defensive hedging, but through an outward-looking, positive, joyous affirmation of our dynamic faith in the essential, eventual goodness of human nature. It is upon this divine spark within the human breast that the security of our lives and our treasures has always and always will depend.—Robert Spencer Carr

740

God grants liberty only to those who love it, and are always ready to guard it.—Daniel Webster

741

The true democratic process rests as much on the principle of respect for the fundamental rights of minorities as on that of majority rule.—George Dewey Clyde

742

Our love of freedom grew largely out of a sense of moral responsibility in politics, which finally reached all the way down to the people. It was conscious of how little, practically, could be accomplished through political power. The modern growth of freedom is less conscious of responsibility or of limits. Modern freedom, a true child of power, thinks of freedom *from* rather than freedom *toward*. What it wants to be free *from* is rival power or law, any kind of restraint.—Max Ways, "The Confused Image America Presents," *Life*

743

There are two kinds of freedom. The first is absence of restraint and compulsion. This, however, is only negative—freedom from something. The second is positive freedom, the power to choose and to perform, freedom *to* and *for* something. Knowledge of the truth helps to remove obstacles and to deliver from compulsion, but knowledge is the very essence of positive freedom, the power of choosing carefully and of being able to act wisely. When Jesus promised that His disciples should know the truth and that the truth should make them free, He was giving them the pledge of abundant life. He spent His years on earth *teaching* by precept and example. Then He sent forth His disciples with the commission to teach all nations.

The work of teaching remains of primary importance in the missionary enterprise.—Henry C. Sprinkle, Jr., *Prayer Manual for Week of Dedication, 1952*

744

The right to profess a heresy of any character, on any theme, is an essential element of a liberal society. The liberal stands ready to defend the honest heretic no matter what his views, against any attempt to curb him. It is enough that the heretic pays the price of unpopularity which he cannot avoid. In some respects each of us is a heretic, but a liberal society can impose no official orthodoxies of belief, disagreement with which entails loss of liberty or life.—Sidney Hook, *New York Times Magazine*

745

Conservatism is a body of ethical and social beliefs which suggests that we should apply the wisdom of the past to the present and future. Above all else the conservative is dedicated to preservation of the dignity of the individual and freedom for all men. —Senator Barry Goldwater, *Newsweek*

746

Satire, making fun of yourself, is the first sign of a sense of security, and the evidence of a strong nation.— Harry Golden, *The Carolina Israelite*

747

Not until right is founded upon reverence, will it be secure; not until duty is based upon love, will it be complete; not until liberty is based on eternal principles will it be full, equal, lofty and universal.—Henry Giles

748

No man in this world attains to freedom from any slavery except by entrance into some higher servitude. There is no such thing as an entirely free man conceivable. If there were one such being he would be lost in this great universe, all strung through as it is with obligations. It is not whether you are free or a servant, but whose servant you are, that is the question. It is not by striking off all allegiance, but by finding your true Lord and serving Him with a complete submission, that you can escape from slavery.—Phillips Brooks

749

No matter whose the lips that would speak, they must be free and ungagged. The community which dares not protect its humblest and most hated member in the free utterance of his opinion, no matter how false or hateful, is only a gang of slaves.—Wendell Phillips

750

All men who are truly free treat all other men as equally free.

751

Tyranny is no sweeter because it is the tyranny of the majority.

752

Rights beyond the rule of the majority are essential to liberty.

753

Having set our course for freedom, we must strike at everything inconsistent with it. That means the end of privilege, which may be defined as any right devoid of a correlative responsibility. Every right involves a duty; privilege enjoys the substance of a right but escapes the obligation that justifies it. Therefore privilege is antithetical to democracy, and if democracy survives, privilege ultimately proves self-defeating.—Henry M. Wriston, *Challenge to Freedom*

754

Toleration, however, is not true liberty when it is only a gracious concession made by the state to the individual. Gracious concessions are incompatible with liberty of religion which is not something that a state, or an absolutist church offers, but that which the citizen claims and the law protects. We have to distinguish, therefore, between "religious toleration" (something conceded) and "religious liberty" (something claimed), two notions which have characteristically been intermixed in the civil and religious contentions of Britain.—Cecil Northcott, *Religious Liberty*

755

In the judgment of the Constitution, some preventions are more evil than are the evils from which they would save us. And the First Amendment is a case in point. If that amendment means anything, it means that certain substantiative evils which, in principle, Congress has a right to prevent, must be endured if the only way of avoiding them is by the abridging of that freedom of speech upon which the entire structure of our free institutions rests.—Alexander Meiklejohn, *Free Speech and Its Relation to Self-Government*

756

Only if the religious forces have the courage and the intelligence to insist that America keep its purposes clean and clear will religious values be enabled to play an active role in the building of the new world.—Wendell Willkie

757

It is worth remembering that our nation had its greatest influence for good and also its greatest security during the last century, when we had little military strength and we were not wealthy enough to give much away.

Our greatness lay in producing exportable ideas.

We showed that men who "feared God and no man" could in freedom produce a spiritual and intellectual richness and material security such as the world had never seen before. We carried our ideas to others, not by force, but by our missionaries, educators, traders, and diplomats.

Our example caught the imagination of men everywhere. To them we were "Liberty enlightening the world," and under the impact of our example tyranny and oppression receded before a rising tide of true liberalism.

Our present task is to find modern ways whereby we can serve the world as did our forebears. We must think more in terms of what is the right thing to do and thus get into harmony with the powerful force of moral law. Religion teaches, and history confirms, that there does exist a moral law which is just as real as physical law.

Those who ignore or violate this moral law are doomed to ultimate failure, while constructive results come to those who conform to the moral law.

—John Foster Dulles, "Our Strength as a Nation," *Advance*

758

America must stay free, and use the force of her freedom and strength in the task of establishing a united world; she must work to that end without ceasing. We, as a nation, must lead the way as the Mount Rushmore four led us.

It is a long and difficult task that is set for us, but those four—and Borglum—believed its successful completion was possible. The world can live in perpetual peace; international relations can, and must, be founded on the simple, elemental teachings of Jesus Christ. But to achieve this, one powerful free nation must lead the way with unquestionable sincerity, fervor, and faith. . . .

Rushmore . . . says . . . in the calm, stern eyes of Washington, in the aspiring light of Jefferson's face, in the compassionate kindness of Lincoln, and in the outspoken candor of Teddy Roosevelt, that American politics and diplomacy have ventured far afield from the principles which these men laid down.—Robert J. Dean, *Living Granite*

759

May I remind you that the Constitution of the United States remains the greatest liberal instrument of government that the hand of man has ever written. Keep you government as your servant. Keep the miracle of America the most priceless heritage of future generations. All through our national history, ours has been the mission of freedom, of liberty, of tolerance, of peace and of the stern refusal to accept for ourselves the jealousies, bigotries, and the passions of the old world.—Senator Karl Mundt

760

True freedom must begin with an inward personal experience. St. Paul said, "You were called to be free." He does not say that freedom is handed to us unconditionally and is therefore something to be taken for granted or boasted about as one of our rights. When a man is called to any position in life, he must have some inner qualification or potential that fits him for it. Similarly with freedom, said John Milton: "Liberty is to be sought from within rather than from without." This means that we may live in a free democratic country, fortified by what we glibly call our rights, but may remain enslaved as long as we are inwardly absorbed by our possessions, our deep-seated prejudices and our untamed desires. A well-ordered political government is of no great advantage unless you and I have free personal government. Indeed the hardest sight on earth is Paul's picture of his own inner enslavement: "I can will what is right but I cannot do it . . . wretched man that I am!" Or the modern businessman who cried out in sheer exasperation, "What am I fighting? I'm fighting myself, I guess. This life which keeps me running after things that really don't matter. I'm right in the thick of thin things and I know it! That's the terror of it. But what can I do? I know better, and do the worse for it." . . . "All self-centeredness is slavery," says Werner Pelz. Freedom demands a showdown with self and in this tremendous encounter "self must go, and you and I must execute the sentence" (Albert E. Day). And the only way to do this is to be embraced by the will of God and to serve it as our highest ambition and desire. Jesus said, "If any man will come after me, let him deny himself and take up his cross and follow me." The worship of self must give way to the religion of the cross which means dying to self in order to live in freedom. Samuel Rutherfurd, the saintly Scot, knew that the price of freedom was to accept the way of the cross: "He that will take that crabbit tree and carry it cannily will yet find it to be such a burden as wings are to a bird and sails to a boat." This is a picture of true freedom. Are we big enough to pay for it?—Donald Macleod, "Big Enough for Freedom," *The Pulpit*

761

Freedom means mastery of our world. Fear and greed are common sources of bondage. We are afraid, beset by anxiety. We do not know what tomorrow will bring. We seem so helpless over against the forces that move on without apparent thought for men. And our inner freedom is destroyed by greed. We think that if we only had enough goods we should be free, happy, and without care. And so there comes the lust for money and slavery to the world of things. The world can enslave; it can never make us free.—Harris Franklin Rall, *The Christian Advocate*

762

God of our fathers, guide us aright! Help us as a nation to keep our poise true! If ever we needed the steadying power of optimistic vision and the support of confidence in a Divine Plan, it is now!

For many years there have come to our shores vast numbers of men of different nationalities—men oppressed and seeking liberty; men hungered and seeking food; men in ignorance seeking education for their children. They have settled here, and now call America home. Wonderfully Thou hast molded us into one people; out of the confusion of tongues has come a common language. All have given hand, brain, life, to make our Republic what it is!

And graciously Thou hast blessed us; but though our resources are vast and our influence wide, forbid that we boast of strength. Well do we know that it is on our righteousness we must stand. Faults we have; some glaring, some secret. Mistakes we have made. We are sorry. Help us by correcting them to prove worthy of the trust Thou hast bestowed on us.

There are among us many who are disheartened and in want. Let us recognize the responsibility we share as brothers in one great nation-family. So may we be generous with our substance toward all who are in distress, constant in our prayers for those who are dismayed by the buffets of life.

Be with those into whose hands the government is entrusted. Keep their minds clear, their judgment keen, their hearts brave, and make their sense of justice unerring. And may they feel, upholding them in the right, the unflinching loyalty of farmer, artisan, and businessman, the people of every calling who lovingly name our country Home!

All we have and all we are we owe to Thee. Conserve for splendid Christian living our manhood, strengthen for life's finest duties our womanhood, protect—as Thou dost hold it precious —our childhood; and help us to do our part conscientiously in the world's great work, filling our place nobly in Thy all-wise Plan—a nation which places its trust in God. Amen.—Irene Avery Judson, "A Prayer for Our Country," *P E O Record*

763

American life is a powerful solvent. It seems to neutralize every intellectual element, however tough and alien it may be, and to fuse it in the native good-will, complacency, thoughtlessness, and optimism.—George Santayana, *Character and Opinion in the United States*

764

Citizens by birth or choice of a common country, that country has the right to concentrate your affections. The name of American, which belongs to you, in your national capacity, must always exalt the just pride of patriotism.—George Washington, "Farewell Address"

765

The most important thing I have learned as a judge is that the heart and soul of America are sound and true and that the intuitive judgment of the ordinary man in the street is in the aggregate something infinitely penetrating and reliable.—Harold R. Medina

766

Intellectually I know that America is no better than any other country;

emotionally I know she is better than every other country.—Sinclair Lewis

767

. . . American liberty is a religion. It is a thing of the spirit. It is an aspiration on the part of people for not alone a free life but a better life, and so I say to you people of the world, I think I know the heart of the American people. I have lived among them; I know them well. And despite the occasional hesitation and doubts, the American people will reach out, will give their utmost to see that this precious thing we call liberty shall not disappear from the world, either in Europe, or in Asia or in America. —Wendell L. Willkie

768

We, in this great American Republic are, and should be, the guiding star for all the world; and if, united with the other nations related to us in spirit and aspirations, we do our full duty, progress will be assured, the peace of the world will be conserved, and we shall set an example that will be emulated all over the world.— Rudolph Blankenburg

769

I want an America which stands tall in the world, not by virtue of its military might, nor its material achievements, but because it is the incarnation of human liberty, of the rights and dignity of man, of justice and honor, and of faith in the wisdom and power of Almighty God.

I want an America so constant to its ideals and principles, so resolute in honoring its commitments, and so true to its full responsibilities for Free

World leadership that our friends throughout the world will never have reason to regret the trust they place in us.

I want an America whose citizens understand the true meaning of freedom. The freedom we cherish is not passive freedom from something—from want, or fear, or trouble, or injustice —but dynamic, indivisible freedom for something—freedom to work out our own destiny according to the pattern of our own minds, and the strength of our own dedication—freedom to help build a better world. America was created by men and women who valued opportunity more than security. They were eager to accept the risks of standing on their own feet in order to enjoy the full rewards of their own enterprise. The Declaration of Independence did not proclaim the rights to happiness, but only the right to the "pursuit" of happiness—the right to roll up our sleeves and work and fight for happiness.

I want an America ever ready to meet any challenge with high courage, moral resolution, and constancy of purpose.

I want an America in which may be heard echoed with conviction on countless tongues these noble words which still ring down the years with the sound of trumpets: "I have just begun to fight." "I only regret that I have but one life to lose for my country." "Give me liberty or give me death." "Eternal vigilance is the price of liberty." "Right makes might."

I want an America whose citizens recognize that the true greatness of our nation does not lie in its high standard of living, but rather in its high standard of life—the standard of life which has been handed down to us by generations of Americans who counted their worth not in terms of what they had but in terms of what they were. They were most concerned with the spiritual values they were able to pass on to posterity. It is freedom—and these spiritual values which are the sustaining power of freedom —which constitutes our most priceless heritage.

I want an America whose citizens have raised their eyes from the horizons of their daily tasks to face their present danger, and who understand the true meaning of the mortal struggle in which we are engaged—the struggle between our cherished ideals of freedom under God and the degrading philosophy of atheistic communism which seeks by every means to reduce humanity to the level of the beast.

I want an America made up of people who recognize that the security of the nation is the responsibility to each individual citizen—not just in some figurative sense, but in actual grim reality. In order to preserve our freedom, we must prove that a free people can, through voluntary effort, continue to accomplish even more than the regimented society. . . . We must not allow the desire for comfort or convenience in any aspect of life to assume greater influence in our plans and activities than the desire to protect our way of life faithfully and well. I want an America whose citizens possess good, old-fashioned moral courage. It is not enough to have convictions; one must have the courage to defend those convictions. The moral coward's motto is: "Don't stick your chin out." The courageous person—

the person who really counts for America—when convinced of the righteousness of a cause, stands firm, no matter what the cost. We must be a nation of tough-minded people with the hardy moral fiber that will not give an inch to the provocations of international gangsterism. We fervently hope that the growth and fruition of ideals in the hearts of men will bring the day when accepted standards of national morality will prevail in the communist world, but until that day dawns, our only salvation is to be ready and willing to confront force with force under any circumstances. We must recognize the necessity to stand without compromise on the principles which have made America great. We must develop the invincible spirit that will not falter in the face of the blackest threat, and a real capacity for moral indignation —one that will inspire us into action at any time or place where evil, injustice, or corruption appears in any form.

In short, I want an America in which every man and woman measures up to the high bench marks of character, courage, and dedication to the tenets of our American faith which were established so long ago by the founding fathers. In the final analysis, not only the very life of America and the perpetuation of our cherished free institutions, but also the liberty of all mankind, depend upon what we, individually, do, or fail to do, day-by-day, throughout our lives. In the words of the poet, written during one of the world's dark periods of tribulation:

Rejoice, whatever anguish rend your heart,

That God has given you for priceless dower,
To live in these great times and have your part
In freedom's crowning hour.
—Wilber M. Brucker, "The True Greatness of America," *Vital Speeches*

770

Liberty has never come from the government. Liberty has always come from the subjects of the government. The history of liberty is a history of resistance. The history of liberty is a history of the limitations of government power, not the increase of it.— Woodrow Wilson

LABOR DAY

771

Christians are responsible for freeing industrial relations of distrust, fear, suspicion, ignorance, pride, and hate. It is the responsibility of the church to create an atmosphere of good will, trust, and honesty. Industrial disputes do not arise primarily over wages, but rather over human relations. One of the difficulties is that the men who actually make the decisions and the men who actually do the work seldom see each other and come to have very distorted ideas about each other. Workers frequently think of top management as "bloated plutocrats," and boards of directors frequently think of workers as "lazy ignoramuses." Neither is true. In fact, in either case they are just men, and there really is very little difference between them as individuals in either intelligence or diligence or faithfulness.

Fear is probably the greatest cause of industrial disputes. Charles Stelzle once said, "The average workman is more afraid of being out of a job than he is of going to hell." He is afraid that the plant will cut down production and that he will be let off; or he is afraid that his foreman will take a dislike to him and find an excuse for discharging him. The foreman or superintendent is afraid that he will not please the manager and, therefore, will fail to be promoted and maybe even get demoted. The top executive is afraid that the board of directors will be dissatisfied with the profits he turns in and find someone else to take his place. The directors are afraid that the stockholders will elect another board, and the stockholders are afraid that the company won't make money and that no dividends will be coming in to them. This fear sets the worker against management. No other aspect of industry is more important than the assurance of steady work, by which the worker can be less afraid of unemployment and the owners less afraid of losing money.

Christians are not so sure, yet, that they know where their responsibility comes in eliminating fear, if it depends upon steady employment. Is it the business of the church to enter into economic discussion? But Christians can be fairly certain that it is their responsibility to help men to know one another so that they no longer distrust one another and so that they will have respect for one another as persons. The church can bring owners, managers, and workers together on one level, in the place of worship where "God is no respecter of persons." . . . We shall never have Christian men and women until we help them to be wholly Christian, which means bringing Christ to the factory. We shall never convert all men until we convert all of a man.—Marshal L. Scott, *The Christian and Social Action*

772

The first conclusion is that the causes of labor conflict and labor unrest are almost always to be found in concrete policies and in objective conditions, not in somebody's villainy. This is in sharp contrast to the popular belief that labor conflict and labor peace are primarily a matter of personalities, of the good boss, and the bad boss, or the good American worker and the bad and presumably un-American worker.—Peter F. Drucker

773

Not enough has been said or written about the act of joining a union as a step to maturity. In the economic and social sphere it can be compared to religious conversion in the sphere of spiritual life. It takes much the same kind of enlightenment to understand that collective aims and collective action are important, rather than the individual struggle to get ahead. Even though this enlightenment is forced upon workers by sheer economic considerations, it is a profound experience and discipline for wider participation in democracy.

Lack of this experience in the personal lives of most business leaders and a great number of the middle-class public goes far to account for disparities between what organized labor is now asking for in our common social economy and what organized industry seems to be seeking.—Carl Holderman

774

Everybody has to work for a living; let's make it as pleasant as possible.—G. D. Bradley

775

We spend millions on machine maintenance. The human being is more important than the machine.—An Alcoa foreman

776

Labor unions have a definite responsibility for the future welfare of democratic society. We cannot pass the buck to others. We have always been selfish in our interests as a class. We have always sought power without assuming responsibility. Now that we have power we must assume the responsibility of underwriting that power—guaranteeing to the public that this power shall be used wisely, and that we as an organization will be an asset, not a liability, to society.—*Causes of Industrial Peace*

777

The worker is not an abstraction, an "economic man," but a whole man with his hopes and fears, his customs and his ideals. It is the same man who is at work and at play, and in our thinking we must avoid building an artificial barrier between the different parts of the worker's life.—T. North Whitehead, *Labor's Relation to Church and Community*

778

Work is not merely a preparation for living; it is the very act of living.—T. North Whitehead, *Labor's Relation to Church and Community*

779

The man who commands effectively must have obeyed others in the past.—Employment Counselor

780

Have thy tools ready: God will find the work.—Charles Kingsley

781

Our generation has seen child labor controlled, the sweatshop outlawed, and starvation wages done away with to a large degree. But we have not always been able to answer satisfactorily the deeper questions of life. Why am I here? Of what use can my life and my work be? How can I discover what God wants me to do with my life? Young men and women with a lifetime of opportunity stretching out ahead are not the only persons to ask such questions. They perplex older men and women, too, who are concerned with finding in their work soul satisfaction as well as economic security for themselves and their families.

All kinds of motives for working present themselves. For some it is the money involved. The dollar sign is written large over the work they do. "How much will I get out of it?" is a normal question. But when this question takes first place, it pushes too many others into the background. For others the striving for "success" is all-important. Of course we want to succeed in life and in our work. Yet we need to be constantly on guard lest that goal be achieved at the cost of a selfish disposition. Some measures of fame, popularity, economic power, and social position are hollow indeed.

Some men and women are the human element of great working machines. While they contribute to only a portion of the whole product, they can say with pride, "I helped make this." Laborers in other walks of life are happy in knowing that their lives are usefully spent in service to their fellow men in furnishing the goods, the services, the instruction, the counsel that is needed. What a person does while he is on his job, how he uses what he earns, the rewards he seeks from his labor, and the view he holds of service to his community and his world are all expressions of his obedience to what God expects of him.

782

For the poor, the economic is spiritual.—M. Gandhi

783

I was early taught to work as well as play;
My life has been one long, happy holiday—
Full of work, and full of play—
I dropped the worry on the way—
And God was good to me every day.
    —John D. Rockefeller, Sr.

784

. . . the greatest of evils is idleness, that the poor are the victims, not of circumstances, but of their own idle, irregular, and wicked courses, that the truest charity is not to enervate them by relief, but to so reform their characters that relief may be unnecessary—such doctrines turned severity from a sin into a duty with the assurance that, if indulged, it would perpetuate the suffering it sought to allay.—R. H. Tawney

785

Archie Gordon, former labor attaché of the British Embassy, tells a story about two British scientists who were watching three construction workers wheeling loads of bricks. Two of the workers were pushing their wheelbarrows. The other was pulling his. Suspecting they had stumbled upon a discovery that could revolutionize the construction industry, the scientists called their staffs for a conference. No one could come up with an answer to the question why one of the workers pulled his wheelbarrow while the others pushed. Consultants from the labor ministry were called in. One suggested that the way to get the answer was to question the workers.

This was done and the puzzled worker was instructed to take his time in answering the question because what he had to say might be of great scientific importance.

"Well," said the worker. "I can tell you why I pull me barrow instead of pushing it. I can't stand the sight of the _____ thing."—Philadelphia *Inquirer*

786

Some of us carve out careers these days, and most of us work away at jobs. But who has a vocation? The word "vocation" means primarily "call." The Bible is full of stories of calls and the response to them. Underlying them all is the thought that man's life is not a series of random happenings. Some shaping idea went into our making, and what we are has a fulfillment to be found in some work that is waiting for us in this world.

Perhaps the best vocation story of all is that of our Lord's baptism and temptation, for in it the call of a vocation is realized with a completeness that can guide us toward a better understanding of our own place in life. "And straightway . . . he saw the heavens opened . . . there came a voice . . . I am well pleased." All of us are capable, in some small measure, of a moment like this in which we are given a true sense of the self that God created us to be. The world opens to us, and behind it we see the shaping power that makes it and us . . . writing a first "A" theme, or teaching . . . a first class . . . repairing a car, or painting a picture . . . the possibilities are almost endless—as many as there are individuals.

It is a moment of power, when we know what we can do and might be. We must pray for the vision and energy that will enable us to say Yes to our call as Jesus did to His. . . . But . . . what are we going to do with this newly felt power? . . . Any power is a temptation—it can be used wrongly. In the wilderness, Satan offers Jesus three ways of using His power. . . . Are we going to use our power first and foremost for physical comfort and personal gain . . . stones made bread? . . . Are we going to use our gifts to impress and overawe people—cast thyself . . . angels shall bear thee. . . . Are we going to worship power for its own sake? . . fall down and worship me. . . . If we answer a dull No to the call, we are left with nothing more than a job. . . . If we answer a thoughtless Yes to the temptation, we set ourselves out on the sharp path of careerism. We must say both the Yes and the No with all our hearts, as Jesus did, developing our possibilities to the fullest, and denying the wrong uses of them. In this balance lies all the difference between job or career—and a vocation.—Mary Morrison, "A Yes-and-No Answer," *The Episcopalian*

787

We must not only try to reach the average individual with understanding but we must make a frank, frontal approach to the leaders—the activists —in trades unions. Like trying to land a rocket on the moon and get it back again, this isn't going to be easy. Indeed, it might qualify as about the toughest educational job in the world today. . . . Eventually, there must be a meeting of minds and a realization of what is feasible if we are not to have the bitter aftermath of grievous economic error. Many . . . have had the experience of talking with some trade union officer under relaxed conditions . . . and of being told . . . that he is no extremist but he must go along with militancy because so-and-so is trying to get his job. Or that he recognizes the current demand is excessive but it is made necessary because the settlement with another union is used as a yardstick. . . . Some have even told . . . that they don't know where it is all going, but that they are powerless to change a trend. . . . One British Columbia labor leader likes to tell management men: "I know I ask for more than would be good for us to get. That's my job. Your job is to see that we *don't* get too much. I have to do my job well or lose it. You don't expect me to do *your* job, too, do you?" This glib shrugging off of joint responsibility satisfies the militant trade unionist as a policy . . . but it generally assumes that contract negotiations are a contest, a duel, even a form of civil conflict outside the laws of economics and, for that matter, outside of law—period. Howard T. Mitchell, *Vital Speeches*

788

The right to strike is too often interpreted as the right to win a strike. But if it is unthinkable that any strike should be broken, if no strike is to be lost, then every strike must be won. The tolerance of mass picketing gives enormous incentive to irresponsible strike-calling and to the wage-price spiral. Until our lawmakers face the implications of this, the labor problem will grow.—Henry Hazlitt, "Business Tides," *Newsweek*

789

One machine can do the work of fifty ordinary men. No machine can do the work of one extraordinary man. —Elbert Hubbard

790

Life is work, and everything you do is so much more experience. Sometimes you work for wages, sometimes not, but what does anybody make but a living? And whatever you have, you must either use or lose.—Henry Ford

791

Capital is a result of labor. And is used by labor to assist it in further production. Labor is the active and initial force and labor is therefore the employer of capital.—Henry George, *Progress and Poverty*

792

It's a big mistake for young men to look only for the glamor jobs. Anybody who is afraid to get his hands dirty isn't likely to go very far. The jobs that have the least glamor on the surface often afford you the opportunity to get the most know-how of the business you're in.—Alfred L. Hammell

793

Management is the marshaling of resources to get a job done.—M. E. Dimock

794

Not labor but leisure will be the great problem in the decades ahead. That prospect should be accepted as a God-given opportunity to add dimensions of enjoyment and grace to life. We have reason to foresee a fantastic rise in demand for and appreciation of the better, and perhaps the best, in art, music, and letters.—David Sarnoff, *Fortune*

795

Life is an unfinished series of wanting things. From the day we are born to the day we die, we want things we don't have. If we didn't, we wouldn't be normal human beings. We would have no reason to eat, work, or get married. All life is a struggle to satisfy more of our wants.—Percy L. Greaves, Jr., *The Freedman*

796

The right way to kill time is to work it to death.

797

The symbol for half the world is the man with the balancing rod. He is the symbol of much, perhaps most, of the world's struggle for a better life. He is ubiquitous in Asia, the spry, lithe, little man (or woman, for there is not much to choose here), traveling along the side of the road with the bamboo rod on his shoulder, balanced by its burdens before and behind.

Sometimes the burdens are great baskets of fruit, sometimes loads of fish, sometimes wood or gravel or sacks of cement. They are not light loads; most of us Western men could hardly lift them. Yet the burden bearers sashay down the road nimbly enough. Indeed the rod—the badge of their servitude—is a loved and cherished possession, and when the bearers stop for a drink or a breath or a sleep, they do not fail to rub their rod and staff with affectionate concern and no little pride.

I think it is this last which most affronts the American. That there should be such toil, and that a man must sometime needs be a pack animal, may be a harsh necessity. But that a man should seem even proud of the emblem of this toil—that a man should make a friend of this symbolic enemy of his manly dignity—this causes this American, at any rate, to think twice about work and what God thinks of it and what men should think of it and do about it.—Stephen F. Bayne, Jr., "Our World at Work," *The Episcopalian*

798

I long to accomplish a great and noble task, but it is my chief duty to accomplish humble tasks as though they were great and noble. The world is moved along, not only by the mighty shoves of its heroes, but also by the aggregate of the tiny pushes of each honest worker.—Helen Keller

799

Work is a divine provision for developing in us self-reliance, initiative, diligence, and other cardinal qualities. Work should be done in a spirit of gladness and gratitude. No day should be closed without the evidence of new and better achievements. Today belongs to us, with its opportunities for useful work and human helpfulness.

In every activity let us do our best, and let the world make its own appraisement. We are what we are. Explanations seldom explain. We can cultivate a fine sense of independence, based upon the assurance that we are loyal to a high standard of conduct. —*P E O Record*

800

Most people like hard work—particularly when they are paying for it.

801

Footprints in the sands of time were not made by sitting down.

802

A bank, said Bob Hope, is a place that will lend you money if you can prove that you don't need it. Similarly, a corporation prefers to offer a job to a man who already has one, or doesn't immediately need one. The company accepts you if you are already accepted. To obtain entry into paradise, in terms of employment, you should be in a state of grace.—Alan Harrington,

"The Personnel Interview," *The Atlantic*

803

Sins for the office worker:

Reading the paper, writing private letters, or dealing with other personal matters during office hours.
Preferring mediocrity to taking the slightest risk.
Believing oneself to be indispensable.
Questioning and criticizing every decision of the management.

Sins for the manager:

Considering authority as a privilege, not as an opportunity of service.
Believing that one can do the thinking for everybody.
Not having the courage to change one's mind.
Not backing up the staff to outsiders.
Not admitting error, or trying to shift responsibility for it on to others.
—"Sins of the Day," quoted in *Newsweek*

804

The wolf will hire himself out very cheaply as a shepherd.—Russian proverb

805

The threat of potential violence and intimidation through the device of the picket line are powerful factors—so powerful, in fact, that nowadays a firm rarely attempts any operations at all if a strike has been called, although it would be within its legal rights to do so. For all practical purposes the alternative of making a bargain with anyone other than the union has been removed. . . . Should a union be allowed to strangle a business economically by arranging with the teamsters to cut off its transportation? It seems to me we might as well ask if a physically stronger customer in a retail shop should be allowed to twist the arm of a shopkeeper in order to drive a better bargain with him.—Edward H. Chamberlin, *The Atlantic,* quoted in *Newsweek*

806

It would be good if something were done to curb the high salaries, the unlimited expense accounts, and the general plush living of so many of the top union leaders, whose moral position as champions of the erstwhile underdogs is seriously compromised by their own self-indulgence. This is not to argue that high union leadership should be restricted to ascetics, but that unionism needs to be a social movement with some idealism, not just the "union business" of which Hoffa speaks. Those who are in it just for the money should be encouraged to leave for fatter pay checks elsewhere. Despite the loss of their bargaining skill, unions in the long run are better off without officers who are concerned more with personal financial gain than with achieving social objectives. Without them it might be more possible for the merged movement, having joined the more conservative outlook of predominantly craft unions to the broader social vision of industrial unionism, to recapture something of the idealism on which the labor movement was built. —Joel Seidman, *New Republic*

807

To be idle and to be poor have always been reproaches, and therefore every man endeavors with his utmost care to hide his poverty from others, and his idleness from himself.—Samuel Johnson

808

Many of us spend half our time wishing for things we could have if we didn't spend half our time wishing.—Alexander Woollcott

809

You can't make dollars by depositing quarters in an easy chair.—Hans Harter

810

He who labors as he prays lifts his heart to God with his hands.—Bernard, *Ad Sororem*

811

The glare of man's technical accomplishment can blind him to the greater realities of existence, and perhaps this is what the traditional Christian admonition to beware of the world really means.

A complete reliance upon technology can do this: It can give a man a false sense of self-sufficiency. It can lead to a false idea of reality. It can lead to making a machine of society, and cogs and gears of men.

We see all of those effects clearly pronounced in those societies, the communist societies, which are candidly materialist . . . times are always desperate for the Christian conscience, but they are also and always glorious in their possibilities to glorify God.—James P. Mitchell, "The Condition of Modern Man," *Vital Speeches*

812

The church is still talking about lilies and sheep to a generation of men who work with coal and steel: it's about time it used a language the industrial worker can understand.—William Gowland, *Newsweek*

813

The best work is done by one who lives the best life he knows and shares.

814

It is not the goods which free enterprise has to offer—but the good.

Not a higher standard of living—but a higher standard of life.

Not the material rewards—but the spiritual blessings.

Not the prosperity—but the freedom.

Not the profits—but the opportunities.

Not the right to receive—but the privilege to serve.

It is a great story to tell. It is an even greater story to live and to practice. By working together . . . the free nations of this world will not only reap the blessings of a rewarding future . . . but through their united strength . . . will earn for their children . . . a just and lasting peace.—Henry J. Kaiser, Jr., "Partnership for a Free World," *Vital Speeches*

815

The hands of a true craftsman are guided by something wages alone cannot buy.

816

I don't think a man has a hobby when he's not working regularly. A hobby is to get a man away from his work.—Burr Tillstrom, *Newsweek*

817

We lose the faculty of effort unless we do some things we do not want to do.

818

Blessed is the man who is too busy to worry in the daytime and too sleepy to worry at night.

819

In the Bible the rank and file may find the highest expression of the dignity of labor and in its opening pages discover the blessing and satisfaction of creative work.

Every one of us has the creative desire to do something, to stand off and behold it when completed, to say with sincere satisfaction and a good countenance, "I have done that and, behold, it is good." From the time when we first put some blocks together to the time when we perform a difficult task or think through a difficult problem, if it has represented something creative, we have taken pride in our accomplishment and, behold, it is good.

The quest for the satisfaction of viewing something we have done, detached from us and our toil, of being able to say, "I did that and, behold, it is good," is a very normal thing. A man's work is not just the price he pays for the right to fill his stomach. In his work he expresses himself. It is the output of his creative energy and his main contribution to the common life of mankind. In the beautiful Creation story there is one musical refrain that answers each act, "and God saw that it was good." This is the timeless truth from the opening pages of the Scriptures that speaks to the rank and file of people everywhere. When we can say that of our work, our acts, our decisions, our life, we have reached the highest expressions of the dignity of labor.

In the Bible the rank and file may also discover the true fellowship of the New Testament—a fellowship that touches the springs of human individuality and helps produce in the common man the pride and joy of good work—a fellowship that helps restore the human solidarity that has been so largely destroyed by mass industrial society.—James Z. Nettinga, *The Bible Society Record*

820

The justification of strikers' picketing, expressed in terms of basic American rights, lies in the guarantees of free speech and of peaceable assembly. What is said or written in this exercise of free speech is governed by the same state laws on defamation that apply to all communication. What is done by such assembly is limited by federal law to peaceful persuasion and by the many state laws against force and violence. . . .

Picketing, as a means to advertise the existence of a dispute and the nature of the grievances, is certainly grounded in fundamental rights. It differs only in mechanics from the statements employers as well as unions often make by way of newspaper advertising. The further removed picketing gets from the principles in a dispute, however, the more may innocent bystanders be injured—not simply by violence but by by-products of the struggle.

In the name of fairness, therefore, this kind of picketing should be held even more strictly to "publicizing the dispute" and to "peaceful persuasion."
—*Christian Science Monitor*

821

An outward-looking people, Americans have characteristically externalized their criteria of happiness, seeking it in the conquest and improvement of their physical and social environment. In the process they have not virtually eliminated one of the chief drives behind all human effort, namely, the fear of poverty. And while making work easier they have also made it more irksome and less meaningful, at least in the more highly mechanized trades. What can substitute for the old drive against hunger and for work satisfaction? Although automation releases some people to more interesting jobs, it may be that an automated society still lacks the compulsion to excellence and "disinterested" achievement. And this may be the missing component of our continuing quest.
—Editorial in *Life*

822

If there is any one lesson from the results of the public opinion polls we have taken in the last ten or eleven years, in asking about labor unions, it would be this: that the public is getting a little fed up hearing labor union people just talk about their rights. The public would like to hear a little talk about the responsibilities of labor unions. If labor could judi-

ciously mix a little talk about the responsibilities of labor unions in with continued talk about the rights of labor, it would have a more receptive hearing on the part of the public. Fundamentally, the public is "proworker." It just happens to be a little bit suspicious of the contention that at this time the best way to help the worker is through the union labor movement, as now run. Despite that, the public would not do away with unions. It just wants to "fix them up."
—Elmo Roper, *Labor and Nation*

823

Self-interest must be harnessed for two reasons. It is too powerful and persistent to be simply suppressed or transmuted. . . . But self-interest must be allowed a certain free play for the . . . reason that there is no one in society good or wise enough finally to determine how the individual's capacities had best be used for the common good, or his labor rewarded, or the possibilities of useful toil, to which he may be prompted by his own initiative, be anticipated.—Reinhold Niebuhr

824

There are no absolutes in justice; our opinions color our decisions.—Marshal Scott

825

A union is a part of a movement. It is internally a political organization.
—C. R. Daugherty

826

It is a paradox that the most individualistic of peoples are now the people among whom the art of combination has reached its maximum.—James Bryce

827

There is no wealth but life—life with all its opportunities for joy, admiration, and knowledge. That nation is the richest which has the greatest number of healthy, happy human beings.—John Ruskin

828

We need a Christian conscience about work problems. Our grandfathers took this for granted. They knew that to be good Christians their religion went to work with them. To be right with God a man was under obligation to work faithfully, to develop his talents, to be careful with his materials, to be honest in what he made, and to be honest in what he sold. If he cheated or was lazy he knew that he was not a good Christian. But when we got into the factory system, we were confused. Neither the worker nor the manager owns the shop or the tools or the materials. Except for the top man, the manager does not make the real decisions, but does only what someone else tells him, and even the top management shakes off responsibility by saying that it is responsible for getting profits to the stockholders. The worker has little choice about his life. He must do what he is told to do. Individual Christians may frequently protest that much which happens is not right, but usually they feel helpless in the situation and accept the system as being nonmoral. Most men excuse what happens by saying, "Business is business, and religion isn't practical in business." The problem is to get a conscience about what we do in groups that is as strong and honest as the conscience we have long had as individuals. This is called a "social conscience." It does not mean that we give up individual responsibility to God, but it means that in those parts of life where the individual must go along with the group, we must make the group responsible to God. We can't long survive on the idea that a man must be a Christian where he eats and sleeps and plays but can be a pagan where he works. We can't give half our lives to God and hold half our lives in a world without God.—Marshal L. Scott, *The Christian and Social Action*

829

Labor legislation is necessary but it involves a risk. Legislation can be a short cut or escape from the voluntary discipline that should come from doing the right thing without a law. Thus, I believe, the need is for keeping the detailed restrictions on unfair practices to a minimum, and for putting the emphasis on responsible collective bargaining. We can pass laws to keep people from certain practices, but it takes more than a law to make a man or a group assume the righteousness that exceeds the law. The law can encourage such righteousness.—Marshal L. Scott

830

God in the board of director's meeting and the labor union would mean strikes in the discard.—Peter Marshall

831

The story of Moses is appropriate to Labor Sunday because he became the spokesman of working people who did not know how, and did not dare, to speak for themselves. This story is a warm and sympathetic account of a long strike, of a walk-out led by a valiant leader of labor. Notice that this story is told not from the viewpoint of the laborers themselves.

It is, furthermore, appropriate for Labor Sunday because the response that was made by Pharaoh to the labor leader, Moses, is the very same response that management has too often made to the spokesmen of labor . . . "You shall no longer give the people straw to make bricks, as heretofore; let them go and gather straw for themselves. But the number of bricks that they made heretofore you . . . shall by no means lessen. . . ."

When unions and management today find it hard to bargain in good faith, the reason is that too many have . . . memories. It was not until well into this twentieth century that management, taken as a whole, moved very far from this position taken by the Pharaoh. . . . Yet it has not all been conflict. There has been class rivalry and class conflict, but there have also been countless individual acts of tender sympathy and compassion. . . . When we stop talking in terms of labels and meet face to face, things begin to change. Labor and management are not irreconcilable opposites. They are people—fallible and capable.—John B. Warman, "We Three," *Pulpit Preaching*

832

When first we heard the Word of God, we thought it was a great tree under which we could sit and rest. Now we find it is a machete which we must pick up and go to work.—An African pastor

833

One person whose mind is up for a worthy cause can move multitudes.

834

Don't get the idea you are Atlas carrying the world on your shoulders. The world would go on even without you. Don't take yourself too seriously.

Tell yourself that you like your work. Then it will become a pleasure, not drudgery. Perhaps you do not need to change your job. Change yourself and your work will seem different.

Plan your work—work your plan. Lack of system produces that "I'm swamped" feeling.

Don't try to do everything at once. That is why time is spread out. Operate on that wise advice from the Bible, "This one thing I do."

Get a correct mental attitude, remembering that ease or difficulty in your work depends upon how you think about it. Think it's hard, and you will make it hard. Think it's easy and it will tend to become easy.

Become thoroughly proficient in your work. "Knowledge is power" (over your job). It is always easier to do a thing right.

Practice being relaxed. Easy always does it. Don't press or strain. Take it in your stride.

Discipline yourself not to put off until tomorrow what you can do today. Accumulations make the job harder than it should be. Don't drag yesterday's burdens along with you. Keep your work up to schedule.

At the start of every day pray about

your work. You will get some of your best ideas that way.

Take on the "unseen partner." It's surprising the load He will take off you. God is as much at home in offices, factories, shops, as in churches. He knows more about your business than you do. His help will make your work easier.—Norman Vincent Peale, *Advance*

835

Samuel Gompers (a Jew), the organizer and long president of the American Federation of Labor, once told Dr. John McDowell, who at his death was a secretary of the Board of National Missions: "You stick to your Jesus; He can do more for the laboring man than anyone else."

836

Eternal Father, Maker of heaven and earth, who didst reveal Thyself to mankind as the carpenter's Son, help us to see the value of all our labor. We acknowledge Thee as the creator of strength for labor, capital for industry, and the natural wealth of Thy creation waiting to bless mankind. Receive our gifts today in recognition of our dependence upon Thee and all of mankind as co-laborers in the work of Thy Kingdom. We pray in Christ's name. Amen.—Hurd Allyn Drake, "Labor Sunday Offertory Prayer," *Everyone*

WORLD-WIDE COMMUNION

837

The Christian fellowship is world-wide. The Gospel of Christ is for all mankind. The Spirit of the Lord is at work among "every people, tongue, and nation." So at communion-time followers of Christ may give thanks for an unbroken family of faith, remembering their Lord at His Table in every part of the earth.

The Sun that bids us rest is waking
Our brethren 'neath the western sky,
And hour by hour fresh lips are making
Thy wondrous doings heard on high.

The first Sunday of October is World-wide Communion Day. Since its inception in 1936, the observance has grown in spiritual significance.

In the winter of 1935 a group of ministers met to study the spiritual needs and possibilities . . . in depression days. They were Raymon Kistler, Charles T. Leber, and Arthur H. Limouze. In the Lord's Supper they saw a great opportunity to unite the membership in dedication to the Lord Jesus Christ . . . they suggested that all Presbyterian churches celebrate one special Lord's Supper each year . . . and asked all foreign missionaries and their congregations to take part. . . .

The Federal Council of the Churches of Christ in America recommended World-wide Communion Sunday to its constituent communions in the fall of 1940.

The wider extension of the Day was developed under the World Council of Churches, which is furthering World-wide Communion Day throughout Protestantism all over the world. . . .

We remember all in our prayers as we come to the Lord's Table, that in the goodness of God and the greatness of His redeeming love, we all may sense our unity in Him who is our peace, even Christ our Saviour.

So be it, Lord; Thy throne shall never,
Like earth's proud empires, pass away;
But stand, and rule, and grow forever,
Till all Thy creatures own Thy sway.
—Marvin C. Wilbur. Department of Stewardship and Promotion, The United Presbyterian Church in the U. S. A.

838

Communion—collection—fellowship—friendship—are all from the same word.

839

I am the Lord's Supper.

I am the memorial celebration of the life and death of Jesus Christ.

I am the symbol of the full meaning of Christ for each individual and for his church.

I am social fellowship made sacred by a fresh appreciation of its most spiritual bond.

I am the means whereby gratitude for and confidence in Jesus Christ are renewed.

I am a rewarding communion with God.

I am Christ pleading that love and harmony should characterize all social relationships.

I re-invigorate aspiration that may have become weakened with too frequent and too intimate contact with the material and human world.

I am a period of quiet contemplation of the meaning of the cross in human experience.

I am a source of strength that is adequate for meeting the losses, the injuries, the thwarted purposes, the unfilled hopes, and the frustrated efforts of life.

I am a challenge to repent of all sin and to lead a life of holiness.

I am an opportunity for meditation wherein personality invoices are made.

I am a service of worship that makes immediately available the grace of God.

I am a vivid reminder of the fearfully destructive power of sin.

I bring to the minds of His followers the costly love of Jesus Christ for all who need a Saviour and the pledge of His completed work.
—Norman E. Richardson, *Central Truths of the Christian Youth Movement*

840

The Lord's Supper was not originated by any man or group of men. It was instituted by Jesus Christ Himself; hence it is of divine origin. As such it is supreme in range and power of influence among all the commemorative events of human history.

Our Lord broke the bread in order that it might be distributed. Each disciple received an equal part of the same loaf. This signified the oneness of their faith and their *equality* in His love. The broken bread and the shared wine betokened that His body would be wounded and His blood shed for the remission of the sins of erring men all over the world. The occasion was a forecast of Calvary.

Whenever and wherever believers partake of the consecrated elements, they bear witness to their faith in the sacrificial, atoning death of God's "only begotten Son." They also bear witness to the transforming power of God's grace in their own lives. Each and all, alike, by this simple act, draw near to Infinite Love and feel an inner compulsion to devote their lives more fervently than ever before to the service of the Saviour's name.

841

True communion never ends with the benediction. To "remember" must be to serve—it was after the Upper Room that Jesus gave the great Commission to His disciples, and His promise to be with them always.—Inez Moser, *Remember*

842

Here I confess my sins and find forgiveness, cleansing, and restoration as I participate in the body and blood of Christ.

Here I come with a "hunger and thirst for righteousness" and find the "goodness of God."

Here I come with my burdens and find them lightened as I am yoked with Him.

Here I come with my sorrows and find the consolation of the One who, though "a man of sorrows, and acquainted with grief," yet brought the assurance of victory over sin and the grave.

Here I come with my doubts and find assurance through Him who is "the way, and the truth, and the life."

Here I come with my hopes for a better world and hear His commission to spread the gospel to all the world and His promise, "Lo, I am with you always."—Inez Moser, *Remember*

843

What He did, at supper seated,
  Christ ordained to be repeated,
    His memorial ne'er to cease;
      His command for guidance taking,
        Bread and wine we hallow, making
          Thus our sacrifice of peace.
Behold, the table now is spread,
  The cup of Love doth overflow.
Let the Bread, life-giving, living,
  Be our theme of glad thanksgiving,
    New indeed before thee set;
      As of old the Lord provided
        When the twelve, divinely guided,
          At the holy table met.
            —Thomas Aquinas

844

Lord, this is Thy feast,
Prepared by Thy longing,
Spread at Thy command,
Attended at Thine invitation.

845

Every time we sit at the Lord's table we profess our unity, and we confess our sin in breaking that unity and determine to be reconciled one to another.—Franklin B. Gillespie, *Forward*

846

It is in the mystery of broken things that man finds the answer in his search to make himself whole. In the beginning grain was broken that men might have flour. This made for food and the resultant bread is often called "the staff of life."

The breaking of bread is a symbol of hospitality, because unless bread is broken we cannot share it with our brother. And until we break bread together we eat it in loneliness.

The breaking of the bread in the sacrament represents the breaking of the body of Christ that it might be a healing for the broken spirit of mankind.

A man's willfulness and selfishness must be broken before he can follow God's way.—Earl Lake, "The Healing of Things Broken"

847

This Sunday, Christians throughout the world will come to the Lord's table. The bread will be broken and the cup will be shared with the faithful. We Protestants do not believe that anything magical occurs as we take the holy sacrament. But we do affirm that by faith we "feed upon Christ." In this sacrament, He enters into us, and we are made partakers of His life. When John Calvin, with his logical, legally trained mind, came to the discussion of the sacrament, he bowed in humility before its wonder and its power. He wrote too of its mystery. While logic could not explain it, Calvin knew, as do all Christians, that the Saviour is known here and that we are made one with Him. The Christian person communes with Christ in a sure, though mysterious, way, in the sacred communion. And we have fellowship with Christians around the world.—Lowell Russell Ditzen, *Today*

848

It is a solemnizing thought that all over the world . . . Christians of every denomination are partaking of the Lord's Supper. The bread and the wine are being shared by a great multitude which no man can number.

At some time in the past every one of these millions of believers stepped out from the crowd and declared himself to be a disciple of Christ. He promised that with God's grace he would put sin behind him and would live as best he could the life that is "hid with Christ in God."

"Except your righteousness shall exceed the righteousness of the scribes and Pharisees, ye shall in no wise enter into the kingdom of heaven . . ." is an excellent meditation on World-wide Communion Sunday. Today of all days we should fearlessly examine ourselves, to see whether we are very much different from those who do not know our Master and have never sat at the table of our Lord.—George William Brown, *Today*

849

It is noteworthy that Jesus began His ministry with a sacrament and ended it with a sacrament. The sacrament at the beginning of His ministry was that of separation and consecration at baptism. With the second sacrament, we have the fellowship of the Lord's Supper. Both were into His death; yet not as something that had power over Him, but as a death that has been followed by the resurrection. For, if in baptism we are buried with Him, we also rise with Him; and if in the Holy Supper we remember His death, it is the death of Him who rose again. There is a wealth of meaning in a statement made, I believe, by one of the most influential theologians, Karl Barth, that the Christian does not live between birth and death, but between baptism and the Lord's Supper. In baptism, the Christian is born. His old self is buried and the new self emerges. Whether in the case of infants or adults, baptism signifies this more as a promise than as an actually fulfilled fact. The direction is indicated rather than the arrival. When baptized children grow to be old enough to decide for themselves that they wish to keep moving in that direction, in many churches they confirm their baptismal vows. In the Lord's Supper there is fellowship with the Giver of new life. It points forward to that Great Supper at the final consummation of His Kingdom. As Jesus' ministry began and closed with a sacrament, so the Christian's life is spanned between these two events, baptism and the Lord's Supper.—Friedrich Rest, *Pulpit Preaching*

850

The account of the Last Supper in Luke 22 surprisingly includes a very unseemly wrangle among the disciples about personal prestige. This at least is realistic. Anyone who knows the life of a Christian congregation intimately knows that persons breed organizational problems and that these problems do not stop short of the communion service . . . it is just there, at the communion service, that we find a means to settle them.

Christ reminds His disciples that the whole significance of what is going on in the Upper Room centers on His role as God's Suffering Servant. They are to share His body and blood, that is, accept what He is about to do for them on the cross. This means, at the very least, that they must act as servants toward one another. They must bear each other's burdens as Christ bears the burdens of the world.—Lewis S. Mudge, *The Servant Lord and His Servant People*

851

The scene in the Upper Room brings us face to face with the bread and the cup; but also with the towel and the basin. The latter are the tools of service; the former the source of strength. We give ourselves away in scrubbing and in service; in receiving the bread and the cup we grow tall enough to stoop and bend over in the act of service.—Donald Roberts

852

Perhaps at first they talked of little
    things
At supper time that evening in the
    spring—
The Upper Room was dim with can-
    dle shine
As Jesus sat with twelve, remembering.
Then quietly He said, "There is one
    here
Whose kiss will bring betrayal by and
    by."
They did not look at Judas curiously,
But each man murmured, "Master, is
    it I?"

Each one looked inward, frightened
    lest he find
A shoddy place where he had dreamed
    of steel,
None placed the guilt on any other
    guest
Who had partaken of that gracious
    meal . . .
When there are hungry in the street,
When I see tears or hear a heart's
    hurt cry
Because someone has failed to keep
    high faith,
May I, too, murmur, "Master, is it I?"

—Helen Welshimer, *My Religion in Action*

853

Since the Last Supper which we commemorate, the centuries have invested the sacrament with a kind of ceremonial dignity which—wholly appropriate in one way—may obscure an important fact. Surely it was no accident that Jesus chose for this central act in Christian worship such a simple, common, undramatic staple of life as a meal. His chosen symbol was not some high point of living, distinguished and precious by its rarity, but the ordinary, thrice-daily act of taking nourishment.

"The Son of Man came eating and drinking"—and apparently for some of the religious people of Jesus' day, this connoted an offensive lack of "spirituality." Misguided Christians a few centuries later tried to believe that their Lord was pure spirit, not lowly flesh and blood at all.

With the sacrament of the Lord's Supper we are reminded of the importance of the material side of life, of the fact that Christianity transforms the most prosaic moments of ordinary living. And on this common denominator of food and drink, the necessities of life for all men, we meet today with people of all colors, speaking all languages, around a table large as the world itself, with the Christ who loves us all.

854

In the communion service, I take the Cup. The Cup symbolizes the death of Christ for my sins. I take the Cup for myself, and thus it becomes the symbol of my share in the sacrifice of Christ for me and for the sins of the whole world.

No one could drink Christ's Cup for Him. No one else could pay the price of sin on Calvary.

Even so it is with me. No one else can take the Cup for me. I must take it and drink it myself, of my own free will and choice. I am the only one who can appropriate the sacrifice of Christ for my sins. I make my own choice—Christ.

The Cup suggests communion. There is fellowship in eating and drinking. I do not take the Cup alone. There are other persons near me at the Lord's Table. We drink it together, and the Cup of Communion binds us together—in Christ.

Moreover, there are millions of others—men and women and boys and girls of all nations, races, colors, and stations in life—who take the Cup. We all commune together. The Cup lifts me above all the barriers which tend to separate people. Christ died for me! Yes, thank God! But also He died for every other individual. No person is excluded. He gave His life that all men might live together as brothers. To everyone Christ says: "This cup is the new covenant in my blood, which is shed for *you*."—Eugene E. Golay, *I Take the Cup*

855

The hands that lift the Cup must do the Master's work.

856

When you come before the Lord's Table you are about to present yourself to the One most worthy of your love and trust and respect. You know something of what that One expects of you; you must be ready. Therefore, you must look at yourself, at your whole life—personal, family, and business—all of it. What have you been doing lately? What things have taken up your time? How have you dealt with your family and your friends? What about your business decisions? There have been mistakes and outright wrongdoings and then a multitude of deeds which can only be called "our best." Most times nowadays, after searching all our motives and applying all our principles and all our knowledge, we can't be certain that what we do is right. Life will not allow us to be pure and spotless. . . . But our intentions so often do not match up with our deeds. . . . When you come to the Lord's Table you must come with an offering, the only one you have: yourself and your life. You must bring all of it, the good and the bad, the stupidity and the error, the blindness and the gladness. . . . Then you ask forgiveness and strength for renewal.—Charles A. Baldwin, *On Coming to the Lord's Table*

MEN AND MISSIONS DAY

857

Now it's a new day for the world mission—our day. And now it's a new kind of mission. The concept of "foreign missions" is obsolete—not because it failed but because it succeeded so well. With only a few exceptions, a church is now rooted in every nation. It is no longer a matter of the religious "haves" going to the religious "have-nots"; now, each church has something to give. The new day calls for teamwork, each nation sharing according to its genius and resources—building together!

858

Until a man has found God, he begins at no beginning and works to no end.—H. G. Wells

859

A true missionary is God's man in God's place, doing God's work in God's way for God's glory.

860

The church started when the Christian went outside Judaism and found that God was not only behind His apostles, He was also out ahead of them. If God is out at work in the nations, we might be used as men were in the Book of the Acts.—Walden Toevs

861

A church exists by mission as fire exists by burning.—Emil Brunner

862

Dr. John A. Mackay declared, "A church is validated as a Church of God not by its organized structure but by its missionary action. Order must always be secondary to mission." Those who give of their substance to the Lord's work help make possible the missionary action which validates the true "body of Christ," the church.

863

Mission is a job. What is foreign about a mission except that it is our job away from home?—Lambert Erickson

864

We've just about abolished the word "missionary." We have a strong conviction that the era of the white man's burden in religious work is over. We are now equal partners.—Murray S. Stedman, Jr., *Newsweek*

865

Every journey has two ends—a place to go and a place from which to come—both ends create mission problems.

866

When the 100-year-old American Presbyterian Mission in the Cameroun was dissolved, a National pastor said: "When the Mission is dissolved it does not cease to exist any more than sugar does when it is dissolved in water. It remains to sweeten the water." The Presbyterian missionaries he said, have become fraternal workers, "brothers who join hands with us."

867

America is the only country where one has to advertise to sell bread.—Dale Turner

868

Several days ago a man came in from a distant village and asked me to go to see his sick daughter. It was a twenty-mile walk for the roads were closed by the heavy rains and I just didn't see how I could go. It would have meant shutting down the clinic and letting the workmen go ahead without any supervision. . . . I gave the man some aspirin for I didn't know what the child was suffering from and sent him back. The next evening he was in again pleading with me to go and see her for she was dying. Again I put him off, pointing out that many others were dying and I couldn't see all of them. So I gave him some more medicine and sent him home. He must have walked all night for the next day he was back again with the girl's mother. They threw themselves on the ground before me. Grasping my feet, they begged and begged for me to go to their village and see their sick daughter. Apparently the girl was too big to carry even if she had been well enough. Their pleas melted my heart and I had to go. I prepared a bag of medicines and bandages for the man told me there were many sick people in his village. We started on the long hike back through the woods and swamps. We arrived at the village after six hours in the hot sun and I marveled how that man had walked over that same path six times in three days in his bare feet.

As I crawled into their little grass hut I could hear the girl's strained breathing and I feared the worst. As I knelt over her emaciated form and felt the burning face I knew I was too late. I told her who I was and that I had come to help her. She opened her eyes and said to me in the Anuak tongue, "Kiperange yi keri oa cong?" "Why didn't you come long ago?" My heart turned to water. Why hadn't I gone immediately? I might have been able to save her.

Those words of that dying girl will never leave my ears and heart. I wish I could shout them in every church and into the ears of every American Christian. Over the last nineteen hundred years God's black children have been crying out, "Why have you waited so long?" I cannot rest or spare myself until I have used every ounce of my energy and strength in carrying life to these dying children of Africa. —W. Donald McClure, *Red-Headed, Rash and Religious*

869

A living church is missionary in its very essence; its members cannot keep to themselves a faith that has changed their lives.—Suzanne de Dietrich

870

Nothing could be worse than the fear that one had given up too soon and left one effort unexpended that might have helped the world.—Jane Addams

871

You must love the poor very much, or they will hate you for giving them bread.—Vincent de Paul

872

Why Foreign Missions? Why take on the loneliness of service at the end of nowhere, the heartache of separation, the frustrations from lack of results? . . . Missions is not a cross-fertilization of cultures. The aim of the church is not to take Western culture to the rest of the world. . . . There was a time when it was thought that if only the Sudanese would wear clothes they would be halfway to the Kingdom. When they put on clothes they became unclean, filled with body lice and fleas. When they live scantily clothed or naked, they can dip in and out of the river two or three times a day to be cooled off and cleaned. . . . During the latter part of the nineteenth century, missions and cultures were inextricably mixed . . .

"Christian" and "Western" must be divorced.

Again, missions is not a crusade to unite different religions. Men say that in Buddhism there is good; in Confucianism, there is good; in Mohammedanism, there is good; unthinking men then say the best in each religion must be molded together into something that is vital and contains the absolute. The church does not embark on a crusade to unite these. Jesus Christ is the center, the One to whom all knees must bow. He is unique; He is God Almighty. He is not some effulgence of God; He is God.

Missions is not an attempt primarily to save individual souls from destruction. God has in His plan something greater. There is not enough personnel, enough time, enough money to do the job this way. The church can work till the end of the world and get nowhere picking out individuals here and there. . . . Florence Padwick . . . said, "Surely the snatching of a few souls from behind Islam's twisted barrier cannot be God's whole plan. There is something else that God has in mind that is in one single word, the church."

Why then should the church engage in a foreign mission enterprise? . . . Because it is the direct command of Jesus Christ; it is the law of life; it is the proof of the gospel; it is the hope of the return of Jesus Christ. Christianity is . . . a heart pierced with the saving knowledge of Jesus Christ and the establishment of His church.

For the missionary searching for the significance of his life, there is a never-ending battle won by the grace of Christ alone. It is a battle with himself, with the clashing of culture and with the unchecked forces of ignorance and superstition.—Marion and Edwin Fairman, *The Tumbling Walls*

873

Narcissus was that beautiful youth of Greek mythology who fell in love with his own reflection in a fountain. Narcissus at last changed into a flower. We were reminded of that ancient story when we visited the home of a church member whose own enormous portrait dominated one wall of his living room. One wonders what this does to discipleship.

We have thought of Narcissus often as we have sat in a pew holding the bulletin with the church's own lovely image on the front. It may be the graceful gothic or simple colonial lines of the exterior; it may be the balanced chancel or great central pulpit of the interior. But why, when the real thing is before our eyes, must we have this image, too? Is the American church infatuated by its own physical loveliness? Ancient words rise to mock this distorted love: "Whoever exalts himself will be humbled." Is our church primarily concerned with preserving its face and figure unblemished? Other words cry out: "Whoever would save his life will lose it." Could it be that the church finds it more pleasant looking at its own touched-up portrait than at the unlovely world Christ came to redeem? Do we hear the Master saying, "I came not to call the righteous, but sinners?"

Narcissus turned into a flower. The myth is a parable, a parable that is a warning to the churches. Vanity turns to insipidity. Infatuation leads to deterioration. Self-preservation means self-destruction. Sermons turn to saccharine. Narcissus on Sunday becomes a flower on Monday. Suddenly we awake to the fact that the narcissistic church has lost its virility and power. It has ceased to be the church.

The image of the self on Sunday bulletins may thus suggest a deeper malady. The disease is not healed by treating a symptom. There are various cures for the parochial mind and shrivelled heart. The mission of the church . . . can help people see beyond the local church . . . as it reaches out to heal and to lift. Here are vistas into a world Christ came to redeem. Here is a view of God's people in larger perspective. View the church as mission.—*Mission Today*

874

I don't feel inclined to get off the earth just because some people dislike my religion. Internment and death are simply the normal risks that are inherent in our state of life, a small price to pay for carrying out our duty —in our particular case a privilege because it would associate us a little more intimately in the cross of Christ.— James Edward Walsh

875

The only kind of church which can crack the modern world is one in which each man is a missionary. There are thousands of missionary tasks and each must find his own.—D. Elton Trueblood

876

Mission work is many things, but mostly it is slugging against ignorance, indifference and insensibility. In this group, some will learn to read and write, some won't. Some will hear the Bible stories and come to grips with the Christ, most won't. But whether they learn or not, whether they are converted or not, the job is still the same—to keep putting out all we know of Christ in the name of Christ. The light continues to shine in places like Gereif (in the African Sudan) and the darkness overcomes it not!—Marion and Edwin Fairman, *The Tumbling Walls*

LAYMEN'S SUNDAY

877

Man knows demanding hungers of a sort which are not shared by the others. He never quite succeeds in satisfying these hungers which are peculiar to him, try as he will. But try he must—and he does. It is these unsatisfied hungers which drive us on toward that achievement which is uniquely human. The pressure of constant desire for extra-animal satisfactions is the thing which makes man man; it is also the thing which drives him to God.—Bernard I. Bell

878

The idea that God . . . is not a being of caprice and whim as had been the case in all the main body of thinking of the ancient world, but is, instead, a God who rules through law . . . that idea has made modern science, and it is unquestionably the foundation of modern civilization.

It is because of this discovery, or because of the introduction of this idea into human thinking, and because of the faith of the scientist in it, that he has been able to harness the forces of nature and to make them do the work that enslaved human beings were forced to do in all preceding civilizations.—Robert Millikan, *Vital Speeches*

879

There can be no conflict between science and religion. Science is a reliable method of finding truth. Religion is the search for a satisfying way of life. Science is growing—yet a world that has science needs, as never before, the inspiration that religion has to offer. . . . Beyond the nature taught by science is the Spirit that gives meaning to life.—Arthur H. Compton

880

At every crossway in the road that leads to the future, each progressive spirit is opposed by a thousand men, self-appointed to guard the past. Let us have no fear lest the fair towers of former days be sufficiently defended. The least that the most timid among us can do is not to add to the immense dead weight which nature drags along.—Maurice Maeterlinck

881

The longer I have lived the more strongly I have felt the harm done by the practice among so many men of keeping their consciences in separate compartments; sometimes a Sunday conscience and a week-day conscience; sometimes a conscience as to what they say or what they like other people to say, and another conscience as to what they do and like other people to do; sometimes a conscience for their private affairs and a totally different conscience for their business relations. Or

again, there may be one compartment in which the man keeps his conscience not only for his domestic affairs but for his business affairs, and a totally different compartment in which he keeps his conscience when he deals with public men and public measures.
—Theodore Roosevelt

882

Christ wanted men to see, to see far and to see truly. To get that kind of vision requires avoidance of hypocrisies and group prejudice which distort the vision and make men imagine they see what is not really there.—John Foster Dulles

883

It is well to trust in God, but after we have done our best first.

884

If trouble comes, it'll keep our religion from getting rusty. That's the great thing about persecution; it keeps you up to the mark. It's habit, not hatred, that is the real enemy of the Church of God.—Charles T. Leber

885

Man-made law cannot change the hearts of men. High standards of integrity, fairness, generosity, and brotherly love come from within. When Jesus came to expound the law of righteousnes and to write it into the hearts of men, society began to be transformed, but only because *individuals* were transformed *first!* The late Dean Inge said: "In direct opposition to Marxian Socialism, we are taught that from within, out of the heart of man, comes all that can exalt

or defile him."—Admiral Ben Moreell, "True Leadership," *Vital Speeches*

886

Every right-thinking person wants to make his life purposeful. Above all, he seeks happiness and inner peace. Philosophers and theologians have told us, and experience over the ages has confirmed their findings, that we can attain this goal by availing ourselves of God's aid. Our efforts to do this is the practice of religion.

What is "religion?"

Webster says, "Religion is the service and adoration of God—in pursuit of a way of life regarded as incumbent on true believers."

James said, "Pure religion and undefiled before God and the Father is this, to visit the fatherless and widows in their affliction and to keep himself unspotted from the world."

And Karl Marx said, "Religion is the opiate of the people."

I suggest: "Religion is the search for a satisfying way of life, so conducted that, with faith and by His grace, we can approach closer to God, thereby learning *His* purpose *for us*— and how we can best serve that purpose."

This concept is based on my belief that man yearns for truth, goodness and beauty; that he wants to see these values expressed in the specific issues of his daily living; and that this can be done by understanding those laws which govern the good life for man.— Admiral Ben Moreell, "True Leadership," *Vital Speeches*

887

In religion there are no professionals, everyone is a priest but the "priesthood of all believers" requires educated people. Everyone has a right to his own opinion only when he has earned it. One has to know what it is all about if decisions are to be in the hands of "the priesthood of all believers." Decisions must be met with an adult and a mature mind.—Paul S. Wright

888

A Christian is a man who finds privilege unbearable.—W. R. Mathews

889

Until the *men* of the church carry their God-given responsibility, and not until *then,* will the church be what it should be. It is amazing to find the number of men who have their religion in their wife's name. Their theme song might well be:

Take my wife and let her be,
Consecrated Lord to Thee,
Help her now Thy will to see,
   But please, dear Lord, don't count
      on me.

What we need is for the men of the church to render a new stewardship of time, energy and influence. The secret of Protestantism has always resided in its lay power. It began as a laymen's movement. Christian propaganda can only win in the world by lay participation, each man doing his part in his own way.—William Samuel Meyer, "Wanted: Manpower"

890

"Where do we begin?" Each man begins with himself before God, then moves out to act as a man of God in a world full of critical problems. Such men of God take responsibility and practice that responsibility in a democratic way, and the place to begin to practice democratic responsibility is right in the local church.—John Sutherland Bonnell

891

Two-thirds of our colleges and universities do not require their students to study American history. Only one fourth of our colleges and universities require American history for admission. . . . What fertile ground to teach the strong points of Marxism! How can you love a country you know so little about? . . . Any man who reads Karl Marx and Engel and embraces communism and knows not the theory and practice of Christian democracy should go down to the dust from which he sprung, unwept, unhonored and unsung. I am not sure that the preservation of our so-called way of life is the most important issue now confronting us. "Belief in God" may be the more important challenging issue throughout the world this hour. One half of the world is pressing a ruthless war against religion and against the concept of a Creator. The other half is largely apathetic.

We must believe that God is with man in history and that he has not left the world to be run by men worshiping a social formula. Dr. Reinhold Niebuhr has for me summed up the Christian case for democracy. He says: "Man's capacity for justice makes democracy possible, but man's inclination to injustice makes democracy necessary."—Branch Rickey, Newsletter to Presbyterian Men

892

Christian is as Christian lives, gives and loves. . . . It is great to work in such a time; whatever be the immediate future, we know that God in Christ will triumph by way of His investment in us all; and we can go forward with utter faith in Him and His way of life.—Paul C. Johnston

893

We are forced in a day like today to seek the ultimate answers to primary questions. Too many today are refugees from responsibility. Too many are refugees from God.—Clifford E. Barbour

894

Hate is the most destructive force in the world. The church is trying to substitute love for hate through its teaching of good will, the Ten Commandments and the Sermon on the Mount. Hate will resolve no problems; Christian love can solve every problem.—Frank Totton

895

Man is a religious animal, and if he holds aloof from public worship he starves and stunts his highest instincts. If a man is to come to his full stature, he must come to it inside the church.—James W. Clarke, Newsletter to Presbyterian Men

896

Shame on us, laymen, when sometimes we have treated our religion like cancer. We have never wanted anybody to discover that we had it.—Louis Evans

897

It is harder to share life than to take life. Most men are more willing to send their son to take life than to share life. . . . We will never really live our lives and survive our death until we learn to share the life that comes in Jesus Christ.—Charles T. Leber

898

To be true man in the real sense of the world is to be God's man. . . . The true Christian is the servant . . . as Christ washed His disciples' feet He was the kneeling figure which was the next day to be a crucified figure. . . . It is only as servant that mediocrity becomes greatness.—John A. Mackay, Newsletter to Presbyterian Men

899

The laymen constitute the only "bridge" over which Christ can move from the church to the community. . . . When the minister dismisses us . . . at the end of a Sunday service, he impliedly says to us: "I have done my very best to inspire you, to bring you closer to God, and to show you how you should live as Christian disciples. Now go out into the world, to your homes and your various places of business, and show people by your example what it means to be a Christian. And remember, please, that there is no ministry, no preaching, that is so powerful as the example of a Christian life.—Wilbur LaRoe, Jr.

900

The areas where this new age must win its victories are where laymen live —politics, business and finance, racial relationships, the great professions, community service, the church itself, where ministers come and go, but where the abiding continuum is the great body of laymen.—Harry Emerson Fosdick

901

A certain troubled pastor had a dream one night. In this dream, he and his officers agreed to move a heavy bus, whose motor had gone dead, up a hill. He said to them firmly: "Now you get behind and push and I will pull." All went well at first, but the pulling became steadily harder and finally exhausting. The minister stopped to pant and wipe his streaming brow. Then, looking back, he saw to his consternation that all his elders and deacons were seated inside the bus. When the pastor awoke, he saw that the dream was a true parable. Few of us who teach or preach or organize have not had something like that experience.—D. Maurice Allan, "The Layman in the Church and the World," *Presbyterian Outlook*

902

Where three are gathered together, there is a church, even though they be laymen.—Tertullian

903

The most important and most effective minister in any American community is not necessarily the one who preaches from the high pulpit of the church. A most telling ministry is now functioning in and through the lives of those who make up the membership of the church—the laity. Russell J. Humbert, *Adult Class*

904

The son of a prominent industrialist debated for some time about whether to enter his father's firm or become a clergyman. "It's up to you to decide *which* father's business," said a friend. The boy finally entered the family firm, because—as he put it—"I discovered that the question of 'which father's business' was not mutually exclusive. I saw that I might have a very real ministry as a layman on the job, not only in the work I did, but also in the way I permitted my life to touch the lives of those working beside me."—Laymen's Movement for a Christian World

905

Men do not reject the Word of God or the works of God because they are "smart," but because they are "hard." —Frank E. Lindgren

906

We have enough stupid Christians. We need more literate Christians.— Ernest Yarrow

907

Men's lives, like rivers, become crooked from following the paths of least resistance.

908

What is the use of running, if you are not on the right road?

909

Too many people are thinking of security instead of opportunity; they seem more afraid of life than of death. —James F. Byrnes

910

Civilization, besides providing a better framework for it, has something else in common with happiness: both are by-products of some other goal. Happiness is notorious for entering back doors; and no civilization ever rose without some higher aim, such as justice, peace, the liberation of the mind, or the glory of God. Conceivably we might some day find ourselves, after some final victory over our environment, at rest in the "empty, swept and garnished house" of Matthew 12:44; and even if all its inhabitants are decent, fed, adjusted, well-intentioned and purged by psychoanalysis, their last state will be worse than their first.

Long before then it will be necessary, and probably inevitable, that Americans discover the *internal* quest for happiness, which is the highest use to which leisure can be put. There, within the sun-struck privacy of the individual heart and soul, is the ultimate human frontier. If millions are exploring, in joy and freedom, the neglected unknown within themselves, a few at least will be finding metaphysical horizons that far transcend this nation, this century, or the very idea of civilization. Some of those few may even enlarge the boundaries of human thought, and thus fulfill the highest purpose of any civilization, which is to learn new truth about the human spirit and its Maker.—Editorial in *Life*

911

God will not look you over for medals but for scars.

912

Nothing contributes more to cheerfulness than the habit of looking at the good side of things. The good side is God's side of them.—Ullathorne, *Humility and Patience*

913

Religion should be our steering wheel—not our spare tire.—Charles L. Wheeler

914

There are parts of a ship which left to themselves would sink. The engine, the shafts, the steel girders—all taken out of the ship would settle to the bottom of the sea. But when those heavy steel parts are built into the frame of a ship, the ship floats. So it is with life. That wound of a friend, that business failure, that son's death —such sorrow taken singly would sink us; but when these are fitted into the framework of life whose Builder and Maker is God, they keep afloat. Yes, all things, good and bad, can be carried on the voyage of life, if we keep our love and trust in the goodness of God.—Ralph W. Sockman, *Gates of Beauty*

915

Blessed is the man whose calendar contains Sunday.

Blessed is the man who is faithful on a committee.

Blessed is the man who can endure an hour in a place of worship, as well as two hours in a place of amusement.

Blessed is the man who loves his church with his pocketbook as well as with his heart.

Blessed is the man who has grace and gumption enough to leave his critical spirit on the sidewalk when he comes to church.

Blessed is the man who loves his own church enough to praise it.

916

I have worked out a method which I apply in solving . . . problems . . . my formula is this: 1. First, I consider with great care all the known evidence in connection with the problem. 2. Then I pray for help in solving the problem. 3. Afterward, I put the problem on the shelf, so to speak, and try to forget all about it. 4. During the next week . . . I listen for some sign of the voice of God. It usually comes out of a clear sky while I am taking a walk, talking to someone, reading a book, or relaxing. 6. I follow what I believe to be God's prompting. 7. I dismiss from my mind every other possible solution to the problem.—Harry A. Bullis, "God Is My Senior Partner," *American Magazine*

917

There is nothing noble in being superior to some other man. The true nobility is in being superior to your former self.—Hindu proverb

918

My business is not to remember myself, but to make the absolute best of what God made.—Robert Browning

919

"If God did not exist, it would be necessary to invent Him." At any rate, we have invented concepts which, considering that they are only substitutes, have done His job as best they could. One cannot normally expect a child to act as a mature trustee of any institution; one can much less expect a concept to substitute for a God who, by nature so to speak, eludes all attempts to describe Him satisfactorily. Nor can one refrain from smiling at these attempts. Some of them would make you think God was your uncle; they would even prod you to act accordingly. After all, you would tend to think a rich uncle more benign than, and prefer him to, a father who is without illusion about you and knows your worth. Whether paternalistic or avuncular, most of our concepts of God show how worthless men can be.

Of necessity, these concepts are anthropomorphic. This is particularly the case when they originate in the inflationary imagination of sentimental or mass religiosity, or even when they explain the unfolding of a religious novel. But whatever the theological or philosophical connotations may be, this anthropomorphism often means nothing more than that we worship the God we deserve. We create God in our image or, as Erdman Harris says, "The believer phrases his understanding of the divine in terms of the highest values he can conceive at the moment and within his particular frame of reference." And God becomes no more than the ideal man.

To be sure, glibness about this matter may show mere smartness; it is not necessarily enlightening. For this is a religious problem *par excellence*, since man everywhere is limited by the very words through which he seeks to transcend his limitations. In the Bible itself God is referred to as a shield, as One who is "mighty in battle" and "teaches" the soldier's hand to war. He is paternal, even maternal, a shepherd, a friend, a bridegroom, a husband.

Why is it, then, that the modern ways in which especially popular religiosity designates God should make us shudder? What is wrong with designations for God as a "Porter" or the "Fellow Upstairs"? Why are such expressions more objectionable than certain Biblical ones which are no less down-to-earth and just as fragile?

It is not the modern phrase which can (or must) be objected to so much as the understanding it expresses of the self and its relation to other selves and the world. By contrast with the Biblical instances, these modern, popular appellations suggest only that the deity is viewed as a missing link in man's unsuccessful attempts to grasp the meaning of his self and of the world. For this reason, the deity becomes just a global hypothesis, a mere cog of an intricate machine, whether friendly or formidable. And thus the conception of God as the Cosmic Pal is but another development in the series of universal anthropocentrism. We drag God into everything and besot ourselves.—Gabriel Vahanian, "The God We Deserve," *The Nation*

920

True, there are those who do not desire to live nobly or honestly. Some individuals prefer lust to love, poverty to riches, lowliness to fame. But no matter what our choice, we must be honest with our motives, consistent with our aims, and in harmony with self. Sincerity cements all our parts and rips the mask from the real face God has made for us.—George Christian Anderson, "The Unknown Self Within You," *Your Life*

921

Observe a man's actions; scrutinize his motives; take note of the things that give him pleasure. How then can he hide from you what he really is?—Confucius

922

"I ain't much but I'm all I got," said Noah to the Lord in *Green Pastures*.

923

If every man would heal another man, soon the whole world would be healed.

924

"The one secret any man finds hardest to keep," our venerable pastor told us, "is his own opinion of himself. It's fine to believe in ourselves, but we mustn't be too easily convinced."—Burton Hillis, *Better Homes & Gardens*

925

Never be satisfied with yourself.—A. Walton Roth

926

No one objects to a man being himself if he's trying to do better.—G. Norman Collie

927

Be what you are. This is the first step toward becoming better than you are.—Julius Hare

928

Sure the world is full of trouble, but as long as we have people undoing

trouble we have a pretty good world.
—Helen Keller

929

Sin has four characteristics: self-sufficiency instead of faith; self-will instead of submission; self-seeking instead of benevolence; self-righteousness instead of humility.

930

Sin is man's declaration of independence of God.

931

The principal thing in this world is to keep one's soul aloft.

932

Why can't temptation be like opportunity and knock only once, disguised beyond recognition?—Oren Arnold, *Bluebook*

933

One of Boris Pasternak's characters in *Dr. Zhivago* says that untruth came in Russia when "people imagined that it was out of date to follow their own moral senses," and that "the main misfortune, the root of all the evil to come, was the loss of confidence in the value of one's own opinion."—Stewart Meacham, "The Voice of the People," *The Nation*

934

It is astonishing what obedience will do for a person who has been careless. Renewing of the mind comes by obedience to a pattern of thinking and action. This is the way we prove what we need to know. We complain at the restrictions of the Christian life if we have only contemplated it and have not been obedient to it. But once we have been obedient to the Way, we are no longer at odds with it. For the renewing of the mind makes new creatures of us. Some people have the hopeless way of thinking that, since they cannot control their lives here, finally God will take them home and there they will be transformed by the power of God. Surely, if we have no desire to accept God by faith here, we shall not desire Him when we see Him in heaven. If we have no interest in proving the will of God here, we shall surely not want it proved to us in heaven. The transformation begins here or not at all.—Lyman W. Winkle, *Today*

935

I continue to believe that this world has no superior meaning. But I know that something in it has meaning; it is man, because man is the sole being to insist upon having a meaning.—Albert Camus, "Letters to a German Friend," *Catholic World*

936

All men are ordinary men; the extraordinary men are those who know it.—G. K. Chesterton

937

It is useless to think that we can get along without a conception of what man is, and without a belief in ourselves, and without the morality to support this belief.—D. H. Lawrence, quoted by William Walsh in *The Nation*

938

The small things are the powerful things; that bacteria causes the damage was the finding of Pasteur.—Glenn Clark

939

Dead men look worst when they look alive.—Herbert Gold, *The Optimist*

940

The Myth of Sisyphus, the first of Camus's two important philosophical essays, reveals a new depth in Camus's own thinking. The question raised in the beginning of his book is: How can a life that has no meaning best be lived?—Bernard G. Murchland, "Albert Camus: Rebel," *Catholic World*

941

If Christians do not rejoice, it is because they do not live up to their privileges.

942

God gave us imaginations to compensate for what we aren't, and a sense of humor to console us for what we are.—Burton Hillis, *Better Homes & Gardens*

943

He who floats with the current, who does not guide himself according to higher principles, who has no ideal, no convictions—such a man is a mere article of the world's furniture—a thing moved, instead of a living and moving being—an echo, not a voice. The man who has no inner life is the slave of his surroundings, as the barometer is the obedient servant of the air at rest, and the weathercock the humble servant of the air in motion. —Henri Frederic Amiel

944

Humility does not spring from distrust in one's self but from trust in God. It is not inconsistent with humility to know something of one's capabilities. It is inconsistent to be proud of these things as if you made them yourself.—Robert Burns McAulay

945

From the point of view of morals, life seems to be divided into two periods. In the first, we indulge; in the second, we preach.—Will Durant

946

A lot of people make the mistake of thinking they are going to have as good a time in hell as they did getting there.—Dan Bennett

947

I need courage to be honest—
Honest in my use of words
Honest in accepting responsibility
Honest in dealing with myself
Honest in dealing with my fellows
Honest in my relations with God.
—Howard Thurman, "Meditations of the Heart"

948

What we know not, teach us;
What we have not, give us;
What we are not, make us;
What we have been, forgive us;
And toward what we should be and shall be
Guide, guard and direct us for Jesus' sake. Amen.

949

My own experience over many active years convinces me that if men will only take their personal and business problems to God humbly, and listen to Him receptively, their confusion and pessimism will give way to optimism, and this will lead them to the achievement of their dreams. Faith in God gives men faith also in themselves and their future. And that kind of faith results in the traditional tough-minded optimism which founded our country and is the hope of its future.—Harry A. Bullis, "God Is My Senior Partner," *American Magazine*

950

For it is the part of a truly great man not merely to be equal to great things, but also to make little things great by his own power.—Basil, *Letters*

951

Good and evil are different as their names imply. But, in my own humble opinion, they are both of them aspects of my Lord. He is present in the one, absent in the other, and the difference between presence and absence is great, as great as my feeble mind can grasp. Yet absence implies presence, absence is not nonexistence, and we are therefore entitled to repeat, "Come, come, come, come."—E. M. Forster, *The New Republic*

952

Life is nothing but a play and a pretense, and His will must be done, however much we rebel at it.—R. H. Benson, *The History of Richard Raynal Solitary*

953

God is always with us, why should we not always be with God?—Ullathorne, *Humility and Patience*

954

Blessed is the leader who has not sought the high places, but who has been drafted into service because of his ability and willingness to serve.

Blessed is the leader who knows where he is going, why he is going, and how to get there.

Blessed is the leader who knows no discouragement, who presents no alibi.

Blessed is the leader who knows how to lead without being dictatorial; true leaders are humble.

Blessed is the leader who seeks for the best for those he serves.

Blessed is the leader who leads for the good of the most concerned, and not for the personal gratification of his own ideas.

Blessed is the leader who develops leaders while leading.

Blessed is the leader who marches with the group, interprets correctly the signs on the pathway that leads to success.

Blessed is the leader who has his head in the clouds but his feet on the ground.

Blessed is the leader who considers leadership an opportunity for service.
    —"Beatitudes of a Leader"

955

A great deal of talent is lost in the world for want of a little courage. Every day sends to their graves obscure men whom timidity prevented from making a first effort; who, if they could have been induced to begin, would, in all probability, have gone great lengths in the career of fame. The fact is that to do anything in the world worth doing we must not stand back shivering and thinking of the cold danger, but we must jump in and scramble through as well as we can. It will not do to be perpetually calculating risks and adjusting nice chances. A man waits, and doubts, and consults his brother, and his particular friends, till one day he finds that he is sixty years old, and that he has lost so much time in consulting relatives that he has no time to follow their advice.—Sydney Smith

956

The world has a way of giving what is demanded of it. If you are frightened and look for failure and poverty, you will get them, no matter how hard you may try to succeed. Lack of faith in yourself, in what life will do for you, cuts you off from the good things of the world. Expect victory and you make victory.—Preston Bradley

957

An unknown psychologist listed three reasons why mistakes are made: Someone did not know. Someone did not think. Someone did not care. So the best way to avoid mistakes is: to know what you are doing; to think while you are doing it; and to really care whether or not it is done right.

958

If the Christian Church were a pillar of fire leading the peoples of the world, instead of an ambulance corps bringing up the rear as it so often seems to be, communism probably would never have been born.—Helen Shoemaker, *The Secret of Effective Prayer*

959

The word which God has written on the brow of every man is Hope.— Victor Hugo

960

The most exhausting thing in life is to be insincere.—Anne Morrow Lindbergh

961

We are our own devils; we drive ourselves out of our Edens.—Goethe

962

A hundred times every day I remind myself that my inner and outer life depend on the labors of other men, living and dead, and that I must exert myself in order to give in the same measure as I have received and am still receiving.—Albert Einstein, *The World As I See It*

963

What does the Will of God mean to you? Something to dread or resent, or is it a shout of triumph?—Ethel Banks

964

Jesus, my faith is not enough. Lend me some of Yours.—George Hale

965

It may be that God has so ordained the laws of human inter-relationship that we can help one another not alone by our deeds but also by our thoughts, and that earnest prayer may be the exercise of this power in its highest terms.—Harry Emerson Fosdick

966

Recently a minister approached twelve different men in his congregation asking them to accept the responsibilities and duties of Elders. Each refused saying he was not worthy. Such humility is not a virtue. "A part of the appeal of Jesus lies in His extraordinary balance. He combines confidence and humility." Most of us have known someone whose unlimited self-confidence made him unbearable; we have known others whose humility made them weak. But one whose humility saves him from arrogance and whose confidence saves him from weakness, is moving in the direction of the mind of Christ.—Willard W. Strahl, *Strength for the Day,* ed. by N. E. Nyggard

967

A fool—for Christ! The laughing-stock of the world! I am that, indeed. More than half my life has been spent as a fool for Christ! The so-called pleasures of the world have fled from me. In my leisure hours I have never enjoyed a motion picture. Instead, I have kept myself glued to the rubbish heap.

Each day of my life has been marked with tears. People consider me obstinate, narrowminded—a subject for ridicule. Picked up from the streets of lewdness and placed at the foot of the cross, I found myself in a small group of hypocrites and heretics, where I was unwelcome. They spurned me as a pagan, a socialist, and a superficial creature.

But I do not mind at all. I have been caught by Christ. A slave to the cross! The world's fool!

Expressed in other terms, I am starting out to climb the mountain of holiness, leaving behind all earthly things. If this is to be a fool I cannot help it.—Toyohiko Kagawa, *Today*

968

It takes few words to tell the truth. —Chief Joseph of the Nez Percé

969

I would that my life were to God as his hand is to a man.—Sir Thomas Browne

970

I don't wonder that men have felt they were related to God! I don't wonder that they have felt that they were given something which has made them masters of the world. Give them responsibility, give them the will and determination to help God as we must in order to put this world in order.— Gutzon Borglum

971

Every Christian must be himself the holy land where Christ is born and where He dwells.—Henry Sloane Coffin

972

It is perfectly possible to tell a lie without saying anything untrue. As a matter of fact, the most effective liars are those who never deliberately say anything that is not so; they simply tell a piece of the truth and refuse to tell all of it.—Henry Hitt Crane, *Your Life Counts*

973

Nothing can bring you peace but triumph of principles.—Ralph Waldo Emerson

974

The greatest enemy of progress is not bad men, but good men who have ceased to grow.

975

We cannot evade the consequences of our own acts and attitudes. They become a part of us. We are what we are, not what we pretend to be. No man gets to heaven on his wife's religion. No young person can trade forever on his parent's reputation. No normal person can rightly blame his friends or his environment for his downfall. We determine our own destiny.—Charles M. Crowe, *Sermons on the Parables of Jesus*

UNITED NATIONS DAY

976

We felt it appropriate that the material to represent the earth on which we stand, as seen by the light of the sky, should be iron ore, the material out of which swords have been made and the material out of which homes for men are also built. It is a material which represents the very paradox of human life; the basic materials offered by God to us may be used either for construction or for destruction. This leads our thoughts to the necessity of choice between the two alternatives. . . . We want to bring back in this room the stillness which we have lost in our streets and in our conference rooms. In that setting we want to bring back our thoughts to great and simple truths, to the way in which the light of the skies gives life to the earth on which we stand—a symbol to many of us of what the light of the Spirit gives to man. We want to bring back the idea of worship, devotion to something which is greater and higher than ourselves. . . . We were trying to create a meditation room where men of all kinds from all regions of the world would have a place where each could find his God.—Dag Hammarskjold

977

I'm a believer in God and the ultimate goodness. When I was a little girl, there was a revivalist meeting in our church. I got a tremendous urge to become a believer. I prayed about it, I thought of nothing else; I wrestled and I anguished. Then all of a sudden one day it came over me I was going through an unnecessary lot of agitation. There didn't have to be a violent change in me; I'd been a believer all along. It's been as simple as that for me ever since. Here's something else I believe: that one day it's going to come over a lot of people who are shouting and carrying on now against equality for the Negro, that they've really had good will toward him all along and that association with him is just as easy as believing is for me.

When I was a member of the United States delegation at the U. N. I understood better, I think, than others serving with me a great many things that motivated the hopes and pleas and demands of the little nations, particularly those whose people are dark-skinned. How much my people could contribute to our government's understanding of these other nations! But at the same time my government is learning more about my people, because it's concerned now with the world. So this is good, good for my country and my people, I believe this.

You see, I care so much about my country. I've sung all over the world, or very nearly, and I've loved the opportunity I've had to travel. But east, west, home is certainly best. Only I worry about it. I felt this anxiety, or perhaps an urgency, especially when I was working at the U. N. You see when you have a good set of china that gets a crack in some of the pieces, you begin using it for second best, and then finally you put it away or give it away. If you're in a shop and you try on a dress that has a tear or some conspicuous imperfection, you put that aside and take another one. But you can't put away or give away, or turn aside from, a nation that has a crack in it. And a nation that doesn't acknowledge itself as made up of *all* its parts has a crack in it.

Something else I think of often about my country a man said in a speech to my class at school, so you can guess how long I've remembered it. He said you can't put or hold something down without bending over or in some way lowering yourself. You have to get down to that same level. I'm so proud of my country I hate to think of it stooping or bending to hold down some of its own people.— Marian Anderson, "My Life in a White World," *Ladies' Home Journal*

978

The United Nations believes, and rightly, in a new concept of victory in war—victory for humanity—by ending wars through international conciliation before they have been fought to their bloody conclusion in sheer military victory.

There is no dishonor in negotiation and no shame attached to striving for peace. Indeed, in our times, it is only the strongest of nations which can strike effective blows for peace. To work for peace is a source of national strength. For let us not forget that peace itself is a powerful weapon in the world. It carries a commanding appeal for most people. Never in history have a nation and people had the opportunity that we now have to display greatness.—Ralph J. Bunche, "The World's Best Hope for Peace," *Advance*

979

I don't like to talk about co-existence. I don't mean we have to go to war, but we are up against a religion. The only way you can destroy a religion is with a greater religion. This is a fight which will not be a spectacular one for many of us, but I believe that the way you live, day by day, the kind of character you build, the kind of morality you live up to, will decide this struggle. What the church has lacked, what America has lacked, what we are lacking in the new generation coming up is "the sound of trumpets in the morning."—Bishop Gerald Kennedy, *Time*

980

To some of the men on the stage that day, a dream of the ages was about to come true. The bright vision was at hand, the vision of a world without war, the end of aggression, the renunciation of armed force as an instrument of national purpose, the banishing of a specter that had haunted mankind since the beginning of time. It was June 26, 1945. . . . One by one, the fifty men mounted the stage of the Opera House in San Francisco. The flags of fifty nations gleamed in the great hall. One by one, the representatives of those nations signed the document which lay open on a long table. It was the Charter of the United

Nations. So began the great experiment. Could it succeed?

Here were fifty nations, big and small, weak and strong. They were in different stages of political and social development. Their cultural memories were different. They lived under different systems of government. Most important, they held widely different attitudes about the relation of the individual to the state, and the basic rights of men. Still, it was a shining vision. . . .

The United Nations is fifteen years old now. What is its image in the eyes of ordinary people all over the world? What do they think of its accomplishments? Do they think it has made the world a better place to live in? . . .

The majority opinion: The United Nations has done pretty well in its first fifteen years.

The minority view: It hasn't worked, primarily because it is powerless to settle the great struggle between East and West.—Relman Morin, *Associated Press*

981

On the international scene we Americans face a dilemma. We are sure that the freedom of people in many nations in the world today is being completely ignored. Yet how can one nation secure freedom for the citizens of another nation? We faced this dilemma at the time of the Hungarian revolt. To a limited extent we can help by offering asylum to those who escape to freedom. Beyond that, our only channel for "doing something" is the United Nations.

This organization, with all its faults and weaknesses, does represent the majority of the nations of the world.

It can keep channels of communication open. As long as our countries are there, sharing in debate and discussion, the citizens of the free nations of the world have at least a chance of helping to bring freedom to more people. An international organization can at times bring pressure on a nation, or censure it, as another nation cannot. Today, the United Nations stands as the bulwark of hope for political freedom.—Cynthia Wedel, *The Glorious Liberty*

982

The United Nations can best be described as a drilling outfit, drilling toward world peace and brotherhood. —Douglas Lauderdale

983

The world has this place to try to settle differences. Without it, the nations would have not a place to do so. —Tong Chiu

984

The United Nations is not to blame for the failures. The responsibility must be shifted to the nations concerned.—Gunnar Wiberg

985

With all its faults, the United Nations is a living organization which has gone further toward organizing security than any other body in modern history—and this result has occurred at a time of great threats to the peace of the international community.—Henry Cabot Lodge, Jr., *Advance*

986

In World War II an American soldier wounded on a battlefield owed his life to the Japanese scientist, Kitasato, who isolated the bacillus of tetanus. A Russian soldier saved by a blood transfusion was indebted to Landsteiner, an Austrian.

A German soldier was shielded from typhoid fever with the help of a Russian, Metchnikoff. A Dutch marine in the East Indies was protected from malaria because of the experiments of an Italian, Grassi; while a British aviator in North Africa escaped death from surgical infection because a Frenchman, Pasteur, and a German, Koch, elaborated a new technique.—Raymond B. Fosdick, *Within Our Power*

987

The United Nations owes its existence to the work of human minds and hearts across many generations. Its roots run back into lives that should not be forgotten. Some twenty-seven centuries ago, there appeared on this planet the first of the great prophets of ancient Israel, Amos. He lived at a time of comparative prosperity in the two kingdoms into which his people had been divided after the death of Solomon, but the evil he saw was all the more disgusting. . . . In the world of Amos's day, each nation had its own god and its own moral code. But here was a man, a very humble man, to whom had come the germinal insight that there was one God, a just God, above all the nations, and one moral order to which all should conform. . . . The United Nations is an expression today of that same outreach toward the universal that we find in Amos. It includes people of all religions and no religion. But without the feeling in the hearts of many people that they should seek universal standards of right in the relations of the nations to one another, the UN would never have come into existence. This is the element of idealism that helped to create it and that is present at all times to test its work.—Justin Wroe Nixon, "The UN and Our Religious Heritage," *Advance*

REFORMATION SUNDAY

988

Protestant people don't know history. If they did, Protestantism would be surging forward today as a mighty movement, single-hearted in loyalty, constrained by an overwhelming sense of mission.

If Protestants knew history they would understand that it was the Reformation in its manifestations which gave to our civilization freedom and the free society.

If Protestants knew the history of modern civilization they would know that no stable democracy has ever arisen without Protestant nurture, direct or indirect.

If Protestants knew history, they would know that a freeman's religion demands a freeman's society and that, conversely, a freeman's society demands a freeman's religion.

If Protestants knew history, they would know that the freedom of conscience is the basic freedom, without which every freedom is superficial or meaningless.

If Protestants knew history, they would know that unless a man can be depended upon to rule himself by an informed and responsible conscience, he is destined to be ruled by an external authority.

If Protestants knew these things, they would know that Protestant Christianity is greater than the sum total of all its denominations and that it is by far the most important movement in the world today. Without it, democratic societies cannot preserve their freedom. Without it, new democratic societies cannot be successfully established.

If Protestants knew these things, every Protestant would become an evangelist; the spirit of religious vocation would be reborn in laymen; tithing, and more than tithing, would be the common practice; Protestant missions would be permeating every forgotten place in our nation and flowing out across the world to lay the only foundation that can be laid for the building of truth, of justice, of freedom, and therefore of peace.—*The Protestant World*

989

Being justified really means being on good terms with God. Paul taught that those who heard and received the message found that it produced in them faith so that they were able to trust God and receive His grace, or His loving concern and His saving power, far beyond anything expected or deserved. So Paul said, "By grace have you been saved through faith." And he insisted that all this comes from a personal experience of fellowship with God.

Obviously, no authoritarian church, with its traditions and ceremonies and sacraments, can do this for a person. With God, he must work out his own salvation. The examples of prophets, priests, and sages may help, but they will not suffice. The reasoning of the mind and the prompting of conscience are valuable, but not nearly enough. Paul spoke of being "justified in Christ" and thus he linked together faith, grace, and God's own living and saving Son.—T. Otto Nall, *Plain Facts About Protestantism*

990

Protestantism is democracy in religion. The Protestant church is dependent on the loyalty of its adherents. Protestantism suffers from the fact that many non-Catholics in this country refer to themselves as Protestants even though they are not members of a Protestant church.—Hampton Adams, *Protestantism*

991

"Luther's soul was tormented by the fear that he was a sinner condemned by God," writes Walter Russell Bowie. "Then one day a new light broke upon him, which in its results was like a miracle. He was reading the words of the Apostle Paul. 'The just shall live by faith.' So that was the real meaning of the Gospel! Life would come not by works but by faith. Not by what a man had to try to do but by what the love of God had done already. Not by fastings and scourgings and by all sorts of desperate efforts supposed to win God's mercy, but by the mercy that was declared in Christ. Jesus was not most of all the Judge; He was the Saviour. He, Martin Luther, poor sinner though he might be, through the love of Jesus crucified was already saved!"

Whenever a man becomes aware of the real meaning of "The just shall live by faith," the Reformation has come alive in his heart. The Reformation is not just an event that happened years ago. It is a light that must break upon everyone.—Editorial in *National Council Outlook*

992

The Reformation was . . . a time when prophetic voices spoke out to reaffirm for their own time those great and original Christian convictions which are the wellspring of our Christian life. These convictions can never be spoken sufficiently often. They are good now for men of our age no less than they have been for men in every age.—James A. Pike, "A Time of Reaffirmation," *Advance*

993

According to the philosopher Alfred N. Whitehead's famous aphorism, religion is what a man does with his solitariness. This may fall short of a definition of religion in its entirety, but that it is a part of Christianity and a woefully neglected part, which of us would deny?

Let me point out to you, as you stand in that strangely solitary condition, that the chief characteristic of it is freedom. You have detached yourself from everything that would hold you down to the world, and God Himself lays no violent hand upon you, compelling you to move either this way or that. You may do as you like. You are free.

No man can know the meaning of Protestantism, which I believe to be the essence of the Christian gospel, without coming to this position.

The Evangelical Christian shares with the Catholic the belief that the church is the great mother of our souls. We should not know the gospel at all if it had not been transmitted to us by our fathers in the faith. We have a debt that we cannot repay to all saintly and honest men who have gone before us, leaving behind them for our benefit their wisdom and their example. We are dependent upon and beholden to the church for the truth and beauty of God which are conveyed to us by the liturgies of its priests and the utterance of its prophets.

The danger to Protestants is that accepting these as the total of the fact of religion they will slip over into the non-Protestant position of having no moment of faith of their own which they do not derive from others. They will not make a basic decision without appeal to priest or bishop to direct them; they will never set forth their belief out of their experience but will rely rather on a time-honored statement from some ancient source; they will never utter a prayer out of their own misery or joy except in the form they have learned by rote from a prayer book. We shall all resist any attempt to disparage the code or creed or cultus of the churches—but we must be equally on our guard lest the life of our faith be restricted to these things.

Protestants today have a special heritage to preserve at this point. They will not save their freedom in this age, wherein all the tides of their culture seem to be sweeping them toward the commanding state and the authoritarian church, unless they give themselves time to experience it.

Freedom as a tradition is celluloid and hollow: it will perish. Freedom as a philosophical conception is abstract and thin: it will not hold against the pull of actualities. Freedom as experience—the experience of a soul alone with God—that is the very stuff out of which the heroic in history is made. . . . Now comes the ultimate question: What shall a man do with his freedom? And when he is alone with a man on a cross, he knows the ultimate answer: *A man shall commit his free self to God for service in the world.*—Douglas Horton, *The Missionary Herald*

994

The Protestant spirit is one of freedom and liberty in spiritual matters. It is not freedom from religious responsibility or the demands of truth. Rather, it is freedom to think for one's self, freedom to follow the truth wherever it leads, freedom of conscience and the right of private judgment, and freedom to choose one's own course in religious affairs. It considers that all men are created free and equal, that all have access to God through Christ, faith, and prayer, and that to whatever church we may belong we are Christian brothers and one in Christ if we accept Him and His way of living.—Paul E. Folkers, *What Every Protestant Should Know*

995

The dictionary tells us that *to protest* is "to affirm with solemnity." In all seriousness, therefore, a Protestant is first and foremost a witness, one furthermore who easily becomes a martyr for what he believes. For his testimony is a personal affair. Indeed, Scripture shows us God constantly singling out individuals as He deals with men. In His sight, each and every individual soul stands naked. His gospel is the truth that makes men free. In this light it appears as the antidote to totalitarianism. Far from apologizing, therefore, for 260 denominations, we are ready to affirm that if Protestantism were true to itself, it should count denominations not by the hundreds, but by the thousands. Nay, there are as many units in our ranks as there are Protestants in the land.—Emile Caillett, *Intercollegian*

996

Protestantism believes in the church. The charge is often made that Protestantism so overemphasizes the individual as to produce an atomistic result, with no real doctrine of the church. It must be acknowledged that this is the point at which Protestants have been weakest. The full synthesis of liberty and unity has never been achieved by either Catholicism or Protestantism. But the ecumenical movement of today is a clear indication that Protestantism cherishes the ideal of community as well as of individuality. If the note of the universal fellowship of all the people of Christ is late in coming to adequate embodiment, we can at least rejoice that it has now clearly emerged into the Protestant consciousness. Protestantism always leaves room for free criticism of the church in the light of God's revelation of His will in Christ, but at the same time struggles for the realization of the Christian community as one Body of Christ throughout the world.—Samuel McCrea Cavert, *Protestantism, a Symposium*

997

Reformation means more than a historical event; it symbolizes man's witness of the truth in love. The connotation of the word "reformation" is "restoration of conditions to a former good state; a return from bad to good," or, understandingly applied, a back-to-God movement, a return to our God-given state of freedom, God alone being Lord of conscience. . . .

Reformation, consequently, means an ever-recurring soul-stirring act in the life of the individual or group. The spiritual reformed believes he has been called by God to witness for and defend under all circumstances the absolute sovereignty of his Creator, Lord, and Judge. . . .

Reformation Day symbolizes the Christian's true faith and zeal which is based solely on acceptance of and reliance upon the Word of God. To believe His revealed will is to bring its wondrous message of justice, mercy, and love in Christ Jesus to the four corners of the world at the expense of comfort, and life itself, if necessary. So help us God.—K. W. Schalk, *Monday Morning*

998

In Protestantism the influence of the preacher is dependent almost completely on the moral character of the man, the depth of his own religious experience and understanding, and his ability to teach and inspire Christian faith. The preacher is a guide in the Christian life. If he is a true preacher of Jesus Christ he, like the vicar in Oliver Goldsmith's *The Deserted Village,* "lures to brighter worlds, and leads the way." But according to the Protestant conception the individual Christian is his own priest. The preacher may pray for him, but he too must pray. The preacher may help him see his sins and phrase his confession, but the sinner's own heart must utter his repentance. And God will grant forgiveness direct to the penitent. Every disciple of Christ, according to the teaching of Protestantism, is his own priest.—Hampton Adams, *Protestantism*

999

The word "protest" has, of course, a negative as well as a positive meaning. To assert something is to deny its opposite. The man who affirmatively "protests his loyalty" will, by that very act, protest *against* the imputation that he is disloyal. So "Protestant" indicates a strong affirmation of something and, at the same time, a spirited opposition to its contrary.—Winfred E. Garrison, *The World Call*

1000

The word "Protestant," when applied to members of the original movement, meant "one who bears witness to his faith," or "one who testifies that he has had an inner spiritual experience." The word itself comes from two Latin words *pro* and *testare,* which mean "to testify for."—Roy L. Smith, *The Christian Advocate*

1001

In the year 1505 a serious-minded young German who had been harried by a sense of guilt entered the Erfurt Convent in the hope that the church might be able to furnish him with the spiritual guidance he needed.

If ever the Roman Catholic Church had a chance with the soul of a young man, it had that chance with Martin Luther. He did everything the church asked him to do. He fasted, confessed innocent acts as if they had been mortal sins, appealed to the Virgin, besought assistance from all the saints, and spent long vigils in pathetic and fruitless search after God and peace.

Eight years of this sort of thing passed, and he was just as much burdened as when he began. Then one night, while alone in his little cell with his New Testament, he chanced upon the words, "The just shall live by faith" (Romans 1:17). In a moment a divine illumination of great truth dawned upon his mind.

The forgiveness of God is not something that can be bought with sacrifices, vigils, and penance. It is a free gift that awaits all who will appropriate it, confident that the love of God has made it available to the penitent who is truly sorry about his sinning.

This principle is so well established . . . that it is difficult to realize how revolutionary it sounded to those who heard it for the first time. . . . Protestantism solemnly asserts that . . . the forgiveness of God can be obtained "without money and without price." This glorious right was made available to everyone through the death of Jesus.—Roy L. Smith, "Why I am a Protestant," *The Christian Advocate*

1002

At the turn of the century you may recall that Frank Lloyd Wright was commissioned to build a hotel in Tokyo that would withstand earthquakes. He built it on the principle of elasticity rather than rigidity. Instead of going down to rock he went down to mud and floated its foundation on mud. The walls were not joined, but loosely hinged. Only flexible materials were used. He was thought crazy at the time, but when the terrible earthquake struck Tokyo in 1923, devastating the city, the Imperial Hotel alone stood the shock and saved countless lives.

Well, that's our faith as Protestants. The church that will withstand the shocks of our turbulent civilization must have the strength of elasticity rather than of rigid uniformity. Against this church, as our Lord promised, "the gates of hell shall not prevail." —Harry H. Kruener, *Why Am I a Protestant?*

STEWARDSHIP SUNDAY

1003

When I give nothing:
I cast a ballot in favor of closing my church.
I discourage others.
When I give less than last year:
I show my disapproval of the work that has been done.
I favor curtailment of the work at home and abroad.
When I give grudgingly and of nesessity:
I shall find no joy in my giving.
I shall not receive the Lord's richest blessing; for it is written that the Lord loves a cheerful giver.
When I refuse to make a subscription in advance:
I make it difficult for my church to make plans for the year.
When I give systematically:
I shall make it possible for my church and for my denomination to plan work in advance and to live within income.
I shall make it much easier for my-

self. I know, from past experience, that the accumulation of small obligations soon becomes burdensome.

I shall find real joy and satisfaction in my giving.

When I give less than one tenth of my income:

I do less than that which was required of the poorest of the Jews.

When I give proportionately:

I shall be blessed in my giving, whether the gift be large or small. "For if there be first a willing mind, it is accepted according to that a man hath and not according to that he hath not."

I shall probably increase my gifts; I know the Kingdom causes need increased support, and that I have not been giving in proportion. I must ask myself whether or not my giving has increased with my income.—John A. McAfee, *When I Give Nothing*

1004

The soul of a man is in his gifts, because they are a part of a man's life. Money is life. It is the honest reward for honest labor. It is the symbol of a man's strength. It is the evidence of his talent. Truly, it is a part of his life. Thus, when a man gives, he gives a part of his life. This, then, is the deeper meaning of stewardship—to give, to share, to surrender—knowing that in it all the soul of a man shall be revealed.—Arnold Hilmar Lowe

1005

I have found that there is a tremendous joy in giving. It is a very important part of the joy of living.—William Black

1006

If a person can be religious and spiritually-minded among his treasures, surely he can be trusted elsewhere.

1007

Tightwads can't take it with them either, but longevity records show they can stay with it here longer than other people.

1008

Thankful, regular giving develops a genuine recognition of the everyday blessings of life as gifts from God and a strengthening of the desire to serve and worship Him.—Mrs. James H. Woods

1009

Recently a Christian man remarked, "I get so many appeal letters every month I can't even take time to read them."

His friend replied, "Of course. . . . If you lived behind the Iron Curtain, you would not get such letters. Or, if you lived in a country of poverty, you would not be able to respond. You should thank God you live in a country where you have the privilege of giving."

1010

God has created us and placed us on His earth to be stewards of His riches. All that we touch, all that we earn, all that we possess, all that we save, is not really ours. We may have a title or deed to it, but it can never be ours in the final sense. It is God's and only God's. It is but given to us to use while we dwell on earth. We belong to Christ, and Christ belongs to God. Life is a trust, and we are stewards of that divine trust. We witness of that as we give to our church and its mission.—Edward J. Vobra

1011

The New York Times, commenting editorially . . . on the flight of young Robert Hill to Dr. Schweitzer's hospital in Africa with four and a half tons of medical supplies worth $400,000, said, "This is an excellent illustration of the fact that the human heart is essentially warm and responsive. If a need can be made known or an appeal dramatized there is almost always a response. It was Robert's own simple human warmth that brought about this happy result."

Robert Hill, thirteen-year-old Negro boy, son of a U. S. Army sergeant stationed in Italy, read about Dr. Schweitzer's hospital in Africa. He wanted to help with a bottle of aspirin and asked the Allied Air Forces commander in Southern Europe if one of the planes could just drop the bottle at the hospital. An Italian radio station heard about the incident and told the story on the air. After hearing the appeal on the air, many persons wanted to send drugs for Dr. Schweitzer. French and Italian government planes flew the drugs to Africa, and Robert Hill flew, too, with the $400,000 worth of medical supplies.

"I never thought a child could do so much for my hospital," said Dr. Schweitzer.

Commented *The Times*, "Perhaps in this case only a child could have." —Editorial in *The Union Signal*

1012

A nation needs to pray for things it has—for things it has not earned—for gifts from men now dead.—Frederick Brown Harris

1013

Every gift, said Pindar, though it be small, is in reality great if given with affection.—*Christian Observer*

1014

Fools can make money. It takes a wise man to know how to use it.

1015

Money itself is lifeless, impotent, sterile . . . but man . . . using money . . . may feed the hungry, cure the diseased, make desert places bloom and bring beauty into life.—John D. Rockefeller, Jr., *Life*

1016

Does money bring happiness?

The question is hardly original, but the row it has provoked in the obscure Italian village of San Marco d'Urri was surely unprecedented.

The money arrived last November when every man, woman, and child in San Marco was presented with twenty-five shares of Bank of America stock worth $1,200 and paying $47 a year in dividends. "Maraviglioso!" the villagers cried when bankers, TV cameramen, and news photographers arrived from Genoa and slogged the last half mile into town on a muddy mule path. The church bell tolled and there was lofty praise for the two brothers, Victor and Joseph Saturno, who had sent the money from America. Rich and childless real-estate operators in Reno, Nevada, they had wanted to create a memorial to their father, Leopoldo, who had spent his youth in San Marco. "Che generosita!" the villagers agreed.

Everyone, that is, except the terrible-tempered widow Virginia Cassinelli, 82, who, in an age of payola, refused to sign up for her share. Claiming it was the work of the devil and hurling lurid curses, the widow forced her son, Mario, 65, and her daughter, Gentile, 63, to give up their shares, too. The village, she argued, was going to the dogs. . . .

When the villagers started squabbling over their new wealth, it seemed the widow might be right. Youths swaggered around in fancy new trench coats and the silence of the once peaceful countryside was ruined by the roar of scooter bikes. Worse still, a feud developed over what sort of "thank you" gesture San Marco should make.

One proposal was to change the name of the village to Saturno (that wouldn't cost anything, but was finally discarded as too niggardly). Then a statue was proposed but rejected on the ground that San Marco has no piazza to put it in. Finally, the 220 inhabitants of the upper part of the village decided to build a church in honor of the Saturnos. This would save them walking half a mile to the church in the lower part of town. But the sixty-four residents of lower San Marco objected. They preferred a bust of Papa Leopoldo in front of the present church.

"You want the church and the statue, too," complained upper San Marco.

"Well, you've got the wineshop and the television—you can't have everything," shouted back lower San Marco.

Then a small boy got a bright idea.

Why not a statue of Leopoldo, halfway between the upper and lower levels of the village?

"Magnifico," the villagers agreed, and for a while it seemed that even the widow Cassinelli would approve. First she sent son Mario out to claim his share. Next, she sent daughter Gentile. But Gentile was trapped in a sudden six-foot fall of snow and barely made it back to the widow's one-room shack. It was a warning sign to the widow. "The devil's behind this," she wailed. . . . "We'll pay for all this gold in some terrible way. Just you wait and see."—*Newsweek*

1017

We are living in a dynamic world, presenting constantly new and challenging situations. In such a world the church cannot remain static. Heretofore, it has coasted along comparatively easily, but now the situation demands that it shall do something as strenuously different as when airplanes finally achieved power and speed enough to crash the sound barrier. We have to break through into a new dimension of vision and giving. The old pattern simply will not suffice. How this shall be accomplished will demand the best thought and consecration of all of us. I am, myself, convinced that the . . . church must not merely do a little better than it has done before but must somehow gain a totally new perspective and a commitment commensurate with the demand for its witness and service.—Paul S. Wright

1018

Many people regard their giving as an expense and make it as small as they reasonably can. What one gives to religious causes is not an expense. It is an investment—the best that one ever makes.

God is a bountiful God. He multiplies spiritually and materially what we invest in His work. Behold every harvest field! It is not loving that empties the heart nor giving that empties the purse.—Warren H. Denison, *Stewardship Notebook*

1019

Most of us go through our days and weeks and years so intent on our own problems that neither what we see nor what we hear makes any impression as to the needs of the other person. We often become so absorbed in ourselves that our fellow men become no more than automatons. The only job in the world is *my* job. *I* am the only person who really has anything to do. Nobody has problems like *mine*.

But every normal person we meet— in the home, on the street, at work, or at worship—is facing some problem or carrying some burden that a smile, a cheerful greeting, or a show of interest might help to ease. Those who seem to need help least may be the ones who need it most.

Giving is at the root of friendship. Giving something that another wants, needs, and accepts gratefully. Giving material things has been the beginning of many friendships, but friendships grow and endure only through gifts of the mind and of the heart. . . . David Dunn, in . . . "Try Giving Yourself Away," tells an amazing story of how an unusual hobby brought happiness to himself and hundreds of others. Things he gave never cost money— just a little time, a little of himself.

. . . Every individual must give what *he* has and in his own way, Mr. Dunn points out. Sincerity is an absolute requirement. . . . Most parents love their children and see a lot in them that is praiseworthy, but parental desire for perfection in their offspring prompts adults to concentrate on faults rather than to praise for virtues. Parents who give *themselves* to children are not liable to know firsthand the meaning of delinquency. If employers and employees would give more of themselves to each other, every phase of industry would profit, and strikes might pass into history. Men in public life need to give themselves instead of *taking for themselves*. Human desires are the same the world over. Every person wants companionship, approval, love, and understanding—intangibles that all of us can give when we are willing to make the effort. And it does take effort. Even five minutes of companionship with some persons can be difficult. Tolerance often has to pinch-hit while we strive for understanding, and approval sometimes requires arduous searching. Beginners in this high adventure of self-giving might do well to select those to whom giving is easy. If we wish to live in a world of warmth and friendship instead of a desert of loneliness, we must give ourselves, the only giving that really counts. With each giving we learn to give more effectively.—Emma Kidd Hulburt, editorial in *The Union Signal*

1020

In our day charity has acquired an institutional character. Individuals have only limited opportunities for doing good. Modern man knows that his greatest responsibility consists in improving institutions. In the depths of his conscience he knows that he will have to give the Sovereign Judge an account not only of his personal conduct but of the efforts he has made to solve wage and housing problems, and to promote world peace. He knows that a few private acts of charity will be no dispensation.

We have reached the heart of our problem. If all that we have said is true, Christians should now be the most active workers in the fight for social justice and international peace. Many today, even some non-Christians, see that Christianity is the only force capable of giving meaning to civilization. We agree yet we cannot hide the fact that for more than a century, despite certain brilliant achievements, Christianity has failed to meet this obligation. It has failed because many Christians . . . have been motivated by an egoistic anxiety for their own personal salvation and by an exclusively self-interested concern about things temporal. These Christians have forgotten the bond that links these two activities. They have disregarded their absolute obligation to further the reign of God's law, which is justice and charity. First, they must be converted to this law; else they can never influence civilization.

The collapse we are witnessing today is not that of the social doctrine of the church because this doctrine has been but laxly applied. The collapse is that of a Christian world not truly Christian. Yet the world is turning even now to Christianity. It is not the world that doubts Christians, but Christians who no longer believe in themselves. They do not believe in the social efficacy of their faith. Their dis-belief springs from a bad conscience Lastly, their disbelief is a form of laziness and a kind of comfort that dispenses them from effort. They settle down with pleasant hopes about the hereafter and they dispense themselves from working for the betterment of man's temporal condition. But things are not quite that simple. It is in struggling for the present city that the future city is won.—Jean Danielou, "Hope and the Christian," *Commonweal*

1021

Stewardship is concerned with nothing less than man's responsibility to God as he participates in the whole technological-industrial-distributional system of his environing context. For stewardship is the active recognition of the sovereignty of God over His whole creation—over the creative and productive processes in which men share, and the uses to which they put all of the resources and means that come under their care and control. Stewardship within the church of Christ, as it calls for support and ministers to a radically materialistic generation, can only be viewed in this larger frame.—Albert T. Rasmussen, "Stewardship in an Economy of Abundance," *United Church Herald*

1022

Christian giving is God's divine plan to make us like Himself; it reveals our religion and bares our souls; it is prophetic and has to do with the inner life; it creates an inner sensitiveness and gives a keener vision to His work and plans.—Warren H. Denison, *Stewardship Notebook*

1023

What giving does for and to the giver: I am not speaking of the accomplishments of giving—what it does for causes—but the human values that giving liberates and develops. A gift always does something to the giver. It makes him better or worse. "Must I give again?" or "I just must give again!" The emphasis is not primarily on the amount, but on the proportion, the spirit, the method. There are wrong and right ways to give. We get from our giving what we put into it. If our giving is niggardly, unsympathetic, thoughtless, forced, too small a share, our lives will portray similar characteristics. How many there are who shrivel and die spiritually in the very activities that should produce strength and vitality of character. But if our gift is from gratitude, devout hearts, sacrificial spirits, we grow characters of strength and purity. The accomplishments of giving depend primarily on the giver, not on the gift.—Warren H. Denison, *Stewardship Notebook*

1024

Christian commitment means dedication to a life which is accountable to God and as such it can never be partial. We cannot commit our own personal lives without also seeking to commit our family life and our communities. God is sovereign over our total lives or we are only paying lip service to the sovereignty of God and actually living as if man could be God.

Man is the creature of God, but we constantly act in some parts of our lives as though we thought we could be independent creators apart from God. Divided, distraught, fearful personal lives result. Confused, unwanted and unloved children and spouses also result from mixing ourselves up with God. Competitiveness, and irresponsibility for others are the inevitable fruit of trying to be more than we humans can possibly be.—Doris Webster Havice, *Guide Posts*

1025

The story is told of the man who was entirely self-centered. He lived enclosed in mirrors; everywhere he looked he saw himself. Then appreciation, admiration, adoration, and reverence entered into this man's life and grew until the mirrors became windows through which he looked out and beyond to something other and greater than himself.—Christian Hymnways

1026

For most of us the financial program of the church is an unfortunate necessity to be kept as small as possible rather than a way in which we may function as members of the worldwide Body of Christ through regular sharing of a significant portion of our income. Too many of us have been using the irresponsibility of others as an excuse for our own irresponsibility.—Edwin B. Towle

1027

You are to be congratulated that your church has invited you to participate in this every-family visitation canvass. It is a high honor, a gracious, challenging, spiritual privilege, a lifetime opportunity. You are using the Master's methods, too. He gathered the Twelve and Seventy, laymen from every walk of life as you are, then trained and sent them forth by twos with assignments to conduct interviews explaining the work and needs, arousing interest, and securing generous support.

The Every Member Canvass is one of the best known methods of teaching Christian stewardship. Church and Kingdom finance is directly related to the spiritual life. A church may not be successfully financed simply because it gathers sufficient funds. They must be secured on Christian stewardship principles and motives. Your primary emphasis is to develop the life of the giver and enrich his spiritual experience. Yours is not a secular drive but a spiritual challenge. It is not merely to underwrite budgets for local expenses and benevolences, as important as they are, but to develop character, and to persuade men, women and youth to become good stewards of their possessions.—Warren H. Denison, *Stewardship Notebook*

1028

Sitting across the dinner table from the Galilean, Zacchaeus is pictured as bragging of his authority, his possessions and his self-importance. Through it all the Master sits silently. His eyes pierce with conviction the heart of this man's foolish life. Finally Zacchaeus went to the porch, and told the waiting mob that he was willing to pay back, restore and give away, for at last he had found that "things" did not matter. When he returned to the table, Jesus said, "Zacchaeus, what did you see that made you desire this peace?" Came the reply, "Good Master, I saw mirrored in your eyes the face of the Zacchaeus I was meant to be."—Lloyd C. Douglas

1029

Three workmen fashioning a cross,
On which a fourth must die;
Yet none of any other asked,
"And why, and why, and why?"
Said they, "This is our business,
Our living we must earn;
What happens to the other man
Is none of our concern."
—Clyde McGee

1030

One way to look upon the church budget is as a list of expenses to be pared to the minimum so that our giving may be as small as possible. This makes the whole matter a reluctant and painful business, bereft of joy. The results are likely to be inadequate to meet even a very modest budget. The cause of Christ suffers. A "more excellent way" is to see the church and its budgeted program as a way and an opportunity to respond in gratitude to God's love. Then, instead of asking, "How cheaply can I get by?" we ask, "How much can I possibly give to further the work of Christ in the world?" Investing substantially of one's self in this way leads to real joy and satisfaction. This prevailing attitude is one important mark of the true church.—Edwin B. Towle

1031

Every impulse of generosity, when carried to fruition, gives a diastole to the soul which lifts it one step closer to the gates of heaven.—Kendall Weisiger, *The Rotarian*

1032

I have learned that money is not the measure of the man, but it is often the means of finding out how small he is.—Oswald J. Smith

1033

The smallest deed is better than the greatest intention.

1034

We have not realized what the gospel is if we have not felt the compulsion of stewardship with respect to it. "I am entrusted with a commission, a stewardship," said Paul.—D. T. Niles

1035

Stewardship is what a man does after he says, "I believe."—W. H. Greever

1036

But the duty of Christian giving is always there; if that duty has not been taught because for a time others were supplying all the church's financial needs, there was a serious gap in that church's life and teaching.—V. S. Azariah

1037

It is irresponsible to think that Christians can find time and money and strength for everything that everybody else does, and that with spare money in spare time with spare strength they can serve the ends of God's Kingdom.

The great pearl is bought only by selling small pearls. Where no pearl has been sold, there obedience to the demand of the Kingdom has not begun.—D. T. Niles

1038

The world does not take the church seriously because the church is not serious. The world is suing us for divorce because of nonsupport. Religion is more complicated than mathematics.—Paul Calvin Payne

1039

We have now to realize that human society is sick almost to death and that nothing short of radical conversion will bring it to life and hope.

To the end that the world may be converted to genuine Christianity, we must raise huge sums of money for the preaching of the gospel in all ends of the earth and for a needed service to individuals and communities.

More than that, we must ourselves be converted to genuine Christianity. To God and His purpose for mankind we must dedicate ourselves, our minds, our hearts, our pocketbooks, our personal ambitions.

God has never had on His side a majority of men and women. He does not need a majority to work wonders in history, but He does need a minority fully committed to Him and His purpose. In the world today Christian stewardship is a necessity.—Ernest Fremont Tittle

1040

If there is one key word in church canvassing, that word is "communication." More canvasses have been spoiled for lack of adequate communication than for any other cause.

No canvass can be a success unless the people can hear of it and be heard from. Real communication is a two-way street, and if either side of the street is blocked the whole project is most likely to be unsuccessful.—Richard Byfield and James Shaw, *Your Money and Your Church*

1041

Years ago a man knelt with his pastor and prayed as he committed himself to God to tithe. His first week's pay was $10 and the tithe was $1. As he grew older, he became more prosperous, his tithe was $7.50 a week, then $10. He moved to another city and soon his tithe was $100 a week, then $200, then $500. He sent his friend a wire, "Come and see me." The pastor arrived at the man's beautiful home. They had a good time talking over old times. Finally, the man came to the point, "You remember that promise I made years ago to tithe. How can I get released?" He continued, "It's like this, when I made the promise, I only had to give a dollar but now it's $500. I can't afford to give away money like that."

The old pastor looked at his friend, "I'm afraid we cannot get released from the promise, but there is something we can do. We can kneel and ask God to shrink your income so you can afford to give a dollar."—Thomas A. Clark, *Gratitude to God*

1042

Giving to the church has far-reaching implications. When you give of your time you are not really giving time but life. When you give of your talent you are not really giving talent but the portion of your life expended in developing, cultivating, and using that talent. When you give money you are giving the portion of your life expended in gaining money. Stewardship then is not really the investment of time, talent, and treasure in the Kingdom of God, but the investment of self.

The statement "a moment used cannot be regained," is only partly true. It is true in that the portion of your life expended in that moment cannot be relived, but certainly the money received in exchange for that moment of your life can enable your life to be reinvested. A man who misuses his money is cheating himself out of his rightful heritage of the double use of time. By the same token, a man who uses his money wisely receives the double blessing and benefit of being able to expend his life twice for righteousness. This is one of the great joys of Christian stewardship—two for the price of one.

Many times people have been heard to remark that it is not necessary to give money to the church as long as one is a faithful worker. Here again, it should be perfectly clear that they are using their lives only once in the cause of Christ. Christ has asked for the totality of man. He requires an accounting of time, talent, and treasure. To withhold any element is to present God with only a partial accounting of your stewardship.

God has entrusted you with one life. He thus affords you the opportunity to be a good steward of that life. In the two letters written to the Christians in Corinth we find three of the characteristics of a good steward.

First, it is required of stewards that they be found trustworthy. You have been entrusted with one life. The more of that life you return unto God the better steward you are. To betray the trust God has shown in you is to betray the very meaning and blessing of life.

Later, in the second letter . . . we read that "each one of you must do as he has made up his mind." This indicates that stewardship is a volitional act of the will. Each man must make up his mind whether he will faithfully discharge the life God has entrusted to him. To give or to withhold is the question facing man. Either way he decides, but only one decision makes him a good steward.

The conclusion of this verse reads "for God loves a cheerful giver." Joy is a characteristic of a good steward. To give out of a sense of compulsion is to miss the joy of stewardship. When giving is done joyously it is a free expression of man's love for God.

Christian stewardship is the stewardship of life. A good steward will be found trustworthy in his willful expression of love toward God. Because he has truly expressed his love, his relationship with God will be one of great joy.—Robert L. Bell, "Two for the Price of One"

1043

There are the poor rich, possessed by their possessions; and the poor poor, whose poverty is not merely of things but of life itself. There are also the rich poor, who may not have many things, but who have an inner treasure; and the rich rich, who possess their possessions.

Christ, who though He was rich became poor, is not alone a challenging example, but the unfailing source of power to solve the problem of poverty and riches. How many of the Master's words deal with the problems created by the disparity between people in the matter of their possessions! How many economic and social schemes profess to draw their inspiration and authority from His words! In the Christian view, equality does not mean leveling down but leveling up. The true disciple of Jesus is neither a miser nor a spendthrift, but a steward.—William Hiram Foulkes, *Today*

1044

A study of stewardship as it is found in the Bible will reveal that God's basic purpose in this whole business of giving is the enrichment of the life of the giver. This is one of God's great plans to make our spirit like His.—Fred P. Register

1045

Christian stewardship is a far more significant part of our faith than we often realize. It is a call to each of us to leave our self-centered lives as individual persons, as families, as a church fellowship, as world-bound people, to move on to the far horizons which God sets before us. Through it all Jesus is walking among us again, and He is summoning us on to the higher levels of service and witness. May we respond and move on to the far horizons of the Christian way.—Edward J. Vobra

1046

The great medieval philosopher, Moses Maimonides, once said that giving is most blessed and most acceptable when the donor remains completely anonymous.

1047

You can't outgive God.

1048

Poverty is one of the bitter curses; it leaves no right to be generous.

1049

The hand that in life grips with a miser's clutch, and the ear that refuses to heed the pleading voice of humanity forfeit the most precious of all gifts of earth and of heaven—the happiness that comes of doing good to others.—Amon G. Carter

1050

What you are is God's gift to you; what you make of yourself is your gift to Him.—*Survey Bulletin*

1051

Nothing that is God's is obtainable by money.—Tertullian, *The Christian's Defence*

1052

Churches deny their faith when they venture only so far as they can be sure that they can see the way.—Roswell Barnes

1053

To be rich in admiration and free from envy; to rejoice greatly in the good of others; to love with such generosity of heart that your love is still a dear possession in absence or unkindness—these are the gifts of fortune which money cannot buy and without which money can buy nothing. He who has such a treasury of riches, being happy and valiant himself, in his own nature, will enjoy the universe as if it were his own estate; and help the man to whom he lends a hand to enjoy it with him.—Robert Louis Stevenson

1054

The rich young ruler was rejected because he would not straighten out his money matters. Zacchaeus faced his and was accepted. Jesus was even willing to lose the man.

"Today is salvation come to this house." Zacchaeus had straightened out his money concerns.

1055

The purse of the people is the real seat of sensibility. Let it be drawn upon largely, and they will then listen to truths which could not excite them through any other organ.—Thomas Jefferson

1056

Money may be the husk of many things, but not the kernel. It brings you food, but not appetite; medicine, but not health; acquaintances, but not friends; servants, but not loyalty; days of joy, but not peace and happiness.—Henrik Ibsen

1057

The value of money is not simply what the government stamps on the face of a coin. The important value is what you attribute to it.—Robert C. Dodds, *Two Together*

1058

It is easier to renounce worldly possessions than it is to renounce the love of them.—Walter Hilton, *Scale of Perfection*

1059

On his deathbed, Alexandre Dumas, the famed French writer, was told by his disappointed son that there were only a few coins left in the family treasury.

"How wonderful," enthused the elder Dumas. "That's precisely the sum I had with me when I first came to Paris. Imagine, living like a king for half a century and it hasn't cost me a cent!"—*The Bedside Bachelor*

1060

One morning a Scotsman named MacLeod was interrupted by a call from his bank.

"Mister MacLeod," said the banker, "you've overdrawn your account by some $64."

But MacLeod was prepared for him.

"A wee favor, m'lad," he purred back at the banker, "look it up in your book and tell me our financial relationship just thirty days ago . . . if ye'll be so kind."

The banker did so, and reported that thirty days before MacLeod had had a balance in *his* favor of $117. "Aye!" bellowed MacLeod, "and did *I* call *you?*"

1061

The writer who understood money best was Dostoevski. In the *Brothers Karamazov* when Dmitri has humiliated an officer, he sends his younger brother Aloysha to make up to the man by offering money. The man refuses to take Dmitri's money, saying that no amount of money can gloss over the humiliation his young son saw him undergo. He throws the money away. Aloysha, priest though he is, retrieves it because he knows that tomorrow the man will accept it. —Harry L. Golden, *The Carolina Israelite*

1062

For my own part, I believe that honor and money nearly always go together, and that he who desires honor never hates money, while he who hates money cares little for honor. —Teresa of Jesus, *Way of Perfection*

1063

I believe that every right implies a responsibility; every opportunity, an obligation; every possession, a duty.—John D. Rockefeller, Jr.

1064

The rich man is not one who is in possession of much, but one who gives much.—John Chrysostom, *Homilies*

1065

What a man does for himself dies with him. What he does for others lives forever.

1066

He is no fool who gives what he cannot keep—to gain what he cannot lose.—Jim Elliot

1067

Most giving is done because the giver is actuated by his emotions which have been stirred by the needs which have been presented to him.—George E. Lundy, *Successful Fund Raising Sermons*

1068

Christian stewardship is the practice of the Christian religion. It is neither a department of life nor a sphere of activity. It is the Christian conception of life as a whole, manifested in attitudes and actions.—W. H. Greever, *Work of the Lord*

1069

The Society attitude is Olympian, but benign. It is aristocratic but, as we all know, uneasy lies the head. The Society attitude is what gets Society people accused of being snooty and stuck-up, but it is actually not a snooty or stuck-up attitude. Part of it is a heightened sense of social responsibility. The Society attitude is zealous and dedicated but somewhat martyred. Society people feel put upon. "How much can we be expected to do?" sighs a Society lady, carrying in her sigh the implication that without her efforts hospitals would swarm with vermin, foreign missions would abandon themselves to the heathen, girls without number would go wrong and museums of art would collapse. As a matter of fact they might, because Society has been both wise and generous with its time and money. The late Mrs. Norman Whitehouse . . . was acting in the best traditions of Society when . . . she came out in favor of the forty-hour week. It would give the working classes, she said, "more time for cultural pursuits." What a revolutionary thought this was! Up till then it had been assumed that a worker's time, when not devoted to toil, was devoted to drink.

But Society people are not the only possessors of public spirit. Miss Gertrude Ely, who feels that the social cachet attached to "charity" has destroyed much of the effectiveness of it, told me this story: A Philadelphia gentleman, soliciting funds among his Society friends for a worthy cause, found himself, because of a similarity of names, at a modest Quaker home . . . (Philadelphia's large Quaker population has never played much part in its Society). So as not to embarrass the lady of the house, he explained his mission and rose to go. "Very well," said the Quakeress politely, "I'll give thee seven million dollars."—Stephen Birmingham, "Who Are Real Society?," *Holiday*

1070

Nothing is ours to keep for ourselves. Money, talent, time, whatever it may be that we possess, is only ours to use. This is the great law written everywhere.

1071

Money doesn't always bring happiness. A man with ten million dollars is no happier than a man with nine million dollars.

1072

Stewardship . . . is the church's effort to think through as fully and coherently as possible the meaning of its faith and life.—T. A. Kantenen, "A Theology of Christian Stewardship"

1073

Whatever man loves, that is his god. For he carries it in his heart; he goes about with it night and day; he sleeps and wakes with it, be it what it may— wealth or pelf, pleasure or renown.— Martin Luther

1074

Where your pleasure is, there is your treasure; where your treasure, there your heart; where your heart, there your happiness.—Augustine

1075

May you find your greatest happiness in knowing where your treasure truly is.—Russell Loesch

1076

To share—a verb with an interesting range of synonyms. Some meanings are: to participate, to cooperate, to distribute, to dole. A participating, co-operating worshiper knows there is no stewardship in mechanical and occasional distribution or doles.—Wade L. Carter

1077

The characters in Nevil Shute's book *On the Beach* are forced to a reappraisal of the things which are really most important in life because they know that they will die soon. A blanket of radio-active force, unleashed by thermo-nuclear explosions in another hemisphere, is descending upon them. How often we are forced to a re-evaluation of our own scale of values when we are confronted by forces which we cannot control. Is it not true that most of us are continually "on the beach"? Now is the time for us to awake out of sleep and determine what accounting we will make to God for His goodness to us.—Lee J. Smallreed, Jr.

1078

Illusion is a comprehensive ill. The rich man who deludes himself into behaving like a mendicant may conserve his fortune although he will not be very happy.—John Kenneth Galbraith, *The Affluent Society*

1079

No man ever went bankrupt because he tithed.

1080

God wants to give us something, but cannot, because our hands are full. There's nowhere for Him to put it.— Augustine

1081

It is easy to want things from the Lord and yet not want the Lord Himself; as though the gift could ever be preferable to the Giver.—Augustine

1082

Jesus said to the rich young man, "Sell all that thou hast and come, follow me." And the young man went away sorrowful, for he was very rich.

Years passed. The rich young man pursued his accustomed ways, but zest for the old life was gone. Often as he rode over his vast estate or entertained his cronies at the banquet table, there would come upon him a strange sadness which to dispel required ever-increasing diversions. He added to his estate, built ever larger storehouses for his goods, and tried to brighten his days with the splendor of gold. He was successful in a measure. His money bought lands, houses, and friends, but nothing could purchase for him release from the haunting memory of the words heard in his youth, "Come, follow me."

Sometimes in the security of the great hall of his home, surrounded by his admirers, he would humorously tell the story of how once in his careless youth he had almost been persuaded by a long-haired prophet in the big city to give up his inheritance and join a little group of religious fanatics who soon afterwards had been broken up by the authorities. This never failed to rouse the company to laughter. But as the years passed, for some reason, he could not be induced, even in his most stimulated moments, to recite the story.

If in his advanced age he was thought somewhat queer, no one mentioned it to him. No one ever asked him why he was given to muttering to himself the incomprehensible words, "The price was too great; he had no right to ask so much." He came to his end not without the honor and respect of men. It is probable that he was accorded a magnificent burial, although when or how he died, or where his burial place is, are incidents unknown. Indeed, no one remembered even to write down his name.

1083

In a newspaper column recently I read a reference to "The Department of Eternal Revenue!" The idea was most intriguing, and I couldn't help but let my mind wander or leap to the church of the living God. In at least two important senses the church is a department of eternal revenue. The church seeks to bring to all people the benefits of living the eternal life. It is the agency which not exclusively but uniquely dispenses the lasting qualities of life . . . equally impressively, the church is always available as a channel for our giving. This is its sacred and beholden duty. It cannot—it dare not—do otherwise. Its task is limitless for it prays and it works to transform "the world into the Kingdom of God." It must, therefore, be an open-ended contract between God and His people. It pours itself out in service to the community and the world. Its only limit is the limit of our affection and our giving.—Ernest A. Yarrow

1084

Rings and jewels are not gifts, but apologies for gifts. The only gift is a portion of thyself. Therefore the poet brings his poem; the shepherd, his lamb; the farmer, corn; the miner, a gem; the sailor, coral and shells; the painter, his picture; the girl, a handkerchief of her own sewing.—Ralph Waldo Emerson

VETERANS' DAY (ARMISTICE DAY)

1085

A worthy, righteous peace is the fruit of effort. You don't get peace, you don't retain peace just by being peaceable. You get it, if it is worth having, by a constant willingness to work and sacrifice and risk for it. . . . If you think by just keeping peaceable and never going to war that you can get a just peace in this world, you are wrong.

That is the one way in which to surely lose peace . . . peace is made up of manly courage, fearless virility, readiness to serve justice and honor at any cost, and a mind and a heart attuned to sacrifice . . . only the strong can promote and preserve a righteous peace . . . idle and futile is the voice of the weak nation, or the craven nation, when it clamors for peace.—Frank Knox

1086

Peace will never be entirely secure until men everywhere have learned to conquer poverty without sacrificing liberty to security. Peace will be uncertain as long as great sections of mankind live under systems of discrimination and exploitation, racial or economic, which make them militantly conscious of loyalty to the advancement of their own race or class rather than of loyalty to the human family. We and our descendants will have our work cut out for us even if we are free from the immediate threat of another world war. Temporary peace will not become permanent except as men make the rich resources and technology, which today chiefly serve the few, the benefactors of all mankind. There can be no greater challenge to the human spirit.—Norman Thomas, *Appeal to the Nations and Afterward*

1087

There must be, not a balance of power, but a community of power; not organized rivalries, but an organized common peace.—Woodrow Wilson

1088

We should wage war not to win a war, but to win a peace.—Paul Hoffman, *Peace Can Be Won*

1089

International confidence cannot be builded upon fear, it must be builded upon good will.—Herbert Hoover

1090

The body of the Unknown Soldier has come home, but his spirit will wander with that of his brothers. There will be no rest for his soul until the great democracy of death has been translated into the unity of life. Isolation ends at the edge of the grave. Whatever the estate of the dead, they are not divided by prejudice of race

or nationality. To them, at least, all things are common.

But that is not good enough. If there are to be no more wars, the men and women of the world must put their hearts and minds to the task of bringing us all into comradeship this side of Jordan. There is need of some living symbol of unity. Blow, bugles; blow—not for the unknown dead, but for the plain and palpable brotherhood of life.—Heywood Broun, *Collected Edition of Heywood Broun*

1091

Too often peace has been thought of as a negative condition—the mere absence of war. We know now that we cannot achieve peace by taking a negative attitude. Peace is positive, and it has to be waged with all our thought, energy, and courage and with the conviction that war is not inevitable. . . .

When events call for firmness as well as generosity, the United States waged peace by pledging its aid to free nations threatened by aggression and took prompt and vigorous action to fulfill that pledge. We have actively sought and are actively seeking to make the United Nations an effective instrument of international cooperation. We proposed, and with the eager cooperation of sixteen other nations put into effect, a great concerted program for the economic recovery and spiritual reinvigoration of Europe. We joined the other American republics and we now join with Western Europe in treaties to strengthen the United Nations and insure international peace and security. . . .

A secure and stable peace is not a goal we can reach all at once and for all time. It is a dynamic state, produced by effort and faith, with justice and courage. The struggle is continuous and hard. The prize is never irrevocably ours. To have this genuine peace we must constantly work for it. —Dean G. Acheson

1092

There never was a good war or a bad peace.—Benjamin Franklin

1093

It wouldn't be so bad if civilization were at the crossroads, but this is one of those cloverleaf jobs.—*The Rotarian*

1094

Military power is . . . ineffective when it lacks a moral and political base. It is the fist of a hand; but the hand must be attached to an arm, and the arm to a body; and the body must be robust before the fist can be effective.—Reinhold Niebuhr, "The Limits of Military Power," *New Leader*

1095

A neutral country is one which has the power, if the need arises, of defending its neutrality against all comers. A country that survives only by the tolerance of others is not a neutral. . . . Let us call things by their right names. . . . In none of the last wars has the neutrality of any country been respected by the belligerents if the belligerent thought the occupation of the neutral country would be advantageous to him.—Konrad Adenauer

1096

It is more glorious to slay war with words, than man with steel, and it is true glory to secure peace by peaceful means.—Augustine

1097

As long as war is regarded as wicked, it will always have its fascinations. When it is looked upon as vulgar, it will cease to be popular.—Oscar Wilde

1098

You can't say civilization don't advance, however, for in every war they kill you a new way.—Will Rogers, *Everywoman's Family Circle*

1099

War is mankind's most stupid and tragic folly.—Dwight D. Eisenhower

1100

War is old, pathetically old, tragically futile, hopelessly antiquated.— W. H. P. Faunce

BOOK WEEK

1101

Read the preface first, go in through the front door. Read the old books— those that have stood the test of time. Read them slowly, carefully, thoroughly. They will help you to discriminate among the new ones. Read plenty of books about people and things, but not too many books about books. Read one book at a time, but never one book alone. Well-born books have relatives. Follow them up. Read no book with which the author has not taken pains to write in a clean, sound, lucid style. Life is short. Read over again the ten best books that you have already read. The result of this experiment will test your taste, measure your advance, and will fit you for progress in the art of reading.— Henry van Dyke

1102

The bulwarks of our liberty are men and women who read and think.
—Admiral Chester W. Nimitz

1103

Through books . . . ideas find their way to human brains and ideals to human hearts and souls.—Dorothy Canfield Fisher

1104

Persons who read more write better, speak better, think better. And it goes without saying that they know more. As a result of a knowledge of the past they can think better about the present and future.—George Gallup, "You Can't Get Ahead Today Unless You Read," *Ladies' Home Journal*

1105

When I get a little money, I buy books; and if any is left, I buy food and clothes.—Erasmus

1106

The man who is fond of books is usually a man of lofty thought and elevated opinions.—George Dawson

1107

It is the books we read before middle life that do most to mold characters and influence our lives.—Robert Pitman

1108

Books are each a world.—William Wordsworth

1109

If this nation is to be wise as well as strong, and if we are to live up to our national promise and our national destiny, then we need more new ideas from more wise men reading more good books.—Senator John F. Kennedy

1110

These rare books are as much a part of academic equipment as test tubes and Bunsen burners.—Cecil Byrd

1111

"If you raise your children 'by the book,' " our pastor told the Young Married Club at church, "better make up your mind which one—comic, bank, or Good Book."—Burton Hillis, *Better Homes & Gardens*

1112

Everywhere I have sought tranquillity and have found it nowhere except in a corner with a book.—Thomas à Kempis

1113

A good book is the precious lifeblood of a master spirit, embalmed and treasured up on purpose to a life beyond life.—John Milton

1114

Perhaps above all else, the literature gives a powerful impression that the search for the philosopher's stone has not ended; it has only taken on new form and is carried on under new circumstances. The market for magic still appears to be very much alive, as it presumably was in far antiquity.—Louis Schneider and Sanford M. Bornbusch, *Popular Religion*

1115

Literature is a transmission of power. Textbooks and treatises, dictionaries and encyclopedias, manuals and books of instruction—they are communications; but literature is a power line, and the motor, mark you, is the reader.—Charles P. Curtis

1116

Books are the quietest and most constant of friends: they are the most accessible and wisest of counselors, and the most patient of teachers.—Charles W. Eliot

1117

No one knows how born readers are produced, but we can put books in their way and in the way of less happily born, in the hope that proximity will have its effect, as it does in the formation of more mundane habits.—Reuben A. Brower

1118

He hath never fed on the dainties that are bred in a book; he hath not eaten paper as it were; he hath not drunk ink; he is only an animal, only sensible in the duller parts.—William Shakespeare

1119

In literature as in love, we are astonished at what is chosen by others. —André Maurois, *The Art of Living*

1120

Two goats found a pile of discarded movie film in a trash heap. As one of them finished off a film and its container, the other noted that it was from a well-known title, and asked, "How was it?" The other replied, "Better than the book."

1121

If for some peculiar reason a law were passed that forbade people to talk about books they read, reading would be cut 90 per cent.—Ian Ballantine, *The New York Times* Book Review

1122

Language is the armory of the human mind; and at once contains the trophies of its past, and the weapons of its future conquests.—Samuel T. Coleridge, *Biographia Literaria*

1123

To consult with the wisest and the greatest men . . . use books rightly.— John Ruskin

1124

Literature is the best and easiest way of acquainting one people with another.—Maxim Gorki

1125

During a sales conference two men said, "I am so busy that I simply have no time to do any reading." The real meaning of those words is, "I am so busy that I have decided to commit slow mental suicide."

Suppose they had said, "I am so busy that I simply have no time to eat any food." Their failure to eat would lead to death by starvation. There is no essential difference between the mind and the body in the need for food for each. A body becomes healthy through eating proper food and taking proper exercise. The mind becomes stronger and more effective when it is nourished with proper ideas and when it is exercised creatively.

Actually, "I have no time to read," is one of the silliest of excuses. Another meaning of those words is, "I have no desire to read." Even if one does no more than use periods of unavoidable delay to do one's reading, a surprising amount may be done.

There is little excuse for anyone failing to get an education. One does not need to spend any money for books. Usually there are public libraries where books of all sorts may be obtained without cost. Men get what they desire and in the measure of their desire.—Thomas Dreier

1126

If anyone finds that he never reads serious literature, if all his reading is frothy and trashy, he would do well to try to train himself to like books that the general agreement of cultivated and sound-thinking persons has placed among the classics.—Theodore Roosevelt

1127

According to the pollsters, the number of Americans who claim to be reading a book is only half the number who own an automobile.—Charlton Ogburn, Jr., "America the Expendable," *Harper's* Magazine

THANKSGIVING

1128

Focusing the American feast on anything less than God Himself has certainly not been the fault of our nation's chief executives. One wonders if there is any expression of the presidency which has been as constantly and as consistently in harmony with our holiest life as are the annual Thanksgiving Day proclamations which issue from the White House.

To read those documents is to get a quick review of the last eighty years of our history. Many of them list in detail the timely and special reasons for which citizens ought to be grateful on this day. Abraham Lincoln, who revived the celebration of Thanksgiving Day, pitched his proclamation in the key in which his successors have sung. Without exception they cry out: "Thanks be to God!"

Abraham Lincoln wrote: "I do, therefore, invite my fellow citizens in every part of the United States . . . those at sea . . . those sojourning in foreign lands to observe . . . a day of thanksgiving and praise to our beneficent Father who dwelleth in the heavens. . . ."

Theodore Roosevelt declared: "We live in an easier time and in more plentiful times than our forefathers, the men who with rugged strength faced the rugged days; and yet, the dangers to national life are quite as great now as at any previous time in our history. It is fitting that we should . . . set apart a day for praise and thanksgiving to the Giver of Good. . . ."

Woodrow Wilson said: "In a spirit of devotion and stewardship we should give thanks in our hearts and dedicate ourselves to the service of God's merciful and loving purposes."

Franklin D. Roosevelt proclaimed: "To set aside in the autumn of each year a day on which to give thanks to

Almighty God for the blesings of life is a wise and reverent custom."

. . . Surely, Thanksgiving Day gives us its finest blessings when we echo the prayer of Christ: "Father, I thank thee."—F. Eppling Reinartz, *Advance*

1129

There is a difference between a superficial thanksgiving and a sacrificial thanksgiving. It is easy to hold a thanksgiving service. It is much more difficult to translate thanksgiving into life. . . . We may translate thanksgiving by sincerity of devotion and worship . . . and by simplicity of service . . . and the sacrifice of love.—Fred R. Chenault, *Pulpit Preaching*

1130

Gratitude is from the same root word as "grace," which signifies the free and boundless mercy of God. Thanksgiving is from the same root word as "think," so that to think is to thank.—W. P. King, *Pulpit Preaching*

1131

"He doesn't have to say 'thanks,'" said a woman to the mother of a small child after giving him some candy while they were waiting in an airport.

He may not have to say "thanks" but he will grow into a better man if he does.—E. Paul Hovey

1132

The only people with whom you should try to get even are those who have helped you.—John E. Southard

1133

Thou that hast given so much to me. . . . Give one thing more—a grateful heart.—George Herbert

1134

Everybody knows how to express a complaint, but few can utter a graceful compliment.

1135

We thank Thee, our Father, for life and love, for the mystery and majesty of existence, for the world of beauty which surrounds us, and for the miracle of our conscious life by which we behold the wonders of the universe.

We are grateful for the ties which bind us to our fellow men; for our common toil in industry and marts of trade; for our joint inheritance as citizens of this nation; for traditions and customs hallowed by age through which our passions are ordered and channelled.

We thank Thee for the faith of our fathers by which we claim kinship with the past and gain strength for the present; for the love of dear ones in our homes and for the enlarging responsibilites and sobering duties of our family life; for the serenity of old people who redeem us of fretfulness; and for the faith and courage of youth through which we are saved from sloth.

We are not worthy of the rich inheritances of our common life. We confess that we have profaned the temple of this life by our selfishness and heedlessness.

Have mercy upon us that we may express our gratitude for Thy many mercies by contrition for our sins, and that we may prove our repentance by lives dedicated fully to Thee and to the common good, through Jesus Christ. Amen.—Reinhold Niebuhr, "A Prayer of Thanksgiving," *Advance*

1136

When our Pilgrim Fathers instituted this anniversary, it was for them no holiday. They were separated by the breadth of the ocean from home and family and friends. Neither were there abundant harvests nor "peace, prosperity and wealth" for which to give thanks. A bleak prospect confronted them and foes surrounded them. For what, then, did they give thanks?

The root of their thanksgiving was the conviction that an overruling providence had enabled them to lay the foundations of a new commonwealth in which freedom of thought, of worship and of political action were assured for free men everywhere. On that first Thanksgiving Day, they dedicated themselves to that ideal.—Raymond Calkins, "The Meaning of Thanksgiving," *Advance*

1137

I am thankful that I live in a land where everyone may salute the same flag.

I am thankful that I live in a land where, regardless of race, everyone may take part in national ceremonies. . . .

I am thankful that I live in a land where the future seems bright and hopeful, rather than dark and hopeless. . . .

I am thankful that I live in a land where the youth of all races have a tomorrow, rather than in my native land where the youth of the race is without a tomorrow.

I am thankful that I am happy and free.—Prayer of a sixteen-year-old Jewish refugee.

1138

No day in the civil year of any other people has quite the significance of Thanksgiving Day for Americans. It grew from very definite religious roots, and although some of its manifestations in our day are not very religious, yet the proclamations of all the presidents have recognized that God is the giver of all our blessings, and that we must give Him our individual as well as our united thanks. One of the most significant acts of our Lord Jesus occurred during the institution of the Last Supper: "And he took the cup, and gave thanks." Let us also give thanks for all things; they come from the hand of God.—Henry Barraclough, *Today*

1139

The psalmist was conscious of having received abundant mercies from Jehovah; everything he possessed had come from God. He sensed too his obligation to express his thankfulness to God for all His benefits. And just as evidently he desired to find an adequate measure for the response he should make to his obligation. What is the standard of thankfulness to God?

By what standard shall we measure our response in thanksgiving? The average Jew of Jesus' day asked, "How much?" and the answer was, "The tithe." Zacchaeus adopted a larger standard and placed half of his goods at the disposal of the poor. But when Mary broke the box of ointment for the anointing of Jesus, she was prompted not by necessity or by generosity; she was prompted by her love for Jesus! This, then, is the finest measure of thanksgiving, a thankfulness which springs from love.—William C. Skeath, *Today*

1140

Shakespeare called thanks "the exchequer of the poor." Let us thank God that He has made it possible for us to give something back to Him.— William C. Skeath, *Today*

1141

O Lord, that lends me life, lend me a heart replete with thankfulness.— William Shakespeare

1142

The Pilgrims made seven times more graves than huts. No Americans have been more impoverished than those who set aside a day of Thanksgiving. . . . The more that we have to be grateful for, the less grateful we are. For some Thanksgiving is not a holiday but a hollow-day.

Three things are necessary to restore Thanksgiving to its rightful place: a genuine sense of gratitude for America, a deletion of the infantile tendency that sends us crying to Washington for all our wants, a rebirth of the principles of our ancestors, and a willingness to say "thank you" to our families, our neighbors and friends, and most of all to God, the source of light and life, and to His Son.—H. E. Westermeyer, Walla Walla (Washington) *Union-Bulletin*

1143

We said, "Lord, we thank Thee for food."

And He said, "Have you thought of the farmer, who with faith and hope tills the ground, and plants the seed, and toils the long months until the harvest?

"And of the gardener who, with bending back, fights his untiring battle with frost and storm, weeds and insects?

"And of the drivers of trucks; and of the handlers of trains; the pickers, the sorters; the toilers in the intense heat of canneries?

"And when last did you show your thanks by a kind word, and with patience when service falters, and by concern for a fair price and a fair wage?

"And have you thought of the world's hungry millions: of the children who have never had enough to eat, of mothers who starve that their children may eat; of wasted food and restricted production and empty stomachs; of filled shop windows and hungry men wearily pacing the street?"

And we heard a voice saying, "I was hungered and you gave me no meat."

We said, "Lord, we thank Thee for clothing."

And He said, "Have you thought in humility and penitence of the Negro and the tenant farmer, ill-fed and poorly housed, his back bent beneath the boiling sun to pick the cotton?

"And of the lone herder on the windswept hill, patiently watching his sheep?

"And of the women and children at the hot silk vats?

"Of men and women standing day after day in the monotonous whirl of many machines, weaving cloth and wondering, 'Will my job be here tomorrow, or will the mill be closed again?'

"Of the tailors bending over their

needles, many of them in ill-ventilated, ill-lighted workshops?

"Of the patient salesgirls behind many counters?

"When you bought your latest bargain did you ask, 'Who made it and where, under what conditions?'

"And when you spoke your thanks for warm clothing, was it with a touch of shame that you live in a world in which so many suffer for want of clothing and that you have done so little about it?

"Did you think of what terror the winter holds for countless millions across the world with only rags to keep out the cold, of children without shoes, of men who must work without comfort?"

And we heard a voice saying, "I was naked and ye clothed me not."—Herman J. Sweet, *Baptist Missionary Review*

1144

Matthew 15:32-38 and John 6:5-14 tell us of two meals, very large ones, one served to 4000 and the other to 5000. Even the most experienced of us would find this a big task. We would wonder how we would ever get enough plates (even leaf plates) for so many, let alone food. As it is told in the Bible, it seems to have been done very simply and easily. The story begins with the concern of the disciples for the hungry people when they asked Jesus to send them away to try to get food for themselves. The little boy who was willing to give up his own meal is an important part of the story, and so is the loyal obedience of the mystified disciples as they went about seating the people. The climax comes when Jesus takes the little lad's simple food into His own hands, looks to heaven in thanks, blesses and breaks it, and it becomes enough to feed all those tired, faint folk, with something to spare.

There are many interesting places in this story where we might stop and meditate with profit and joy. Let us think of the way Jesus gave thanks and blessed the food before He or anyone else put it to their mouths. In modern words, this is what we call a grace before meals. As we read about Jesus . . . we find that He seems to have a habit of asking grace before meals. Where did He learn to lift His heart in grateful thanks for His daily food? I am sure He learned this in His home. Are you surprised that . . . we seem to know so little about His home? If we list thoughtfully every single mention of Mary and Joseph in the Bible we shall find that we know more than we thought we did about them and why God chose their home for His only Son to grow up in. Two sons who came out of this home are a sure proof of its quality: Jesus, so right and wholesome in every relationship, and James, who became the wise, strong head of the early church. Such children only come out of a home where God is a living presence and worshiping and loving Him are as natural as breathing. . . . In order that everyone in the home may have a close and happy relationship with God, we must relate Him to all the everyday experiences of our lives.

Food is an important and enjoyable part of every normal child's life. So to understand that God is the One who provides this good food with the father's and mother's help, and to feel thankful to Him for it, is the first and simplest step in creating an atmosphere of joyous appreciation of the loving Heavenly Father's care. When the saying of grace is made an experience of genuine worship, it is of real help in a child's learning to pray. . . . Gradually the child may come to the place where he wants to say grace himself. Then he may be helped to express thanks in his own words, or he may memorize a short, very simple form of prayer. It seems wise to encourage the use of original prayers much of the time, however, if the saying of grace is to be a vital experience for the child. . . . A child should never be asked to say grace as a means of showing off before relatives or friends. If these prayers of a child, growing out of his everyday experiences, are interpreted . . . most of this praying may well be prayer in its highest form, simply fellowship with God. This is growing towards God, as Jesus did.—Mrs. J. L. Goheen, *Bulletin Agricultural Missions, Inc.*

1145

Thanksgiving is unique among holidays. It is not a religious holiday in quite the same sense as Easter and Christmas, but we do render the day meaningless if we fail to give thanks. It does not, like Independence Day, mark the founding of a nation. Rather it marks the founding of a spirit—that of gratitude.

1146

When the American colonies were being established, the settlers endured many privations. Being devoutly religious, they brought their problems to God on days of fasting and prayer. On one occasion when it was proposed to appoint another day of penitence and humiliation, a sensible old colonist said that he thought they had brooded over their misfortunes long enough; that it seemed high time they should remember all God's mercies toward them. He proposed that instead of a fast they should keep a feast, and from that time Thanksgiving Day has been an annual observance in America.

One proven antidote for pessimism and despair is the attitude of gratitude, "giving thanks for everything to God," as St. Paul urged.

In our kind of world, preoccupied with crises, is there any good reason for thanksgiving? Like our fathers before us, we can also take life for gratitude and that's thanksgiving! We can gratefully remember that behind all the perplexities of modern living is the fact of the incredible bounty of our Father's world.

In 1795, President Washington asked the nation to observe a Day of Thanksgiving. He asked the people to gather in their churches and to humbly and fervently pray to God that He might prolong the blessings of this nation to us; to ask God to imprint in our hearts a deep and solemn sense of our obligation to Him for the blessings. He closed his plea with these remarkable words: "and finally to impart all the blessings we possess, or ask for ourselves, to the whole family of mankind."

When we take the earth and life for gratitude, we are led to share with others. Appreciating the sheer miracle of life, we see that life is a field of honor on which it is intended by the Lord of all that we should be expendable for the sake of others.

Gratitude can lead individuals and entire communities to join in promoting the welfare of the human race!

1147

Oh, Pilgrim Fathers, we, your sons,
　Rededicate your way;
By giving thanks to God for all,
　On this Thanksgiving Day!
　　　　　　　—Cal J. Aisenbrey

1148

Strange how little and how seldom we thank God for God! . . . We think *things.* We thank God for what we get or are and are glad to know that "he rewards those who seek him," but we never really arrive at the soul of appreciation until we are grateful that God *is.* . . . Knowing that He came from the Father and that to the Father He would return, Jesus had it in Him to thank God for God at a time when thinking God was hard and thanking God was harder. But this was the vision splendid. He knew God for what He really is. . . .

Speaking from the human angle, it would not be far off to say that a Christian is one who majors in appreciation. . . . He rejoices in God. God is his chief and sustained enthusiasm. He senses the Christlike character of cosmic control. He appreciates God as a goodness, a wisdom, and a power beyond the ways of men. . . .

The average prayer of gratitude runs something like this: "Father, I thank thee *for.* . . ." What ardent *for* prayers we are! What are these prayers except acknowledgments for favors? Jesus has not impressed us with the fact that He stood in the receiving line. He rejoiced in recognizing. He had looked God full in the soul.

He was sure of a relation. Hence, He was wont to pray: "Father, I thank thee *that.* . . ."

We are not to split hairs over words. One can so say *for* as to mean *that* and so say *that* as to mean *for.* The former was done by Joyce Kilmer when he wrote: "And oh, thank God *for* God!" the latter was done by the Pharisee, who thanked God *that* he was not as the publican. Yet the difference is colossal: *for* something received; *that* God stands revealed! "Veil after veil have we lifted, and ever the Face is more beautiful." It is easy to thank God *for*; it takes insight and inspiration to thank God *that.* . . .

It is only if you know this God that you know all there is to thank Him for. Christian appreciation comes out of Christian experience. . . . "The Father is greater," said Jesus. I always feel sorry for those who are unable to see the personal in God. They seem to me to miss the glory of His being.

"Thus," said Isaac Penington, one of the greatest of the Quakers, "hath the Lord been teaching me to live upon Himself and not upon anything received from Him but upon the Life itself." "In Him we live and move and are."

The longer you love God, the more you will find out that His love passes understanding. That is the reason for limitless gratitude. Most people do not apprehend God enough because they do not appreciate Him enough. . . .

All too many thank God merely for favors received. Do not the heathen likewise? Not so Jesus! He had better sense and better taste. His gratitude was not thing-centered but God-centered. . . . Those who have His mind have His gratitude. They thank God for *that*. They thank God that God *is*, is *more*, is *other*, and is *here* to stay. They thank God for *God*.— John M. Versteeg, *Adult Student*

1149

"It is a good thing to give thanks unto the Lord." Across the uncertain ways of space and time our hearts echo those words, for the days are with us again, when, at the gathering of the harvest, we solemnly express our dependence upon Almighty God. . . .

In giving thanks for the greatest harvest in the history of our nation, we who plant and reap can well resolve that in the year to come we will do all in our power to pass that milestone; for by our labors in the fields we can share some part of the sacrifice with our brothers and sons who wear the uniform of the United States. . . . —Franklin D. Roosevelt

1150

As a nation much blessed, we feel impelled at harvest time to follow the tradition handed down by our Pilgrim Fathers of pausing from our labors for one day to render thanks to Almighty God for His bounties. Now that the year is drawing to a close, once again it is fitting that we incline our thoughts to His mercies and offer to Him our special prayers of gratitude.

For the courage and vision of our forebears who settled a wilderness and founded a nation; for the "blessings of liberty" which the framers of our Constitution sought to secure for themselves and for their posterity, and which are so abundantly realized in our land today; for the spirit of unity which has made our country strong;

and for the continuing faith under His guidance that has kept us a religious people with freedom of worship for all, we should kneel in humble thanksgiving . . . in contrition for our sins, in suppliance for wisdom in our striving for a better world, and in gratitude for the manifold blessings He has bestowed upon us and upon our fellow men.—Dwight D. Eisenhower

1151

Devoutly grateful to divine Providence for the richness of our endowment and the many blessings received, may we continue to give a good account of our stewardship by utilizing our resources in the service of mankind.

May we have the vision and courage to accept and discharge honorably the responsibilities inherent in our strength by consecrating ourselves to the attainments of a better world . . . and by offering thanks to God for the bounties vouchsafed us and by re-dedicating ourselves to the preservation of "the blessings of liberty" envisaged by our forefathers in the preamble of our Constitution.—Harry S. Truman

1152

With our great heritage of freedom and spiritual strength, let us stand before the world as a people joining in Thanksgiving for a way of life dedicated to faith in our Creator.— George T. Mickelson

1153

Were thanks with every gift expressed,
    Each day would be Thanksgiving;
Were gratitude its very best,

Each life would be Thanksliving.
—Chauncey R. Piety

1154

When all the colors of Indian Summer have streamed down the winds of Autumn, and the first snows have melted the mountains with winter's promise of water for another year;

When the bloom has gone from the last rose and the bountiful earth has yielded up to a free and industrious people its annual contribution of food and clothing and fuel;

When Nature herself seems to pause and gather strength for the long sleep of winter while our good earth renews her energy; and the rosy wind-burned cheeks of childhood reflect the lights of home in early evening:

Then it is ordained that the people of this free Christian republic give thanks to Almighty God for the blessings of liberty; for the peace and tranquillity that have attended us at home and abroad; for the snows that fill our reservoirs with the gift of clean pure water; for the glory of growing children, and for the right to worship and speak and talk and print what we will; for the right to walk this earth in dignity as individual human beings. . . .

It is fitting . . . to pause in solemn thanksgiving . . . in our churches, our homes, and at our tables, for the blessings of another bountiful year, and for our freedom and liberty and its guarantee of dignity for the individual human being in this nation under God.—Robert E. Smylie

1155

Thanksgiving Day, so distinctively American, is symbolic of a spiritual attitude toward life which makes a man superior to his environment. Gratitude depends not upon where a man lives or how much he has, but upon what he is. It has little to do with a man's outward circumstances.

If the Thanksgiving spirit depended upon physical or material well-being, then our first Thanksgiving Day should have had its origin in the Jamestown Colony in Virginia, which enjoyed marked comfort and prosperity, rather than in the Plymouth Colony in New England, which suffered untold hardship, misery, and destitution. Thanksgiving has more to do with a man's spiritual attitude than with his physical and material condition. The thankful heart is found as frequently among those who have little as among those who have much.—John Homer Miller

1156

A thankful heart is not only the greatest virtue, but the parent of all the other virtues.—Cicero

1157

Lord, it is Thanksgiving Day.

For the fathers and founders of my country who laid its foundations well;

For the pioneers who felled its forests, tamed its rivers, tunneled its mountains, tapped the riches of its prairies;

For the hardy adventurers who sought out its mines, planned and dreamed its cities;

For the saints and prophets who made its laws, set up its system of government, gave their lives for its liberty, set up its schools and churches and homes;

For these, O God, I give Thee my thanks,

And for all that is now, I praise Thee on this Thanksgiving Day,

Save me from petty and selfish pride.

Grant that I may be willing to pass on from my own life something to enrich the spirit of my country,

Spare me from the willingness to receive much from the past and to contribute nothing to the future.

May my purposes and those of other young people be such that, if the nation knew them, it would count them to be its chief reason for gratitude on this Thanksgiving Day. Amen.—Percy R. Hayward, *Epworth Herald*

1158

Hearken unto us, O God, and incline Thine ear, that we may lift our spirits in thanksgiving.

We would make a glad song of praise;

Let it be heard in the sigh of the wind across the great wheat fields that roll away to meet the mountains.

Let it be heard in the mines, deep within the earth, where the sinews of peace are being strengthened and made perfect.

Let it be heard in the hum of the tireless factories, weaving the warp and woof of plenty.

Let it be heard in the city, where commerce plies its shining silver needles of communication.

Let it be heard in the country lanes, where bright leaves cover the earth, as Thy love and care cover us.

Let it be heard in the constant memory that all men are brothers;

that if anyone be hungry, sick, or cold, all will taste the bitter cup, for that no man lives to himself alone.

Let us give thanks for Thy lovingkindness and Thy tender mercies, and may we show forth Thy spirit in all our ways as we walk life's highroad on this Thanksgiving Day.—Elsie Smith Costello

1159

Thanksgiving was never meant to be shut up in a single day.—Robert Caspar Lintner

1160

For the old sweet fashions of nature,

For the ritual of the seasons,

The wonder of seed-time and harvest;

And the sky over all,

Deepening as we gaze—

Let us give thanks.

For the flowers of divine grace and human kindness;

For the love that heals our hurts,

And the mercy that lifts us when we fall—

Let us give thanks.

For the thorns that require careful handling,

For the disciplines that train us for strength and honor,

For the sorrows that subdue to sobs and weld us in love to our kind—

Let us give thanks.

For our country and its laws.

For home and family and dear love of comrades

And for all who interpret to us the way and will of the Eternal.

Let us give thanks.

—Jesse Halsey

1161

We are warned often, and rightly so, that we Americans are missing the true meaning of Thanksgiving. We pause in the midst of our feasting, our overflowing bounty, to give a fleeting thanks.

In true thanksgiving we need to compare ourselves with God and not with other people. The Pharisee's trouble began right at this point. . . . When we compare ourselves with God and not with other people, we are all in the same boat. For all have sinned and come short of the glory of God. . . . Let us forget how much we have done for God, and remember what He has done for us in Christ, and what He is continuing to do for us every day. More than anything else in the world we ought to Thank God for Jesus Christ.—George R. Hendrick

1162

"Before theology comes doxology." John Baillie thinks thankfulness is the germ of religious response. The very fact that a man is thankful implies Someone to be thankful to.—Eliot Porter, *Forward*

1163

Thankfulness is a way of looking at life, and it brings its blessing even though it may be difficult. If Jesus could practice thanksgiving in spite of all the difficulties of His day, you and I will find reason for thankfulness in the commonplace routine of our private lives. Thus we shall find ourselves strengthened in spirit to meet the pressing problems that are everywhere. Today my step will be a little lighter because I have said in my heart, "Father, I thank Thee."—Hugh Ivan Evans, *Monday Morning*

1164

It would seem to have been a poor time for thanksgiving when the sons of Jacob came down to Egypt to get food in time of famine. . . . For Jacob and his sons, who lived in the land of Canaan, this was a time of great anxiety. Several years of plenty had been followed by years of drought, and there was a widespread famine. But God had providentially raised up Joseph to superintend a plan to conserve the abundant harvests of the plentiful years to carry through the years of drought. There was to be food for Egypt to share with the rest of the world in time of need. That was something to be thankful for. . . . Joseph had suffered much at the hands of his brothers . . . but now he had risen to a place of power in Egypt. When he made himself known to his brothers, they were terror-stricken. What justified vengeance would Joseph take upon them? . . . instead of vengeance, Joseph saw God's leading in history. . . . Through Joseph the hungry world would be fed and his tribe would be permitted to grow into a nation under the protection of Egypt.

May it not be that God wants to use our nation to set an example to the world by our patience and high purpose? . . . We can have a true Thanksgiving only when, beyond the material blessings, we see the hand of God, His providential leading, and can say with Joseph, "God sent me before you to preserve life. For the famine has been in the land these two years; and there are yet five years in which there will be neither plowing nor harvest.

And God sent me before you to pre-serve . . . and to keep alive for you many survivors. So it was not you who sent me here, but God." As the most prosperous nation in the world, shall we thank God not only for our prosperity, but for His providential leading and His call to world service.
—Park Hays Miller, *Presbyterian Life*

1165

A little schoolboy living in the most poverty-stricken part of a great city found his way into a mission Sunday school and became ·a Christian. Not long after someone tried to shake his faith by asking him some puzzling questions: "If God really loves you, why doesn't He take better care of you? Why doesn't He tell someone to send you a pair of shoes?" Thinking a moment, with tears rushing suddenly to his eyes, he replied: "I think He does tell somebody, but they are not listening." Are we listening to that still small voice of God? If you know someone who is in need, express your gratitude by sharing with them. Try it—just once.

1166

Remember—for a Christian thanks-giving, we must *give* thanks.

ADVENT

1167

The story of God's dealings with His people is marked by invasions. . . . God invaded the heart of Abra-ham and he answered by his trek across the desert to invade a strange land. God invaded the Children of Israel, calling them out of bondage in Egypt.

They responded and became the in-vaders of Canaan. God touched the lonely prophets who in turn moved into the court and market with their disturbing, "Thus saith the Lord." An invading God gave rise to an invading people.

As we approach Advent we recall the Great Invasion. By it all invasions are judged. It happened in Bethlehem of Judea—so none could doubt that it was a real invasion. Mary, the stable, the animals, and the shepherds make vivid the fact that this was no phoney invasion, but was right into the center of man's life where he lives and sleeps and eats and struggles. Ours is the story of a God who cares and shows it by costly invasion.

In the Christian's calendar Thanks-giving comes after Advent. That is the proper order. Prudent men, quite apart from the Christian faith, might find it good policy to give thanks for comforts and privileges. But Christians give thanks because of Advent, the Great Invasion. This gives us some-thing to shout about. So Thanksgiving is linked with Advent—or should be.
—S. Macon Cowles, Jr., "The Great Invasion," *Mission Today*

1168

The name Emmanuel assures us that through Jesus, God entered into our human affairs to be with us to guide, to empower, to discipline, to save, to offer the life abundant.

This idea of Emmanuel—*God with us*—is the central message of the Ad-vent season. . . . If we utilize this sea-son to impress . . . that God is with us in all our affairs, the idea may take hold sufficiently not only to influence our Christmas practices but to stay with us throughout the next twelve months. The Advent emphasis, while seasonal, must be an enduring influence in our lives. When Jesus comes into human life He comes to remain. Therefore, if we . . . can interpret the meaning of Emmanuel . . . we will put into their possession a priceless truth—that God is with us all the time. Emmanuel is with us in joy and sorrow, in sickness and in health—and should influence our observance of Christmas.—Earl F. Zeigler, "Uneasy Conscience About Christmas," *Church School Worker*

1169

To the thousands present it was a never-to-be-forgotten moment. A beam of light from Arcturus scientifically directed threw a switch at the Century of Progress Exposition and in the twinkling of an eye the great fair sprang into full view in all its dazzling splendor. For those who had planned it and labored for years to produce it, it was a proud moment when they could say, "Behold the achievements of man through a hundred years."

Infinitely greater, and not to be mentioned in the same breath with the accomplishments of man, was the moment when the Creator lifted His voice and spoke the momentous words, "Let there be light." Instantly the whole creation thus far completed stood forth in its rugged majesty. Darkness had given way to light.

Jesus came into a sin-darkened world. To a groping and bewildered people He announced: "I am the light of the world." A new day had dawned. Man was no longer to walk in darkness, but in the full illumination of the heavenly Light.

The season of Advent comes and once more the Christian Church lifts her eyes to hail the threefold coming of the Light, which is Christ.

In the fulness of time He came, redeeming the world and bringing life and immortality to light.

To each succeeding generation He comes, bringing forgiveness and salvation to the individual, with power to walk in the light.

On the day of the Lord He shall come in glory and power to judge the living and the dead. Then shall the portals of the City of Light be flung wide. Come, Lord Jesus, come. . . .

1170

And behold, as the Christmas season came again, I turned unto the Familiar Story told by Luke so long ago.

And I began to read as follows:

"And the angel said unto them, Be not afraid; for behold, I bring you good tidings of great joy which shall be to all the people: for there is born to you this day in the city of David a Saviour, who is Christ the Lord. And this is the sign unto you: Ye shall find a babe wrapped in swaddling clothes, and lying in a manger."

Believest thou what the Angel sayest?

And he said unto me, I know not whether to believe or to doubt.

And I said unto another, Believest thou what the Angel sayest? For my own Heart knew not whether to believe or to doubt.

And the Other answered me, Never have I heard such a Voice from any Man. Could it be that we have heard an Angel? If it was an Angel that spoke, then I believe. But if not an Angel, I believe not.

Then there spake unto us the Eldest

of the Shepherds. And he said unto us, The Angel meant what he said. And my Council is that we go at once unto the City of David and see what the Lord God hath brought to pass.

And we believed the Aged Shepherd. And we went unto the City of David. And we found the Mother and the Babe, even as the Angel had said.

And as I dreamed of my Experience of being among the Shepherds of Bethlehem, there came unto me this Thought:

Behold, the Lord hath spoken much through His Word. And People ask the Meaning thereof. And the Voice of the Aged Shepherd seemed to come to me again and again, saying, The Angel meant what he said.

And this Saying hath strengthened me; for it teacheth me to have Reverence and Respect for the Word of God. And when I read what the Word sayeth, I seek not to avoid the Meaning thereof by devious Interpretations, but I strive to take it in its Simplicity.

For I believe that God meant what He said. And that is sufficient for me to know.—"The Angel Meant What He Said," editorial in *Westminster Adult Bible Class*

1171

Ask any historian of antiquity how matters stood in the Roman dominions when the angels sang over Bethlehem and you will find that they were singing above the clatter and clash of a crisis as acute as any. . . . History is a sure cure for latter-day blues. In sizing up our time it is right that we should get down to earth, but there is no point in going underground where we can't see the sky. When the angels sing, we have to be out in the open to hear them and looking upward to see that they are there. There have been many crises up through the ages. Yet here we still are, and the world is still inching forward! Perhaps there is something in what the angels say, after all.

Of course, if we ask what exactly an angel is, no man knows the answer. Are angels real beings, in the same way that God is and we are? If they are and it were important for us to know it, we should probably have been given an opportunity to meet some of them and examine them under test conditions before now. Or are they creatures of myth, personifications of an idea? In either case, we are in no doubt as to what they mean.

The name by which we call them means "messenger." In both Hebrew and Greek of the Bible, it means simply that; the same word is used for a human messenger on any errand. The angels of heaven are the messengers of God. For the shepherds in St. Luke's fragrant tale, whether it be fact or legend, the angels' message was to announce the birth of a deliverer for troubled mankind with the splendid promise that men of good will should find peace in His train. That message sums up what the men who first knew the man Jesus experienced in knowing Him, and what His followers still feel as securely as they feel their own being: that here God Himself was coming in from outside upon our little realm of space and time, to set things right, as men could never do.

That is a terribly hard thing for our minds to accept, disciplined as they are to a notion of natural law which seems to exclude anything ever happening except what human knowledge, if it were wide and deep enough, could fully account for in terms of measurable causes and consequences. That modern notion of natural law is certainly sound, as far as it properly goes. To it we owe all the natural sciences, with all the rewards, and of course incidentally the penalties, which they have brought along. But one suspects that we commonly carry it too far . . . is it true that we are shut up in a closed system of cause and effect wholly within the space and time with which we now have direct acquaintance? If it were true, how could the unexpected ever happen? Yet the unexpected is always happening. Is it simply because we do not yet know enough to be aware of what is bound to happen, that things so often take us unawares? . . . Good and bad both occur unexpectedly, and we are as much at a loss to explain the one as the other. Yet history would seem to say that the balance is on the side of the angels.

That is religion's verdict, also. For at bottom, beneath all creeds, religion is the affirmation of life. . . . Religion is the hopeful and constructive tone in living. It cannot be proved ahead of time, but it works out in practice. Moreover, the sages of faith, the experts in this type of approach to life, tell us that by the very attitude of hopefully expectant attention, looking for something wonderful to happen instead of something horrible, we open the sluices from our side for the life force, for God, to send through His floods of aid to us in our necessity. The short word for that order of expectancy is prayer; and we all do pray,

either toward God or away from Him, every time we hope or despair.

Whether we realize it or not, God is still coming in from outside upon the little closed system of our thinking and living, individually and collectively, if we will let Him in . . . in the darkest hours we are foolish to despair. And the more calmly we hope, waiting for sunlight beyond the tunnel and moving steadily ahead while we hope, the sooner will rescue come . . . only he who is faithless in a vital sense beneath all formal religion, only he who perversely denies life itself, can doubt but that mankind has a bright future. For the children . . . Christmas is a festival of story, song, and gifts, next door to fairyland. For us, their elders, it is a reminder of the angels' song and what it stands for. Deliverance is at the door. Help will come from outside, the unpredictable will happen again, and as often as it is needed. It will come to save mankind, in harmony with our highest hopes, and in spite of the worst that men can do. "It came upon the midnight clear, that glorious song of old . . . !" And the angels are still singing.—Russell Henry Stafford, ". . . And the Angels Are Still Singing," *Advance*

1172

If only the innkeeper of Bethlehem had known that the King was coming he would never have been so curt or abrupt in his remarks; he would never have said: "There is no room in the inn!" "If I had known. . . ." "Of course, if I had known who they were. . . ." But he did not.

Shutting his door on Christ, taking his lantern and going to bed, sleeping while the angels sang and the King appeared—here is a picture startlingly true of mankind's attitude today. We too have no time for stars. We too are often overbusy and too preoccupied to sing with angels, "Joy to the world! The Lord is come; Let earth receive her King." And yet, we dare not say: "If I had known!" Rather, in this Advent season we must exclaim: "I know. I know that He is come to seek and to save that which was lost."

There is something decisive about His coming. Beautiful as is the story of His lowly birth and sacrificial life, it is indeed more than an account of a good man who came to establish His Kingdom of love. He is a King who makes demands upon our love and loyalty. The world has too often denied that Advent claim. It has tried to get along without Him too long . . . the better world for which we hope and pray can come only when His will becomes our will, when we acknowledge sincerely with our "I know" that He is our new-born King.

1173

What a difference there is between a command and an invitation! Caesar commanded and the people obeyed, even though that very obedience meant acting against their own wishes and desires. The invitation of Jesus to those who would follow Him is often unheeded and unanswered. Is it because there is no real desire in the hearts of those who would be His followers to accept the requirements of discipleship?

As the Christmas season approaches, may we accept with earnest determination the invitation found in the words of one of the great carols: "O come, all ye faithful, joyful and triumphant, O come ye, O come ye to Bethlehem; Come and behold Him, born the King of angels; O come, let us adore Him . . . Christ the Lord!"—Donald F. Lomas, *Today*

1174

The question comes to us . . . "Are you celebrating Christmas the same way you did ten years ago? Are you trying to keep this observance a childhood anniversary, when you recapture the spirit of Christmas as you once knew it?" . . . there are, after all, many kinds of Christmases.

There is the children's Christmas: Santa Claus, reindeer, the chimney, "If you aren't good. . . ." Baby Jesus, camels, wise men, shepherds, animals and the manger.

There is the Christmas of hymns, carols and Scripture brought us by our choirs. They use a theology which no longer finds thinking acceptance among some of us, a vocabulary of words like "Emmanuel," "The Dayspring from on High," "Rod of Jesse," "The Morning Star." Because we do not read our Bible as the infallible source of all wisdom, and quote it as proof, many are not familiar with the references. Our choir children learn the words as so many syllables.

There is the "business" Christmas: the idea of gift-giving gets under way before Thanksgiving—decorations, promotion on every hand.

Now the family is all grown up; no dolls or trains to buy, but more costly gifts. To such the question comes: "What do you want to get from Christmas?"

Is it the Story of a Babe, surrounded by carols, legends, a halo of glory? Is it disillusionment resulting from a changing pattern: "The bottom dropped out!" "Something to get through with!" "So commercialized!" "Just a social exchange among people who already have more than they need"? Or is it something deeper than the show of things back of the excitement and mystery of childhood Christmases?

What do we mean when we sing with Phillips Brooks, "Be born in us today"? Did Jesus come once for all time, or is He continually coming, a little different in each age? He has come as a king, a lowly carpenter, a teacher, a healer of physical and mental ills, as the Son of God, and to some the Son of Man and nothing more. These all are interpretations of how people have wanted to think about Jesus.

Our children say, "Is this story true? Is there a Santa Claus?" Gradually we substitute for the jolly old gent, who gives us presents, a number of Santa Clauses, ourselves as one. We plumb the depths to find the real truth behind this "Spirit of Christmas."

So we come to the Christmas story. "What will you do with the Christ?" is the important question. Did His coming stop with a particular century, or is He born in each one who will accept Him and His way of life?

Suppose during this month, we search each day for a way in which we may make His life a part of our own. Each day holds the opportunity of an extra; a letter written of appreciation to someone who has helped us— to an old friend or a teacher—our pastor—a member of our family—a missionary far away from homefolks at this time of year. Suppose we regard as one of our Father's children the taxi driver, the clerk in the store, the individuals who service our homes. Perhaps we may find time to call on a lonely person, or replace a cherished resentment with an act of outgoing kindness.

The curious thing about this way of life, once it is started, is that one finds it hard to keep ahead of the game. One sends a loaf of fresh-baked goods as a gesture of concern, and back comes some simple yet choice gift in response. "My joy I give unto you" is no empty phrase, after all. Perhaps Advent may become an all-year-round *Advent-ure!*—Doris Brenner Stickney, "What Doth the Lord Require?"

1175

In paradise it was conceived,
  A perfect dream of God;
'Twas fed and nourished
  Within the shelter of His arm.
It gently stirred; then growing
  Fought for life 'til dawn,
When angels bore the gift to earth
  And in a manger
    Love was born.
          —Edith Hazzard, *Fiat Lux*

1176

It was close to Christmas time in the wooded mountain territory of the Northwest. There was a great deal of excitement among the citizens and rangers of that area—a five-year-old boy was lost.

More snow fell as the searchers looked frantically in every cave and on every mountain side. But no Bobby could be found. As evening came, the weary, heartsick father turned back home. Dejectedly he kicked against what seemed to be a log in his path. But when the snow fell lose, a small boy stretched, sat up, and exclaimed: "Oh, Daddy! I've found you at last!"

Now—who found whom?

The bleeding heart of the older man knew that it was he—and not Bobby—who had done the searching and the finding.

During these Advent days—as we hasten toward Bethlehem with accelerated step—men sometimes talk about finding God. Learnedly, they speak of the search for God and the discovery of the divine.

But it was not God who was lost, it was we! Nor was it we who found God, it was God who found us. He found us outside, and He brought us into the fold of His grace and forgiveness through the Christ-child of Bethlehem.

Today, as we ponder the wonder of God's love as revealed in the Christmas miracle, we thank Him for having found lost mankind and for having brought us into the warmth and light of Bethlehem's manger.

1177

Go down the road to Bethlehem.
It's quiet there,
  Except for angel-songs in lofty key
  Outsoaring far the shepherds' jubilee.
It's wondrous there,
  Where wise men kneel, their endless journey through,
  And rise, how changed! The heavens and earth are new!
It's holy there,
  As Mary whispers, rapt in prayer, in fear,
  "The riddle of the world lies answered here!"

Go down the road to Bethlehem.
It's God who's there.
            —Church World Press, Inc.

1178

"Advent," declares Dr. Lilley, "proclaims to us that Christ the Son of God, has come. He comes down His own secret stair to speak to us about our own personal obligations." Here is the heart of the Advent message: God has done something which is of deep personal concern to every one of us.

This is the fact that many people miss during the season of preparation for Christmas. . . . All too frequently the experience of Christmas has been thoroughly frustrating for some people. In the hurly-burly of preparation they lose sight of its religious message and after the carols are sung and bells rung, the silence is oppressive. Christmas has no intrinsic significance . . . it is so difficult for secular-minded people to grasp what caused John Newman to write: "God's presence, and His very Self, and essence all-divine." . . . Our horizons are so limited to the things we see that no longer are we awed by the thought of an eternal mind that embraces all creation. Advent is a time of expectancy but it is also a time of wonder. We've lost the majesty and magnificence of Advent when we no longer react to it with glad surprise. . . . To make Advent a higher experience than ever before, it will be helpful to capture the meaning C. H. Dodd put into it when he wrote: "The Word is uttered in a *Man,* who, living among men, shows forth the splendor of the divine nature in terms of personal character and social action, and so finds us where we live."

Here we have a vision of Advent

that cannot fail to challenge our thinking and claim our devotion. Advent points to an event—"The word became flesh and dwelt among us." It deals not with a folk tale; it presents a fact of history. And this fact is not restricted to the locale of a village inn, but bursts the narrow frames of tribal story and embraces all history and moves it with revolutionary strength. Advent looks ahead to Christmas with the steady assurance that this event can occur again whenever the Spirit of the Christ lays hold upon human character and makes a new creation.—Donald Macleod, *Monday Morning*

BIBLE SUNDAY

1179

I am the Bible.

I am a library of sixty-six books.

I am the world's best seller.

I am more than a mere book; I am a force that overpowers opposing systems of thought.

I am the rock upon which civil liberties and social freedom rest.

I answer the question: Who and where is God?

I was written by minds saturated with consciousness of God.

I am published in more languages and dialects than any other book that has ever been written.

I am cherished by millions of people as being the only concretely available and infallible rule of faith and practice.

I am the Word of God as set forth by inspired prophet, law-giver, genealogist, priest, historian, poet, essayist, story-writer, moralist, seer, and theologian.

I set forth the way of life that leads to abundance and satisfaction of experience.

I tell the story of the great drama of redemption.

I am the meeting point of man's effort to discover God and God's revelation of Himself to man.

I inspire devotion to truth and purity of life purpose.—Norman E. Richardson, *Central Truths of the Christian Youth Movement*

1180

A man may learn from his Bible to be a more thorough gentleman than if he had been brought up in all the drawing rooms in London.—Charles Kingsley

1181

Generation after generation new light has broken out of the Holy Book, and there is still more light to break forth from it, if men will search the depth of its divine meaning. The Bible is a world power, and we release the power only as we read and ponder and incarnate the great truths which are set forth in its pages.—Charles Edward Jefferson, *Searching the Scriptures*

1182

This age needs a new inoculation of the Bible. It is the tonic we need when our hope "blood count" is low. If we could take into our systems more of its good cheer, its poise, its courage, its quiet confidence in the long processes of life, it would act for us as the keel does for the ship; it would hold us steady in the time of storm, and keep us from bobbing aimlessly around.—Albert William Beaven, *Rejoicing in Hope*

1183

The "fore-edge" Bible, which was first introduced into England in the seventeenth century by Samuel Mearne, bookbinder to the king, has unique decorations on the edge of the volume. A skillfully concealed picture of Christ was painted by an artist in such a way that it became visible only when one took up the book and started to open it. The picture was made by painting a design on the front edges while they were fanned out and clamped in a slanting position. When the Bible was closed, with pages tightly shut, the art work could not be seen, but when the pages were flexed as one began to open the book, the likeness of the Savior was plainly evident . . . beneath are the words of Jesus: "It is I myself; handle me, and see."

The artist is suggesting that we can never see Christ in an unused Bible. But if the Book is opened by people with expectant minds, Christ will appear to them in such a way that they will see Him not only as the Jesus of history but as a living Lord who seeks to be the daily companion of His disciples.—Walter Dudley Cavert, *Ours Is the Faith*

1184

When the days are dark, men need its light. When the times are hard, men need its comfort. When the outlook is discouraging, men need its confidence. When despair is abroad, men need its word of hope.

The Bible is not a book of political maxims or of economic theories. It is not a book of maxims or theories at all. It is a book of living principles. Its spirit is the spirit of brotherliness and good will. It is a summons to helpfulness: "Bear ye one another's burdens." It is a summons also to self-respecting independence: "Let every man bear his own burden." It teaches charity, but also justice. It calls us to the giving and serving which the strong owe to the weak, and those who have to those who lack; but it also strikes straight and clear at the moral defects in individuals which are responsible for a large part of the poverty and suffering of the world; and also at the moral and economic defects in society, in business relations, and in the distribution of the common resources of the world, which are responsible for the remaining part.

Christ is the only hope of individuals and of society. And the Bible is the only book which tells His story. It alone preserves His words, which are the spirit and life. It alone records His deeds by which He saved the world, and would save it now if we would obey Him.—Robert E. Speer

1185

Unless we form the habit of going to the Bible in bright moments as well as in trouble, we cannot fully respond to its consolations, because we lack equilibrium between light and darkness.—Helen Keller

1186

"Speak to the children of Israel that they go forward." They have been going forward ever since. That is the great message of the Bible. Confucius taught his disciples to walk in the footsteps of the fathers. The Bible teaches us to start where our fathers left off.

1187

To every area of the human situation the Bible becomes the timeless wonder of God's eternal truth, as when it spoke to the skeptical chief of an African village who was listening to a missionary read one of Paul's Letters from the Bible. When the missionary had finished, the chief asked, "When did you say that was written?"—"About nineteen hundred years ago," replied the missionary. "Now I know you are a liar," exclaimed the chief. "That was written about our village." Much too up-to-date, indeed!—"The Timeless Wonder," editorial in *Bible Society Record*

1188

Men do not reject the Bible because it contradicts itself, but because it contradicts them.

1189

The Bible differs from the sacred books of all other religions. They all speak of God who demands and man who acts, while the Bible speaks of God who acts and man who benefits from God's actions.—Archbishop Lehtonen of Finland

1190

A Bible in the hand is worth two on the closet shelf.—Earl Riney

1191

The Bible has always been a book of amazing power. No other book has influenced and transformed Western civilization so profoundly, nor could another conceivably do so again.—Julius A. Bewer, *The Prophets*

1192

Any book, to be fully understood, needs to be read against the background of the environment which produced it. This is especially true of the Bible, whose message was first of all addressed to the contemporaries of the inspired authors. They delivered that message not only in the current idiom but in the literary structures with which their countrymen were familiar. Some knowledge of these modes of expression, then, is necessary to the study of the Bible. Without this background, we are in danger of misunderstanding the import of the Biblical writer's thought and so of losing the divine message contained in it.—Neil J. McEleney, "What's Happening to the Bible?," *Catholic World*

1193

For the man who knows where he is going, sign posts are short cuts to the road he wants to travel. For the man who is unsure of the turning, sign posts are guide points. For the man who has lost his way, the sign post is a friendly hand pointing the way back toward familiar surroundings. The best sign posts in my life have been those great books, beginning with the Bible, that lie within the reach of most of us who know the value of sign posts.—"Rocking Chair Speeches of a Reading Man"

1194

As I look about me, I see no heaven upon earth. In my own time family ties have become looser and looser. They may be broken without censure or comment. Among certain classes, children are cast off or neglected; and among other classes, children have no respect for their parents, whom they coldly let suffer and die in poverty. Hunger for land and riches has no bounds. People of small means are exploited by corporations organized for the purpose. From him who hath little all is taken. Men seek public office, not for the benefit of their constituents, but for private gain. Fraud and embezzlement are common occurrences. A lie is a virtue if one can get away with it. Our minor courts are often run in the interest of political parties. Justice, which once had a home there, has long since taken flight to the heavens above us. Murder goes unpunished. War has a continuous existence, like the germs of the most deadly disease. When one war ends, another begins somewhere else. It is a dark picture.

And yet, against these sinister forces are always working the Biblical ideals of personal and collective conduct which lie embedded in our fundamental laws. New means and devices for detecting crime have been discovered. People are watching the action of our courts with eyes more alert than a generation ago. Nations are uniting in efforts to prevent aggressive wars. When crises arise, men of integrity come forward to assist in affairs of state and nation. State and federal laws are being enacted to mitigate greed and the exploitation of the public. As private charity has weakened, the state has come to the rescue of the sick and the afflicted, orphans and neglected children, widows unable to care for their children, and the growing number of men and women who reach old age with no means of support. This is what Jesus Christ would preach and urge were He still among us in the flesh.

The struggle between light and darkness may go on forever. But there is no reason for despair. As long as our civilization lasts, the Bible will call us back to the banner of honesty, justice, and mercy.—Wilbur L. Cross

1195

We read the Bible devotionally when we read it for the purpose of cleansing our spirit, refining our temper, and deepening our devotion to God . . . read it as a means of grace . . . pay no attention to verse or chapter divisions. They are a mechanical device introduced for the sake of convenience of reference, but are often an encumbrance to the reader. Never read the Bible by verses. You cannot read Dickens or Tennyson . . . so. Read on! Do not stop when you come to obscure words or unintelligible expressions. Read on! When you come upon a word you do not understand, do not look it up in a dictionary, read on! Save the hard words for some day when you want to study. Do as you do at the dinner table when you are eating fish. When you come to a bone, you lay it aside and go on eating. The table is no place for the study of anatomy. When you use the Bible (devotionally) as a form of food, lay the bones aside and go on eating.—Charles E. Jefferson

1196

The Bible introduces us to a group of men who, in a very real sense, come to be part of our acquaintance. They are almost our contemporaries. There are millions of people today who are better acquainted with the personal experiences of men like Moses and Abraham, Isaiah and Jesus, than they are with the persons who live next door. By the very nature of the case, Bible characters are profoundly influential. They could be far more so if we would cultivate them. It is particularly important for us today to get the lesson of some of these past experiences.—Albert William Beaven, *Rejoicing in Hope*

1197

The Bible is always concrete. It tells us about man by telling us about men. As Dean Hodges has said, "Its pages bring before us a long procession of people. Its precepts are embodied in persons. It is akin, not to the dialogues of Plato, but to the plays of Shakespeare; that is, truth is not reasoned out, but acted out." In the Bible, for the most part, people do not argue about good and evil. They live, and in their lives we see what good and evil are. Even when, as in the case of the books of the prophets, or in the Epistles of St. Paul, there are long messages of inspiration or of warning, and of explanation as to what religious faith should mean, these messages are never abstract utterances, but the warm and living counsel of men who in their own souls were wrestling mightily with the great issues they proclaimed.—Walter Russell Bowie, *The Light Shineth in Darkness*

1198

The great figures of the Bible do not stand still. They may start from poor beginnings, but they do not end

there. They may sin, but they are not satisfied with sinfulness. Even Jacob dreams his dream of the ladder set up from earth to heaven. Selfish and crafty as many of his instincts were, he too had within him a sense of his need of God if his life were to be complete. He began as the deceiver who crept off with his brother's birthright; he ended as the man who, having learned deep lessons, wrestled with God and prevailed.—Walter Russell Bowie, *The Light Shineth in Darkness*

1199

A story is told about a college professor who sat in the waiting room of a hospital while his wife was having a baby. He began reading a book and became so completely absorbed in it that he forgot where he was and what was happening in another part of the building. A nurse came to the door and said: "It's a boy." Without lifting his eyes from the book, the absentminded professor made the same response that he did at home when told that a college boy was waiting to see him: "Ask him what he wants."

The prophets of the Old Testament looked forward to the coming of a Messiah. The New Testament opens with the announcement that Christ has come. Why was it that God entered into human life in the form of the Babe born in Bethlehem? What is it that Christ wants? The Bible gives a plain answer. He asks us to give our attention to the revelation which He brings from God. He seeks to make plain to us the nature of the universe in which we live. He wants us to understand that back of it is a God who loves us so much that He is willing to suffer on the cross to reconcile us to Himself and to one another.—Walter Dudley Cavert, *Today*

1200

The Bible reveals the mind of God, the state of man, the way of salvation, the doom of sinners, and the happiness of believers. Its doctrines are holy, its precepts binding, its histories are true, and its decisions are immutable. It involves the highest responsibilty, will reward the greatest labor, and will condemn all those who neglect its sacred contents. Christ is its grand subject, our good its design, and the glory of God its end. Read it slowly, frequently and prayerfully. Read it to be wise, believe it to be safe, and practice it to be holy. It should fill the memory, rule the heart and guide the life.

1201

Youth needs inspiration to great daring and noble personal living. Others have found it, and I gladly testify that I have found it, in the pages of earth's greatest book—the Bible.—Amos Alonzo Stagg

1202

If the Book has suffered from its friends—its misguided friends—it has also endured through the ages the attacks of its open enemies . . . yet, faced by all these obstacles, the thing which could not happen has happened. The unbelievable has taken place. It is the Lord's doing, and it is marvelous in our eyes. For we are today the trustees of a Book which literally dominates and completely permeates English literature.—Charles Frederick Wishart, *Coverdale Speaks*

1203

The Bible is addressed to me, and as I read it a demand that God made of somebody else becomes God's demand of me. A sin that hindered the obedience of somebody else is shown to be my sin too. Another god that somebody else worshiped I recognize as my own.

But are there not passages in the Bible which are only informative and tell me nothing about my relationship to God? There are and there are not. For a passage which for years was only informative may suddenly become an imperative for me.

I may not therefore make up my mind in advance that any portion of the Bible is irrelevant for me or for today.

Others had read the demand of Jesus asking the rich man to sell all that he had. When C. T. Studd read it, he said, "That is for me." Others had read the call of the prophet of the exile for sacrificial suffering that redeems. But when Jesus read it, He said, "That is for Me."—D. T. Niles, *For Today*

1204

The word "provide" is related to the word "providence." The providence of God means simply the actions of God in which He provides for and takes care of the things He has created.

The Bible rejects all notions of chance, fortune, and fate. Life has purpose and meaning because God controls and guides His creation. This control is shown in two ways. What are commonly called the "laws of nature" are only ways in which the providence of God is described. The sun does not "automatically" come up. This is the working of God.

The second way in which God's control is seen is in the events of history. Any prayer for particular events assumes that God is active in shaping and directing events. This includes the events of your life. This was the point of view of the Apostle Paul when he wrote, "We know that in everything God works for good with those who love him. . . ."—Hubert Morrow, *Thy Will My Will*

1205

Often in other countries I have held in my two hands before a congregation my own Bible in English and another in the language of the people with whom I was worshiping. The two Bibles were a symbol of our common heritage of faith and of our oneness in Jesus Christ, our Lord. The Bibles themselves often spoke far more eloquently than I could of the faith we share and of our common task to witness for Christ in the world and to advance His Kingdom in the hearts and lives of men.—Theodore F. Adams, *The Book for Everyone*

1206

The heroes of faith . . . never dreamed of defending the Word of God. On the contrary they must needs release the Bible that it might defend them. If they could speak to us today we think they would say, "This time-tried transcript of God's way and will to men needs neither your apologetics nor your apologies. Unloose it that it may do its proper work in human hearts, unfettered by tradition or prejudice, unembarrassed by forced and fussy 'defenses,' by twisted and distorted meanings read into it, by the devices of Satan who can 'quote Scripture for his purpose.' See to it that the Word of God is not bound. Release it for souls hungering after God; for those who mourn; for sin-sick and weary and doubting men and women; for pilgrims who walk with faltering feet through the valley of the shadow.". . . Solemn voices hail us out of the past. Shadowy hands beckon to us from the unborn generations that are yet to be. Clouds of invisible witnesses look to us from the eternal world. They trust us and we dare not fail.—Charles Frederick Wishart, *Coverdale Speaks*

1207

People who know the Bible, and have been moved by its great ideas of God, and of man, and of what God wants to make of man, will not consent for more than a time to conditions which depress and annul the surging response of their spirits to the invitation of life and faith.—John A. Hutton

1208

The Bible is the most astounding book ever written. The languages in which it originally appeared have long since joined the ranks of the dead, but the words of this ancient book have been reincarnated in the living speech of every continent on earth. Constantly being translated into new languages and dialects, the Bible is rapidly becoming the universal possession of the spiritual life of the race. Civilizations crumble, but the Word of God endures. Fashions pass over the face of the earth, but the supreme value of this library of eternal truths remains in the unalterable loyalties of the human spirit.—Paul B. Kern, *The Bible in a Time of Confusion*

1209

Without this book America could not have become what she is; and when she loses its guidance and wisdom, she will be America no more.—Odell Shepherd

1210

O for a thousand tongues to sing
   My great Redeemer's praise,
The glories of my God and King,
   The triumphs of His grace.

Thus sang Charles Wesley. With the Bible now translated into many more than a thousand dialects and languages, the prayer of Wesley has come to pass. Just as on that first Day of Pentecost when all the people assembled heard the Word in their own language, it is now possible for most of the people of the world to see and hear in their own tongue the Word of God as recorded in the Bible.

But a closed book on a shelf will not tell a story.

Are we doing anything to help someone to hear and read the Bible in his own language? It may be our next-door neighbor or, through missions, someone in a faraway place.—E. Paul Hovey, *Today*

1211

The Scriptures have not been translated into these thousand tongues because the people who spoke all these tongues demanded it. But they have been translated because . . . men and women of many nations, finding that this foreign Hebrew and Greek Book spoke to them as no other book spoke —aye more, had the very message of life for them—determined that their own people should have it and that other people ought to have it too.— Eric M. North, *And Now . . . in a Thousand Tongues*

1212

The Bible is one of the solid facts of Christianity. What it is, is not affected by what men think of it. Changing opinions about the Bible do not change the Bible. Whatever the Bible was the Bible is. And what it is, it has always been. It is not men's thoughts about the Bible that judge it. It is the Bible which judges men and their thoughts. It has nothing to fear but ignorance and neglect. And the church need have no other fear on its account. The Bible will take care of itself if the church will distribute it and get it read.—Robert E. Speer

1213

As our nation faces the future, it must have guidance. We cannot trust to the happenings of the hour; for some unforeseen crisis may arise, and the nation may be driven on the rocks. We must face frankly the great problems that confront us and plan the course which we should take. We have solved difficult problems in the past, and if we follow the light which led our fathers, we will be able to see our way in the future. America is facing some serious problems . . . George Washington said, "It is impossible rightly to govern the world without God and the Bible."—Alonzo W. Fortune, *The Fountain of Life*

1214

Life inevitably brings problems, and our attitude toward these problems helps to determine what life shall mean to us. Life in our modern world is so complicated that these problems are numerous and are difficult to solve. Instead of having these problems worked out for us, we need light that will enable us to work them out for ourselves. The Bible is an invaluable source of help. It is a book of human experiences, and the men who gave us the record of these experiences were illuminated by the divine Spirit. In helping us to solve our problems, it becomes for us a fountain of life.

We all have our particular problems, and there are a few that are common to all of us. It is these common problems that are the most important. Most of us are confronted by the problem of making a living, and it is serious for many people. Heads of families are unable to solve this problem, and young people are afraid to undertake the establishment of homes, because they can see no solution for it.

The Bible does not solve the problem, but it does throw light upon it, so that those who are working at it can see their way more clearly.—Alonzo W. Fortune, *The Fountain of Life*

1215

The Bible has made a supreme contribution to popular education. More than any book or force in history, it has been the great liberator of the human mind. It has burst open the prison doors of superstition. Its translation into each new language has been a classic event in the educational advance of the people speaking that language. The reign of illiteracy begins to come to an end in the life of a people from the time the Bible comes among them, and they are free to listen to its message.—John Alexander Mackay, *The Truth That Makes Men Free*

1216

It is most wonderful to read the Bible at such a time. How alive it suddenly becomes and how real! It really gives you the impression of having been written specially for prisoners and for prison.—Martin Niemöller

1217

Clearly and definitely the Bible sets forth the basic truth between God and man. Man is told he is not the creator and ruler of the universe. The Bible reminds him constantly that he is but a created being. God is the Creator and Lord of the universe. Men's role, therefore, will always be the humble one of the creature learning to know something of the Creator. Only as man realizes this truth will he come into the right relationship with God. That is why in the Bible when God is mentioned, the words "know" and "understand" are so often used: "Be still and know I am God. . . ." "But let him that glorieth glory in this, that he understandeth and knoweth me."—T. Z. Koo, *For the Healing of the Nations*

1218

The Bible has had the peculiar ability to survive the collapse of civilizations with which it has been intimately associated, and to bring light to the dark ages that have followed.—Kenneth Scott Latourette, *The Light That Will Not Go Out*

1219

Everyone who has a thorough knowledge of the Bible may truly be called educated; and no other learning or culture, no matter how extensive or elegant, can, among Europeans and Americans, form a proper substitute. Western civilization is founded upon the Bible, our ideas, our wisdom, our philosophy, our art, our ideals, come more from the Bible than from all other books put together.—William Lyon Phelps

1220

The Bible's message of God is a message that was given in history. The patriarch and kings and prophets of whom it tells were men whose actions and whose words have their full meaning for us only when we realize the conditions they faced and the kind of world in which they lived.—Walter Russell Bowie

1221

It is not enough to read the Bible regularly; we need to read *devoutly* and *expectantly*. The ears of our spirits should be tuned to hear what God wants to say to us. Horace Bushnell found that the Bible was dull when he was dull: "When I am really alive, it opens, and reveals depths even faster than I can note them."

We cannot tell just when or through what passage of the Bible God will speak to us. He tries a variety of ways to reach us, as He did with Elijah in the cave on Mt. Horeb. Elijah could not detect God's presence in earthquake, wind, or lightning. But then to his heart came the whisper of a still, small voice.

If we do not hear the still, small voice of God speaking to us out of the Bible's pages, it is because our spirits are deaf, for we cannot hear Him with the physical ears. We will hear Him only if we read expectantly and attentively, wondering what word He has for us out of the experiences of the seers of old.—*Pathways of Prayer*

1222

Today, Christianity is passing through a fiery ordeal of judgment. Leader and people are seeking for an authority which will not only remain unmoved, but which will give them a point of advantage from which to move out with new power and zeal. That authority is the Word of God.—Elmer George Homrighausen, *Attend to Your Reading*

1223

"Suffering here—glory hereafter," is the thought furthest from the Bible's life-renewing teachings. Its own message is, "Ye are now come to the city of the living God." It does not prepare us for heaven; it does not command us to wait for immortality. It tells us to take earth and make it heaven by doing and giving, because it is a joy to do and to give.—Helen Keller, *The Book for Everyone*

1224

Bible people lived close to the desert. The dry and parched land they knew well. Many times they hoped for water that their living would be sustained. One of their writers, Isaiah, in describing the hopes of the people, speaks of waters breaking out in the wilderness and streams in the desert. They sought life-giving water. As they digged their wells and drank gratefully, they related their thirst and their satisfaction to God, the object of their lives. For many, His choice messenger, Jesus, became the water of life.

In our time, there are deserts. Our hurried business living is often a parched land. We, too, are thirsty for a well of water or a stream in the desert. If we will do so, we can drink freely of the water of life. The Holy Bible contains words of comfort, ideas of courage and strength, and if we will turn to its pages regularly, we will quench our thirst and satisfy our hunger.—Kenneth Clinton, *The Holy Bible*

1225

The Bible has profoundly influenced all great Christian literature. It is the river supplying many pens, and a river that never runs dry. It is simple, direct, and glowing with memorable passages. Magnificent prose, superb poetry, and incomparable short stories insure it a place in the confidence of future generations. Moreover, it touches every phase of life from the deepest sorrow to the loftiest joy. Included on its priceless pages are narrative prose, swift drama, comforting poetry, warm exhortations, lofty visions, beautiful lyrics, legal counsels, statistical summaries, personal letters and, far surpassing all, the immortal words of our blessed Master. In all the earth there are no words of throbbing truth, of shining beauty, nor any words so conducive to good living as the Psalms, the sayings of Jesus, and the teachings of Paul!—John Edward Lantz, *Bible Lessons for Youth*

1226

The Bible is the cornerstone of all great literature. Upon it rest many other literary structures, but none challenges its power in the building of human lives. Boys and girls of every generation need its condolences and inspirations just as much, if not more, than good food and virile exercise. And seeking men and women of all time need its wisdom and guidance. Of all the contributions of man to posterity, that of the Hebrews is unquestionably the greatest.—John Edward Lantz, *Bible Lessons for Youth*

1227

George Bernard Shaw once said that he could not remember ever learning to read and so concluded that he was born literate. I cannot claim that much but I began reading at a tender age and have been reading for more than forty years. Yet I cannot think of a book that I would label "The Book for Everyone," save one. That, of course, is the Bible. Everything else is dated, parochial, or specialized. But the Bible knows no limitations.

It is "The Book for Everyone's Sins." There may be some new ones discovered but I never heard of them. All the betrayals of the soul, the lusts of the flesh, and the evils of the spirit are confronted in the Bible. So much of the shocking descriptions of modern literature appear to be more like small boys writing bad words on walls, than an honest revelation of human nature. But the Bible dares to begin with the worst and look into the dark places of the human soul. It probes and reveals spiritual pride which most of us are too insensitive to recognize, or cover up with the selfish claims of hypocritical virtue. A generation that is Biblically illiterate never knows itself truly, for it never knows how bad it is or could be. Only the Bible finds every man and makes him understand that he must begin the human adventure by confessing: "I am a sinner."

The Bible is "The Book for Everyone's Hopes." What ambition does a modern man have that a man in the Bible did not have long ago? What fine scheme for success do we dream about today that was not considered and described in the Bible? "The mighty hopes that make us men" are all there and still rise up within our hearts. There are found in the Bible the dreams for the better life, the longings for the good life, and the desires for the best. There, also, are the false hopes of the world and the hypocritical mirages of the senses. There is no other book to so help a man separate the false from the true. It is the Book that leads us to the hope that "does not disappoint us, because God's love has been poured into our hearts through the Holy Spirit which has been given to us."

The Bible is "The Book for Everyone's Salvation." We need to be saved not only from hell, but from fear, from frustration, from compromise, from isolation, from meaninglessness. If there is one clear thing about human nature, it is a need to be saved. If any man doubts this, let him read history both ancient and modern, and contemporary fiction. The Bible begins with tragic questions but it leads to glorious answers. For it leads us to God in Christ who sought us when we were lost and died for us while we were yet sinners. The Bible brings a shout of triumph into our dull world and a song of victory into our saddened hearts. Bible men are led through the valley of death and despair to the proclamation of their great Redeemer's praise. Of a truth, here is "The Book for Everyone."—Bishop Gerald Kennedy, *The Book for Everyone*

1228

In the middle of the nineteenth century Henry Rogers wrote a remarkable book entitled *The Eclipse of Faith.* In the book was a chapter called "The Blank Bible." It related a dream. By a sinister miracle the letterpress of every Bible in the world was deleted. Every Scriptural passage in any book whatsoever similarly disappeared. It was as if some profane darkness had covered the earth, and the literature and much of the history of the world was left in shreds and tatters.

When people had recovered from their bewilderment, they began to try to remember Bible passages. By dint of stupendous effort the whole Bible was at last recovered from the memories of men.

Henry Rogers's book emphasizes the rich contribution that the Bible has made to the literature of all nations, to understanding of ancient history, and as a source book of Christian theology.

If every verse of the Bible were suddenly to disappear as described in *The Eclipse of Faith,* it is very doubtful whether our present generation could recover the entire Bible from memory.

The greatest loss imposed by such a tragedy would not be to literature, history or Christian theology, but it would be the loss of the one Book in the world which is "The Book to Live By."—John Sutherland Bonnell, *The Book to Live By*

1229

There are two things the Bible never takes into consideration. These two things mean nothing to it. They are these:

The Bible never takes geography into consideration. It leaps across the barriers of the nations and disregards the frontiers of peoples. It is at home in every land and language.

Then, too, it never takes time into consideration. Time means nothing to it. Written thousands of years ago, it is as relevant today as when the words were first recorded. It is meant for all lands, all languages and all times. The Bible belongs to the ages.—Joseph Richard Sizoo, *What Darkness Cannot Dim*

1230

The Bible not only mirrors our longings, it also resolves them. If it is true that a hand reaches up wistfully out of the night, it is also true that a hand reaches down to us. It is never enough to know that man seeks God; what he wants to know is if there is Someone somewhere who hears and answers. The Bible does not leave us in the dark long; it is really a two-way street. Up that road man travels to God through prayer and supplication and fasting; but down that road God travels to man through visions and revelations and communion until they meet in Christ, the Word of God made flesh.—Joseph Richard Sizoo, *What Darkness Cannot Dim*

1231

The Bible's strength is in its power to interpret life in terms of its tragedy and its glory. The Bible frankly speaks of sin, not to belittle man, but to reveal it to him, bring him to himself, and offer him forgiveness and new life. Thus is man remade.—Elmer George Homrighausen, *Attend to Your Reading*

1232

The Bible has the singular quality of taking hold of a human spirit and transforming it; which truth is the day's hope.—William T. Ellis, *The Book That Has Power*

1233

Dusty Bibles are a sign of arid spirits.—William T. Ellis, *The Book That Has Power*

1234

The Bible is a book on religion. True religion is indispensable to good character and high morals.—Ellis Adams Fuller, *One World—One Book*

1235

Bibles are cheaper than bombs. They build where bombs blast.—Ellis Adams Fuller, *One World—One Book*

1236

In parts of America and England there may be more Bibles available than there are people to read them. Everywhere else in the world, among Bible readers there is Bible famine.—*The Book of All Nations*

1237

De Quincey says that there are two kinds of literature—the literature that instructs and the literature that moves; the literature that informs us and that which stirs us to action. The Bible measures up to both requirements. It instructs and it moves.—John Sutherland Bonnell, *The Book to Live By*

1238

Not only does the Bible lead us to God. It leads us also into a larger understanding of the problems of daily living and how to deal with them.—William Walter Peele, *The Bible, a Light and Guide*

1239

The Bible points out to us how God wants us to live, and what He wants us to do in the making of a better world.—William Walter Peele, *The Bible, a Light and Guide*

1240

This Book is far more than man's book. It is God's unchanging Word sent to man, that he may have a chart and compass for his voyage and that he may have a staff upon which to lean in weary hours.—Billy Graham, *The Book of Hope*

CHRISTMAS

1241

I am Christmas.

I commemorate the birth of Jesus Christ.

I bring good news and good cheer to millions of people.

I demonstrate how God can incarnate Himself in a human being.

I am the birthday of the Christian faith.

I bring the message of peace on earth made possible by the Prince of Peace.

I honor lowliness of mind and purity of heart.

I put God definitely within the series of historic events.

I show how godliness may be subject to the law of growth and development.

I am celebrated most appropriately as a religious festival.

I call attention to the spiritual capacities of newly-born children.

I bring encouragement to those of lowly birth.

I place the wisdom and the holiness of God within man's reach.

I identify religion with human experience enriched by God's self-revelation.

I celebrate the beginning of a life in which God was made real and immediately approachable.—Norman E. Richardson, *Central Truths of the Christian Youth Movement*

1242

The birthday of Jesus was first set on December 25 in the year A.D. 354. For several decades prior to that time the Eastern Church had been celebrating the event on January 6. But leaders in the Church at Rome were aware of the urgent need for a Christian observance to be a substitute for the pagan orgies which commanded the interest of the people during the month of December.

The Romans had observed a holiday for several centuries which they called *Saturnalia.* It began on December 10 and came to a climax on December 24.

That date marked the time when the sun turned from winter toward spring. At its best, the holiday dramatized the promise of new life as the sun shone with warmer rays, and the days became longer.

The pagan rites were extravagant orgies of feasting, dancing, and immorality. Leaders of the Christian movement were aware that many people were willing to accept Christ and the tenents of faith, yet saw no reason why they should give up the gaiety and pleasure which they had always enjoyed at that season of the year.

It did not seem strange to set the birthday of Jesus to coincide with the observance of *Saturnalia*. After all, the leaders argued, Jesus was the Sun of the spiritual world. His coming to earth brought the assurance of new life and hope to all the people.

The theory which led to the choice of December 25 had some justification, but the Christian leaders did not take into consideration the fact that many pagan customs would be carried over into the observance of the birthday of Jesus. So Christmas was burdened from the beginning by numerous ideas and practices which had nothing whatsoever to do with the birthday of the Christ.

The pull of paganism upon the observance of Christmas has never been released.—G. Ernest Thomas, *Rediscovering Christmas*

1243

Dear Innkeeper:

I was a guest at your inn a few weeks ago. My visit to your city was unpleasant—the Romans were enrolling me for another of their miserable taxes. And the stay in your hostel did not improve matters.

I am a patient man, innkeeper. One must be if he is to be a merchant. I can forgive you for many inconveniences. I can overlook the fact that your wine was poor and your bread stale.

But, innkeeper, there are several things I cannot forgive. For my private room, you charged an unreasonable price. And it was about as private as the market place. The stench from the stable was unbearable.

No sooner had I fallen asleep than I was awakened by shouts of "Hallelujah, the King is born!" I saw a group of shepherds in front of the stable. I could see them by the light of bright stars. I ordered them to be quiet, but they paid no mind. At long last, they disappeared into the stable and it was relatively quiet again.

Five minutes later, I was awakened again, this time by the crying of an infant. Strangely enough, the cries came from the stable. I looked out again and, through the open stable doors, could see the infant and its mother. I yelled down to keep the baby quiet, but apparently they didn't hear me.

I could not sleep for the rest of the night. It was the most miserable night of my life—and all because of those people in the stable.

If you are going to permit your high-paying guests to be disturbed by those who pay less and are less, then I hope you are prepared to suffer great financial loss. You will never get anything from shepherds and a family which had to be housed in a stable.

With great displeasure, I remain,
Silas of Jerusalem
—Michael Daves, "Letter to an Innkeeper," *Together*

1244

Phillips Brooks said the wonder is not that extraordinary signs should have surrounded the birth of our Lord; the wonder would have been if a man of such marvelous saving power, so increasingly and mysteriously potent in human history, had come into the world with no outward indications that His birth was a momentous event.

One thing is certain: The stories of the birth of Jesus which we have in Matthew and in Luke are perfect symbols of what He was to mean to all mankind. They do not *in the least* exaggerate His significance for future generations.

The fact that Herod killed all the babies in Bethlehem symbolizes the undying hatred which every Fascist ruler from that day to this has had for Jesus and His gospel. Some of them have been willing to use religion for their ends, but the real Christ and the real Christianity have always called out from them the most murderous opposition. But Providence outwitted Herod, and has outwitted the Fascists again and again.

On the other hand, the humble shepherds on the hills of Bethlehem received the announcement of His birth with great joy. To the poor in spirit and to the meek, and to those who hunger and thirst after righteousness, the news of the coming of Christ is a source of inexpressible joy.

How contrary to the picture men would naturally have painted are the events surrounding the birth of Jesus.

Think of it—the King of glory was born in a stable! Selfish people were snoring away in the inn, leaving the young woman to pass through the great crisis of her life among the oxen. And His cradle was on the hay in a manger. As Marcus Dods says, the great of the earth were as unconscious of the significance of the birth of our Lord as were the big-eyed oxen, calmly chewing their cuds in the stable. And that has been true all down the ages. The great have been oblivious to really great events.

And then the angelic annunciation was made not to the chief priests or the doctors of the law in Jerusalem, but to shepherds. It was as though a great event today were proclaimed from heaven not to the churches or the clergy, but to the night switching gang in the railroad yards. Everything is unexpected. Instead of rabbis and priests coming to Bethlehem to see the infant Christ, it was these shepherds from the hills, and the Magi from the far-off heathen country, who made the pilgrimage to the manger.

And thus it is today. We are perpetually surprised at the way in which men from unfavorable backgrounds are eager to know about Christ and do Him honor; and surprised also by the way people highly privileged by birth and education are unfeelingly indifferent to the good news He brings.

But the universe is back of Jesus. The stars proclaim Him, and angelic choirs celebrate His birth. In spite of all the darkness and the sorrow, we are privileged to believe that the ultimate reality is music. The heavens are telling the glory of God, and in due time the earth will listen and rejoice.—Rollin H. Walker, "The Message of Christmas to the World," *The Christian Advocate*

1245

The major portion of Dickens' *Christmas Carol* is devoted to Christmas Eve and if one is not careful the picture of Scrooge on the night before Christmas is the only one remembered. So vividly does the author picture him with his egotism and meanness that we can hardly forget it. We ought, however, to remember that this is Christmas Eve!

Looking at the end of the story we see an entirely different character, one we would not recognize as the same person in the beginning of the tale. The miserly old man is transformed. In religious terms, he has been converted.

This story relates what we know to be a fact in life. The bad can become good; the mean can lose their selfishness; those opposed to Christ may become His followers.

In the beginning Scrooge was not ready for the angelic song, "peace on earth, good will toward men." He was self-centered, bigoted and prejudiced. But Dickens surrounded him, the ghost of Jacob Marley being the exception, with characters representing the type of life he wanted Scrooge to live. He gained Scrooge's interest by means of the three spirits and they presented both sides of the argument, for and against brotherly love. As the advantages in favor of brotherly love mounted up, Scrooge developed a real desire for that type of life. The result was that he was convinced and converted. Waking from his dream to find the bed-post was his own and that "best and happiest of all, the time before him was his own, to make amends in."

That "awakening" begins "Scrooge's Christmas" which turns out to be strikingly different from the Christmas we had been led to believe he would observe.

We have too long remembered him only as "that old skinflint, Ebenezer Scrooge," and not as one who "knew how to keep Christmas well, if any man alive possessed the knowledge."

We are prone to think of his Christmas as a Christmas without hope. But such a picture of Christmas is the one seen through the eyes of Scrooge on Christmas Eve—the night before Christmas. The night before the idea of "peace on earth, good will toward men" caught hold of him. Jesus once said, "Unless you turn and become like children, you will never enter the kingdom of heaven." Scrooge came to enjoy Christmas just as much as did Tiny Tim. He was different when he understood the meaning of Christmas.

Will Christmas ever change us? Will we hear the angels sing? Will the spirit of Christmas turn us to good will and peace? Will the world have a Scrooge's Christmas in which we seek to help and save all mankind?— E. Paul Hovey, "Scrooge's Christmas," Hot Springs (South Dakota) *Star*

1246

The miracle of Christmas is not in the fulfillment of its promise of peace and happiness and good will, because after two thousand years the world is still waiting for a universal way of life without cruelty and injustice and violence. The real miracle is that it is remembered and observed as a

Holy Day after so many centuries have passed, because of the wonderful faith that sustains it.

Jesus said that the heavens and the earth would pass away, but that His Word would not pass away. In the twenty centuries that have intervened, mighty men have been forgotten. Powerful nations have fallen. The great heights to which the giants of history ascended fade into the perspective of time, and what they did and said loses importance. But the gentle words of Jesus, which asked of man only that he treat his brother as himself, have a power that grows with the years.

Christmas comes as a benediction and a blessing upon the affairs of a confused and stumbling world. Each year that reaches this beautiful day is made better and cleaner for the spiritual experience that attends the retelling of the lovely story. Every life is enriched and made fruitful by the joining of hands and heart that is inseparable from homes and families made bright by the Christmas observance.

1247

The star that shone on Judean hills years ago would have failed if there had been no shepherds to see the star, then seek the newborn King in Bethlehem. Success for the star was assured only by human channels present to carry its message. Human eyes caught the shining light and reflected its bright story through the world to men. Tens of millions of Christians have caught that light reflected into their hearts by other humans.—Ruth W. Rippey, *P E O Record*

1248

No wonder we love Christmas. Once every year we retell this old story to ourselves; in poetry, prose, song, art. And, as the great historian said, we too are softened and transformed.—Norman Vincent Peale, *P E O Record*

1249

God has no birthday. Every human being has a day he can look back to as the time of his beginning. With God there is no beginning and no ending, so we cannot think of His birthday. Yet, in a beautiful way, He has made it possible for us to celebrate the day when His love showed itself in human form—the birthday of Jesus.

This is the deepest meaning of Christmas. Everything else stems from this central fact that it is the birthday of the Son of God. "Love came down at Christmas," wrote Christina Rossetti. God's love was shown in Jesus, who was born of a human mother and wrapped, like any tiny baby, in swaddling cloths and laid in a manger, because there was no room in the inn. —*Pathways of Prayer*

1250

A miser must have a wretched time at Christmas, for Christmas is pre-eminently a time of generosity. God set the example when He gave His own Son; the wise men followed it, when they gave their gold to the Christ-child; and in proportion to our share of the Christmas spirit, we are walking in their footsteps today.— John T. Faris

1251

Everybody'd be happier this Christmas if we'd just cut the cost and revive the reverence.—Oren Arnold, "The Head Man," *Bluebook*

1252

Selfishness makes Christmas a burden; love makes it a delight.

1253

The Christmas spirit never asks, "How much *must* I do?" but "How much *can* I do?"

1254

Don't expect too much of Christmas Day. You can't crowd into it any arrears of unselfishness and kindliness that may have accrued during the past twelve months.—Oren Arnold, "The Head Man," *Bluebook*

1255

Christmas—that magic blanket that wraps itself about us, that something so intangible that it is like a fragrance. It may weave a spell of nostalgia. Christmas may be a day of feasting, or of prayer, but always it will be a day of remembrance—a day in which we think of everything we have ever loved. Then we will realize that He who has led us down through the labyrinth of years, born two thousand years ago, showed us the way, saying that we would have peace on earth if we love one another.

It's been a long trek. Some have wearied, some have sought a shorter way, some have turned back when the road was rough, others have failed to heed the road signs. But no matter what havoc disobedience has wrought, a brush dipped in the milk of human kindness will obliterate the picture, heal the wounds, dissolve the hates— love will find a way.

There was a gift for each of us left under the tree of life two thousand years ago by Him whose birthday we celebrate. The gift was withheld from no man. Some have left the packages unclaimed. Some have accepted the gift and carry it around, but have failed to remove the wrappings and look inside to discover the hidden splendor. The packages are all alike: in each is a scroll on which is written, "All that the Father hath is thine." Help yourself to happiness.

What greater gift than the privilege of sharing, of having, of being, of giving, of knowing, and of loving. In the innermost recess of every man's heart is a desire to be happy and to be loved.

What better resolution could we each make for the New Year than that we carry a lighted candle in our heart, lighting other candles as we go so there may be left no dark corners? Then each shall reveal to himself the splendor of God's gift to man.— Augusta E. Rundel, *P E O Record*

1256

"The heavens declare the glory of God." The first Christmas night must have been like many other nights which the townspeople and shepherds had known, until suddenly a heavenly messenger appeared, "bringing good tidings of great joy, for all people." Then and there the new "skyway to hope, joy, and peace" was opened to all the world. Down its shining path came the heavenly hosts "declaring the glory of God" and announcing salvation to mankind. . . .

Those "skyway declarations" become a vital part in the celebration of the Christmas season. . . . The heavenly host and the star may have seemed a phenomenon to that generation, but down through the centuries, their "skyway declarations" have become a reality in the hearts of mankind.

Too often we do not know how to value the incidents which occur in our generation. Everyday events may be epoch-making, just as this wonderful experience which heralded the coming of our Lord and Saviour was in that day. Someone has said, "In the ordinary things of life God often reveals His perfect plan."—Edith K. Stanley, "Skyway Declarations," *The Union Signal*

1257

The challenge of simplicity is a magnet to the human spirit. Much of the beauty of Christmas lies in its challenge to look further, deeper, until we find its secret in the heart of God. —Dale Evans Rogers, *Christmas Is Always*

1258

In his autobiography, *The Unexpected Years,* Laurence Housman describes the staging of his Nativity play in London. The law prohibited anyone from acting the part of the Deity and the British censor granted a license only on the condition that the Christ child was not to be seen. A concealed bulb lighted the inside of the manger and created an appearance of heavenly radiance. After the departure of the shepherds and the Magi, came a scene when the child was supposed to be asleep. This was to be a highlight of the pageant when all eyes focused on the Babe while people meditated on the mystery of the incarnation. All lights were to be extinguished except the one in the manger. Somehow the stage manager made a mistake and turned off all the illumination. In the silence and darkness a hoarse whisper was heard, "Hey there, you switched off Jesus." Mr. Housman said the incident was "a little symbolic of what happened spiritually in the course of the production." It is also an illustration of what occurs in our personal lives, our homes and our churches. Jesus easily gets "switched off" by our carelessness or neglect.— Walter Dudley Cavert, *Ours Is the Faith*

1259

A while back I griped out loud that I never could think what to give people for Christmas. My pastor friend overheard me and next day sent me this list:

To your enemy, forgiveness.
To an opponent, tolerance.
To a friend, your heart.
To a customer, service.
To all men, charity.
To every child, a good example.
To yourself, respect.
—Oren Arnold, "The Head Man," *Bluebook*

1260

The most complete and best-known account of the birth of Jesus is in the Gospel of Luke. We read it, or hear it read, several times during every Christmas season; and we never grow tired of the beautiful story. Perhaps that is because we find ourselves fitting into the events, and hear for ourselves the angelic chorus.

First, we meet the shepherds, "abiding in the field, keeping watch over their flock by night." They were the common people of the time, not the mighty or the influential. And they were about their usual tasks, faithful in their accustomed place of labor. We are common people, too, and we are trying in our way to be diligent in the work which God has appointed us.

Suddenly upon the quiet scene there bursts the vision of the angelic host, and there is heard the chorus proclaiming the birth of the Saviour "in the city of David." The shepherds were startled and "sore afraid" at what was taking place, as we would be if the same thing were to happen to us. Yet, because the wonderful announcement came to those ordinary shepherds, we are encouraged to believe that God still speaks to His people, whoever they are, so long as they are receptive to His voice. Perhaps to us, this very Christmas, there will come an especial awareness of God's nearness.

Then the shepherds journeyed to Bethlehem to see the Christ-child. They represent those men and women who are responsive to the divine invitation. Their search was rewarded, for they found "the babe lying in a manger." We, too, may find Him when we seek Him with our whole heart.

Finally, the shepherds "returned, glorifying and praising God for all the things that they had heard and seen." They must return to their common duties, which henceforth would bear an uncommon glory. All life will be glorified for the Christian who finds again the Saviour in his heart.

1261

There is a name applied to Jesus which we use all too little, "Dayspring"

—The Dawn. How expressive is that name! It was indeed the dawn of a new day when He was born. A new day for the world, a world then in its darkest night.

A striking passage in the novel *Giants in the Earth* shows the effect of the birth of a child on a community. This story of Norwegian pioneers in Dakota territory is full of hardships and anyone who has lived through the winters of that area can appreciate O. E. Rölvaag's stirring description:

"A grey waste . . . an empty silence . . . a boundless cold. Snow fell; snow flew; a universe of nothing but dead whiteness. Blizzards from out of the northwest raged, swooped down and stirred up a greyish-white fury, impenetrable to human eyes. As soon as these monsters tired, storms from the northeast were sure to come, bringing more snow. . . . 'The Lord have mercy! This is awful!' said the folk, for lack of anything else to say.

"Monsterlike the Plain lay there—sucked in her breath one week, and the next week blew it out again. Man she scorned; his works she would not brook. . . . She would know, when the time came, how to guard herself and her own against him!

"But there was something she did not know. Had it not been for the tiny newcomer, who by mysterious paths had found his way into the settlement on Christmas morning, the monster might have had her way; but the newcomer made a breach in her plans—a vital breach!

"Most marvelous it was, a sort of witchery. A thing so pitifully small and birdlike . . . there was no substance to him, really nothing. Only a bit of tender flesh wrapped in pink silk. . . . But life dwelt in every fibre of it. Yet hardly life—rather the promise of it. Only a twitching and pulling; something that stretched itself out and curled up again—so fine and delicate that one was afraid to touch it with rude hands."

Anyone who has ever read the novel will remember that it was the coming of this baby that kept the little settlement in existence. They had been ready to give up—to quit.

How like the story of the birth of Jesus. His coming changed things. The powers in control were overcome as was the terrible winter which almost overpowered the Dakota pioneers. The hearts and lives of these settlers were transformed by the coming of the Christmas child, as the first Christmas Child transformed the whole world.—E. Paul Hovey

1262

It is such an easy matter to criticize the innkeeper. But have we made room for Jesus? What shall we say of our Christmas preparations? How will we observe the coming day of Jesus' birth? The tree, lights, ornaments, gifts, parties, and all the other outward observance of the holidays no doubt will be there. But is that all? Where is Jesus? Remember: "There was no room for them in the inn" some 1900 years ago. Is there today, when your heart is in the inn, and you the innkeeper? There will be many who in the next few days will say to their Saviour: "True, Christmas first of all is a festival in honor of Thy birth. But, I am sorry to say, in my heart there is no more room for Thee."

Christ is first in *Christ*mas. What part will He play in your Christmas? Will there be room for Him in your celebration? Will there be room for Him in your heart? Will you find time to worship Him in a service of your church? He came to bring heavenly gifts to you—forgiveness of sin, eternal life, and salvation. These are expensive gifts. They cost Him dearly. The price was His life. Only by suffering the punishment of your sins, only by dying in your stead, could He redeem you. Is it then unreasonable that He should make a claim on you, since "He bought you with a price?"

No room for Him in the inn of your heart? Then, if you would know the real joy of Christmas, make room for Him today.

Ah, dearest Jesus, holy Child,
Make Thee a bed, soft, undefiled,
Within my heart, that it may be
A quiet chamber, kept for Thee.
—Arthur W. Meyer, Hot Springs (South Dakota) *Star*

1263

The best gifts a church can give are rich and colorful experiences, opportunities for loving service, joyous music to hear and sing, the age-old story in the words of the Bible . . . these are the church's own, and their value is unequalled.

1264

How fortunate we are, not only that God's Son came to dwell with us, but that He came as a little child! The Babe in the manger cradle in Bethlehem was helpless and dependent like all babies everywhere. And, even amid the poverty of simple people in a dictator-ruled land, He was surrounded with the tender care and loving solicitude that good mothers and good neighbors always lavish on little ones.

The cause of children and the blessed relationships of the family were exalted on that first Christmas night. They have never been the same since the Christ-child came.

Besides, His coming was another evidence of the relationship that God the Father wants each of us to have with Him. We are His children, and we need Him. Our spirits are restless, our strivings are vain, until we achieve this Father-and-son relationship that was symbolized when He sent His Son as a little child. It is the Father's will that we should be dependent, receiving food, shelter, and all other material benefits as gifts from His hand, taking our standards and values from Him, thinking His thoughts after Him, becoming at last workers together with God. "Whosoever shall not receive the kingdom of God as a little child, he shall not enter therein," said Jesus when He had grown to maturity. And behold, from Bethlehem onward He has shown us the way!

1265

Christmas comes as if from another world. It is always something of a miracle, a mystery, a kind of surprise. Our ordinary days run along in dull succession; our lives seem unexciting if not drab, and what we do a tiresome part of an endless routine. And then the "spirit" of things changes, and in the midst of the drab and dull and the tiresome and the commonplace, God comes making things new. There's a lilt of something heavenly in the voices of friends, and the poorest of us seek to enjoy the wisdom of making

gifts, and even in the darkest of this world's troubles we find a star to give us hope.

Yet it is not an easy thing to keep the great meaning of Christmas clear and unobscured in a world as filled as ours with scrambling anxieties and blundering haste. We may exhaust all our energy before the day of Christmas comes and have no strength for its joy or place for its peace. If we are to keep Christmas at all well, we will need purer motives and a more profound innocence. There will be many satisfied to enjoy its consequences as they may be known in a world incredibly gladdened and made generous for a few days, but for Christians there is a precious and more fundamental joy at the very source of Christmas itself—it is the heartening visitation of the Eternal to this troubled world. If there be any gratitude in us for this month or this world so incredibly gladdened by that first Christmas, then we will turn inevitably to the sanctuary where music may articulate our gladness, prayer make plain our thankfulness, and all that is worship deepen the understanding of our joy and of that event from which all our joy has come.

1266

Heaven once more draws nigh unto the earth. The whole world thrills in elation and expectancy at the rustle of angel wings. The faces of mankind light up with hope when God hangs a new star in the sky. The dark shadows of life vanish and disappear when the glory of the Lord shines round about us. An angel speaks, an angelic choir sings and the whole world, in awe and wonderment, goes to Bethlehem to see this thing which is come to pass. It is Christmas. God is thinking about you and me, loving us and giving us a Saviour. It is the holy night. God is very near this night.

There is a Saviour for this world. Many plans have been outlined and many specifications have been drawn for a better world. Some have been inspiring and beautiful, some have brightened man's horizon for a fleeting moment, some have just been dreams. All have come to naught because this is a world of sin and evil and selfishness. Jesus came to save the world and make a new heaven and a new earth. He speaks and light and hope spring anew in the human breast. He bids us "Follow Me," and those who follow enter into life and do great things. He looks with compassion on the multitudes and their faces light up with joy and courage. He walks down the paths of mankind and every place and every task becomes holy. He sees men idle in the market place and bids them to go work in His vineyard. He sees men filled with sin and evil and He goes forth to die, and those who believe in Him are forgiven and live new lives. He comes forth from the dark tomb and says, "I go to prepare a place for you." He who has known our troubles, He who has been here, says, "I will be with you alway." The world has a Saviour. It is Christmas.

1267

Most Christians undergo something of the experience of Joseph and Mary. Things did not go as Joseph had planned. Outside interests invaded, plans had to be changed. The baby's place of birth was not as they would have wished it to be.

Many of the cherished dreams of the Christian are crowded out, left by the wayside; and feelings, like those of Mary as she thought of her baby's safety, take over our minds. We may be like Joseph, wanting to provide the best but finding ourselves amid circumstances that require us to make the best of whatever is available.

In spite of all the worry and anxiety, Mary and Joseph welcomed Jesus on that first Christmas. In our parties and engagements do we miss Him or is He thrust aside? Do we see Him in some child who has found the love and true joy of Christmas? Do we possess the Christmas spirit as found in the wise men, the urge to seek Christ until we find Him, and then worship Him and offer the gift of self? Christ enters the life that welcomes Him in love.—E. Paul Hovey, *The Upper Room*

1268

In a sense the early Christians looked backward to Christmas. Most of them, we may safely guess, knew in experience the reconciliation wrought by His death and the power released by His resurrection before they ever heard the strange story of His humble birth. But not many generations passed before Christians were celebrating with every kind of human rejoicing the very heart and center of their faith—that God became man. In the fourth century, Constantine, the first Christian Roman emperor, for good or ill, decreed that the pagan festival of the winter solstice should be combined with the church's celebration of the nativity of her Lord. From that time onwards, and perhaps with growing confusion, there has been a mixture of pagan jollification and Christian rejoicing. That is why every Christmas we must deliberately and thoughtfully look backwards . . . to the first Christmas, stripped of all the romance, decoration and sentimental association. . . . We need to see afresh the stark humility of God's irreversible decision to become man. We need to see with clear fresh eyes that we live on a visited planet and that by God's choice God and man are irrevocably joined together. . . . The real wonder starts here. For surely we cannot grasp in anything but a formal way the meaning of our redemption, unless we know for certain that the figure on the cross was truly God-become-man. We cannot be convinced of the relevance of the resurrection even though we give assent to the resurrection stories of the Gospels, unless we believe that the immeasurable God became human—as truly human as we are human—and yet conquered the black terror of death. The ascension of Christ witnessed with joy by a few early Christians means almost nothing to us unless we see it as a demonstration of the fact that God takes humanity with Him back into the timeless realm of heaven . . . only the Christian faith dares to state that God really became man, that from the time of that event, now nearly two thousand years old, God has identified Himself with man. There is no revoking of that position, and the Son of God does not cease to call Himself the Son of man. Our values, our treatment of our fellows, our quality of living, indeed our whole attitude towards life and death derive ultimately from what happened in the

stable of an inn. That is why with reverent imagination and with humble minds we must year by year look backwards to the first Christmas.— J. B. Phillips, *Backwards to Christmas*

1269

Why did God's Son come into the world at just the time He did? Why did He not come earlier—or later? Would He have come at all if man had not sinned? In what sense did He come in the "fullness of time"?

These are questions that come to the mind of all Christians who think seriously about the meaning of God's coming to earth in Jesus Christ. Though we cannot know the final answers, the questions point to an important fact in our belief about God —that Christ came into the world at a definite time and for a specific reason.

God has never left Himself without a witness in the world. In the Old Testament He was known through the patriarchs and prophets. It is our faith that God revealed as much of His nature in every age as men could understand; but this understanding was slow in coming, and it was not until the way had been well prepared that the Son was sent into the world. God would not force man to be receptive. And in the fullness of time, when all was ready, the Son came—and this was the first Christmas.

The questions of why and how, important as they are to an intelligent discussion of the Scriptures, do not allow us, as persons, to avoid the truth stated by Angelus Silesius, the seventeenth-century German poet, "If Christ were born in Bethlehem a thousand times and never in you, you remain forever lost." Until He has been "born in us," we are lost forever.

The conditions for Christ's coming into our lives are no different from those of His coming into the world that first Christmas. That is, God will no more force Himself into our lives than He forced the innkeeper to receive His Son. We may leave the door shut. We are not puppets. We cannot be saved against our wills. We may say, "There is no room."

Has Christ been born in your life? Will He come again into the "inn" of your heart this year as you celebrate? Or will you hold Him at a distance of 2,000 years, talking interestedly about His birth at Bethlehem, but not at all about His coming to your house?

This Christmas open wide the doors of your heart and home and "prepare Him room." And when once He has come, the questions of how, where, and why will fade away when you realize that the greatest Christmas of all is Christ born in your heart. He cannot —He will not—come into the life of any person until that person is ready to make the full response.—Harold L. Fair, *Adult Student*

1270

The inn was proud and crowded, the stable was humble and with an empty stall. Only in a humble and uncrowded heart and mind can awareness grow. I sometimes think no one can know greatness until he has reached the place where he says from his heart, "I am scarcely worth bothering about. I know nothing." Then he has made an empty room. Then there is room for the Christ to come in; there is room for the lovely Kingdom of Light to emerge and rule; there is a building

that life can use where once there was only a crowded, noisy, unavailing inn. . . . Mortals are immortals unaware. Make room, make room, it is life you are crowding out.—Celia Caroline Cole

1271

I will light the candle of *Hope* this Christmas. Hope is the mood of Christmas—the materials are a newborn Baby, a family, and work. Even in the grimness of our world, babies are being born—and an endless procession of births is life's answer to death. Life keeps coming on, keeps seeking to fulfill itself, keeps affirming the possibility of hope.

Hope is the "growing edge"! All around, worlds are dying out, new worlds are being born; all around, life is dying—but life is being born. The fruit ripens on the trees, while the roots are silently at work in the darkness of the earth against a time when there shall be new leaves, fresh blossoms, green fruit. Such is the growing edge! It is the one more thing to try when all else has failed, the upward reach of life. It is the incentive to carry on. Therefore, I will light the candle of Hope this Christmas, that must burn all the year long.— Howard Thurman, *Christmas Worship in the Home*

1272

The day of joy returns, Father in Heaven,

and crowns another year with peace and good will.

Help us rightly to remember the birth of Jesus

that we may share in the song of the angels,

the gladness of the shepherds,
and the worship of the wise men.

Close the doors of hate and open the
    doors of love
all over the world.
Let kindness come with every gift,
and good wishes with every greeting.

Deliver us from evil by the blessing
    that Christ brings,
and teach us to be merry with clean
    hearts.

May the Christmas morning make us
    happy to be Thy children,
and the Christmas evening bring us
    to our beds
with grateful thoughts, forgiving and
    forgiven, for Jesus' sake. Amen.
    —Henry van Dyke

1273

O come, O come, thou day so bright;
We welcome thee with song and light.
Come, Christmas day so glad and fair,
And tell of Jesus everywhere.
Rejoice, rejoice, glad tidings tell
For He shall come, Emmanuel.
    —Ione Catton

1274

When Christmas comes to us each
year, there is a certain spirit that seems
to pervade all our hearts and lives.
It is a spirit that is contagious, and
more and more it is a spirit that en-
circles the globe. Year by year other
nations are added to those who already
celebrate Christmas.

Christmas is a memorial day. It
brings to our remembrance the birth
of Christ, who was born centuries ago
in a manger in Bethlehem. And from
that time until now a new spirit has
entered the world and continues to
grow in volume and intensity. The
song of the angels, "Glory to God in
the highest and on earth, peace, good
will to men," is becoming the song of
the multitudes as well as the song of
the heavenly host, which first praised
God over Bethlehem's manger.

What is this spirit? First, let me say
that it is the spirit of song. Christmas
is a festival of song. It is a time when
Christendom praises God. In the
second place, it is a spirit of youth.
It is a time when we become young
again. In the third place, it is playtime.
It is a time when we lay aside the
more sordid things, our worries and
our cares, and play. It is the spirit
of giving, a time when it becomes more
blessed to give than to receive. For
God so loved the world that He gave.
The wise men or the Magi who came
from the East brought their gifts to
the Lord. In appreciation of God's
gift to us we give our lives and service.

Best of all, Christmas means a spirit
of love, a time when the love of God
and the love of our fellow men should
prevail over all hatred and bitterness,
a time when our thoughts and deeds
and the spirit of our lives manifest
the presence of God.—George F.
McDougall, "The Spirit of Christmas,"
Huron College Bulletin

1275

One Christmas Eve, little Babs,
granddaughter of Mary Roberts Rinehart, was out riding with her famous
grandmother when they passed a large
orphan home.

"That," pointed out Mrs. Rinehart,
"is a place where little boys and girls
live who haven't any fathers and
mothers. Would you like to visit them

and take them something nice for Christmas?"

Babs looked hard at the great building.

"Yes," the child finally agreed, "I'd like to do that." She pondered a moment, then added, "I think I would like to take them some fathers and mothers."—Adrian Anderson, *Coronet*

1276

The star is the symbol of Christmas. As we enter again into the blessed season of Christmastide, we shall be guided by a star as we make our pilgrimage to Bethlehem. We shall find that the general background of the scene is the same: the stars, the feeding sheep, the rapture of faithful hearts. And yet, with each recurring year, new visions of splendor and significance break upon our astonished eyes.

As we approach the village we shall see in the distance the star shining overhead. Over the hills the angelic serenade will be heard: "Peace on earth, good will among men." We must journey into the village and search out the inn. We shall find it filled, with no room for weary travelers.

We must go to the stable. There we shall behold Joseph and Mary and the infant Jesus. Our attention will be centered on the Babe of Bethlehem. Shepherds who have followed the gleam will be our companions. They will have come down from the hills to make their offerings of love and praise. God's love shall be made manifest in the Holy Child lying in the lowly manger at Bethlehem.

As we gather again this year around the manger, in the stable at Bethlehem, in the midst of its humble surroundings, let us look with deepened awe and wonder on the figure of One destined to become the center of all human history. By His career and teaching He is to revolutionize the thinking of the world. His coming into the world is the most perfect demonstration of God's love that mankind has ever known.

Let us, therefore, follow reverently the leading of the star and take our places around the manger where the miracle of Christmas was brought to pass. As the result of our pilgrimage to Bethlehem and of our fellowship with the Christ-child, may we find a new significance in the festival of His birth.

1277

Let good Christian men rejoice! But let us know in heart and mind exactly why we rejoice. Many around us will enjoy themselves behind the many masks of Christmas. But they will relapse into joylessness, fear, and anxiety unless the One whose birthday we rightly celebrate becomes to them real, alive and contemporary. It is we who are Christians who hold the secret behind the façade, but it was never meant to be a secret; on the contrary, from the beginning it was meant to be "good tidings of great joy which shall be to all people." By thought, by prayer, by every tried and untried means, let us do all that we possibly can to make known that astonishing mystery, which is also a historical fact, that God became one of us that we might become like Him.—J. B. Phillips, *God with Us*

INDEXES

INDEX OF CONTRIBUTORS AND PERSONS MENTIONED

(ITEMS ARE LISTED BY SELECTION NUMBER; NUMBERS IN ITALICS INDICATE A PERSON NAMED WITHIN AN ITEM.)

TOPICAL INDEX

(ITEMS ARE LISTED BY SELECTION NUMBER)

309